SACRAMENTO PUBLIC LIBRARY

828 "I" Street

D0481620

THE
CRUSADER

ALSO BY TIMOTHY STANLEY

Kennedy vs. Carter:
The 1980 Battle for the Democratic Party's Soul

THE
CRUSADER

THE LIFE
AND TUMULTUOUS
TIMES OF
PAT BUCHANAN

Timothy Stanley

Thomas Dunne Books
St. Martin's Press ✹ New York

THOMAS DUNNE BOOKS.

An imprint of St. Martin's Press.

THE CRUSADER. Copyright © 2012 by Timothy Stanley. All rights reserved. Printed in the United States of America. For information, address St. Martin's Press, 175 Fifth Avenue, New York, N.Y. 10010.

www.thomasdunnebooks.com

www.stmartins.com

Library of Congress Cataloging-in-Publication Data

Stanley, Timothy.
    The crusader : the life and tumultuous times of Pat Buchanan / Timothy Stanley.—1st ed.
        p. cm.
    Includes bibliographical references and index.
    ISBN 978-0-312-58174-9 (hardcover)
    ISBN 978-1-4299-4128-0 (e-book)
    1. Buchanan, Patrick J. (Patrick Joseph), 1938– 2. United States—Politics and government—20th century. 3. Conservatism—United States—History—20th century. 4. Nixon, Richard M. (Richard Milhouse), 1914–1994—Friends and associates. 5. Reagan, Ronald—Friends and associates.
6. Political consultants—United States—Biography. 7. Presidential candidates—United States—Biography. 8. Journalists—United States—Biography. I. Title.
    E840.8.B83S73 2012
    973.927092—dc23
    [B]   2011035926

First Edition: February 2012

10 9 8 7 6 5 4 3 2 1

To Mother

Sola quae filios gessit amorem verum novit.

CONTENTS

Part Two

A PEASANT IN REVOLT

Introduction

P at Buchanan's home is a museum to lost causes. In his living room, there is a portrait of Robert E. Lee on one wall and a painting of himself on another. "That's from when I ran for the presidency in 1996," he told me. A fan copied it from the dust jacket of one of his books and gave it to Pat as a present. "People send me all sorts of stuff." In a glass cabinet there's a pitchfork. "They called me 'Pitchfork Pat,'" he explained, "from when we won the New Hampshire primary in 1996 and I said, 'The peasants are coming with their pitchforks!' I've got a gold pan from Alaska somewhere . . ."

Advisor to two presidents, three times presidential candidate, inventor of right-wing TV punditry, Pat Buchanan's story is the story of modern conservatism. The black-and-white photos on his walls chart its long march from Barry Goldwater to Ronald Reagan, the uncertain happiness of the 1980s, the bitter squabbles of the 1990s, the Bush wars, and the Tea Party revolution. In all the pictures, Pat looks the same—tall, well dressed, intelligent, and always about to tell the one about the nun from Sligo. There is a common misunderstanding among liberal commentators that conservatives are either mad or bad: Jesus freaks or shills for big business. Pat defies those stereotypes. He is clever, self-aware, compassionate, and frustrating. And he has been indispensable to the Republican Party. He put terms like "hardball," "silent majority," and "culture war" into common usage and helped turn the GOP into a populist movement. He has enjoyed power, but never been corrupted by it. Most of the men in the photos let him down. Nixon went to China, George H. W. Bush raised taxes. Even Ronald Reagan left too many things undone. Pat Buchanan served the Republican Party loyally for three decades. But his greater loyalty to conservatism and the folks who fill its ranks led him to break from the GOP. That is why, today, he is a prophet in the wilderness (or cable news, as some people call it).

On one shelf in Pat's house is a bust of Lenin that he picked up when he stayed in the Kremlin with the "Old Man," Richard Nixon, in 1972. "Another tribute to another lost cause?" I asked.

"Oh, no," said Pat, misunderstanding me. "I think we won that one."[1]

Throughout his career, Pat Buchanan defined American politics as a battle over culture. He didn't just fight to cut spending and lower taxes, but to protect a way of life and the people who prayerfully lived it. When the Cold War ended and the battle between capitalism and communism was over, he articulated the coming of a new conflict between Christianity and liberalism. He entered the 1992 primaries in an effort to take away the Republican nomination from President George H. W. Bush. Pat's candidacy started out as a tax revolt by the right, but it evolved into a populist conservative revolution that rolls on today.

On August 17, 1992, Pat Buchanan fired his first shot in the American culture war. The Republican National Convention gathered at the Houston Astrodome to renominate George Bush. Although he was easily beaten in that year's primaries, Buchanan had done well enough to earn a prime-time speech.[2] Speaking from the podium, he poured scorn on the Democratic Party and its July convention—a "giant masquerade ball . . . where 20,000 liberals and radicals came dressed up as moderates and centrists in the greatest single exhibition of cross-dressing in American political history." The Democrats had nominated Bill Clinton—a man, said Pat, whose foreign policy experience was "pretty much confined to having had breakfast once at the International House of Pancakes."

For the conservatives, the Clintons were the Mr. and Mrs. Mao of the culture war:

Elect me, and you get two for the price of one, Mr. Clinton says of his lawyer-spouse. [The audience booed.] And what does Hillary believe? Well, Hillary believes that 12 year olds should have a right to sue their parents, and she has compared marriage as an institution to slavery and life on an Indian reservation. [The audience gasped.] Well, speak for yourself, Hillary. [The audience laughed.] Friends, this is radical feminism. The agenda Clinton and Clinton would impose on America—abortion on demand, a litmus test for the Supreme Court, homosexual rights, discrimination against religious schools, women in combat. That's change, all right. But it is not the kind of change America wants. It is not the kind of change America needs. And it is not the kind of change we can tolerate in a nation that we still call God's country.[3]

The audience burst into applause. First Lady Barbara Bush politely joined in. Around her, Pat's "peasant army" broke into a chorus of "Go Pat, go! Go Pat, go!" and Mrs. Bush asked herself what had become of the Grand Old Party of her youth. She didn't recognize most of those faces in the crowd—the men in cowboy hats, the women with pro-life buttons, the young people who howled like wolves at everything that dreadful man said. They had chased her husband across the country in primary after primary—calling him "King George," a liar, a coward, and a traitor because he had raised their taxes to fill a hole in the budget. These people had no understanding of the intricacies of good government. Worse still, they had no breeding. *Was this "racist" Pat Buchanan really the future of the Republican Party,* she thought? It all seemed so "very extreme."[4]

At the podium, Buchanan said, "There is a religious war going on in our country for the soul of America. It is a cultural war, as critical to the kind of nation we will one day be as was the Cold War itself." On one side were anarchy, permissiveness, secularism, perversion, stagnation, and the Clintons. On the other side was God, family, patriotism, hard work, and Pat Buchanan. This was the new liberal vs. conservative struggle as Pat saw it, and there were Democrats and Republicans on both sides. For all his faults, President Bush was "a defender of right-to-life, and lifelong champion of the Judeo-Christian values and beliefs upon which this nation was built." So Pat urged his voters to stick with the Republican Party. For now.

The convention fell silent as Pat turned to the riots that had torn Los Angeles apart that April. Fifty-three people were killed and nearly 2,000 injured, 3,600 fires were started, and 1,100 buildings destroyed. Korean- and Asian-owned shops were targeted and Koreatown was a war zone. Pat visited Los Angeles a few hours after the rioting ended. He told the convention that he met some young men serving in the National Guard and asked them what they had seen.

> They had come into LA late on the second day, and they walked up a dark street, where the mob had looted and burned every building but one, a convalescent home for the aged. The mob was heading in, to ransack and loot the apartments of the terrified old men and women. When the troopers arrived, M-16s at the ready, the mob threatened and cursed, but the mob retreated. It had met the one thing that could stop it: force, rooted in justice, backed by courage.

Buchanan saw that confrontation as a metaphor for America. The riots were the product of liberalism's war against Christian moral doctrine and the nuclear family. The conservative movement was the last line of defense against total social collapse.

> Greater love than this hath no man than that he lay down his life for his friend. Here were 19-year-old boys ready to lay down their lives to stop a mob from molesting old people they did not even know. And as they took back the streets of LA, block by block, so we must take back our cities, and take back our culture, and take back our country.[5]

He didn't mention it, but in the 1992 Republican California primary Pat carried Koreatown.[6]

There were people in tears by the end of the speech. Diana Banister had come all the way from California to see it. Watching Pat Buchanan eviscerate his opponents on TV's *Crossfire* in the 1980s had encouraged her to convert to Catholicism. "Catholics in the arena—like Pat—seemed to understand conservatism better than anyone else," she explained. "He was so articulate, so informed. He was always able to get in with a last dig." When he declared in November 1991, Diana took a bus from California to New Hampshire to campaign for Pat. She wrote songs and painted signs on the way. Ten months later, she stood in the Astrodome crying. "It all culminated in that speech. It was beautiful. He brought us to highs and lows and we understood that we were hearing something significant. The speech was prophetic. He saw something before others saw it—that there was going to be a big war between us and the liberals."[7]

Rachel Maddow, then a nineteen-year-old who lived with friends in Philadelphia, saw the speech on TV. She had just come out as a lesbian. Maddow didn't much care for politics, but watched Pat transfixed. "Pat's culture war speech at the Republican convention hit me right between the eyes," she said many years later, now a TV host on MSNBC. "He was, without euphemism, declaring that my own country was at war with me. I get it intellectually and strategically now, but at nineteen, I only got it emotionally." The speech was one of the things that encouraged her to get into political journalism. It was "positive polarization," she said, dividing the country in two and reaching out to the bigger half.[8]

Watching the convention from his campaign war room, Bill Clinton agreed. In his opinion, Buchanan had "played to the dark side of middle-class insecurity." But Clinton was savvy enough to know that it might work. Pat's job wasn't to win liberals and centrists over to the Republican Party; it was to break off from the Democrats all those voters who hated the progressive, tolerant politics that Clinton felt he was trying to promote. Pat Buchanan's speech heralded the beginning of a new era of partisan politics. The Republicans wouldn't be content to call Democrats dumb anymore. They were going to call them sacrilegious perverts as well.[9]

Moderate Republicans sat on their hands. They thought that the speech's variety of social conservatism was out of date, that independent voters wanted something more tolerant and aspirational. Reps. Jack Kemp and Newt Gingrich called it "counterproductive." Asked how Buchanan's pitch would play in Wisconsin, Republican governor Tommy Thompson replied, "I don't think it will." Sen. Richard Lugar of Indiana said: "Pat's message is not a very appealing one for most Americans, and it's not a winning message. You don't build majorities by excluding whole groups of people, and you don't have to be nasty to be conservative."[10] Rep. Bill Green of New York was "shocked. His effort to turn a political campaign into a religious war was profoundly un-American."[11] Gov. William Weld of Massachusetts could barely hide his disgust. "I want the government out of your pocketbook and your bedroom," he said.[12] Even Pat's friend Peggy Noonan (a conservative speechwriter) said that he looked "slit-eyed and thuggish."[13]

The press helped turn the speech into a vote loser. One TV pundit quipped, "The most significant delegate here in Houston this week is God."[14] Anthony Lewis in *The New York Times* wrote, "The sleaze was so thick on the ground in Houston, the attacks so far-fetched, that some people may be tempted to dismiss them as funny. Not I. I remember Joe McCarthy."[15] The bestselling author Molly Ivins said of Buchanan's speech: "It was probably better in the original German." Columnist Dave Barry wrote that the convention may have been "dominated a little too much by the religious right, especially as they opened the second night by burning a witch." Why, a journalist asked Pat Buchanan, did so many people take an instant dislike to him? "It saves time," he shrugged.[16]

All the people with power and influence denounced the speech. Yet the day after, George Bush leaped eight points in the polls. Pat Buchanan's "nasty" speech cut Clinton's lead from seventeen points to just three.[17]

Play Pat Buchanan's 1992 convention speech to someone and you can probably tell by their reaction what side of the culture war they are on. Liberals presumed that its ugliness would make Pat Buchanan unelectable and consign his brand of conservatism to the trash heap of history. Moderate Republicans used it as an excuse to try to purge the radical right from their party, with mixed results. But for many conservatives, the speech defined their struggle against liberals in both parties. "It was not a declaration of war," said veteran right-wing activist Richard Viguerie. "It was a counteroffensive. The liberals had been waging war against American values for twenty years and Pat was the first person who ever hit back. The guy who hits back isn't the guy who started the fight. He's just defending himself."[18]

Millions of Americans agreed enough to vote for Pat Buchanan in 1992, 1996, and 2000. Thousands campaigned for him, some of whom became big-name conservative celebrities. In 1992, actor Mel Gibson gave an endorsement.[19] When Pat came to the town of Wasilla, Alaska, in the 2000 Republican presidential primaries, he was greeted by Mayor Sarah Palin. The mayor wore a "Buchanan for President" badge.[20]

This book is partly about people like Sarah Palin, for whom Pat Buchanan at one time spoke. It is the story of how conservatives tried to turn the Republican Party into a vehicle for their values. They had moments of triumph, but they saw out the Cold War frustrated and divided. In the scramble for new ideas that took place in the 1990s, their movement almost imploded. Pat Buchanan the speechwriter, tired of watching politicians mangle and betray his words, hoped that his presidential campaigns might tie the GOP to a new "conservatism of the heart." He thought that an emphasis upon cultural traditionalism and nationalism could create a new majority out of anxious middle-class Americans. When he failed, he quit the Republican Party and became a bestselling author instead. But his spirit remains and some of his positions—on guns, immigration, abortion, gay marriage—have become Republican articles of faith.

Whatever the social context, at the center of this book is Pat Buchanan. He is a controversial figure, so I have avoided passing judgment. It is better simply to tell his story from beginning to end and let the reader make his or her mind up as to whether he is a visionary or a brute. It is important to begin at the beginning because Buchanan's life was shaped by his happy memories of America in the 1950s. Like many conservatives, Buchanan sensed that paradise got lost in the 1960s. But while other right-wingers sold out to the future, Pat kept the faith of his childhood.

One of his devotees offered this fascinating insight:

> Of course, Pat's favorite move is *The Godfather*. And that makes a
> lot of sense if you think about it. It's all there: the Catholicism, the

devotion to father figures both real and adopted (Pop Buchanan and Richard Nixon), the violence in his youth, suspicion of authority. And most of all, loyalty: loyalty to friends, loyalty to family, and loyalty to the past. Pat Buchanan is basically an Irish Michael Corleone.[21]

Part One

A Courtier to Kings

ONE

The Georgetown Gang

Politics is biography. Many conservatives became conservatives by reading Ayn Rand or Milton Friedman at college. Not so Pat Buchanan. He learned his philosophy at the dinner table and in the playground, and he *felt* it before he defined it and could put a name to it.

Pat's conservatism is full of the sights and sounds of Washington, D.C., in the 1950s, where he grew up. Reading his memoir *Right from the Beginning*, you can almost smell the incense and home cooking; almost hear the school bell call the boys to prayer and the soft *click-click-click* of rosary beads as they run through fingers at nighttime prayer. His was a nonpartisan, "street-corner conservatism." A conservatism that came, wrote Buchanan:

> of absorbing the attitudes and values my mother learnt in a German–Catholic family of eight, which she left as a girl of seventeen to become a nurse in southeast Washington. It was the conservatism that came from being raised alongside eight brothers and sisters by a Scotch-Irish and Irish father, an Al Smith Democrat, whose trinity of political heroes consisted of Douglas MacArthur, General Franco, and the junior Senator from Wisconsin they called Tail Gunner Joe . . . Not until my twenties did I learn to conscript the intellectual arguments of the sages to reinforce the embattled arguments of the heart. When a boy approaches manhood, he gives

or denies his assent to what he has learned in home and school and church . . . To me the lessons of those years, however uncomplicatedly they were taught, retain the ring of truth.[1]

Patrick Joseph Buchanan was born into a family of Confederates, Catholics, and rascals on All Souls' Day, November 2, 1938.[2] His father, William Baldwin Buchanan, was a successful accountant and his mother, Catherine Elizabeth Crum, was a former nurse. They lived in Georgetown, a mixed German and Irish neighborhood, fanning out east and north from Georgetown University and Holy Trinity Catholic parish. Pat had six brothers and two sisters: William Baldwin Buchanan Jr. (born in 1936), Henry (Hank) Martin (1937), Jimmy (1940), Kathleen Theresa (1941), Jonathan Edward (1947), Angela Marie (1948), Brian Damien (1950), and Thomas Matthew (1953). The youngest girl, Angela Marie, was nicknamed "Bay"—the boys' gibberish version of "baby."[3] Pat was called "Paddy Joe" and was a troublemaker from birth. When his older brothers were toddlers, on their knees at the foot of each cot praying the Our Father, the Hail Mary, and the Glory Be, baby Pat would shout impatiently from his pen, "Holy Mary, Mother of God, pray for us sinners now and at the hour of our death, amen!" One night, the brothers had enough of being upstaged. After lights out, Pop heard screams coming from their bedroom. He ran upstairs and found Pat covered in milk and blood. After he had interrupted his brothers' prayers yet again, Hank had stolen Pat's glass milk bottle and smashed it over his head.[4]

Children in the 1940s and 1950s were expected to sustain a few cuts and bruises. The Buchanan boys played at war in the streets and Pop put up a punching bag in the basement. The boys "hit the bag" for four sessions each week, 100 times with the left, 100 times with the right, and 200 times with the "old one-two." Pop also set up a boxing ring in the hope that one of the boys would get into a fight with a neighbor and he could referee it. It was Hank, a natural athlete, who delivered. One summer's day, Pop Buchanan looked out of the window and saw Hank being chased up the road by a bigger boy. Not five minutes had passed before he had them both in the ring, the family gathered around, as he shouted "Keep your right up!" to his golden son. Hank was doing badly until he delivered a hard right; his opponent cracked his head against an exposed iron girder and his knees bent. Hank saw the opening and thumped him to the floor. Satisfied, father declared a knockout. He proudly christened his son "Hammering Hank."[5]

Gangs of boys divided Georgetown into different neighborhoods. They conducted wars for land and cigarette cards, wars fought with bows and arrows and imitation guns wielded like sticks. In this urban jungle, infant Pat was at a disadvantage. He was an odd-looking kid—tall, gangly, and "walleyed" (both his eyes stared away from the nose at strange angles). Pat longed to become a pilot, but was told early on that he would never make it because he had trouble judging distances. The doctors operated on his eyes and forced him to wear enormous glasses.[6] He was a magnet for bullies. One day he was assaulted by a boy three years older than he. Poor walleyed Pat ran screaming to a kid called Jimmy Fegan. He told him what had happened and asked for protection. Fegan went to see the culprit and messed him up with his belt. The kid got the message and backed off. Pat offered Fegan his loyalty in the never-ending war for the streets. He later reflected: "I learned the importance of good friends and the difference between being tough and being mean. That [bully] was mean, and Jimmy Fegan was truly tough. In politics, the same distinctions exist."[7]

L ike all good Catholics, Pat went to a parochial elementary school. In first grade, over a hundred children squeezed into two small rooms. All attended a daily Mass at 8:30 a.m.; first confession came upon reaching the "age of reason" in the second grade. When the boys entered the sixth grade, they had the opportunity to be altar boys. This meant serving at three separate weekday Masses, usually at 6:30 in the morning. On Sunday there were six Masses to choose from (6, 7, 8, 10, 11 a.m., and noon). Senior servers assisted at Benediction on Monday night, when five altar boys helped adore the Host.[8] Little Pat's world was full of mystery and devotion.[9] One night, he was woken by his father and taken to the Sacred Heart Church on 16th Street. There the Nocturnal Adoration Society met to pray before the exposed Blessed Sacrament in the early morning hours (because, according to the parish magazine, "so many of the worst sins are committed at night"). "The protection that God offers is similar to that which I give you," Pop Buchanan whispered to his son. Life is full of suffering and pain; that is as it should be. But with moral and spiritual training every bit as rigorous as "hitting the bag" in the Buchanan basement, walleyed Pat might just make it through.[10]

By the age of thirteen, most of the Buchanan boys were smoking in alleys and fighting in the schoolyard. That's when the nuns handed them over to the Jesuits, lest their souls be lost forever. The Jesuit-run high school, Gonzaga, was housed in a squalid neighborhood. There was a whorehouse on the other side of the street. During the Latin class, the boys translated Virgil while watching the ladies across the road come out and take a cigarette between clients. Gonzaga was a good school but many of its pupils harbored a sense of exclusion, as if—in the words of one student—they were "being educated downstairs."[11] That made the boys competitive and touchy. Pat was taught (to a very high standard) logic and reason, but with the sole aim of defending the faith in argument with snobby Protestants.[12]

The Gonzaga boys learned a strict interpretation of the Catholic dogma that "Outside the Church there is no salvation." Beyond the "one Holy Catholic and Apostolic Church" there was only Hell and death. Their singular salvation gave American Catholics a big stake in the Cold War.[13] Pat was taught about the 1917 visions at Fatima, where the Virgin Mary appeared to three Portuguese children and delivered three prophetic "secrets." The second secret warned that Armageddon was inevitable unless Russia converted to Catholicism. Entrusted with this insight into the will of God, American Catholics felt a personal calling to fight Russian Bolshevism. The persecution of the Church in Eastern Europe and the end of missionary activity in Red China confirmed the atheistic evil of communism. Many anticommunists were driven by real politick, or a fear that the Soviets would crush temporal freedoms.[14] The boys at Gonzaga thought the Soviets were literally Satanic.

There was no legitimate alternative to "the Gospel truth," only lies. While the rest of American society struggled to deal with the tough questions posed by sex, Beat poetry, rock and roll, sociology, psychiatry, James Dean, and the Civil Rights Movement, the Gonzaga boys had a magnetic self-confidence. To emphasize the clarity of choice between Catholicism and everything else, Pop Buchanan would grab one of his boys' hands and hold a lighted match against the palm. He would say: "See how that feels; now imagine that for all eternity."[15]

In Pat's world, pain was a given, maybe even a blessing. He learned to revere St. Lawrence, who was roasted on a spit when he tried to bring the Good News to the Romans. "Turn me over," he said to his executioners with a beatific smile. "I'm done on this side."[16]

A s Pat entered his adolescence in the 1950s, America was a land of plenty. The Greatest Generation—the men and women who lived through the Depression and the Second World War—had built their country into a super-power. As the empires of Europe crumbled, only the Soviet Union could rival its military and political clout. American products were in demand across the world, and U.S. dollars flooded into Europe by way of Marshall Aid. Industry boomed, churning out Chevys and Fords that ended up on the streets of Paris, Havana, and Tokyo. Average wages were high and the economy could sustain near-full employment.[17] The cost of living was low enough that a single work-ing man, like Pop Buchanan, could keep a housewife and a family of nine, his grandmother, and an African American servant under one roof. In 1951, he moved his clan to a huge house on Utah Avenue, where the boys had a whole acre of garden to play in. The Buchanan family's rise from the working class to the middle class in one generation was emblematic of America's leap to great-ness.[18]

The mansion on Utah Avenue wasn't big enough to contain the Buchanan boys, though. As they grew bigger and tougher, they became a menace on the streets. Maureen Dowd, who later worked as a journalist for *The New York Times,* lived in the neighborhood. Her brother, Michael, fled the night that he was asked by the Buchanans to help throw a motorbike over a wall. Michael recalled that "We regarded the Buchanan boys with the same awe and fear that Romanian peasants spoke of vampires." Maureen claimed that Pat "and his brawling brothers were the scourge of Washington's Catholic community. Boys at parochial schools all over the city would huddle on Monday mornings to whisper about the latest Buchanan hooliganism. Did you hear how they crashed a party and beat everyone up? Did you hear how they stuffed a hapless drunk in Ocean City into a garbage can and rolled him into the sea?" The Fifties were great for men like Buchanan, Dowd argued, because white "boys were gods." But for African Americans, girls, and weaklings, it was terrifying. The Buchanans were titans. "Some bullies are cowards," said Michael Dowd. "But the Buchanans were not. They were extremely intelligent and a little crazy. You knew if you got in a fight with them, you'd better be ready to fight."[19]

The fights were usually over one of two things: beer and girls. Steal a beer and you were guaranteed a sucker punch. Steal a girl and you might never walk again. By the time he was fifteen, Pat drank every Friday and Saturday night. A six-pack would usually suffice; you could get half a dozen Gunthers for a dollar. The bigger the boy, the bigger the intake. The Kadow twins were notorious for starting every evening with at least twelve cans inside each of them. At parties, the Kadows and the Buchanans had "chugging" matches to see who could put away the most. Keg parties were held most weeks. A keg could be purchased for $14 and during the summer the Buchanans and Kadows would take over Aerlie Playground and sit around in their underpants getting drunk. When the police showed up they split into the trees.[20]

Drink, girls, and gangs all led to a nightly routine of fistfights and bloody noses.[21] A favorite pastime of the Buchanans and the Kadows was crashing private parties. A network of informants let them know when and where one was taking place. Pat turned up on the doorstep at 8 p.m., dressed in a suit and tie. The father of the house opened the door and Pat pretended to be a friend of his son. In a Brahmin accent he implied that he attended one of the local private schools (Landon or St. Albans) or was doing premed at Princeton. Bowled over, the father welcomed him in. By the time Pat made it downstairs his cover was blown—but it was too late. He opened up the basement doors and in walked the Kadow brothers with a keg of beer over their shoulders, followed by the entire pack of Buchanans. The atmosphere grew tense; one by one the girls left. By midnight all that was left was the cobelligerents. "And then," recalled Pat, "the action would begin." By the time the police were called, the basement was awash with booze and blood.[22]

It was impossible to run away from a fight. If one boy was scrapping, then everyone else had to get involved—whether he was innocent or not. Buchanan wrote: "That somebody stood by friends in trouble . . . was, in those days, about the highest compliment you could pay; and virtually the worst term that could be used about anyone was that he was 'chicken,' someone who, when fighting started, ran out on friends."[23] Loyalty was repaid with a night in a cell or a heavy fine. But that was all right. The keg parties and the policeman's baton were all part of the chaotic cycle of sin and redemption. The Buchanan boys respected the cops who busted up their parties and chased them into the trees, and the next morning the gang lined up outside the confessional to lay it all before God. Pat Buchanan was mischievous, but he was no anarchist.[24]

A dolescent Pat's loyalty to the faith, family, and the system that raised him made him strong and self-confident. But it sometimes left him insensitive to the perspectives and feelings of others. The fact that Washington, D.C., was segregated passed him by. Pat wrote in his memoir: "In the late 1940s, and early '50s . . . race was never a preoccupation with us; we rarely thought about it . . . The Negroes of Washington had their public schools, restaurants, bars, movie houses, playgrounds, and churches; and we had ours. Neither community could have been called rich."[25]

There is anecdotal evidence that, like most kids of their generation, the Buchanan boys were ethnic chauvinists.[26] Their next-door neighbors on Utah Avenue were a Jewish family called the Bernsteins. One night in 1958, Bill and Hank invited a crowd of local hoods to the Buchanan place to watch a football game and get drunk. When it finished, they went out onto the front lawn at midnight and improvised their own game. They woke the Bernsteins up with their noise, so Harry Bernstein got into his car and drove up to the Buchanans' front door to complain. The boys swarmed around his vehicle and tried to tip it over. Bernstein swore he heard cries of "Get the Jews!" He reversed home and called the cops. When they showed up, Hank told them to get lost and slammed the door in their face. Later that night, beer bottles rained down on the Bernstein rooftop.

Harry's daughter, Karen, couldn't confirm if her father had correctly heard the Buchanan boys say, "Get the Jews!," but she was sure of one thing: "They didn't like the Jews. There's no question about it. I don't think they woke up every morning with a prayer, saying 'Thank you God for not making me a woman

and a Jew,' but they didn't like 'em. They would call us dirty Jew. I don't necessarily know that Pat Buchanan himself said those words . . . He was thirteen
years older than me. It was just understood how the Buchanans felt about us."

Years later, Pat said this was "nonsense." He pointed out that his father had
two Jewish clients who were treated like family; one attended Pat's wedding.
And when Bay became U.S. Treasurer, she mailed the Bernsteins a commemo-
rative dollar. Karen conceded that the Bernstein boys gave as good as they got
with ethnic jibes and fights: in one spat the Buchanans threw watermelon
rinds over the garden wall, and the Bernsteins sprayed seltzer water back.[27]

Whatever the truth about his racial views, throughout his career Pat refused to express guilt for any offense he *may* have caused minorities. "Racism
is the obsessive preoccupation with the subject of race," he wrote in his memoir. "The racist sees everything in life, education and politics, from the stand-
point of race." Pat was satisfied that this definition didn't describe him. The
Buchanan family didn't wear white robes and burn crosses, so what was there
to apologize for? Life in segregated Washington bred in Pat Buchanan a fatal
blind spot on race.[28]

Pat's earliest political influence was his father. Pop Buchanan told his son
that he used to be a Democrat, but that the Democrats had let him down
on the biggest issue of the day: communism.[29] One of Pop's heroes was Gen.
Francisco Franco, the Spanish dictator. Pop was furious with how American
liberals had joined forces with Marxists to try to overthrow him. The general
had kicked the Reds out of Spain and, despite whatever his secret police may
have done, he was still a friend to the Catholic Church. Only a "chicken"
wouldn't support a friend in a fight, said Pop.

Many parts of the Democratic Party and the American left supported the
Spanish republican opposition to Franco—the popular front alliance of liberals, anarchists, and communists. American sympathizers ignored reports of
republican atrocities against the Church that occurred during the Spanish
Civil War. But Gonzaga was awash with stories of relics, churches, and mon-
asteries being looted and defiled. Thousands of clergy were murdered. Nuns
were raped. In Ciudad Real, a priest was castrated and suffocated with his own

sexual organs. The parish priest of Navalmoral was put through a parody of the Crucifixion—whipped and crowned with thorns—and then shot. Synagogues were burned down as well. To the Buchanans, the Spanish republicans were devils and Franco a veritable St. Michael. They struggled to understand why Roosevelt gave away so much land to the communist monsters at Yalta, and why Truman failed to stop China going Red in 1949. Either these men were fools or complicit.[30]

Pop Buchanan said that the one man in politics who understood the problem was Republican senator Joe McCarthy. On February 9, 1950, McCarthy gave a speech at Wheeling, West Virginia, that claimed to expose the extent of the Marxist infiltration of American society. Holding a piece of paper aloft, he said: "The State Department is infested with communists. I have here in my hand a list of 205 . . . names that were made known to the Secretary of State as being members of the Communist Party and who nevertheless are still working and shaping policy in the State Department." The accusation rang true with a public that was terrified by Soviet expansion overseas. Committees to investigate un-American activities sprang up across the country. In the Senate, McCarthy and his allies tore into those accused of aiding and abetting the enemy. Some accusations were hysterical, some unveiled genuine security threats.[31]

Teenage Pat Buchanan saw spies everywhere. He decided that the Democratic administration of Harry Truman was soft and infiltrated by traitors. News of atrocities in Korea, where Americans were fighting the communists for control of the country, upset him. "I was reading horrible reports of American trucks driving over the bodies of wounded American troops . . . 'Why doesn't Truman drop the atomic bomb on the attacking Chinese armies who are killing thousands of Americans?' I recall asking myself. Five years before, he had dropped it on two defenseless Japanese cities . . . Maybe Pop is right about Truman, I concluded."[32] American voters agreed. Korea and McCarthy helped elect the Republican ticket of Dwight Eisenhower and Richard Nixon in 1952.[33]

McCarthy's reputation today is poor. He picked a fight with the army and was censured in the Senate. His career faded and he died of an alcohol-related illness in 1957.[34] But the Buchanans adored Joe McCarthy. What mattered to them, said Pat, was not "precisely what he said," but "what they understood him to be saying." They understood him to be saying that the American establishment—both Democrat and Republican—had betrayed the men who fought at Normandy and Iwo Jima. The establishment seemed to have handed a third of the world over to communism and created cozy jobs for themselves in a massive bureaucracy that was out of touch with the concerns of ordinary Americans. McCarthy was a populist. His fans raged against the domination of society by privileged elites. Like all populists, he proposed simple solutions to complex problems—solutions that typically involved toppling the powerful. Every question could be answered by trusting the people. As Thomas Jefferson wrote: "A little rebellion now and again is a good thing."[35]

The Buchanans held strong opinions on most subjects but they couldn't vote. Washington, D.C., only permitted voting in presidential elections in 1961 and the mayor was appointed. There was no local politics. Bay recalled: "Our local newspaper was *The Washington Post* and the headlines were all national. So we didn't talk about stuff like the little leagues. Foreign policy and communism were local politics to us . . . I guess that's why it mattered so much." National politics was debated at the dinner table. Bay's place was beside her mother and she watched in awe as her brothers shouted each other down, her father refereeing from the sidelines.[36]

Pat recalled: "Every one of us was opinionated and we were all taught not to back down. Whatever our positions lost in logic might be recovered in invective. If you never quit an argument, presumably you never lost. To make oneself heard as the argument got intense, we got louder and louder. The only one who could halt the uproar was my father."[37]

It was "*Crossfire* in training," observed Bay, although she felt it did have some intellectual value. "Everything you said was torn apart, so you had to be careful about what you said. You needed to have facts to back up a point. No one would let you get away with saying something stupid that couldn't be supported . . . I went to college and was surprised to meet liberals who couldn't sustain an argument. Everything we believed had run the test of that dinner table."[38]

Nothing in those family debates, besides the agreed weakness of liberals on fighting communism, suggested Pat Buchanan would grow up a partisan Republican. His friend, the philosopher Paul Gottfried, was surprised that he did: "There was little in his background to suggest that he was GOP . . . His father had been a Democrat, they were all urban Catholics. And there were many, many labor people who felt the same way about communism that Pat did . . . Perhaps if he had been born a little earlier [before FDR gave away Eastern Europe and Truman 'lost' China] then he might have been a Hubert Humphrey Democrat."[39] The Kennedys loved Joe McCarthy as much as the Buchanans. Joe dated their sisters and was a regular guest at their home in Hyannis Port.[40]

But there were conservative lessons in Pat's childhood. Growing up in rough, Catholic Washington convinced Pat that life was an earthly anarchy overseen by a celestial order. It was wrong, as the liberals tried, to legislate away the anarchy and usurp the order. But it was also wrong, as the free market fundamentalists tried, to pretend that the anarchy is pleasant and the order doesn't exist. One must accept the anarchy and submit to the order, with an active determination to survive and be saved.[41]

And there was one thing that the Republicans had that the Democrats didn't: red-blooded Red-baiters like Richard Milhous Nixon.

Every summer, the children of D.C. went touting for work. One year, Pat and his friend Millard Crouch landed a job at the Burning Tree golf club in Montgomery County. The labor was dumb and boring. The boys spent hours sitting on the caddy log drinking Cokes, waiting for a customer. Then they would carry their bags across the eighteen-hole golf course in the burning sun for $2.50, sometimes a 50-cent tip. Several times Pat sat and watched as President Eisenhower went out to play. His Secret Service men trailed behind with fake golf bags containing rifles, picking through the rough for snipers.

Besides Pat and two others, all the other caddies were black. The African Americans had seniority, so always took the first players to arrive; but then this was their full-time occupation. They got two or three jobs a day, made $10 or $15 with tips, and left the white boys to stew on the log. Pat's best bet was to land a late-afternoon tee-off when the veterans were already out on the course. One afternoon, when Pat and his buddy Pete Cook were the last two on the log, Buchanan saw the club pro bring out the tartan bag that belonged to the

Vice President of the United States. A little while later, a black limousine pulled up to the clubhouse and Richard Nixon stepped out. Pat was picked to be his caddy.

Nixon was in his forties and enjoying himself as Vice President. He had power and money, and a great deal of respect. He was Vice President of the number one world superpower and perhaps the most influential anticommunist of his generation—the man who exposed Hiss as a Red agent and who beat liberal Helen Douglas out of a Senate seat, by telling voters that she was "Pink right down to her underwear." Pat was in awe of him. Nixon was tall—taller than Buchanan expected—gravelly voiced, and tanned. He was also a lousy golfer. Nixon was a klutz, a man uncomfortable in his own skin who fought a running battle not to put a foot through a window or staple his own tie to the desk. His shots were "stiff and jerky." He took a long time to size up the ball, aim the club, retract the arm in a short, sharp snatch, and then—inevitably—send it flying into the woods. "Tough break, Dick," said the other players every other hole.

Nixon might have been a poor golfer, yet—recalls Buchanan—"from the comments his fellow players made, you would have thought we had the young Palmer out there." Nixon slunk a ball 150 yards down the fairway in something that was almost a straight line and someone said, "Great shot, Dick, a real beauty!"

"Your game is really improving, Dick," added a general, which made Pat wonder what it had been like a year ago. When the ball dribbled off the fairway or rolled into the sand, Pat spotted a shared look of pain on the other players' faces. "Tough break, Dick," they would say. Nixon whacked one into the middle of the forest and it took them ages to finally find it "three shots from civilization."

Back at the hole, the general cupped his hands to his lips and shouted, "Take one, Dick, and put it on the fairway!" People needed to get home for dinner.

But Nixon looked happy. He told jokes and laughed a lot. Nixon might not have had the other fellows' breeding or education, but he made up for that by playing at buddies and talking the language of the power elite. The lexicon was colorful. At one point on the tee he jerked around and shouted out, "Those fucking Democrats have cut our cocks every chance they get!" Later, they came upon Sen. Stu Symington of Missouri—the man who had questioned Joe Mc-Carthy's honor and finished his career. Nixon greeted him like an old friend. "Hey, Stu, they're voting up on the Hill; why aren't you there?" the Vice President shouted. "Tell 'em to shove it," Symington hollered back.

This looked like the Greatest Generation at play. Here, in a man's playground, partisan differences counted for nothing. Money and influence was what bought you a stake in the game. Democrats, liberals, Republicans, conservatives—all were equal on the golf course. That day, Pat learned firsthand how alike elites often were; how they shared a language and a macho camaraderie that outlasted whatever they might say in front of the camera. At one point, Nixon took a break from demolishing the tee to relieve himself in the bushes. Buchanan joined him. The two men stood side by side peeing into the grass; the caddy from Georgetown and the Vice President from Yorba Linda. Neither knew how close they were destined to become.[42]

TWO

License to Kill in St. Louis

I n 1956, Pat was accepted to study at Georgetown University. As the 1950s drew to an end, America had to grow up. But Pat dug his heels in. In 1959, he turned twenty-one and came down with a nasty case of arrested development. In January he contracted mononucleosis, which laid him out for three weeks. Then he was diagnosed with a form of arthritis known as Reiter's Syndrome. The sufferer gets pains in the joints (particularly the knees), has difficulty urinating, and may get inflammation in the eyes. The disease ended any hope of entering the army. Pat would forever live with the jibe of liberal critics that he was an armchair hawk.[1] For the next twenty years Buchanan got by on a combination of pills and frequent spells off work.

Pat spent the summer of 1959 in bed with Reiter's, wracked with pain.[2] As soon as he recovered, he returned to his unhealthy lifestyle of drink, women, and trouble. One Saturday night in October, Pat was driving along O Street with a date when he was pulled over by a patrol car. He wound down his window and the officers accused him of speeding. Pat denied it, using language that would make a beatnik blush. He said that his girlfriend had been watching the speedometer and would testify that he stayed below thirty.

"In that case," said one cop, "suppose we make the charge passing at an intersection?"

As he wrote the ticket, Pat told him in "X-rated language" what he thought of him.

"Out!" shouted the cop. "Get out of the car!"

The policemen led Buchanan to the back of his patrol car, but he refused to get in. The cops decided to make an example of him, and Pat went down fighting. One officer tried to push him onto the backseat and Pat put his boot up his backside, kicking him out onto the pavement. The other officer rained down blows, but Buchanan gave as good as he got. "I was ahead on points," he swore, "'til they brought out the nightsticks." One cop worked over Pat's head and neck, while Pat delivered a couple of sucker punches to the other guy. He made it out of the car, but a citizen ran to the aid of the police and pushed him back in. Pat told him where he could shove his "citizen's arrest." Safely inside, the cops locked the door and got into the front seat. They watched in awe as Pat threw himself against the glass partition between them and the back, calling the wrath of St. Michael down on them.

They drove him to the station. Waiting for him was a semicircle of eight cops, slapping their clubs against their palms, looking for an excuse to use them. Pat stepped out of the car and politely bade the arresting officers good night as they were rushed off to the hospital.[3]

The O Street Incident was among the "great, dumb deeds" of Pat's life. He called his date expecting support. She yelled down the phone, "You oughtta have your mouth washed out with soap!" Pat's hand was broken and in a cast. The police charged him with assaulting an officer and he got out on a $2,000 bond. Georgetown University told him not to return. Pop intervened and got the exclusion reduced to a year's withdrawal and no scholarship. Pat was put to work in his father's accountancy office. He prayed that this wasn't how his life would end—buried beneath a pile of tax returns and balance sheets.[4]

It was while working for his father that Pat first picked up a copy of William F. Buckley's conservative magazine *National Review*. He recalled that his reaction was "not unlike that of John Keats, 'On First Looking into Chapman's Homer.'" Pat fell in love with Buckley's uncompromising conservatism, particularly its apocalyptic take on the Cold War. He was impressed that Buckley was both a Catholic and a Republican. While most other Catholics were backing Jack Kennedy for president in 1960, Buchanan and Buckley had both concluded

Kennedy was insufficiently anticommunist, and were supporting Protestant Richard Nixon instead.[5] Pat admired Buckley's mystical way with words, his ability to lift conservatism from a thing of economic logic to a thing of spiritual beauty.

By the time he put the magazine down he knew he wanted to be a journalist: "to become a writer like the best at *National Review*." The most prestigious school of journalism to go to was Columbia University in New York City. But it required straight As to get in. Determined not to wind up an accountant, Pat returned to Georgetown a changed man. He got up early each morning, took classes until noon, went to business school at night as a backup plan, and was in bed by 10:30 p.m. He later wrote: "Being expelled was among the best things that ever happened to me . . . It ended adolescence . . . Now, I, too, had a goal in life, a destination toward which to channel my talent and energy."

Buchanan spent his last year at Georgetown plowing through English literature. His taste was traditional and Romantic. He wallowed in metaphor and imagery, and he admired the ability of great American writers to stir a primitive response in their readers. He adored Melville and Poe, for they spoke of evil as a concrete thing present in men's hearts—not the by-product of circumstance and institutions. Man could not be perfected; all the artist could do was list his wrongs and warn of mistakes to come. Pat read and reread *The Waste Land* by T. S. Eliot, a lyrical warning of the demise of Western civilization. Eliot spoke of seeing "fear in a handful of dust," and Pat knew what he meant. He sensed that the foundations of his own world were beginning to crumble.

Buchanan was also developing an interest in rhetoric, studying political speech as if it were poetry. He found in the works of his favorite orators "a musical quality, as though the words are actually marching in cadence." He grew to appreciate the rhythm and meter of good speech and, with a finer ear for tone, the ability to build a symphony from vowels and consonants.[6]

Working hard, Pat was determined but not necessarily happy. In his final year, his Georgetown tutor asked him, "Patrick, what is the matter with you?"

"Nothing," he replied. "I was booted out of here; now I'm back; I'm staying out of trouble, and I'm doing my work."

"You're doing splendidly," said the tutor. "That is not the problem. The problem is, every time I look over in your direction you look as though you're going to explode. What is the matter with you? Why are you so angry?" Pat couldn't answer. He seemed lonely at Georgetown. His family and friends had graduated and he wasn't comfortable with strangers. He was perfectly charming, but he missed the clan. Buchanan knew he was born to defend the truth and that he wanted to write. But he was still uncertain about the future.[7]

B uchanan graduated third in the class of 1961 and made it to Columbia. The journalism school was as strict as a Jesuit college. The professors taught their students how to write the perfect report, usually in a formal style suited to *The New York Times* or *The Washington Post*. Poetry and punditry were frowned upon. Television journalism was banned. Pat was surprised by the "seriousness, bordering on stuffiness and sanctimony" that pervaded the faculty. "Some students and teachers seemed to carry the weight of the world; a look of barely suppressed pain was always on their faces. Some were downright grim." All were liberal.[8] Pat's conservatism stood out a mile. His friend Don Oliver recalled that they used to sit around in dormitories drinking coffee and discussing loudly "the advantages of fallout shelters . . . We did it to stir up trouble and have people say, 'Who are those conservative assholes?' "[9]

The one fight that Pat had at Columbia—which should be placed into the context of the *hundreds* he had at school in Washington, D.C.—was legendary. Journalists talked about it for years. One critic remembered it like this:

> It was a primal punch thrown from way downtown in the reptilian brain stem of the young and resentful Pat Buchanan. The site was the World Room of the Columbia journalism school; the occasion was a Christmas party for the professors and the class of 1962. Wildly drunk and mysteriously enraged, Buchanan walked over to Kim Willenson, now international managing editor of UPI, and without telegraphing his grievance, socked him hard in the right eyeball. Willenson hit the canvas. They briefly wrestled and shouted obscenities until the dean, Richard Baker, broke them up. Flooring the smartest guy at the school, an arrogant pinko from Madison,

Wisconsin, meant Christmas in excelsis for the kooky Georgetown bruiser whose boyhood idols were Joe McCarthy and Generalissimo Francisco Franco. Not the least bit embarrassed by his thick mick manners, Buchanan exulted through the night, hydrating his hangover with a case of Pepsi.[10]

Why did he do it? Willenson floated a couple of ideas. He might have hit on a girl that Pat was keen on, or it might be because his parents had picketed Joe McCarthy. Perhaps it was simply that Pat was a Neanderthal. Willenson claimed that Pat liked to say nice things in polite company about the American Nazi Party in an effort to start a fight. The truth was beyond Willenson's understanding. A few hours before the fight, Pat had cruised around with Don Oliver. Oliver told him that Willenson had insulted him and he was going to give him a black eye. Pat said he was with him. The Buchanan family code stuck: If your friend is in a fight, whether victim or perpetrator, you join in on his side. Later at the party, when Willenson made a move on a girl he was interested in, Pat told him he was a sleaze. Willenson swore back, not knowing that Buchanan had a prior commitment to slug him. He made good on his promise.[11]

Pat was astonished at his immediate notoriety. Willenson and the students presumed the fight was political, that Buchanan was a brown shirt in the making. But anyone else who'd grown up in Georgetown would have done the same thing. Pat concluded that the Willenson incident showed the gulf between liberals and "the real America." A real American "would have reacted the same way: a thirty-second fistfight was no big deal. . . . To us, someone who threw that kind of language in your direction was insulting you and looking for a fight; and, if you took that without responding, something was wrong with you, not him." These kids had no respect, no honor. In the shock that greeted the Willenson incident, Pat saw a forewarning of the press's opposition to Richard Nixon's strong-arm policies in Vietnam, its reflexive pacifism. Although this time around the liberal establishment was on Buchanan's side. The students so loved him that they commemorated Willenson's black eye by walking around in eye patches.[12]

. . .

Pat graduated from Columbia in 1962. Straightaway, he landed a job at the St. Louis Globe-Democrat in Missouri. Life in St. Louis was sweet. The newspaper was solidly conservative and the editor, Richard Amberg, appreciated Pat's attacks on Democrats or the local, communist-infiltrated branch of the NAACP. Amberg was a replacement for Pop, a muscular conservative who encouraged his protégé to push the boundaries of good taste. Of an editorial target, Amberg once advised: "Slice him from rectum to belly button." Buchanan wrote his parents: "I have a license to kill."[13]

Pat's first public cause was one usually associated with liberals. Shortly after landing the job, he convinced the Globe-Democrat to run a campaign for reform at the Missouri Penitentiary. A Catholic priest had sent ex-cons to see Buchanan to petition his support. He was horrified by what he heard: several prisoners crammed into a single cell, routine male rape, and an administration, headed by Warden E. V. Nash, that permitted the hardest cons to run the prison.[14] Pat was invited to write an article for The Nation about the jail. Obviously moved, he documented "the gambling, drugs, sex affairs, poor physical facilities and low morale among the guards. What makes these problems . . . next to insoluble in Missouri is the physical makeup of that 47-acre amalgam of walls and cells. The rambling, unorganized premises can conceal a thousand knives. A typical cell has two bunks, an overstuffed chair, shelves of canned goods, a homemade table, walls plastered with obscene pictures . . . An acceptable solution—one providing both rehabilitation and prisoner safety—cannot be found until that 128-year-old anachronism overlooking the Missouri River is scuttled."[15]

The debate over the Missouri Penitentiary helped elect a reforming governor. Nonetheless, the Globe-Democrat kept up the pressure for prosecuting Warden Nash. One Friday in November 1964, Pat wrote a front-page editorial taking Nash apart. On Saturday morning, the front page of the rival St. Louis Post-Dispatch read "Warden Nash Kills Self." The relentless attacks had been too much for Nash. They crippled his career and destroyed his self-esteem. He returned from a party with his wife and shot himself. Later, Pat discovered that Nash had had emotional problems, but he was still shaken. Buchanan arrived home late at night for Christmas and found his father waiting in the gloomy kitchen. Pop told him that it was all right, that it wasn't his fault. But it was a lesson in the price of playing hardball; some men couldn't take it.[16]

As the reform effort at the Missouri Penitentiary hinted, American society was changing in the early 1960s. The Civil Rights Movement challenged the racial consensus that governed D.C. and Buchanan attended the March on Washington, where Martin Luther King Jr. declared "I have a dream." He felt ambivalent toward the movement. On the one hand he admired King's bravery and the dignity of peaceful protest. On the other hand, he suspected that civil rights causes were being hijacked by far-left elements who wanted to tear America apart. Pat saw most things in terms of freedom vs. communism, and feared the Civil Rights Movement was aiding the latter. Editor Amberg fed Pat information on Martin Luther King Jr. donated by the FBI. Buchanan told his readers that King was "sometimes demagogic and irresponsible in his public statements, dangerously naive in his choice of associates and negligent of the consequences of his words and deeds."[17] But the public didn't appear to heed the call, and Pat's views seemed increasingly outside the mainstream of American political life.

Since the New Deal, the Republican Party had drifted to the center. The Democratic Party's coalition of blue-collar workers, ethnic minorities, liberals, and women voters looked unbeatable, so Republican presidential candidates stole many of its ideas, pledging to protect Social Security and Medicare. The GOP was dominated by an east coast clique of wealthy Brahmins who, every four years, picked their own nominee in smoke-filled rooms.[18] Their choice in 1964 was the billionaire liberal Nelson Rockefeller but, to their surprise, he faced strong competition from an unabashed conservative.

The scion of Arizona department store magnates, Barry Goldwater wanted to demolish the New Deal welfare state, roll back regulation, and cut taxes. He argued for a more aggressive stance toward the Soviets overseas and pledged full support to the embattled government of South Vietnam—hinting that he might entertain the use of nuclear weaponry. Goldwater was "Mr. Conservative," but he posed a threat to the Republican establishment.[19] As a result, even the *Globe-Democrat* refused to endorse Barry Goldwater in 1964.[20]

Nevertheless, Pat Buchanan was one of thousands of conservative activists who went wild for the Arizona senator. To quote Buchanan: "What attracted me . . . was his principled militancy. When people called us the 'radical right,' they had a point. *Radix* is the Latin word for 'root,' and Barry Goldwater wanted to return America to her root ideas of constitutionalism and limited government." In the sense that he wanted to return power to the people, Goldwater was more a revolutionary than a conservative. Barry Goldwater was Robin Hood with a Stetson and a department store.[21]

Gearing up for the primaries, Goldwater presumed he would be running against President John F. Kennedy. He wanted a straightforward fight between a Massachusetts liberal and an everyman conservative. But Kennedy was assassinated in November 1963. His replacement, Lyndon Baines Johnson, was a Texan with populist instincts. Promising to fulfill Kennedy's legacy, he pledged to desegregate the South and build a Great Society with taxpayers' dollars. The Civil Rights Movement had brought poverty and racism to Americans' attention. Johnson's liberalism caught the public mood.[22]

Barry Goldwater won the Republican nomination in 1964. He broke the grip of the east coast elites and gave western and southern conservatives a bigger role in their party. In the long run, this made Ronald Reagan's nomination in 1980 possible. In the short term, it allowed the media and the Democrats to paint the Republicans as dangerous and crazy.[23] Goldwater's complex constitutionalist opposition to civil rights legislation sounded like a play for the votes of bigoted southerners. If it was, it worked: Goldwater carried five states in the South. But he got whipped everywhere else.[24] The *St. Louis Globe-Democrat* reported that liberal-minded state authorities in Minnesota held a mock election in a St. Cloud prison. Two burglars stood in for the Goldwater-Miller ticket and a robber and a forger for Johnson-Humphrey. The President swept St. Cloud with over 60 percent of the vote.[25]

For his followers, Goldwater's defeat was hard to take. He had tried to stem the tide of liberalism, to break the waves of change that were lapping at Middle America's feet.[26] Pat sensed that the America of his childhood was disappearing fast. He could see it happen every Sunday in church. In the early 1960s, the

Catholic Church set about reforming itself, searching for relevance in the age of the atom.[27] Services in Latin were ditched and the ancient Tridentine Rite effectively outlawed. People started saying the Mass in their own tongue, rewriting the liturgy to suit local custom. From silent prayer, they embraced noisy participation. Children's choirs and tambourines were all the rage. Marble altars were torn out and replaced with tables—the Mass was now said facing the people in the style of a communal meal. The priest became more of a man than a servant of God, friendlier, less likely to use violence in the classroom, more likely to pull out a guitar and sing "Kumbaya."

The reformed Church engaged in "dialogue" with other faiths and conceded that God might be found in their temples, too. Evangelization all but ceased. The Church embraced new social responsibilities in preference to its ancient devotion to saving souls. Liberation theology taught that Christ was a socialist warrior who had fought for the poor against the rich. Rosary crusades were replaced with protests against nuclear bombs. The Church swapped its war against communism for a campaign for peace and plenty.[28]

American Catholics went along with these changes with remarkable docility. Perhaps they were welcomed; perhaps they seemed apiece with the liberated, egalitarian mood of the 1960s. But imagine Pat's shock the day he entered a church—the church in which he had been baptized, confirmed, and raised—to find that everything had changed.[29] Some traditionalist Catholics said that Marxists had infiltrated the Church hierarchy. Some even said that the Holy See was vacant and the Church no longer had a Pope.[30] Pat was no schismatic, but he did regret the changes. Like many traditionalists, he attended the Tridentine Rite whenever he could—gathering with a few others in priest holes all over D.C., the rite said in a whisper lest the bishop hear. And Pat saw a link between political and theological liberalism. As the 1960s wore on, he witnessed Catholic priests marching against a war on communism in Vietnam. He heard Catholic priests celebrate the economic system of Eastern Europe as a humane alternative to capitalism. He thought that the men he had been taught to call "Father" were behaving like children.[31]

Traditionalism created a paradox among orthodox Catholics like Pat. On the one hand, Buchanan longed to obey. On the other hand, to preserve anything worth obeying he had to fight the authority of reforming priests and bishops. Traditionalism turned conservatives into unlikely revolutionaries.[32]

Pat served two years at the *Globe-Democrat* before getting itchy feet. The paper gave him plenty of work and an associate-editorship, a remarkable accomplishment for a man of just twenty-six years. But he wanted to do something to help fight the liberals and St. Louis was too far from the action.

On December 9, 1964, Richard Nixon came to speak at Belleville, Illinois, just fifteen miles from Pat's home. The Vice President had made a new generation of fans during the general election, stumping hard enough for Barry Goldwater to look like he actually wanted him to win. Buchanan thought Nixon could unite the party and triumph in 1968, that the Republicans could put a man in the White House who would kick the communists out of South Vietnam. Pat's friend Don Hesse, the *Globe*'s cartoonist, was throwing a cocktail party for the Vice President at his home. Buchanan called him up and asked if he could orchestrate an introduction.

At the party, Hesse found the right moment and introduced a nervous Pat to the Vice President. "We've met before," said Buchanan, and recounted that summer afternoon at the Burning Tree golf club.[33] Nixon had changed since then. As Vice President he was the brash heir to the throne, a shoo-in after Eisenhower retired. But Kennedy's victory in the 1960 presidential election had stopped him in his tracks. He ran to become governor of California in 1962 and was beaten again. The world had presumed that it wouldn't have Nixon to kick around anymore. But he had clawed his way back.[34]

His eyes, remembered Buchanan, "were bright, savvy, experienced, cautious, weary, and broken."

"I hope you're going to run again in '68," said Pat. "And if you are, I want to be on board early."

"Before we get to 1968," chastened Nixon, "the Republicans will have to win in 1966, or the nomination won't be worth anything. That's what I'll be working on this coming year." The Vice President was playing it cool—doing everything necessary to win the nomination but to do so without seeming eager. He asked Buchanan what he did for a living.

"I'm assistant editorial editor," he replied, which sounded slightly absurd.

"But do you *write*?" demanded Nixon.

"Three or four editorials a day, Mr. Vice President, on local, national, and foreign issues." Nixon pumped Buchanan for information, the questions coming so fast that five minutes felt like an hour. This was Nixon's technique—to see what and how much someone knew, to gauge their usefulness and then, if necessary, return later for more.

"I need someone to help handle my correspondence," the Vice President finally said. "It's getting too much for me alone. And also to help me write a monthly column I've signed to do. I might be in touch." Then he complimented Buchanan on his date to signal that the interview was over. Nixon worked the room and Pat went home. The next day, Pat "debriefed" Hesse to find out what happened. The Vice President was impressed, Hesse reported. On the forty-five-minute car ride home, he had talked about nothing else but Buchanan.[35]

Pat waited by the phone like an anxious suitor. He had just about given up when, on December 19, he got a call at his desk from New York. It was Richard Nixon.

"Can you come to my offices for a chat?" he asked. Pat wasn't sure he could take a day off work and suggested that he run it past his publisher. Nixon said "okay," and rang off. A few minutes later Amberg entered Pat's office, looking dazed. Richard Nixon, the former Vice President of the United States, just called and asked if he could give Buchanan a day off work to visit him in New York.

"Do you think I should go, sir?" asked Pat.

The publisher looked at him like he was mad and said, "Of course!"[36]

Nixon was holed up in a law firm in New York called Nixon, Mudge, Rose, Guthrie, and Alexander. His job gave him the time and money to do better things, like tour Asia and the Middle East as a sales rep for Coca-Cola. He fielded calls at his desk from the White House and the Republican National Committee and lived in a prestigious apartment on Fifth Avenue, just a floor below Nelson Rockefeller. He was comfortable but frustrated. Nixon missed the intellectual puzzle of politics.[37] A nervous Pat Buchanan sat down in front of him and the Vice President immediately launched a barrage of questions. Where did Buchanan come from, what did he know? Where did he stand?

What did he think of Romney, of Rockefeller? ("*While the conservatives do not want Romney, sir, they will not accept Rockefeller.*") What did he think of Goldwater? ("*He'll never run again, sir, but the Goldwater conservatives are the key to the nomination.*") What did he think would be the issues in 1966? If Buchanan worked with him on a syndicated column, what should they write about? How did he stand on a surtax, on civil rights, on Vietnam? What should be done there?

Nixon had no obvious ego; he was untroubled by contradiction. He struck Buchanan as "the least ideological statesman I ever encountered" and, as such, a first-rate conversationalist. Nixon's mind was supple and complex. Conversation took the pattern of a fugue. It began with a simple theme ("*What do you think of President Johnson's approach to Vietnam?*") that the two men would explore; then Nixon would offer a variation ("*Can we negotiate with the North Vietnamese in good faith?*"), and another ("*Or should we bomb Hanoi?*"), and another still ("*And what part will China play in all this?*"), until every possible twist on the original theme had been examined and exhausted. Throughout, Nixon nodded and smiled and moved the music on fast, so that those providing the answers could be fooled into thinking that he agreed with them—when in fact he was simply exploring all options. They talked for three hours and, by the end of it, Buchanan was convinced that Nixon would rather level Beijing than recognize Red China.

And Nixon would telegraph what he wanted to hear by making a strong assertion, but suffixing it with "or am I wrong?"

"You're not as conservative as Bill Buckley, are you—or am I wrong?" he asked. If anything, Pat Buchanan was *more* conservative than William F. Buckley, but Nixon had just called the Buckleyites "more dangerous" than the right-wing John Birch Society.

"I have tremendous admiration for Bill Buckley," replied Buchanan. Nixon nodded and moved on. The answer was a good one; it hinted that he was a conservative, but was savvy enough not to say so.[38] Nixon offered him the job. Again, Buchanan insisted he run it by his overwhelmed publisher, who the Vice President called and requested he give Pat a leave of absence. Pat left the office exhausted. He flew back to Missouri, gave his furniture away to a pretty girl, and said good-bye to St. Louis.[39]

THREE

A New Old Man

P at was joined in the Nixon office by a pretty secretary called Shelley Ann Scarney. Shelley grew up in the tiny historic district of Detroit known as Indian Village. In the 1950s, she graduated from the University of Michigan with a degree in political science. Shelley went east in search of work and found herself in Washington, D.C. A friend offered her a job as a secretary in Vice President Richard Nixon's office. She was part of a small staff—no more than twenty-five—located in the Senate building, just across the hall from Jack Kennedy's office. She stayed there for the length of Nixon's term. Softly spoken, with measured words and a careful smile, she was the perfect personal assistant. Shelley often made the time go by quicker with typing contests with the other girls. During the 1960 presidential campaign, she traveled with the candidate to every state in the Union. One of her jobs included phoning D.C. from the airport, taking down news stories in shorthand, and then typing them up for the Vice President to read in his hotel.[1] After the 1960 defeat, Shelley went to work as a legal secretary; but dutifully returned in 1962 to help out with the California campaign. She was perfectly settled in a better-paid job when, one day, she got a call from Nixon to say he was thinking about another run for the presidency. Would she help?[2]

The good and faithful Shelley Scarney walked into Nixon's New York office and found that there was a new boy on the staff. Nixon's permanent secretary, Rose Mary Woods, was where she always was—in the outside office on the typewriter. The Vice President was in the main office, chatting to someone on the phone. But sitting behind a huge pile of mail, hidden by a plume of cigarette smoke, was a young man from Georgetown called Pat Buchanan. Three years later, Shelley would marry him.[3]

Pat deferred to Shelley straight away. Of the two, she was by far the more politically experienced and closer to Nixon. But Shelley noticed that Pat already had an almost familial relationship to the Nixons. The Vice President delighted in Pat's chutzpah and confrontational conservatism, his "eccentricity and encyclopedic knowledge."[4] Pat called the Vice President "the Old Man." A mutual friend, Richard Moore, said, "I often thought that if Nixon had a son, he would have liked to have Buchanan."[5]

Pat had hundreds of letters to answer and newspaper articles to underline and summarize. Yet most afternoons, Nixon would call him into his office for an extensive interview. Buchanan's answers were jotted down on the Vice President's yellow legal pads. They were wonderful dialogues, full of penetrating analysis and wit. The Old Man would bounce ideas off Pat, encouraging him to disagree and challenge his assumptions. But when it turned dark outside, Nixon would wrap it up and go home; leaving Pat to finish the mail and write the Vice President's column. It wasn't unusual for the working day to only begin at 9 p.m.[6]

Every person on Nixon's staff reflected some aspect of his character. Like Buchanan, Nixon came from a nonelite background and was a conservative by instinct. He had fashioned an image for himself that was ordinary and antiestablishment—a spokesman for the "forgotten American."[7] He fancied himself as an everyman, although their conversation was far from barroom. Pat never spoke with the Old Man in the language he had heard him use back at the Burning Tree. They talked philosophy and religion, along with the minutiae of public policy. But both felt, given the weight of power and influence stacked against them, that they had to play tough to get what they wanted. Nixon taught Pat to fight with words, to kick a man with adjectives as he curled up on the floor begging for the bell. Pat stayed up late in Nixon's office, punching the typewriter keys like he was hitting the bag in Pop's basement; one in the eye for Lyndon Johnson, one in the eye for Nelson Rockefeller.

Nixon had intelligence and soul: There were times when he would wellup or get angry, but also moments of incredible objective insight and political genius. When he moved to New York, Pat Buchanan swore fidelity to the Nixons and joined their clan. Pat surely felt welcome enough to bum cigarettes off Mrs. Nixon, who Pat remembered as a "lovely lady" who "kidded" around the office and got "right in to all the politics." Her wit was somewhat sardonic. She had suffered terribly on the campaign trail in 1962, and asked her husband not to do it again in 1968. But she was often in the office, with an unfiltered cigarette dangling between a here-we-go-again smile.[8]

Nixon started his comeback with a tour of congressional districts during the 1966 campaign. Pat was by his side, crashing on cots in motels and ferrying him to and from the airport in hired cars. The era of social reform was grinding to an end. Johnson had achieved much, but the pace of change was too fast for some. Many whites feared that the government was trying to tamper with the "ethnic purity" of their communities, workplaces, and schools; that expanded welfare meant robbing from the hardworking middle class to give to the lazy poor.[9] African Americans, frustrated with broken promises on poverty and racism, tore up the inner cities. In 1966 and 1967, fires burned in Atlanta, San Francisco, Oakland, Baltimore, Seattle, Cleveland, Cincinnati, Columbus, Newark, Chicago, New York City, and Detroit. The Detroit riot lasted five days and 43 people were killed, 467 injured, 7,231 arrested, and 2,509 stores looted. Johnson had promised too much to too many too soon, said Nixon.[10] The 1966 effort was a success for the Republicans; they gained forty-seven seats in the House and three in the Senate.[11]

Richard Nixon was back.

By the end of 1967, there were 485,600 American soldiers in Vietnam. One of those serving was Jimmy Buchanan, so Pat backed his brother and backed the war. American views about the righteousness of the Vietnam War fluctuated throughout the 1960s, but support for the troops was consistently high. It was tough to accept that people's husbands, sons, and fathers were dying for nothing in the paddy fields of Southeast Asia; so many people refused to believe it.[12] The war was going badly, Pat Buchanan argued, not because it was immoral or unwinnable, but because it was improperly fought.[13]

On January 30, 1968, the Vietcong launched an offensive against Saigon and overran the U.S. embassy. Media images from the siege shattered confidence in the Vietnam project and Johnson's poll figures plummeted.[14] The next day, Buchanan and Nixon flew to Nashua, New Hampshire, to file for the first-in-the-nation presidential primary. They left it to the very last minute, booking the Vice President in a motel under an assumed name. In New Hampshire, the Old Man relaunched himself as a New Nixon. The Old Nixon was a gutter-fighter; the New Nixon was a world statesman—a thoughtful public servant who promised to unite the nation and bring "peace with honor" in Vietnam.[15] He declared his candidacy with a dignified letter to 150,000 people in New Hampshire written by Pat Buchanan. It spoke of Nixon's years in the political wilderness and the opportunities it offered to learn about the problems facing America. "I believe," he concluded, "that I have found some answers."[16]

Buchanan's most well-defined role in the campaign was the production of news summaries that kept Nixon in touch with the mood of the country. Pat would tear through the early editions looking for relevant stories; he would cover the copy in red ink and highlight the paragraphs that he wanted Shelley to retype on thick paper. Pat often stayed up past midnight working on it, then he'd hand it to Nixon as he boarded his jet in the morning—who flicked through it once or twice and handed it straight back. It might have seemed like a lot of effort for a throwaway glance at a sheaf of papers, but relations with the press were crucial to the success of the campaign. The New Nixon was an image, not a man. The image had to be perfectly pitched to the media, so knowing what turned them on and what turned them off was important.[17]

Nixon sensed that President Johnson was in trouble. Minnesota senator Eugene McCarthy had entered the Democratic primaries to protest the war. McCarthy was an urbane, witty man with a laconic disposition that served him well on television. Where Nixon was buttoned down and driven, McCarthy was spontaneous and lazy (one of his staffers complained that, even in the crucial days of the campaign, he never rose before 9 a.m.).[18] He peppered his speeches with ruminations on Catholic thought and his message was essentially conservative—that the U.S. government had overreached itself in Vietnam, that all attempts to improve man were likely doomed to failure.[19] McCarthy had been written off as a protest candidate but, after the embassy siege, he looked like a real threat in the Democratic New Hampshire primary.[20]

On the Republican side in New Hampshire, Nixon's only real opponent was Michigan governor George Romney. Romney hoped to run strong on an antiwar ticket, but exposed himself to ridicule when he told a TV interviewer that he had been "brainwashed" into supporting the Vietnam War. Nixon's private polls showed him leading Romney 7–1, but he still told the press that it was going to be "pretty close" and that defeat wouldn't knock him out of the race.[21] Romney ran a good campaign throughout January and early February 1968, doing three or four meetings a day and drawing big crowds. Buchanan implored the Old Man to hit the state hard but, as always, Nixon preferred caution. "Let him kill himself up there," he said. Too much campaigning in 1960 left him irritable and ugly. So Team Nixon limited his appearances to three days, then flew him down to Key Biscayne for rest and relaxation. He returned to New Hampshire "looking," Pat said, "like a million dollars." Romney buckled under the strain and pulled out. "I learned an important lesson about going the distance," said Buchanan. "Nixon was like a boxer who took all the punches and was left standing . . . He understood that sometimes the winner is the guy who hangs on in there and exhausts his opponent."[22]

But, still, Pat was nervous. The New Nixon hadn't yet been tried out on the voters. Until he proved himself as a vote getter, the nomination was far from secure. In a Boston hotel bar in early February, Pat was approached by a queer-looking fellow with a torn suit and a bad comb-over. The journalist introduced himself as Hunter S. Thompson. Thompson told Pat that Nixon was "a hopeless bum with no hope of winning anything." It was getting late and Buchanan invited him to continue the argument in his room. Between them they finished off "half a gallon of Old Crow" whiskey. It was obvious, Thompson wrote later, that Pat thought the journalist was "stone crazy." But why, demanded Hunter, did a man with obvious "good sense" hang around an old fraud like Nixon?[23]

On March 12, Nixon won the New Hampshire primary with 78 percent of the vote. Antiwar Republicans wrote in Rockefeller's name, giving him 11 percent and suddenly making him the new man to beat. California governor Ronald Reagan said he might enter, too. Among the Democrats, McCarthy took 42 percent to President Johnson's 49 percent. The challenger claimed a moral victory.[24] On March 16, Robert Kennedy declared his candidacy for the Democratic nomination, splitting the antiwar movement.[25] Pressure mounted on Johnson to campaign properly, and he announced that he would give a major speech on Vietnam on March 31. Nixon was flying back from visiting his daughter and asked Buchanan to wait for him at the airport and listen to the speech on the radio. A huge media pack gathered on the runway. Pat stretched out in the car, put his feet up on the dashboard, and listened to the President make yet another offer to halt the bombing in exchange for serious peace talks. But then Johnson added that, at this crucial time, the presidency must stand above partisan bickering. And so, "I shall not seek, and I will not accept, the nomination of my party for another term as your President." Pat sat bolt upright. Nixon was touching down. Buchanan leaped out of the car and ran down the runway, trying to get to him before he reached the press. Breathless, he whispered Nixon the news: President Johnson was out of the race. The media swam around. The Old Man gave them a bloodless smile.

"Well, it looks like this is the year of the dropout," Nixon said. And with Johnson gone, the White House looked like his for the taking.[26]

Pat was Nixon's advance man. He traveled to wherever the Vice President was going to give a speech, usually on a small prop plane that had all the ballast of a jelly on strings. A white-faced Pat would meet with the local GOP committee and ask them what the Old Man should talk about—local crime rates right down to the price of milk.[27] He passed all the info back to headquarters from a phone box across the street. "So Nixon would come and get up and say 'We've got inflation and the price has gone right up down at so-and-so's store'"; and the crowd would gush at the thought that the former Vice President knew so much about their little town. Later, Pat graduated to Nixon's on-the-road speechwriter. The Old Man had his own speech: Buchanan provided an additional three paragraphs that was aimed at the locals. Nixon would recite his standard fare, pause, take Buchanan's paragraphs out of his pocket and read them, and then return to global affairs. Nixon understood the maxim that "all politics is local."[28]

Nixon knocked out Rockefeller in Nebraska and Oregon. Reagan was doing no better than Rockefeller, although Nixon declined to enter the June 5

California primary. Reagan's sweep across the state actually gave him a slight plurality in the total votes cast in the primaries. That same night, Robert Kennedy also won California, placing him a step closer to the nomination.[29] Pat went to bed weighing up all the pros and cons of another Nixon vs. Kennedy election. At 3 a.m., a call came through to his hotel room. Someone had shot Bobby Kennedy. Pat stared at the ceiling and went numb. His hand trembling, he phoned through to Nixon and told him the bad news. He already knew. Nixon's daughter and son-in-law had watched it as it happened live on TV—the singing, the dancing, the shots, and the screams.

"What do you want to do?" asked Pat.

"Give me three paragraphs on law and order," Nixon said wearily. The campaign went on.[30]

T he Republican and Democratic nominations were decided not by votes but by backdoor politicking. While McCarthy took primary after primary, Vice President Hubert Humphrey sewed up the Democratic title by winning the support of party and labor leaders behind closed doors.[31] Nixon was not his party's first choice, either. He arrived at the Republican convention in Miami to discover a surprising groundswell of support for Reagan. Reagan had notched up conservative credentials by taking a stand against antiwar students at the University of California at Berkeley. He couldn't win, but if he cut a deal with Rockefeller, he could deny Nixon the nomination. Only a last-minute endorsement from South Carolina senator Strom Thurmond secured the Old Man's nomination. In exchange for a series of promises on Supreme Court appointments and school desegregation, Thurmond helped convince Southern delegations to vote for Nixon on the first ballot. The Reagan revolt was deferred.[32]

The banality of the New Nixon whitewashed the convention. In his speech he promised peace with honor in Vietnam and a new commitment to tackling poverty. What he offered was not substantive change—policy details were thin—but a reordering of America's priorities. He promised to listen to "the voice of the great majority of Americans, the forgotten Americans—the non-shouters; the non-demonstrators." This was the image that Nixon left in most viewers' minds—one of calm, rational authority on their side against the wreckers.[33] He chose Maryland governor Spiro Agnew as his running mate. Agnew had denounced civil disorder in the city of Baltimore and blamed civil rights leaders for failing to stop it. His nomination was a sign that Nixon was running on a law-and-order ticket.[34]

As was custom, Nixon retired from campaigning during the Democratic convention in Chicago. He spent August with his friend Bebe Rebozo, in Key Biscayne, Florida. Buchanan was his spy in Chicago. As he walked through the crowds sucking up abuse, Pat was shocked by what he saw and heard. The antiwar left descended on the city to protest the coronation of Hubert Humphrey. It was a cacophony of foul language, Vietcong war songs, and Yippie theatrics.[35] At night there was bloodshed. In Buchanan's opinion the beautiful people "got what they deserved." A horde of about 10,000 protestors were met with the full force of Mayor Richard Daley's police, who ruthlessly broke up rallies and marches. The police overreacted, using nightsticks and tear gas to dispel the largely peaceful crowds.[36] The demonstrators gathered in Grant Park, across from the hotel where Buchanan was lodging. He stayed up all night with the writer Norman Mailer, drinking cocktails and watching the fight down below. Daley had imposed an 11 p.m. curfew on the demonstrators and when they failed to move, the police charged them with tear gas and truncheons. Mailer leaned over the balcony and screamed at the cops, "Pigs! Fascists!" Buchanan leaned over and shouted, "Hey, you've missed one!" The Old Man rang through and asked how the convention was going. "Listen to this," said Pat, and he held the telephone up to the window. Nixon listened to the screams below. Buchanan got back on the line and told him the election was sewn up. The Democrats were falling apart. A thousand miles away, Nixon laughed.[37]

The Democratic convention nominated Humphrey but he led a divided coalition. The Democrats were still the majority party in America, but, on the left, the antiwar movement threatened to sit out the general election and, on the right, thousands of southerners and blue-collar workers were defecting to the independent ticket of Alabama governor George C. Wallace. Wallace was hugely popular in the South because he had resisted the desegregation of Alabama's schools.[38] In 1968 he ran on a law-and-order ticket. Taking the South out of contention, he tried to break into working-class votes in northern cities plagued by crime and political unrest. Liberal welfare programs, he said, stole from the working poor to give to the indolent poor.[39] The message and the medium were one in Wallace, who roused audiences to rapturous anger at the "pointy-head" bureaucrats and intellectuals who had hijacked the welfare state and turned it into a tool of social engineering. "I've got a four letter word for y'all," he said to cussing hippies who interrupted his speeches: "W.O.R.K."[40]

A mid-September poll gave Nixon 43 percent, Humphrey 31 percent, and Wallace 19 percent. By the end of the month, Wallace hit a high of 21 percent.[41] Stalling peace talks in Paris and the defections of southern and labor Democrats to Wallace suggested Nixon was heading for a landslide.[42]

Then everything fell apart.

On September 30, Humphrey gave a game-changing speech. Nixon had coasted along, happy to avoid major issues and let the Democrats duke it out. But Humphrey announced that, if elected, he would halt the bombing of North Vietnam. The public responded positively and a few days later a campaign spokesman said that Humphrey would withdraw all troops on January 21, 1969. The antiwar movement began to drift back to the Democrats. Signs appeared at Humphrey rallies reading, "If you mean it, we're with you."[43]

Buchanan got straight on the phone to the Old Man and told him to "Hit Humphrey, hit him hard. Go right at him." Pat thought that Humphrey's posturing was cynical and dangerous—it was the boys in the field who would take the risk if he halted bombing and the Vietcong was able to regroup. But he also recognized that Nixon's only hope was to "drive a wedge between the Democrats." A united majority party would be unstoppable. The peace lobby was back in the coalition and so, too, were northern working-class whites. A campaign by labor had successfully drawn blue-collar workers back from the Wallace ticket. Wallace still held the South, so it was the Democrats who benefited the most from his decline. "I could feel them coming together," Buchanan moaned. "The Democrats were the Union Army. We didn't stand a chance against them." Yet Nixon wouldn't deliver the killer punch. The Old Nixon might have called Humphrey a wimp, but the New Nixon was above that. The essence of his appeal was his lack of definition. To come out strongly either way on the Vietnam issue would scuttle his campaign.[44]

Nixon was haunted by comments he had made earlier in the primary season that he had a "plan" to end the Vietnam War.[45] He had a formulation in mind (involving military and diplomatic pressure) but no definite strategy. Nevertheless, the media in New Hampshire reported that Nixon had hinted at a "secret plan" and the misunderstanding stuck. When Buchanan first got wind of it, he immediately called the Old Man and demanded to know what it was: "Because people were dying and if he had a plan, he ought to share it with the President." But Nixon had been bowdlerized by a media determined to create a story even if he didn't want to give them one. The myth that Nixon was either holding out on the President or playing with an empty hand contributed to a revival of "Tricky Dick" skepticism.[46]

The flashy marketing had backfired. Storming the country, sweating and shouting answers at screaming students, Hubert Humphrey's campaign seemed more real.[47] Someone in the GOP campaign showed Buchanan a poll that put Humphrey at 43 percent and Nixon at 40 percent. Michigan and Texas were lost. Seeing three years of effort drain away, Buchanan broke out in hives on his hands and legs. On election night, Team Nixon holed up in the Waldorf Astoria and watched the returns come in. The popular vote was desperately close; they were waiting for Illinois to break. Mayor Daley was holding out on releasing the Chicago vote, in Buchanan's opinion waiting to see if he could cook up "enough votes to steal it." Nixon had won, but if Humphrey took Illinois the election might be thrown to the House.

Buchanan wandered around the hotel and found a room with an open door and a bath. He got into the tub and fell asleep. A little after 5 a.m., Shelley found him and woke him up. Illinois had been called for Nixon. They had done it. They had won by just 43.4–42.7 percent. Buchanan asked her where the new President was. Shelley told him they had been unable to find Pat so went to Key Biscayne without him.

"What about moi?" Buchanan cried.[48]

FOUR

Speaking Up for the Silent Majority

In the popular imagination, the Nixon White House has the power and mystery of an Ottoman Court—a place of intrigue, dirty money, spooling tapes, soft clicks on the telephone, and long lists of enemies. The reality of those early years was quite different. Nixon delegated a great deal of power. He surrounded himself with a tight coterie of advisors, mostly square young men from business and the media. Crew cuts and thin black ties were typical. The spirit was technocratic, sometimes liberal.[1] When he discovered that Johnson had infested the White House with bugging devices, Nixon had every single one torn out.[2]

Pat brought color. He was now thirty, and one journalist called him "husky, ham-faced, rough looking but with dancing Irish eyes and a bright rapid-fire line of gab." Puffing away on cigarettes and blustering back and forth with newsmen, he could have been a displaced Teamster official—but for his ideology. "He likes to interrupt himself suddenly to ask, somewhat portentously, 'But what can governments do?' or 'It's that old problem: How can one know when one is entering a Dark Age?' Buchanan comes on brash, but guilelessly, so one gets to like him for it."[3]

In the Nixon gang, Pat was the favorite son. He had the swagger of a boy who knew he was loved. Richard Nixon delighted in Pat's mischief. Older sons, who had been around longer, were less impressed. Chief of Staff H. R. Haldeman struggled to control him. He recorded in his diary that Pat went into a meeting with the President on his first day in office to discuss TV and press relations. When he emerged after an hour, Haldeman pointed out that Pat's fly was undone.[4] Buchanan laughed it off. A few days later, Pat arrived for a staff meeting in the Oval Office. The President wasn't attending so Pat, to everyone's horror, sat in his chair.[5] Haldeman worried that Pat's behavior might bring the family into disrepute and asked the Old Man several times to rein him in.

Pat had to learn to defer. President Nixon couldn't be contradicted in the way that Vice President Nixon could. Rather than challenge him directly in the Oval Office, Buchanan wrote long, surprisingly frank memos that said on paper what protocol demanded not be said to his face. When the memos were leaked many years later, Buchanan was shocked to read just how rude he had been—often using adjectives to describe his boss like "gutless" and "aimless."[6] It is difficult to think of any other President who would have tolerated Buchanan's polemical abuse. In conversation, Nixon still used his "or am I wrong?" technique, but no one could now reply with a flat "yes." Instead Buchanan weighed up advantages and disadvantages of a Nixon-originated idea and concluded, on balance, that the administration might move in a different direction. Nixon once told a staffer to pass on the message to Pat that he was to "stop sending me problems without sending me solutions." Pat was respectful, but was still prepared to criticize.[7]

Two of Pat's political brothers on the speechwriting staff were Ray Price and Bill Safire. Their appointments were an experiment in Republican multiculturalism: Nixon's effort to take the best from all backgrounds. Safire recalled: "On the old political spectrum, Price was the liberal, Buchanan the conservative, Safire the centrist; Price a WASP, Buchanan a Catholic, Safire a Jew . . . Price is introverted, I'm extroverted, Buchanan in between." A Buchanan draft might be given to Price to be softened or to Safire to be made more quotable.[8]

Pat's full-time job was publisher of the same daily news summaries he had produced during the campaign. The new dailies were written and edited by Lyndon "Mort" Allin, a former social studies teacher who had been recruited to work as head of Youth for Nixon in 1967. They were run independently of the White House press relations department, giving them an air of factual independence.[9] The summaries were supposed to be a warts-and-all account of press coverage—not filtered to flatter. Buchanan, Allin, and a staff of about four others began compiling stories after the morning news shows. Work started in earnest at 3 p.m. and finished sometime after midnight. A fifty-page report landed on the President's desk in the morning at 8 a.m., with a brief introduction by Buchanan written an hour before. On Monday morning the Old Man received a special weekend edition.[10]

The summaries were anything but neutral. After Watergate, some people said that Pat had poisoned Nixon's mind against the press and the Democrats with selective quoting.[11] There was some truth in that. Pat would advise one of his pals—like Bill Buckley—to write a scathing critique of détente or high taxes on a Tuesday and, on Wednesday morning, it would appear on the front page of the summary marked for special interest. In this way, Buchanan started to get a reputation as the conservative movement's man on the inside.[12] In contrast, Pat quoted selectively from liberal critiques to give the impression that mainstream newspapers were unduly critical of the new administration. On the basis of perceived slights, Nixon refused access to *The New York Times* and *The Washington Post* and forbade his employees to speak to individual journalists. Bill Safire ignored the freeze-out and got a tap put on his phones as a result. It didn't take long for Nixon to see the value in Johnson's bugs.[13]

But the summaries illustrated the limits of Buchanan's influence as well as its potential. If in the mood, Nixon poured through the reports, praised them, and wrote reams of notes on them. A daily summary could generate up to twenty memos from the Oval Office. Some, however, were ignored.[14] When the Watergate transcripts were released they revealed that Nixon privately read for himself almost every single article that Buchanan had meticulously paraphrased anyway: He received daily copies of the newspapers that he disavowed. Pat did not shape the President's view of the media; he confirmed it.[15]

Life in the White House could be melodramatic. Richard Nixon was a passionate man, given to explosions of anger. But these were tempered by a statesman's calm and ability to reflect. What he said in private rarely equated to what he expected to happen in public. Buchanan and other family retainers referred to his occasional bouts of terror as "The Old Man letting off steam." Experienced staffers even joked about his ability to fly off the handle and sometimes encouraged it—almost as a kind of therapy. When compiling the daily news summaries, Buchanan liked to highlight unpleasant things that the North Vietnamese had said about Nixon, underlining words like "gangster" and "capitalist lackey." The President took the bait and wrote "Bomb them!" in the summary margins. Such tirades were cathartic. No one who knew Nixon believed that he meant them or expected his instructions to be followed. Some historians and commentators, poring through hours of tapes and memos, interpreted Nixon's words literally. That is a mistake. Richard Nixon was an intellectual who enjoyed dialogue. He explored every avenue of thought, often putting out controversial statements to test radical ideas and challenge his subordinates. Long after Watergate unraveled and the President resigned, Buchanan reflected that what must have happened was "Nixon told someone to do something and the damned fool actually did it."[16]

There were moments of bitter honesty. Once, Barry Goldwater dropped around for a drink in the Oval Office, Pat in tow. Nixon pointed at his desk and said, "Hi Barry, you want to sit in the chair?"

Goldwater replied: "Hell no, you can have the damn thing." Barry told a story about when he visited Jack Kennedy during the Bay of Pigs invasion. It was going badly and Kennedy was climbing the walls. While JFK went for a walk in the Rose Garden to cool off, Goldwater sat in his rocker to see how it felt. Kennedy snuck back in and said, "Barry, do you want this fucking job?"

Buchanan found that hilarious, but Nixon looked sour. He had felt the sting of Jack Kennedy's snobbery. "The Bay of Pigs was the only time he ever called me, too," muttered the Old Man.[17]

Nixonism was nonideological. It had certain prejudices (Nixon was unlikely to surrender in Vietnam or nominate Gloria Steinem to the Supreme Court), but Nixon's first concern was reelection; he would do whatever it took to stay in office. Buchanan understood that the President was "not a conservative." Sometimes, he even called him a "liberal." But he also saw him as a fine anticommunist. And he sensed that if Nixon could be convinced that a conservative line was popular, then he would follow it.[18]

Pat argued that if the President wanted to get reelected, he had to reach out to the people who voted for George Wallace. The numbers suggested he was right. Nixon got 43.4 percent in 1968, George Wallace 13.5 percent. Together, their vote was nearly 60 percent. So, pound away on crime, Vietnam, and the liberal obsession with civil rights and Nixon had a natural majority to command.[19] But the moderates within the administration said different. Americans might have moved to the right on social issues, but they still expected the government to deliver on welfare and jobs. Take civil rights. Whites didn't want their kids to get bused several miles to a majority-black school in the name of integration. But this didn't mean that they associated themselves with the George Wallace brand of segregation.[20] The conservative vote in the South was fractured. Poor, rural whites, who often expressed racist sentiment, went for Wallace. Middle-class suburban whites, who liked to think of themselves as racially tolerant, went for Nixon.[21]

The administration was torn over what to do. If anyone won the debate, it was the moderates. In conversation with the Old Man, Haldeman laughed about Pat's conservatism. The favorite son was a great speechwriter, conceded Haldeman. On many issues he was probably right. But the American people were not as conservative as Buchanan thought; or, at least, they didn't like to think they were. Nixon agreed.[22]

It was about this time that Pat popularized the phrase "political hardball." Like many of the great lines that came out of the Nixon White House, who precisely invented it is up for debate. But it reads like pure Pat Buchanan.

The press was tough on Nixon throughout 1969. To end the Vietnam War without surrendering, the administration tried to build up the South Vietnamese forces to the point where they could defend themselves. American presence was reduced, although bombing was intensified. In March 1969, America began a secret barrage along the border between Vietnam and Cambodia in an effort to crush Vietcong supply lines. "Vietnamization" and the bombing campaign produced few obvious results. Nixon had pledged to end the war quickly and bring peace with honor. The press said that Tricky Dick had lied.[23]

In October 1969, Nixon called Pat into his office. He had read the daily news summary, which contained two fresh editorials calling him a liar. "He asked me if I could draft a letter to the editors," Pat recalled. "I said, sir, it's already gone way beyond that. We need to play hardball with these people."[24] Buchanan had just finished reading an article by David Broder in *The Washington Post* called "The Breaking of the President." Broder wrote:

> The men and the movement that broke Lyndon Johnson's authority
> in 1968 are out to break Richard M. Nixon in 1969. The likelihood
> is great that they will succeed again, for breaking a president is,
> like most feats, easier to accomplish the second time around."[25]

Buchanan told Nixon that he agreed with Broder. The press wanted to prove its power by bringing him down. Most of the editors were east coast liberal snobs who just couldn't stand to see a man of the people in the White House. "We've got to stand up and go out and defend your policy," said Pat. Nixon agreed and he went to work on a national address.[26]

Nixon wrote the speech himself, but he borrowed a phrase Buchanan had written for Vice President Agnew: the Silent Majority. On November 3, 1969, Nixon took the American people through the steps that led to war and the conditions he was laying down for peace. He finished:

> And so tonight—to you, *the great silent majority* [italics mine] of
> my fellow Americans—I ask for your support . . . Let us be united
> for peace. Let us also be united against defeat. Because let us un-
> derstand: North Vietnam cannot defeat or humiliate the United
> States. Only Americans can do that.[27]

The speech was a hit. The White House received over 80,000 telegrams and letters in support. Over 300 representatives and 58 senators sent their congratulations, and a Gallup poll gave Nixon a 68 percent approval rating. But the enthusiasm was not reflected in the media coverage. The networks followed it with "instant analysis" sessions that gave it a drubbing. ABC's Tom Jarrell said that the speech offered "no quick solutions" and threatened to "polarize" the country. On NBC, anchor John Chancellor opined that "the essence of the speech has been a defense of his plan to end the war that he thinks is working.

His critics think it's not working and it's making the war go on longer, and they will be after him again."[28] The White House was particularly concerned with a glowing spot given by ABC to administration critic Averell Harriman. Its length, twenty-five minutes, rivaled the President's and smacked of an official rebuttal by the network.[29] The morning newspapers were just as bad.

Pat Buchanan learned an important lesson from the Silent Majority speech. He took it for granted that the people he knew at Columbia were liberals; that they were always going to be nasty to a conservative. But he saw that part of the problem was that conservatism didn't play well on TV. Nixon's lawyerly defense of his policies just wasn't interesting enough. He observed:

> That the conservative and the . . . journalist should be as mongoose and cobra is not surprising . . . The virtues traditionally prized by conservatives—party fidelity, commitment to principle, respect for traditional values and established institutions, political consistency— are poison to television news. They need a daily plateful of dissent, action, excitement and drama, which it is fair to say are not customarily the conservative's long suits.[30]

The liberals made good TV. They burned flags and bras. Conservatism is innately dull. "There is a genuine question," said Buchanan, "whether any conservative politician can rivet the camera's attention without ceasing to be, strictly speaking, a conservative." The only way to get noticed was to float conservative ideas in a radical, noisy way. The day after the Silent Majority speech, Haldeman wrote Buchanan and told him to compose a letter to each of the newspapers protesting their coverage. Pat refused. "I said, 'I won't do that.' We need to fight back louder than that." Buchanan suggested they find someone to play hardball with the press. Haldeman wrote back "P. agrees." But "P." was above doing himself. Luckily, there was one man in the administration who was not.[31]

Vice President Spiro Agnew had no intention of going down in history as Nixon's hatchet man: He had ambitions for 1976.[32] But the moment he read the speech Buchanan prepared for him, Agnew caved in.[33] Buchanan sent a draft to Nixon and the President called him into the Oval Office. Nixon flicked through a couple of pages in silence, then sat down at his desk and started writing in the margins. "Let's say this here," he muttered. "And that there; I've always wanted to say that." Pat stood over him and watched as the President poured his soul out onto the page, overjoyed to finally have a chance to speak his mind. He handed the speech back and said, "Let's do it! This'll tear the scab off those bastards!"[34]

On November 13, Agnew put on a show at a Republican conference in Des Moines, Iowa. His hair slicked back, his black eyes darting about the room, he began:

> Monday night, a week ago, President Nixon delivered the most important address of his Administration, one of the most important of our decade. His subject was Vietnam. His hope was to rally the American people to see the conflict through to a lasting and just peace in the Pacific ... When the President completed his address—an address that he spent weeks in preparing—his words and policies were subjected to instant analysis and querulous criticism. The audience of seventy-million Americans—gathered to hear the President of the United States—was inherited by a small band of network commentators and self-appointed analysts, the majority of whom expressed, in one way or another, their hostility to what he had to say.

Agnew laid out, for the first time, the conservative case against the American media. Of course, his biggest issue was the predominance of New York and Washington, D.C., elites who put a liberal slant on everything they reported, but he also challenged the quality and ethics of contemporary reportage— particularly television. Television's constant quest for a potent image had seen facts and intellect sacrificed for sex and violence. "Normality has become the nemesis of the evening news ... Bad news drives out good news. The irrational is more controversial than the rational. Concurrence can no longer compete with dissent." Agnew asked "what is the end value" of television—"to enlighten, or to profit?" Capitalists and hippies were conspiring to downgrade American culture, scraping the bottom line in every sense.[35]

The Des Moines speech set off a firestorm. Liberals accused the administration of undermining free speech. Conservatives were thrilled that someone
had finally kicked back at the left-wing media, sweet revenge for what they did
to Barry Goldwater.[36] The Silent Majority and Des Moines speeches were,
in Buchanan's opinion, "the moment when Nixon really became president." It
was also the moment when Pat became indispensable. Nixon and Haldeman
wanted to leave the Des Moines speech as the last word on the subject of press
bias. Buchanan stood in the Oval Office and argued the opposite: "I said that
we've got to show we're serious, Mr. President. We've got to follow it up." Seven
days later, Agnew appeared in George Wallace's backyard city of Montgomery, Alabama, to flay *The Washington Post* and *The New York Times*, too.[37]

And so began Spiro Agnew's alliterative tour of America. Pat wrote the following for the Vice President to deliver at a Republican meeting in Spring-
field, Illinois: "Ultraliberalism today translates into a whimpering isolationism
in foreign policy, a mulish obstructionism in domestic policy, and a pusillani-
mous pussyfooting on the critical issue of law and order." In other parts of the
country, Agnew lashed out at "an effete corps of impudent snobs," "the 4-H
club: hopeless, hysterical hypochondriacs of history," and "nattering nabobs of
negativism" (the last one was written by Safire). It was clever or outrageous depending on whose coverage you read—but Pat undeniably achieved something
profound. He had gotten the media's attention by injecting the exciting, colorful language of newspaper polemics into political speech. No one could ignore
Agnew as he gabbled and growled Pat's prose into the microphone. He was
a conservative for the TV age: watchable and quotable, and a spokesman—it
seemed to some—for the ordinary man on the street.[38]

But Agnew's crudity came at a price. A cable TV journalist interviewed
voters in a bar in Baltimore to gauge their reaction to their former governor's
speaking tour. They said they loved how he tore into the hippies and the liberals. But they were less enthusiastic when the interviewer asked them if they
would, one day, vote for Agnew for president. Why? One barfly gave a good
answer: "Because I don't want the President of the United States to sound like I
do after I've had a few beers."[39] It was a paradox that Pat would become familiar
with: What made Agnew likable made him unelectable, too.

. . .

The culture wars of the 1960s rumbled on into 1970. The President announced an assault on Cambodia in a televised address on April 30. He denied that it was an invasion, explaining that it was an incursion into enemy occupied territory with the goal of landing a blow against the communist forces in next-door Vietnam. Outraged that Nixon had expanded the war, opponents announced a nationwide student strike and a march on Washington. On May 4, 1970, four students were shot dead at a protest at Kent State University in Ohio.[40] On May 8, in New York, construction workers charged student demonstrators, chanting, "All the way, USA!" and "America, love it or leave it!" They chased the longest-haired down the streets, swiping at them with their hard hats.[41]

On May 9, 100,000 demonstrators occupied Washington, D.C. The mob smashed windows and slashed tires. They camped at the feet of the Lincoln Memorial and dragged parked cars into intersections to stop traffic. A ring of buses was placed around the White House as a barricade. Nearly 12,000 were arrested in the largest mass arrest in U.S. history.[42] Later that month, a terrorist organization called The Weather Underground officially declared war on the U.S. government. From September 1969 to May 1970, there was at least one bomb threat in America every day.[43]

Where did the Silent Majority stand? With the President. A May 1970 Gallup poll showed that 58 percent blamed the students for the deaths at Kent State, 11 percent blamed the National Guard, and 31 percent expressed no opinion.[44] Many people agreed with Pat's take on Vietnam. Veterans felt the protestors were dodging their duty. Their lack of patriotism was a challenge to the sacrifices they had made overseas; their lack of faith in the American project made their own struggle for success seem pointless.[45] Spontaneous expressions of support for Nixon's policies were common. "At dozens of US universities," *Time* magazine reported, "students and faculty have scheduled 'bleed-ins' to provide blood for the fighting men in Vietnam . . . In New York, where 10,000 demonstrators marched three weeks ago in protest against the US role in Vietnam, 25,000 counter-demonstrators jammed Fifth Avenue last week in its support."[46]

Pat rejoiced. He felt sure that if the conservatives duked it out with the liberals, there were enough people on the right to win. He recalled: "Agnew was now the third highest admired man in America, right behind Billy Graham and Richard Nixon. . . . Even though Nixon was a minority president—with both houses of Congress and the press corps against him—there was no doubt: He spoke for the American people. He wasn't at 43 percent anymore. He had 60, 70 percent of the country behind him, hard hats marching down Wall Street beating up demonstrators, and the whole country was on fire; and we had the majority. As we used to say to Nixon, 'Divide the country, sir, and we'll get the larger half.' "[47]

Buchanan urged the President to play hardball all the way to 1972, to manipulate the cultural conflict. Pat told the Old Man to dress down, act up, speak his mind, and confront opponents head on.[48] A memo on giving medals of freedom was typical. Pat wrote that the President could "score one with the forgotten Americans" by snubbing the "high bouncing fairies" on the liberal left. Instead, he should "lay one on Roy Acuff, founding father of country and western music: a Nixon supporter with a special niche in the hall of heroes of the Grand Old Opry."[49]

As the 1970 midterms approached, Pat told his boss to ignore "liberal issues" like "housing, education, unemployment."[50] He promoted a book by political scientist Kevin P. Phillips called *The Emerging Republican Majority* that said social issues could create a new conservative bloc out of voters mostly found in the West, the border South, and the ethnic urban North.[51] Demographically, the Sun Belt was growing while the industrial Northeast was ossifying, its state governments crippled by crime, unemployment, and ballooning welfare budgets. Phillips argued that Nixon should embrace a populist strategy by opposing the cultural values of the Northeast.[52] Critics presumed that this meant playing the race card. This was the so-called Southern Strategy.[53] Seeing an opening, Nixon did as he was told. The President threw himself into the 1970 midterm congressional races to attack with gusto the "radical liberal" elites and their Democratic allies.

It backfired. The aggression made Tricky Dick look less than presidential. The GOP lost twelve seats in the House (although one Republican and two conservative independent members were gained in the Senate).[54] Pat said that Nixon only did badly because the media was against him. Stay the course, he begged. Take a stand, put Agnew on the road, or arrest some more demonstrators, anything other than pander to those damned liberals.[55] But Nixon could do the math. He took the moderates' advice that the people wanted caution, and that they actually did want to talk about "housing, education, unemployment."[56]

The 1971 State of the Union put the administration back onto an orthodox public policy course. Nixon offered a six-part plan that included welfare reform through the enactment of a guaranteed income, an "expansionary budget" to attain full employment, better protection of the environment, more healthcare benefits, bureaucratic reform, and revenue sharing. It was, in the words of Barry Goldwater, a "dime store New Deal."[57]

Pat was disappointed by the new policy, although he was hardheaded enough to understand it and loyal enough not to bolt. Buckley and Reagan complained like hell to Pat that Nixon was selling them out. Buchanan grew worried.[58] In early 1971, he wrote a couple of brutal memos to Nixon that outlined the view of the administration among its conservative critics. "We suffer," he warned, "from the widely held belief that the President has no Grand Vision that inspires him . . . Left and right, both now argue that the President, and his Administration, do not take decisions on the basis of political principle—but on the basis of expediency."[59] "The President," it seemed to conservatives, "is adopting a liberal Democratic program . . . and the President's ability to drag the GOP along behind his proposals makes him a more effective 'President Liberal' than any Democrat could ever be." Conservative voters might sit out the 1972 elections or switch to a Wallace third-party campaign. Worse still, Nixon could also face an internal challenge for the GOP presidential nomination. This incarnation of Richard Nixon was "no longer a credible custodian of the conservative political tradition of the GOP."[60]

Nixon was troubled by what Pat told him, and he okayed a series of meetings with conservatives to flesh out some more right-wing ideas.[61] But Buchanan was a voice in the wilderness. Fellow speechwriter Bill Safire wrote in response to his memoranda on the State of the Union:

Aside from his desire to turn the next election into a Viking's funeral, what is the writer's biggest misconception? Old fashioned purism. The left is the left, the right is the right, and never the twain shall meet. A choice not an echo. I disagree . . . In this transitional era, with liberals and conservatives joining to praise ecology and decentralization, the political center is the place to be.

The White House was running against the ghost of Barry Goldwater's disastrous campaign.[62]

Pat sent another memo to the President saying that he should hit out at antiwar protesters more. Haldeman stepped in to say no. They tried that in 1970 and it backfired. People didn't want to see their President taking potshots at college kids.[63] Buchanan disagreed. What the masses wanted, he said, was a "fighting president," not a "professional president."[64] The Old Man invited his favorite but wayward son to the Oval Office and gave him a fatherly lecture on good politics. His strategy, he said, was to kill them with kindness. He wanted to put the liberals on the defensive by being nice to them.

Pat nodded along, but he didn't agree. If a big man lets a little man disrespect him for too long, then eventually the little man will walk all over him.[65] As it went at home, so it went abroad. Pat didn't like the fact that toughness in Vietnam was balanced by new overtures to the Soviet Union and an emphasis upon the self-reliance of allies; he called the policy "confusing." The "acid test," he wrote the President, would be in East Asia where the Chinese had promised to support regional revolutions. The administration had to take a stand against Red China and reverse the onward march of communism. "I will," said Nixon, with all the sincerity he could muster. Pat left the meeting satisfied that, for all his talk of détente, Richard Nixon would no more parley with Mao Tse-tung than he would go on tour with Black Sabbath.[66]

They had their quarrels, but the Nixon family was tighter than ever. Out of office hours, Pat dated Miss Shelley Scarney, who was now working as the President's appointments secretary. In early 1971, he asked for her hand in marriage.[67] They wed at the Shrine of the Most Blessed Sacrament, with 400 guests including the President and his family. It rained, and in official photographs Buchanan stood holding an umbrella over Nixon and the bride. Mrs. Nixon wore a deep pink linen dress with a jacket trimmed in a band of white-and-pink embroidery. Shelley wore a classic satin dress, with an Empire bodice of Brussels lace and an Edwardian bouquet of tips of stock, white roses, and hydrangeas. The best man was Jimmy Buchanan. At the champagne reception at the Washington Club, President Nixon presented the couple with a gold electric clock inscribed "The White House." He put his arm around his favorite son and the cameras flashed.[68]

FIVE

Mao and McGovern

In their pantheon of devils, many Catholics put Mao Tse-tung on top. Pat Buchanan called him "the greatest state terrorist of them all."[1] Aside from the fact that he probably starved and murdered more people than any other leader in history, Mao drove the Christian missionaries out of China and the Catholic Church underground.[2] The Cultural Revolution was science fiction. Mao tried to redraw individual character by first wiping the slate clean. Ten years of violent scrubbing left China without color, humor, or the consolation of gods. Pat Buchanan loathed Soviet communism but recognized that it was something that had to be dealt with diplomatically, if only to contain it. Red China was an embarrassment to humanity. It should be condemned and isolated.[3]

Richard Nixon disagreed. He and National Security Advisor Henry Kissinger were determined to open up a relationship with China to counter Soviet expansion. In December 1970, the Old Man sent word via Nicolae Ceaușescu of Romania that he wanted diplomatic ties with China. He reduced trade restrictions between the two countries and put a block on anti-Chinese statements coming out of the White House. In April 1971, an American table tennis team visited the Middle Kingdom. Mao's premier, Chou En-lai, sent word that they were prepared to host someone of greater stature. In July 1971, Kissinger flew to Beijing in secret. Soon the world was stunned to hear that President Nixon would visit China the next year.[4]

Pat was horrified.[5] He had once advocated recognizing Albania, China's ally, in order to panic the Soviets into arms talks. But he never imagined that the Old Man would consider sitting down to cocktails with Mao.[6] Later, he observed that "Nixon was a genuine romantic. He really believed in a generation of peace, and that if he put together this balance of forces . . . that he could usher in an era of peace and he would be called responsible for it. I never agreed with that." He found Kissinger's calculating approach to foreign policy un-American.

> Henry believed also in that balance of forces—put China against the Soviets, the Soviets against us, and so on. But I said to him, "Henry, America is a right-or-wrong country. It's not balance that we're interested in: it's that the communists are evil. They're wrong. They're anti-Christian, atheistic communists. That's what appeals to our folks." . . . The reason why I had such a problem with the China visit is that when you're dealing with the greatest mass murderer of all time, you can't go to the Great Hall of the People and sing "Home on the Range" with these people.

Pat said to Kissinger when they first met after the news broke:

> If I can sit down and write a toast to Mao Tse-tung, the most barbaric Asian communist of them all, why are American kids dying fighting Asian communists in Vietnam? You undermine your own moral argument.[7]

Reluctantly, Pat agreed not to protest. He traveled with Kissinger to see Ronald Reagan to explain the strategic necessity of the trip. He also had lunch with William F. Buckley and tried to convince him it was right to go. Buckley was backing a conservative congressman in the forthcoming Republican primaries against Nixon, so it was important to keep as much of the Right as sweet as possible.[8] Haldeman insisted that Pat be the only speechwriter on the trip, as a way, perhaps, of satisfying conservative critics. It could also spread the burden of guilt, forcing a true believer to compromise himself publicly in the hope that he would be too tarred to later condemn the visit.[9]

On February 21, 1972, Buchanan boarded Air Force One for China. As the plane crossed the bright blue Pacific below, he made a suggestion. The Chinese people had never been told about the Apollo moon landing. Wouldn't it be a great tribute to China if, in his first speech, Nixon remarked that American men on the moon had looked down and seen the Great Wall? The Old Man smirked. "It's all very amusing," he said, "but no."[10]

The Americans were greeted at the airport in Beijing by Chou En-lai. The ugly gray tarmac and the communists in their ugly gray uniforms was the first glimpse Pat got of China. The diplomatic issue of height bothered Buchanan:

> The place was like it was run by mad monks, all those people in tunics. The Chinese people are very small, but they got all these tall fellows to stand around the airplane to make us feel short. That's just what the King of the Prussians used to do—get all his tallest people to make foreigners feel like midgets . . . In the photographs Chou stood on steps and boxes. I'm tall. There's no way Chou was taller than me, but he looked it. I'm definitely taller than Chou.

The administration staff was driven to guest lodges while the President was sped away to meet Mao. Pat bunked with the Secretary of State, Bill Rogers, who was furious that Kissinger was taken to meet the Emperor instead of him. Being stuck in the lodge with a grouchy Rogers got to be too much. Pat snuck out and tried to see the real China.

Buchanan and a friend took a car down to the train station. They stood on the platform and waved as the train went by. "It was the darndest thing," he said. "People normally wave when you wave them. These fellows just sat there staring at us." Then they rode to Tiananmen Square. "All these people—so many of them—came out early in the morning and stood in rows and did their tai chi or whatever. They all wore blue uniforms and none of them had cars. There were one or two bicycles. Tiananmen Square is massive and it was totally empty. We were the only car passing through it." The one thing to do in this empty city was to go to the friendship store and buy cheap ivory. "We bought as much as we could . . . I remember that, coming back, we were worried that the plane wouldn't get off the runway there was so much ivory everywhere."[11]

The China visit was thrilling for TV viewers back home. They saw Richard Nixon walk the Great Wall and Pat Nixon tour schools and farms. But for Buchanan it was a depressing bore.[12] One dinner followed another, with round after round of sickly sweet buns washed down with sickly sweet toasts. The operas were communist boy-meets-tractor stuff and the people eerily silent. Pat could see that the Old Man was under Mao's spell, and often a little drunk. Buchanan wrote a toast but it was insufficiently flattering, so Kissinger got on the phone to Price in Washington and asked for a different version. After Nixon had given it at yet another interminable feast, he sat down and winked at Buchanan. Pat was astonished. He had never seen the Old Man so unreserved.[13]

Nixon tipsily assured the communists that there was "only one China" and that they had a legitimate claim to independent, capitalist Taiwan. On the final day, Nixon and Chou signed the Shanghai Communiqué. It affirmed the One China policy and the U.S. pledged to reduce its military presence in Taiwan.[14]

On the plane on the way home, Kissinger recorded in his memoir that Buchanan was "morose."[15] That was an understatement. Both Pat and Nixon's secretary, Rose Mary Woods, felt physically sick with disgust. Rose stared out the window and wouldn't talk. Pat prowled up and down the plane, his eyes flashing with anger. He and Kissinger had it out in the gangway, an old-fashioned Georgetown-style "face-off." Buchanan: "Henry told me that the communiqué was necessary to bring the Soviets to the table. I told him that was bullshit. He had sold Taiwan out." Pat held Kissinger personally responsible and told him so. When he arrived in the U.S., Pat's parents picked him up from the airport. They expected him to glow with pride. Instead he was angry. "That's it," he said. "I'm going to quit."[16]

Pat called Haldeman on March 2 and told him he wanted to resign. Haldeman stalled. He told Pat that the Old Man was resting and shouldn't be disturbed. Buchanan went away and fumed. On March 5, Haldeman discussed Buchanan's resignation with the President. Nixon said, "Let him go." He was furious at reports that Pat was discussing the evils of the communiqué with other conservatives. He had tolerated Buchanan's outbursts all these years because of his intelligence and humor. But this was a step too far. And then, at the moment when he seemed willing to pick up the phone and personally sack Pat, Nixon backed down. Buchanan was family. Moreover, he was useful. If Buchanan went, the conservatives would say the administration had capitulated to the liberals. Better to keep Pat inside the tent.[17]

Nixon came up with a list of reasons why Buchanan should stay. Haldeman called Buchanan and read them to him over the phone. Privately, Pat had already decided that he didn't want to hurt the Old Man. He swallowed his pride and said he would stand by the visit.[18] But the cost of his brashness was that he was denied the leading role in the 1972 reelection campaign that he craved. For several months, Buchanan was frozen out of the inner circle. Ironically, this might have spared him a jail sentence.[19]

W hile Nixon glad-handed tyrants, there was an election going on back home. Pat Buchanan helped out with attack work in the primaries, monitoring dissent in the GOP, and stirring up trouble in the Democrat camp.[20] In the Republican race, conservative congressman John Ashbrook ran in New Hampshire, Florida, and California but never took higher than 10 percent of the vote.[21] The Democratic side was more fun. Pat played the Democratic primaries like a game of chess—move and countermove. If a candidate was up, the administration helped his opponent. When the outsider made a breakthrough, the administration dragged him back down. The frontrunner was Maine senator Edmund Muskie. He had all the endorsements and cash necessary to win, but his dull centrist campaign failed to catch fire.[22] The Democrats had expanded their nomination process to include more primaries and caucuses. Delegates were selected according to a complex system of quotas that favored social activists and liberals. George McGovern, an antiwar Methodist preacher's son from South Dakota, pulled off a surprising second-place showing in the first-in-the-nation Iowa caucus and gained momentum.[23] Pat's team helped out by circulating polls that showed McGovern was more popular than he really was.[24]

Headed into the first primary in New Hampshire, Muskie fell apart on the campaign trail. According to the Watergate hearings, Pat put out forged documents claiming Muskie had said bad things about native French speakers. The conservative newspaper the *Manchester Union-Leader* published the gossip and threw into the mix that Mrs. Muskie was a drunk. Muskie protested outside the *Union-Leader*'s offices and, as snowflakes fell on his cheeks, appeared to cry. Democrats cried dirty tricks. But one man's dirty trick was another man's clever ploy. McGovern placed second again and the antiwar crowd was in the ascendant.[25]

George Wallace, the conservative Democrat, won the Florida primary a few days later. McGovern then scooped the Wisconsin primary, establishing him as the credible liberal alternative to Wallace.[26] It was crucial, said Pat, that Wallace do well in the Democratic primaries but stay out of the general election. Nixon needed to attract his supporters if he was to sweep the South and build a majority. So the President's men boosted him in Michigan and Maryland.[27] Then, on May 15, Wallace was shot while campaigning in Maryland. The administration tried to plant pro-McGovern literature in the assassin's hotel room, but the police got there first.[28] Wallace's injuries put him out of the race. That didn't stop him from sweeping Michigan and Maryland though.[29]

McGovern's honeymoon was short. His campaign was ramshackle and radical, and he never recovered from attacks by Hubert Humphrey, who was running an impressive comeback campaign. Pat made sure that the President said "something nice" about Humphrey to help him.[30] McGovern beat Humphrey but, by the time of the Democratic convention in Miami, he was 34 percent behind Nixon in the polls. Television showed a convention full of feminists, civil rights protesters, antiwar hippies, and Hollywood wannabe revolutionaries. The coverage made a genuine attempt in open democracy look like a freak show. McGovern supporters protested that many of the more radical statements coming out of the convention were from people they didn't recognize. They suspected an administration conspiracy.[31] They might have been right. In a memo dated April 10, 1972 and headlined "Covert Operations," Buchanan wrote:

> We should have as many of these down there [at Miami Beach] as needed to conduct harassment exercises, and embarrassment exercises for the Democrats. They should have no connection at all with the GOP Observation Post, and should be directed out of

here, as they have been in the past. They should be able to help put demonstrations together, get leaflets out, start rumors, and generally foul up scheduled events—and add to the considerable confusion and chaos that will inevitably exist.[32]

When he could find no one better, McGovern picked Sen. Tom Eagleton of Missouri to be his running mate. Days later, McGovern dropped him from the ticket after it was revealed that Eagleton had been hospitalized for depression.[33]

It was all good fun, but implicit in everything Pat did was his suspicion that the President wasn't popular enough to get elected on his own merits. After the Miami convention, he wrote Nixon:

> We should recognize that the operative political reality is not that President Nixon is 34 points ahead—but that George McGovern is 34 points behind. He is there because the American people perceive him to be an ultra-liberal, incompetent and somewhat radical character, surrounded by the types whom they dislike and even despise. As argued some months ago, given the Republican minority in the nation, the only way for us to get in the neighborhood of 64–30 is not only an excellent performance on our side—but a disastrous performance on the other side.

The only way to win—and to win big—was for the Democrats to do poorly. Pat loved the Old Man, but after China he had come to understand what his critics meant by Tricky Dick.[34]

And Pat was excluded from the dirtiest parts of the dirty tricks campaign. He wasn't in on the meeting when Nixon discussed a burglary that occurred at the Democratic headquarters in the Watergate Hotel on June 17, 1972. The President told administration officials to ask the CIA to halt the FBI's investigation into the break-in on the grounds that it was a national security matter. That afternoon, Nixon became part of a criminal conspiracy.[35]

There was more to the Nixon campaign than dirty tricks. In 1972, Richard

Nixon achieved a level of popular support that he had never before enjoyed. The visit to China and a trip to Moscow in May (accompanied by Buchanan) made him look like a peacemaker. On Vietnam, he ended conscription, brought most of the troops home, and, shortly before the election, Kissinger declared that "peace is at hand." Although conservatives disliked his use of price and wage controls to bring down inflation, they worked in the short term.[36] Even the AFL-CIO sat out the election, a tacit endorsement.[37]

And President Nixon's record was often surprisingly liberal (he introduced the first-ever federal affirmative action hiring plan and expanded environmental regulation), though he could play the conservative when needed.[38] Buchanan often argued that Nixon should take a stand against the use of court-ordered busing to integrate schools. Busing was a vote loser, he said: "The ship of integration is going down; it is not our ship: it belongs to national liberalism—and we cannot salvage it; and we ought not be aboard." The best way to win over the Wallace voters was to oppose it.[39] Nixon followed Pat's prescription. When Wallace won Michigan and Maryland in the Democratic primaries, the President called for a congressional moratorium on court-ordered busing. It was a very popular move.[40]

There were encouraging signs for conservatives in other areas, too. Pat convinced Nixon to give federal aid to Catholic parochial schools, in exchange for an agreement by the Vatican not to criticize the policy in Vietnam.[41] In the summer of 1972, Buchanan brought to the President's attention Cardinal Terence Cooke's crusade to overturn New York's liberal abortion law. Nixon wrote an open letter signifying his support for Cooke, although he stressed that he felt abortion should remain outside federal jurisdiction.[42]

Whatever Buchanan thought of the ideologically wayward policies of the Old Man, he was, in Pat's opinion, a thousand times better than the opposition. Pat watched the McGovern campaign with incomprehension. The people involved were alien to him. He called one of them a "screaming fairy" and dubbed the feminist McGovernites "the Butch Brigade."[43] For Pat, beating these people could atone for all the defeats, or unconvincing victories, conservatives had suffered since 1960. Victory, he wrote in *The New York Times*, would clear Nixon's name.

Enshrined in the conventional wisdom of the American Left is the conviction that a quarter of a century ago Richard Nixon was a political brawler, with but a nodding acquaintance with the Marquis of Queensberry. . . . And if his acolytes in the media succeed in having George McGovern remembered before history as the St. Francis of Assisi of American politics, then the rest of us will just have to take consolation in a remark attributed to Voltaire: "history is a pack of lies, agreed upon." A landslide in November would confirm that the people need, maybe even admire, Richard Nixon.[44]

According to the polls, he was right. Richard Nixon cruised to victory.

These were the happiest days for the Nixon family. A few weeks before the election, Nixon invited Buchanan and a few others aboard the presidential yacht—*The Sequoia*—for an informal party. Among the things discussed was Watergate, and within eighteen months half the people at the party would be in court. But for now, the President said it was a dead issue—one that would hurt the opposition more than him. As was his habit, Buchanan wrote a memo recording the events of the evening. Its ironical tone reflects the mix of protocol and familiarity in the relationship between Nixon and his retainers. Reading between the lines, the alcohol obviously flowed and the language was ripe. We might speculate that it was written in a haze the following morning:

> The evening was almost wholly devoted to the discussion of politics—and the political campaign with the President asking questions, eliciting advice, making various judgments about the situation. The mood was jovial; there was much back-and-forth banter between the President and aides; a good deal of humor. Among serious matters was an expression of concern by [one aide] that he had been called by the Grand Jury to testify re: the Watergate, and the President told him to be unconcerned that the opposition would push this matter, that it would cost us some points in the polls, but that it was not a turning issue, and that we would survive it . . . During the conversations in which PJB was involved, as is not unusual, PJB was the foil for presidential humor. The president sug-

gested that a certain individual in Buchanan's terms might be considered a "liberal asshole," to which Buchanan replied that the term was redundant. There were two drinks on deck before a dinner of sweet-corn on the cob and meat, which was outstanding. The evening, again, was not one in which commitments were made—or plans laid, so much as it was a presidential discussion of individuals and aspects of his coming campaign with some of his top political advisors. HRH took notes, as I recall whenever the President made a decision which called for a follow-through. If added thoughts come to mind about this voyage up the Potomac, PJB will jot them down and pass them along in a subsequent memorandum.

PJB[45]

SIX

Watergate

R ichard Nixon won reelection with over 60 percent of the popular
vote. He swept the South but also the North, by breaking into the
blue-collar constituency that ordinarily belonged to the Democrats.
Nationwide, Nixon took 54 percent of union members and 52 percent of
Catholics (compared to just 33 percent in 1968).[1] "While the Nixon landslide
was a victory of the man over McGovern," wrote Buchanan, "it was also a victory of the New American Majority . . . a victory of traditional American values and beliefs over the claims of the counter-culture."

Nothing pleased Pat more than his conviction that he had won the ordinary,
God-fearing people he grew up with over to the GOP. The politics of class and
culture had intersected, giving the Republicans an opportunity to build a
coalition "between the lower and middle-class Democratic center and right"
against the "upper middle-class elite and left." Nixon's victory, he hoped,
heralded the arrival of a new brand of populist conservatism. While liberals
obsessed about fashionable minorities at Manhattan cocktail parties, conservatives were singing "America the Beautiful" with their cultural kin on the
factory floor.[2]

But what next for the President, and what next for Buchanan? Some insiders argued that Nixon needed to soften his image; that he had failed to show
"heart" during the campaign.[3] Pat disagreed. He said that the Old Man won
because, in a contest between a "bleeding heart" and a "heartless, cold, SOB,"

the public chose the SOB. To suddenly develop a human side would look hypocritical and would mean sacrificing the social conservatism that won so many votes. "If we want to get some grades for warmth and heart—I can tell you how to do it," he wrote. "First, we can get RN to give an impassioned pro-Civil Rights speech, tearing into southern and northern reaction, and with tears in his eyes, sing 'We Shall Overcome.' But that is not RN's style, that is not the man—and the first thing one learns on joining Her Majesty's Secret Service is that it is utter folly to attempt to change the man."[4]

If anything, wrote Buchanan, the President should get tougher. He urged Nixon to uproot the Great Society programs as part of a war on inflation.[5] Meanwhile, he called for an affirmative action policy for Catholics in the White House, in order to cement the new relationship with ethnics. "Our future is in the Democratic working man, Southern Protestant and Northern Catholics." So there should be no letup in social conservatism.[6] Nixon was thinking along the same lines. In the New Year of 1973, he promised a conservative revolution, including an expansion of revenue sharing between federal and local government, budget slashing, and tax cutting.[7]

But at the forefront of both men's minds was the press. Pat saw his role in the second administration as the coordinator of resistance to the inevitable liberal backlash. "It will be argued," Pat lamented, "we have to live with [the press]—so let us follow a policy of 'live and let live.' [However] a small, ideological clique has managed to acquire monopoly control of the most powerful medium of communication known to man; and they regularly use that unrivaled and untrammeled power to politically assault the President . . . The interests of this country, and the furtherance of the policies and ideas in which we believe, demand that this monopoly, this intellectual cartel, be broken up." Go on the offensive, said Pat.[8]

Buchanan asked to be made White House Director of Communications. Nixon and Haldeman said no, but they agreed on the necessity for a "counter-attack" program against the media. It is extraordinary to note that, just over a week since a thumping victory, the Nixon White House was already drawing up a fresh list of enemies. The Old Man complained that "90 percent of what the press had written was drivel." He and Pat threw some ideas around for publications that might remind them that they backed a loser, with titles like

"Things they would like to forget" and "the dirtiest campaign in history against a president." The President was bullish, but in high spirits. At the end of the meeting he read Buchanan an anecdote from a biography of Churchill and clapped him on the shoulder. "Pat we've had some good battles together, haven't we?" Then he mentioned in passing that, considering *The Washington Post*'s investigation of Watergate, it might be wise to suspend all the dirty tricks. Pat agreed, but he sensed that Watergate wasn't going to go away as easily as Nixon presumed.[9]

In a news summary, Buchanan warned the President that the media's coverage of Watergate was getting "out of hand." Two *Washington Post* journalists—Bob Woodward and Carl Bernstein—had just identified two White House men—Donald Segretti and Dwight Chapin—as the money men behind the break-in at the Watergate Hotel. Nixon sent Pat a memo telling him to calm down. Who cared about a third-rate burglary? The President assured him that the story wouldn't run for more than a couple of weeks.[10]

The collapse of the Nixon presidency happened in short order. In January 1973, the Watergate burglars were convicted of breaking and entering by Judge John Sirica. In February, the Senate established a committee under Sam Ervin to investigate White House activity in the presidential campaign. In March, an informant wrote Sirica that the Watergate defendants had pleaded guilty under duress; that they committed perjury and that others were involved in the break-in. He claimed that the burglars lied at the urging of John Dean, Counsel to the President, and John Mitchell, the Attorney General. Dean agreed to cooperate with the Ervin committee. The hunting of the President began.[11]

Richard Nixon told Pat Buchanan that he had no knowledge of the break-ins. Pat believed him.[12] He presumed that *The Washington Post*'s investigation was politically motivated, that they were trying to repeal the "mandate of 1972."[13] The mood in the White House was tense and obsessive. There was, said John Dean, "a cancer on the presidency." In an effort to save himself, Nixon cut away all his friends, cauterizing them one after another to prevent the disease from reaching him. At the same time, he became closer to the innocent, as if their ignorance were a vaccine.[14] Pat and the Old Man spent hours in the Oval Office discussing the media's agenda. This wasn't about Watergate, it was about Nixon, wrote Pat: "Individuals are seeking to use Watergate to repeal the democratic verdict of 1972—to discredit with headlines not only the men who may have been involved, but the 'movement' they were unable to defeat at the polls." The President shouldn't apologize for anything, Pat said. The right tone was "sorrow mixed with Presidential anger, at what has been done to him, his cause, and to his presidency."[15]

Convinced that the Old Man was innocent, Pat told him to sack anyone who could not maintain their integrity.[16] Nixon took comfort in Buchanan's loyalty. There was something pure about him, about his conservatism, and his Catholicism. Nixon invited Pat to spend a day and a half at Key Biscayne in late April. Neither of his top aides, H. R. Haldeman or John Erlichman, was there. Both men had been implicated during John Dean's testimony and their reputations were tarnished.[17] Four days later the President went on air to announce Haldeman and Erlichman's resignations. He called Haldeman afterward and drunkenly told him that he loved him like a brother.[18] It was a tough decision for Nixon, but he had to do it. Pat wrote him to say, "To be brutally frank, the choice is now between the President and his friends . . . If they are to survive, they have to do it on their own. The only question extant now, it seems, is whether we're going down as well. If we are not culpable, then there is no moral obligation upon the President to share the fate of those who deceived the President."[19]

The Nixon family was reduced to its tight inner core—the daughters Julie and Trisha, Pat Nixon, Pat and Shelley Buchanan, Ray Price, the new Chief of Staff Al Haig, and a few other favorite retainers. Henry Kissinger, never entirely trusted, continued to gad about the world winning awards—the acceptable face of the Nixon administration. Buchanan was appointed special consultant to the president.[20] He was by Nixon's side when he gave America's backing to Israel during the Yom Kippur War. The President's diplomacy probably saved the world from a confrontation with the USSR, but the Arab world's punitive hike in the price of oil threw the United States into economic crisis. The country was paralyzed, by Watergate and by the cost of gas. Lines gathered outside gas stations and tempers frayed. It seemed like America was running on empty.[21]

In May 1973, the Senate hearings began. In July, Alexander Butterfield, former presidential appointments secretary, revealed that, since 1971, Nixon had made tapes of all conversations and telephone calls in his offices. When he heard, Pat's immediate response was "burn them." In a memo, he advised the President to take them out onto the White House lawn, start a bonfire, and throw them on. The liberals on the Ervin committee were outraged. Where's their sense of humor, or their sense of proportion? asked Buchanan.[22] "Berated morning, noon and night with Watergate, the nation has seen its important business put off, its economic interests and currency suffer in foreign markets, its reputation in the world diminished," he wrote. "There now appears no damage to United States interests that is unacceptable, no political principle they will not rise readily above—to sink their teeth in the President of the United States." Nixon, he pointed out, was no worse than Lyndon Johnson. Johnson bugged his own staff and throughout the 1968 election, Nixon was "bedeviled" by "phony press releases, bollixed schedules and trains chugging out of the station before time." Campaign espionage? Johnson was a veritable Mata Hari: Goldwater's policy documents and press releases were routinely stolen.[23]

The Old Man started to drink heavily. Pat sat in the darkness with him and whispered sweet excuses. The real conspiracy, he wrote, was the press's attempt to force a popular president from office.

> They were right and we were wrong on Watergate—but we have been right and they have been wrong on Vietnam; and social policy. We have been with the country and they have not. And simply because Woodward and Bernstein were correct on Watergate and we minimized it does not mean that in the larger collision between the national media and the Nixon administration, we have been wrong and they have been right.[24]

In September it was Pat's turn to address the Watergate committee. They wanted to talk about the dirty tricks campaign against Edmund Muskie. The

Ervin committee had got hold of some memos that were full of Buchanan's hardball language: "We ought to go down to the kennels and turn all the dogs loose on Muskie," read one. Some liberals were starting to ask if America had a fair election in 1972. To date, all those questioned by the committee had either distanced themselves from the President or proved contrite. They expected the same of Pat Buchanan.[25]

Instead, Buchanan gave the only robust public defense of the President heard during the whole nightmare. His core argument: Nixon only did what all politicians do and, given the Senate's peculiar obsession with his crimes alone, this committee was a witch hunt. Buchanan *looked* unapologetic. His hair was greased back, his scowl fixed and furious—his body coiled to spring across the table and bang Ervin on the nose. "You're looking at the Buckminster Fuller of dirty tricks," said Pat. He called the committee unethical for leaking claims that he was behind the anti-Muskie campaign. He had proposed nothing that was "illicit, unethical, improper—or unprecedented in previous Democratic campaigns." The 1972 election "was not stolen" and Pat was the victim of a "covert campaign of vilification" to "malign" his reputation.[26]

Of course he had recommended that the White House help eliminate Muskie and elevate McGovern. Of course he had ghosted advertisements and letters attacking Democratic contenders, posting false authorships. Of course the administration had taken advantage of the incumbency to derail the Democratic campaign. The burglary was a crime, granted. But "none of the stratagems, overt or covert, had exceeded the limits of time-honored tradition in American politics." When Senator Ervin invoked something pompous once said by President Andrew Jackson in response, Pat pointed out that Jackson was "the father of the spoils system." Watergate, said Buchanan, was all part of the American game of hardball politics. The only reason why Nixon was on trial was because the Democrats were sore at having lost.

It was, said one White House insider, "the only day of the hearings I've really enjoyed."[27] Nixon called it "a public death blow" to the investigation. So humbled was the committee that it canceled the interrogation of another speechwriter, Ken Khachigian, lest he prove as verbose. From thereon, the dirty tricks aspect of the investigation was dropped. The Old Man fell in love with Pat's mind all over again. And, without Haldeman and Erlichman around, he relied on him more than ever.[28]

But the "public death blow" did not do the job. On October 10, 1973, Vice President Agnew pleaded no contest to charges of tax evasion and money laundering and resigned. Two days later, Gerald Ford took Agnew's place. The nightmare rolled on.[29]

P at was at the height of his power. In October, he and Nixon fled the early frost and went down to Key Biscayne for a break.[30] Barry Goldwater joined the men and their wives for dinner. Goldwater was committed to the cause, for now, and he added his voice to the argument that Nixon should stick it out. The family had a few drinks and laughed about the past. Watergate had to run out of steam soon, they said.[31] At the end of the month, the President fired special prosecutor Archibald Cox. The Senate demanded access to the tapes. Nixon offered them transcripts.[32]

The Old Man put Pat in charge of editing the transcripts. Working with what the President chose to give him, Buchanan thought they made his case all the stronger. In his memoirs, Nixon wrote: "When I read Buchanan's report ... I was reassured by the thought that anyone reviewing the tapes would agree with my view that Dean had lied [about my role in the cover-up]." In fact the transcripts were full of enough innuendo, racism, blasphemy, and salty humor to destroy what remained of the President's reputation. But, continued Nixon: "Buchanan was strongly in favor of releasing the transcripts. I shared his belief that if we could survive the first shock waves, the tapes would end up proving Dean a liar."[33]

Buchanan was wrong. The public were shocked by the Nixon revealed in the transcripts: foulmouthed, conspiratorial, sometimes drunk, often abusive about opponents. Only those who shared Nixon's prejudices could have missed how horrible they really were. The Ervin committee said that transcripts were not enough—they wanted to hear the recordings themselves. A battle started over tapes that Nixon argued were private property.[34]

If Woodward and Bernstein's exposé of the final days of the Nixon White House is to be believed, the mood inside the administration was hysterical.

Pat Nixon took to drink. Julie and Tricia, convinced of their father's innocence, spent their time whipping the White House staff into line. They found
an ally in Pat. The President and his friends must hold firm, said Buchanan,
lest the country be torn apart by impeachment proceedings. He sincerely believed that the Senate might be satisfied with censure.[35] The official face of the
resistance, Buchanan did an interview with Dan Rather and, yet again, put
the blame on the press. "What's come up in this country," he said, "is like the
railroads at the turn of the century, the networks in the United States have
gained a position of power and dominance over the flow of ideas and information to the American people which I think is excessive."[36] Pat told a crowd
of conservatives at the University of Pennsylvania to boycott the products of
people who advertised through media outlets that criticized the President. He
seemed oblivious to the fact that the administration was actually guilty of
something.[37]

In January 1974, Nixon visited Egypt and brought Buchanan with him.
The Old Man was greeted like a king. Thousands of Egyptians climbed over
each other to shake hands with the peacemaker. Buchanan noted with sadness
how Nixon was regarded as a crook in his own country, yet a highly respected
statesman abroad.[38] Speaking of the brilliance of Egyptian dictator Anwar
Sadat, Nixon recalled in his memoir: "What he reminded me of, curiously
enough, was that he had a forehead like Pat Buchanan's, and my guess is that
he has the same kind of brain and drive and single-mindedness that Pat has."
In July 1974, Buchanan joined Nixon in Moscow for arms talks. Nixon and
Brezhnev spoke in the General Secretary's office and then walked to a reception at St. George's Hall. Nixon guided Brezhnev by his elbow, introducing
him to each of his staff. He paused at Buchanan and said, "He's liberal,
this man." The Old Man laughed. Brezhnev looked confused.[39] They flew to
Yalta, where Buchanan did some shopping. Wearing a T-shirt and slacks, he
spotted a Vietnamese-made black lacquered chess-backgammon board with
inlaid mother-of-pearl patterns for $108. Buchanan wanted it badly but ago-
nized over whether it came from North Vietnam or South Vietnam. "It must
have been made in the North," joked a London *Telegraph* journalist. "If it
had been made in the South, it would have been better." Pat bought it anyway.[40]

· · ·

By July 1974, the administration staff was on deathwatch, waiting for the President to resign. Nixon veered between deciding to go and wanting to stay. He talked about life in prison. Once he said that there were "worse things . . . There is no telephone there. There is, instead, peace. A hard table to write on." Sometimes he retreated into his study and listened to records. Nixon was passive, despondent. His daughter Julie's husband, David Eisenhower, said he was "waiting for Mr. Nixon to go bananas." He worried that the President might kill himself. Al Haig, at first loyal and convinced of Nixon's innocence, was now simply trying to keep the government working while the Old Man made up his mind to go. But still Buchanan held out. He could only accept the logic of Nixon's resignation if he was guilty of something. And if he was guilty of something then he had lied to Pat.

One day in August, after a meeting of the White House strategy group, Haig asked for Buchanan to wait behind. It had been a good meeting; Pat was upbeat and ready to fight some more. Haig took his usual place at the top of the table and addressed Buchanan. "We've all been living with this agony for a while," he said. "Now we want you to share it with us." A tape had turned up dated June 23, 1972. It was a conversation between the President and Haldeman talking about using the CIA to halt the FBI's investigation into the Watergate burglary: the smoking gun.

"An early tape, or late?" Pat asked.

"Early," Haig replied.

"That was our concern all the way back." Buchanan said flashing an angry look at Ray Price. They had worked together on Nixon's May 22, 1973, statement in which he denied using the CIA to contain the FBI inquiry. They had double-checked and triple-checked and every time the President insisted he was innocent. He had lied to them. Pat asked Haig what was on the tape and Haig told him.

"What do you think he should do?" said Haig.

Buchanan's response was quick. "I think he's gotta resign."

"Basically, you've come to the same conclusion everybody else has," said Haig. "The President is thinking of doing it Monday."

Buchanan requested a transcript. While he waited he argued that the President could not step down saying that he wanted to "spare the country the agony of impeachment." Rather, he should say: "We have to let our own people and everybody else know why it had to be done—because of what's on the tape, because he lied." The transcript arrived and Pat read it aloud. When he came across the smoking words, his fist hit the table. "Jesus Christ!" he said. "He has to resign." When the meeting was over, Pat went and found Shelley. "It's all over," he told her. He suggested they go to a bar and mark the occasion with a "good old Irish reaction."

The problem was how the staff could force Nixon to go. Pat came up with the answer: Leak the tape. "We should step back and let the thing blow," he said. "The President should feel the force of the blast himself." Haig arranged it. When the news broke, Buchanan went to see Nixon's daughter Tricia. "I told her that he had to go," Pat recalled. His word was enough. If Pat no longer supported the Old Man, then the cause was lost. Tricia disappeared to pack her bags.[41]

The Nixon administration had it within their grasp to change politics and change the world. But they threw it away. Pat Buchanan wrote, "It's like Sisyphus. We rolled the rock all the way up the mountain . . . and it rolled right back down on us." His friend Hunter S. Thompson composed a stinging reply in *The New York Times:*

> Well shucks. It makes a man's eyes damp, for sure. But I have a lot
> of confidence in Pat, and I suspect that he won't have much trouble
> finding other rocks to roll. [The difference between Buchanan and
> Sisyphus was that] Sisyphus got mashed . . . and Pat Buchanan will
> survive in the footnotes of history as a kind of half-mad Davy
> Crockett on the walls of Nixon's Alamo—a martyr, to the bitter
> end, to a "flawed" cause and a narrow, atavistic concept of conser-
> vative politics that has done more damage to itself and to the coun-
> try in less than six years than its liberal enemies could have done in
> two or three decades.[42]

SEVEN

In the Crossfire

Gerald Ford had no use for Buchanan's hardball politics. Pat asked to be made ambassador to South Africa, but the new President said no. He quit the White House in September 1974.[1] The Buchanans bought a house in McLean, Virginia. Neighbors included Al Haig and the direct-mail fund-raising genius Richard Viguerie. Senators breakfasted in polo shirts in the local restaurants; congressmen jogged along the highway. The Kennedys owned a nearby compound. On the Buchanan's first night in residence, George and Barbara Bush dropped by with a bottle of champagne to welcome them to the neighborhood.

Without the Old Man to look after, Pat lacked purpose. Nixon sat in his house in California and brooded. Pat grew his hair long and tended his Virginia garden. One day, Al Haig dropped by while Pat was out front trimming a bush. Thinking Buchanan was staff, Haig walked right past him and rang the doorbell.

"Hey, Al, I'm over here," said Pat.

Haig could barely recognize him in jeans and sweater. "Jesus Pat," he said. "I thought you were the gardener."[2]

Pat made some pocket money on the speaker circuit, a hit at business forums and Republican dinners.[3] The *St. Louis Globe-Democrat* took him back as a columnist. He got syndication and, with it, a bigger audience than ever before. As a commentator, Pat was free to say whatever he wanted: the more controversial, the better. Years later, the things he wrote for the *Globe-Democrat* came back to haunt him. But in the 1970s, political correctness was just a punch line in *National Lampoon*.[4] As a columnist, Pat spoke out against affirmative action, the income tax, forcing mothers to work, and the car airbag.[5] It may seem outrageous by contemporary standards, but, back then, Buchanan's confident right-wing prose was zeitgeist defining stuff.

While America's legal and civil institutions embraced social liberalism, a conservative cultural backlash was brewing in the living rooms and pews of middle-class suburbia. In 1975, political analyst Kevin Phillips coined the phrase "New Right" to describe the grassroots organizations sweeping the country.[6] These were single-issue groups driven by opposition to gay rights, détente, abortion, the Equal Rights Amendment (ERA), or the removal of prayer in schools.[7] They came together in broad-spectrum conservative organizations like the National Conservative Political Action Committee (NCPAC, famous for its annual conferences, CPAC) and the Heritage Foundation. These groups promoted a new generation of political leaders—including Richard Viguerie, Paul Weyrich, the antifeminist Phyllis Schlafly, and Howard Phillips—that operated as an informal network: the first manifestation of what Hillary Clinton later called a "vast right-wing conspiracy." At the heart of their operation was a massive direct-mail scheme that kept different people in touch with one another. From his office in Falls Church, Virginia, Richard Viguerie had access to 15 million names and addresses on an IBM computer bank. A person who gave money to "Stop the Baby Killers!" generally gave money to "Stop the Surrender to the Soviet Union!" Every time they filled in a form and sent in a check, they joined a complex web of angry individuals.[8] Pat's columns in the *Globe-Democrat* kept him at the center of that huge countercultural network. Liberal critic Bertram Gross dubbed the New Right "friendly fascism." Pat Buchanan, he wrote, was its very own Joseph Goebbels: Reich Minister for Propaganda.[9]

The New Right represented a subtle shift in conservative priorities, from the pursuit of total liberty to the pursuit of righteousness.[10] Like Barry Goldwater, its activists were critical of bureaucracy and high taxes. Unlike Barry Goldwater, their biggest concern wasn't the size of government but the spiritual health of society. Where government lessened the ability of families and churches to do their job, it should be swept away. Where it might help sustain tradition, it could be granted a small role. For example, Barry Goldwater thought abortion was a private matter between a woman and her doctor. The New Right was ready to allow bureaucrats to force her to go full term.[11]

The New Right could be critical of capitalism where it corrupted public morals, and scathing of corporations that monopolized markets and drove the little guy out of business. They were populists who wanted to usurp the powerful elites that they believed manipulated American society.[12] Some on the right were critical of this blending of conservatism and class war. Chilton Williamson in the *National Review* called it "country and western Marxism."[13]

The 1970s New Right was nonpartisan. It liked George Wallace as much as it liked Ronald Reagan. And it hated Nelson Rockefeller as much as it hated Ted Kennedy.[14] Pat Buchanan spoke for many conservatives when, in 1975, he wrote:

> The right should make it clear that the [policies] being pursued in Washington, by the [Republican] Administration and the Congress, is done against the protest of the right. Conservatives should behave politically as what they are—strangers to the corridors of power, dissenters outside the councils of government, men without power and without responsibility for what is happening.

The Republicans had "not yet decided irrevocably where they stand on the issues of the new era," he complained.

> The party wishes to be thought of as both principled and progressive. It prefers the comfortable, less bitter conflicts of an earlier age.[15]

Buchanan couldn't hide his disappointment with Gerald Ford, the man who sacked him. Ford started out well, Pat felt, when he pledged to cut federal spending and taxes.[16] But when he pardoned Nixon, Ford's poll numbers slumped. The President was a moderate, obsessed with chasing consensus.

Tax cuts were balanced with increased spending on unemployment and healthcare. "The best defense is offense," said the President, but accommodation with the Soviet Union was his top priority. Abortion was not opposed per se, but its legality was to be decided by the states.[17] On New Year's Eve 1975, Pat and a score of other journalists were invited to the White House for an interview.[18] Buchanan reported that Ford's resolutions included: "1. Strengthen moral and spiritual values among 215 million people. 2. Do everything possible to improve the economic circumstances of ourselves . . . 3. Resolve that we have peace with ourselves and peace with the world as a whole."

Pat wrote in reply: "Meaning no disrespect, on [1] some of us look to Rome or Mecca for spiritual leadership, not [Washington]; [2] is an objective which Sen. Strom Thurmond and Sen. George McGovern could endorse; and [3] reads like something the President cut and pasted from one of his Christmas cards." The administration's real resolution? "To be holding in 1977 the same jobs they have in 1976."[19]

Gov. Ronald Reagan decided to challenge Ford for the Republican nomination. Pat was a friendly critic of Reagan.[20] Like many on the New Right, he was unmoved by the governor's obsession with balancing the budget. He felt that the Republican Party's future lay in enticing the kind of voters who went for Wallace in 1968 and Nixon in 1972: blue-collar ethnic northerners and southern Protestants. These people were motivated by a mix of social conservatism and economic populism. Pat said that Reagan had the former, but had not yet grasped the appeal of the latter. Buchanan liked a proposal being floated by Republican congressman Jack Kemp for a 30 percent tax cut. This was the kind of activist conservatism that was pro-growth and attractive to the working man. Pat saw a potential alliance between tax-cutting conservatives and organized labor. Reagan's emphasis upon slashing federal expenditure and privatizing Social Security drove away labor and split the conservative coalition. Pat wondered aloud if the Republican label was itself a hindrance to the conservative cause, if Republicans were too associated with big business and Yankee snobbery.[21]

Reagan and Ford battled it out right up to the 1976 Republican convention. Ford won, but there was just a 117 difference in their delegate count.[22] Despite their skepticism, Buchanan and a group of New Right activists approached Reagan and asked him to run as a third-party candidate. He declined. They also went to see Nixon strongman John Connally and Gov. George Wallace. Pat had the highest hopes for George Wallace.[23]

Buchanan had gotten to know Wallace in the years following his assassination attempt. He visited the governor's mansion in Montgomery and the two men bemoaned the degeneration of the republic.[24] Wallace was dwarfed by the mansion, a broken old man in a wheelchair who lived on a diet of painkillers and regret. Tears filled his eyes when he talked about the terrible things he once said about segregation. His wife, Cornelia, a former water-ski champion, was cheating on him; he knew this because he was bugging her telephone. Nothing without the limelight, Wallace entered the Democratic primaries one last time in 1976. Pat returned from a visit to Montgomery and wrote a column in the governor's honor:

> To this writer, the appeal of Wallace to the workingman has always been a phenomenon easy to understand ... George Wallace ... is the genuine article, a flesh-and-blood figure interesting and appealing as an alternative to the cardboard media candidates from the nation's capital ... The Wallace candidacy has been, since 1964, the primary megaphone through which the working class has protested the growing arrogance and intrusiveness of federal bureaucrats and federal judges.

He urged a vote for Wallace in the primaries.

> [A victory] would produce a tremor [in Washington] such as has not been felt since that July morning in the summer of 1864, when startled federal pickets awoke to see the advance elements of the Confederate army of Gen. Jubal Early maneuvering in the Silver Spring."[25]

But Wallace was easily defeated by a soft-spoken peanut farmer and former governor called Jimmy Carter.

. . .

Jimmy Carter was an unexceptional president. He vacillated between hiking spending and cutting the deficit. An energy crisis produced long lines at the pump: in June 1979, 60 percent of America's gas stations were closed due to shortage of fuel. Already spiraling levels of unemployment and inflation—a phenomenon dubbed stagflation—grew worse. The vulnerable were hit the hardest: In 1980 the black unemployment rate was 10 percent while price inflation was 13.6 percent.[26] Carter scored few points on foreign policy, either. He mishandled the Soviets, who intervened in Angola and the Horn of Africa. They invaded Afghanistan in 1979, a few weeks after the Shah of Iran was driven from his country in a fundamentalist Islamic revolution. Militant Islamic students overran the U.S. embassy in Tehran and took the staff hostage.[27] America was losing confidence in itself. In 1979, 77 percent of people interviewed by Gallup said that the country was headed in the wrong direction.[28]

In everything he did, Carter sent mixed signals. He told evangelical voters that he favored allowing prayer in schools and a ban on abortion. Neither came to pass. In 1978, the administration announced that it would end tax exemptions enjoyed by private Christian schools. The White House received over 125,000 letters of complaint. This battle united the religious right and fiscal conservatives, creating an unlikely alliance between small-town pastors and Wall Street CEOs.[29] Antitax fever gripped the states. In California, voters passed Proposition 13 and slashed property taxes by 57 percent. Massachusetts experienced a "modern Boston Tea Party" when residents voted to cap property taxes to 2.5 percent of the full and fair cash value of the local tax base. In 1979, Rev. Jerry Falwell formed the Moral Majority group, which became the revolutionary vanguard of Ronald Reagan's 1980 election effort.[30]

Pat was the Cicero of this New Right revolt. Putting to use the poetry he studied at Gonzaga, he spent hours sharpening sentences until they virtually sliced the page in two. His columns were shot through with irate beauty, and a little humor. Take his opening salvo in the battle over an ordinance banning discrimination against gays and lesbians in Florida's Dade County:

My fond hope is that the Gay Liberation Front and its political aux-
iliaries receive a long overdue thrashing. For years, pornographers,
liberated feminists, open marriage nuts and homosexuals have
been hogging the news columns and rubbing society's nose in their
value systems. It is time society pushed back.

Close your eyes and listen to the words and you could easily be sitting in a
bar in South Boston, being berated by an angry truck driver at the end of a
long day.

The gays may counter that the American Psychiatric Association
has, of late, dropped homosexuality from its list of disorders. That,
however, tells us less about the nature of homosexuals than about
the moral courage of the APA . . . One need not be a Ph.D. to know
that when some 40 year old male paints his face with rouge and
lipstick, and prances around in women's clothes, he ain't playing
with a full deck.[31]

Pat's most frequent complaint was that America had gone soft on communism. In one column, he asked why the U.S. gave in to every Soviet demand.
He compared Red China to Nazi Germany, arguing that Mao Tse-tung shared
Hitler's genius for torturing his own people while teasing diplomatic and economic concessions out of the West. In passing, he referred to Hitler as "an individual of great courage, a soldier's soldier in the Great War, a political organizer
of the first rank, a leader steeped in the history of Europe, who possessed
oratorical powers that could awe even those who despised him." In the
1990s, Pat's critics leaped on those words as proof that he was a Hitler lover.
In fact, he was paraphrasing a recent biography by historian John Toland. Pat
also called the dictator "racist and anti-Semitic to the core, a man who without
compunction could commit murder and genocide." But it was the claim that
Hitler was a man of "courage . . . an organizer of the first rank" that critics
would return to time and time again, until much of the readership of *The New
York Times* could recite those words verbatim.[32]

. . .

In 1977, Buchanan got an offer to host a Washington, D.C., radio call-in show called *Confrontation*. In pursuit of balance, the producers put him on with Frank Mankiewicz. Mankiewicz had been George McGovern's campaign director in 1972 and had earned a place on Nixon's enemies list. Every morning on WRC radio between 7:45 and 9:45 a.m., Pat and Frank discussed the big issues of the day—sparring back and forth, from left to right. Listeners could call in to offer their opinions. Inevitably most subjects—from world peace to parking fines—came back to Nixon. Buchanan called Mankiewicz a socialist and a libertine. Mankiewicz said, "Buchanan is the last defender of Richard Nixon who doesn't need the approval of his probation officer to go to a radio station." The show had potential but Mankiewicz was too polite. They refought the 1972 election and the result was the same the second time around: Buchanan won.[33]

Mankiewicz got plucked for a better job. He suggested as his replacement the liberal columnist Tom Braden. Braden was the opposite of Buchanan: a WASP, graduate of Dartmouth, professor, assistant to CIA director Allen Dulles, and committed liberal. Braden wore a long trench coat and ruffled sweater and chain-smoked his way through Malboros. He was personable and his writing mixed important events with domestic trivia—his best columns were about the time his son was arrested for smoking marijuana, or when his daughter's pet boa constrictor went missing. The two men first clashed in 1973, when Braden wrote a column critical of Buchanan's role in Watergate. Buchanan sent in a scathing letter of complaint and their pictures appeared side by side, with Braden's response. Both were invited to appear on a radio show to debate Watergate. Braden refused. "I said 'No, I will not confront Pat Buchanan,'" he recalled. "'It wouldn't be good TV because I couldn't stand the guy.'"

In 1977, Mankiewicz asked Braden to take his place on *Confrontation*. This time Braden agreed, because he thought his friend was getting beaten too easily and wanted to redress the balance. His view of Buchanan hadn't improved, if anything it got worse. But the two men had a strange chemistry. "It's balance and complement, with an 'e' rather than an 'i,'" said Buchanan. "When one of us is gone, the show lacks a certain spark. It doesn't have the same liveliness." Braden set the pace. Sitting facing the control booth, he was the one who got the signals for ad breaks. They set up a subject—anything from nuclear proliferation to bad grammar—bantered a bit and then took calls. These came from a mix of cab drivers and politicians—there was a special line reserved for people calling from the Hill.[34]

Eventually, the show stopped taking calls. Braden said this was because they were "too dumb."[35] But the truth was that producers realized that Braden and Buchanan duking it out uninterrupted was far more interesting. It was macho, primitive stuff and the verbal fireworks were fueled by a mix of ideological disagreement and personal enmity. Although they both admitted to a "grudging respect for one another," they were not friends. They did not socialize and barely spoke when not on air. Once, they stopped speaking altogether. Buchanan got upset about something and yelled at Braden to shut up. Braden said, "Well I will shut up," and didn't say anything for two hours. He sat smoking cigarettes, leaving Buchanan to carry the rest of the show. Buchanan was fond of calling Braden a "pointy-headed liberal" and a member of "the Volvo, white wine and cheese set." Braden called Buchanan an "ideological bedfellow of George Wallace" and "a narrow-minded New Rightist." Braden was laconic, relaxed. Buchanan was uptight and angry. But funnier, too.

The guests who dared to go on the show were often ignored. Buchanan and Braden would take a break from their argument to introduce a speaker, and then go straight back into the argument where they left off. One guest, Kenneth Woolack of the Middle East Policy Survey, said, "I felt like I was in a barroom brawl. The only thing missing was the beer bottle over my head." When Pat was ill one week he was replaced by a former priest and adviser to President Nixon, John McLaughlin. Braden found McLaughlin so appalling that he stormed off air mid-argument, got in his car, and drove home.[36]

The producers realized they had a hit on their hands and the show got moved up to a primetime afternoon slot. Running weekdays from 4 to 7 p.m., the ratings put them third in a field of thirty-five. One survey found that 51 percent of members of Congress called *Confrontation* their favorite broadcast. Eventually, they were offered their own TV show—WDVM's *After Hours*—which was broadcast at 11:30 p.m. on Thursday nights.[37]

The TV show was, if anything, even rowdier. To bring things under control, the producers employed journalist Gordon Peterson as a moderator. But Peterson might as well have been in a different room (he once joked on air that he needed a whistle and, a few days later, was sent one by a football coach). Buchanan and Braden, who were still doing *Confrontation* in the afternoons, picked up any argument they had started earlier and ignored whatever guest or topic they were supposed to be discussing. One time, former senator Gaylord Nelson was in the studio to talk about conservation. Buchanan introduced him, ignored him, and quickly forgot he was there. Instead he launched into a diatribe about how little Braden understood about ecology. Braden pointed at Nelson and shouted, "Why don't you shut up and listen to someone who does?" Buchanan had a reputation for not letting people finish their answers, for losing patience with fools. Once, he interrogated the liberal priest-cum-congressman Fr. Robert F. Drinan. Time after time, Pat asked questions and then interrupted as Drinan tried to answer. Eventually, Drinan snapped, "Do you ever permit anybody to finish a sentence?"

"Yes," Buchanan replied. "You just finished one."[38]

In 1982, Buchanan and Braden were invited to run the show on CNN. They dispensed with a moderator and renamed it *Crossfire*. *Crossfire* emerged at a pivotal moment in TV history, when punditry and conservatism were undergoing an image change. Prior to the 1980s, a semblance of civility and deference still permeated TV chat shows. Interviewers presumed that viewers were tuning in to hear their guest speak—not them. But that all changed in the 1980s. Producers looking for more action now expected guests to play their part in a black-and-white struggle between left and right. Luckily, a new generation of punk politicians was happy to oblige. On the right, commentators like Pat Buchanan were so used to giving and receiving insults that they felt no need to hold back on live TV. Some found that they could make a career out of it, and men like Pat, Robert Novak, and John McLaughlin became professional "talking heads." They were the forerunners of people like Ann Coulter, Joe Scarborough, and Tucker Carlson. Pat Buchanan's peers learned how to fashion and craft a stunning one-liner that would make the news and promote the show.[39]

Pat took the job very seriously. He did research and prepared his remarks

before the show, honing ad-libs and put-downs. During the morning he produced a column, spent the afternoon at the radio station, and then the evening
was devoted to *Crossfire*. Pat was busy, but his world was confined to two studios and his house. Shelley, meanwhile, was evolving into a business partner—
the unseen but vital other half of Buchanan Inc. She drove her husband to and
from the studio, underlined facts and theories in newspapers, and even waited
for him in the green room where she hung on every word. Shelley Buchanan
once controlled access to the President of the United States of America. Now
she was the right-hand woman of the right wing's favorite "mouth for hire."[40]

EIGHT

Reagan in the White House

In November 1980, Ronald Reagan won a landslide victory against Jimmy Carter. For the New Right, Reagan's election was as much a triumph over the Republican establishment as it was over the Democrats. Reagan entered the GOP primaries at the head of a coalition of economic populists (who backed Jack Kemp's tax cuts) and social conservatives. He was opposed by George H. W. Bush, who defended the ERA and legalized abortion, and labeled Reagan's tax-slashing plan "voodoo economics." Bush won the Iowa caucus, but Reagan resurged in New Hampshire and swept the primaries. Pat cheered him along, showing up at the 1980 convention as a friendly commentator. Reagan's nomination, said Pat, buried memories of Nixon. The outsiders had won control of the GOP and cleansed it of insider corruption.[1]

The Reagan revolution owed something to Pat's sister, Bay Buchanan.

Bay had a different experience of growing up in Washington to Pat. She was ten years younger and the second of only two girls. While the boys were hitting the bag in the basement or prowling the streets, the girls were sewing and praying. Irish Catholic women were strong and outspoken, but they were expected to defer to their menfolk. Bay watched her brothers argue at the dinner table in awe. She believed every word they said and, by the time she went to college, Bay was Richard Nixon's number one fan.[2]

All the Buchanans sounded and looked eerily alike, and Bay was no exception. At times she seemed to "channel" Pat; in argument, her eyes widened, her fist clenched, and she jabbed the air like a prizefighter. Childhood in Washington was all about family and church. Her parents were convinced that she owed her life to a miracle. In May 1958, when Bay was ten years old, she was rushed to the hospital for an emergency appendectomy. During the summer, she failed to regain her energy. On Halloween, Mrs. Buchanan took her daughter for an X-ray. The tests showed that her liver was swollen to around three times its natural size with hepatitis, and one kidney was shot through with sarcoma. Three separate opinions gave Bay just three months to live.

"We must look at it this way," Pop told Ma. "God was good enough to give us this child for ten years, and now he has decided to take her home." Catholics were taught to play the cards that God dealt them with good grace. Of course, they could ask God to change his mind. The nuns and priests of the Blessed Sacrament church prayed for Bay, as did the Jesuits at Gonzaga. The Sisters of the Society for the Holy Child Jesus ran a round-the-clock prayer vigil: twenty-four hours a day, seven days a week someone in Washington was asking God for a reprieve.

Over Christmas 1958, Bay's condition got worse. The doctors wanted to remove the kidney, although one surgeon said it was pointless. Why put the child through agony when she has only months to live? he asked. Nevertheless, the hospital went through with it. However, when they took the final X-rays, something had changed. The Buchanans were at home having dinner when the surgeon called. "I have a belated Christmas present for you," he said. The cancer was gone and the liver was back to its proper size. Bay was cured. Mrs. Buchanan was convinced that her daughter was the victim of a dirty needle that infected her during the appendectomy. But Pop Buchanan knew otherwise. "There is no other plausible explanation for it," he told Pat, "other than a miracle."[3]

Bay was an active, committed conservative at college in the late 1960s; she was proud of what her brother was doing in the Nixon administration and he gave her a job working accounts in the 1972 campaign. But Watergate disillusioned her. She upped and moved to Australia. When she returned in 1975, she asked Pat what she should do with her life. "Do something you believe in," he said, "no matter how bad the pay."[4] Bay moved to California and volunteered for Reagan in 1976. By 1980, she was the treasurer of his presidential campaign. When Reagan went down to Bush in Iowa, Bay took the blame and resigned.[5] But her loyalty was remembered. When Reagan finally won, Bay was appointed the youngest ever Treasurer of the United States. Every note printed in the early 1980s bore the thirty-two-year-old's signature.[6]

In the late 1970s, Bay converted to the Church of Latter-day Saints. In 1982, she married a Mormon lawyer. Pop Buchanan boycotted the wedding and insisted that his family do the same. Pat didn't show.[7] God spared Bay as a ten-year-old because her parents had been devout Catholics; it horrified Pop that his daughter would walk away from the Church that saved her life. Pat explained it thus: "We could always argue with Pop about almost anything, and we did; but if one of his sons or daughters questioned the faith, he would say, 'If you think that, you can leave my house.' Faith, for him, came ahead even of family bonds."[8]

Only sixty-nine days into the new administration, a deranged gunman tried to assassinate President Reagan. A bullet missed the President's heart by less than inch. He was rushed to the hospital and put on the critical list. Reagan drifted through this nightmare with characteristic charm. "Honey, I forgot to duck!" he told his wife, Nancy, before going into surgery. In the theater he said to the surgeons, "I hope you're all Republicans?" The nation breathed a sigh of relief when he emerged from the hospital fit and strong. His survival broke a cycle of political assassinations that had haunted America since 1963. His Boy Scout pluck gave a sense that the USA was headed in a different, better direction.[9] Jimmy Carter had talked about the state of the nation like a pastor giving a jeremiad. Ronald Reagan only ever preached the Good News.

Prone to speaking his mind and making off-the-cuff decisions, the President was policed throughout his first term by a troika of counselors—Edwin Meese (an ideological conservative), Deputy Chief of Staff Michael Deaver (a loyal retainer), and James A. Baker III (a pragmatic Brahmin Republican). The troika controlled who saw the President and what information reached him. They loved and respected Reagan, but found that without micromanagement he was liable to go off message or give contradictory instructions. Some insiders reported that the White House had the air of a Tibetan monastery. Reagan was the Buddha in residence, elliptical and vague and hidden from public view in his Oval Office antechamber. Meese, Deaver, and Baker interpreted his words and deeds to the press. It was not that Reagan was dim or uninterested. But he was an antigovernment conservative *in* government, a paradox that meant Reagan held power but was not in love with it.[10]

Reagan's philosophical conservatism led him to challenge the totems of the postwar era: big government at home, accommodation with communism overseas. In his inaugural address, Reagan stated, "In this present crisis, government is not the solution to our problem; government is the problem." He cut income tax by 25 percent, simplified the tax code, and deregulated business. During his time in office, the top rate of income tax fell from 70 percent to 28 percent. Caps on fuel prices were lifted and the price of gas fell as exploration went up. After a harsh recession in the early 1980s, the country rebounded spectacularly. By 1988, America had gained 16 million new jobs and inflation stood at just 3.4 percent.[11] Flares and gas lines went out, shoulder pads and junk bonds came in.

Unlike his predecessors, President Reagan believed that communism could be defeated, and he was determined to see it happen under his watch. Reagan supported anticommunist groups around the world, including the Contras in Nicaragua, the Mujahideen in Afghanistan, RENAMO in Mozambique, and UNITA in Angola. In a landmark address to evangelical groups on June 8, 1982, he called the Soviet Union an "evil empire." In October 1983, U.S. troops invaded Grenada to oust a Marxist dictatorship. Reagan, who was personally opposed to nuclear weapons, championed the Strategic Defense Initiative (SDI)—a defense shield covering the U.S. that could shoot down incoming missiles.[12]

Considering Reagan's reputation as a conservative, it is surprising to find that the New Right thought he was the prisoner of moderates.[13] Ideologues were not easily charmed by the President's bonhomie. Some blamed his preppy, moderate Vice President. Paul Erickson, a student Republican activist, judged that "Reagan had great instincts . . . but he was subverted all the way by Bush's

people, who forced conservatives out and put their own people in charge."[14]
Pat was one of those who suspected that the administration underestimated
the communist threat.[15] After he witnessed a press conference on foreign
policy at the White House, Buchanan wrote: "the President was—to put it
generously—at sea. Though charming, appealing, the President rolled out answers like some C-student relying upon a winning personality before oral
examiners to compensate for his skimpy knowledge of the subject at hand."[16]

In 1982, Pat joined the staff of the new conservative broadsheet *The Washington Times*. His editorials regularly accused Reagan of "winging it" on
communism.[17] In his most stinging column, he observed:

> Even under Ronald Reagan, foreign policy appears to be steered in
> critical areas by illusion, inertia, nostalgia. A nationalist foreign
> policy, grounded in the security interests of the US, would, three
> years ago, have shut down the San Francisco consulate, evacuated
> the UN spy center from New York to the Third World, terminated
> contributions to the International Development Association, de-
> manded and gotten vote power over all loans from the World
> Bank, put [the Polish government] in default, cut the contingent of
> Soviet bloc diplomats in Washington to numbers comparable to
> those of the United States in communist Europe. Without belliger-
> ence, but without apology. The principal adversaries of such of a
> foreign policy are the international bankers and finance ministers,
> the foreign ministries of the West and that parasitical class of in-
> ternational bureaucrats numbering in the thousands.

When Reagan proclaimed 1984 as a "year of opportunities for peace," Buchanan wrote that pressure from the European Union, the media, and liberals
had "converted Mr. Reagan into a president of the Order for Peaceful Coexis-
tence."[18]

Domestic policy came in for a battering, too. Pat wrote that, under Reagan,
the "continued socialization" of America had "proceeded apace." Buchanan
demanded to know why the administration would not even discuss "scrapping

the entire federal welfare and income-support structure for working-aged persons, including . . . Medicaid, food stamps, unemployment insurance, worker's compensation, subsidized housing and the rest."[19] In a speech before CPAC in February 1983, Buchanan raged against a compromise deal between Democrats and the administration to push through a $98.3 billion tax increase to protect Social Security. In December 1983, Reagan went along with a gasoline tax hike to finance a highways jobs program. In *The Washington Times,* Buchanan wrote that this bill was "the latest in a series of calculated maneuvers to soften the image of Mr. Conservative into Mr. Conciliation." The "turnaround cut the legs from under those Republicans who, at some political cost, have echoed Reagan's own arguments about the folly of expanding the deficit to create make-work jobs."[20] As the 1984 election loomed, Pat asked, "Is there more than a little truth in the jibe that Republicans, once empowered, inevitably become less conservative and more corporatist; that the GOP is always capable of rising above principle to stand upon the sacred ground of maximized profit?"[21] He later wrote: "Post-November, one question the right must address is this: Given that the populist, nationalist and conservative Republican Party of Ronald Reagan, in power, proved incapable of a clean break with the establishment, globalist and détentist Republican Party of Kissinger and Rockefeller, is a new institution required?"[22]

The New Right was sad to discover that the Reagan White House was mainly concerned with cutting taxes and containing the Soviet Union. The administration had little time for nice words about the Confederacy or a constitutional amendment banning abortion. The troika only followed a cause so long as it was popular.[23] Anything, or anyone, that smacked of controversy was dropped.[24] In 1980, Professor M. E. Bradford was tapped by Ronald Reagan for chairman of the National Endowment for the Humanities. Bradford was an English professor at the University of Dallas—a southern romantic who admired the world of antebellum Dixie and regretted the coming of the twentieth century. He once wrote: "Reaction is a necessary term in the intellectual context we inhabit in the twentieth century, because merely to conserve is sometimes to perpetuate what is outrageous." The nomination procedure looked like a formality, until some administration moderates intervened. They said that Bradford once called Lincoln "a dangerous man"; that he had campaigned for George Wallace and was probably a racist. Bradford lost the job.

Bradford's supporters were shocked by the vehemence of his critics. One of Pat's coworkers at *The Washington Times*, Sam Francis, wrote: "The bitterness felt by many [of Bradford's supporters] was not due so much to losing the post for their own candidate as to what they regarded (accurately in my view) as a . . . smear campaign . . . that insinuated he was, among other things, a Nazi sympathizer." The administration was trying to draw a line between the respectable and the unrespectable right. It would sacrifice old friends to preserve its mainstream image. Anyone on the New Right could be next, even a former presidential aide like Pat Buchanan.[25]

In 1982, Pat invited Allan Ryan onto *Crossfire*. Ryan was the head of the Office of Special Investigations (OSI), which was set up to capture the remaining Nazis fleeing justice for crimes committed during the Second World War. Buchanan said that Ryan used unreliable evidence to persecute naturalized U.S. citizens: "You've got a great atrocity that occurred 35, 45 years ago, okay?" he asked. "Why continue to invest . . . put millions of dollars into investigating that? I mean why keep a special office to investigate Nazi war crimes? . . . Why not abolish [the] office?" Buchanan said that he saw no "singularity" about the Holocaust that justified maintaining a special prosecution office. All the OSI did, he said, was hand propaganda victories to the USSR by confirming a supposed relationship between the anti-Communism of East European émigrés and fascism.[26] The interview earned Pat the condemnation of the Jewish Anti-Defamation League. The ADL officially registered him as a "lobbyist for war criminals."[27]

Pat was not alone in criticizing the OSI. Lyndon Johnson's former Attorney General, Ramsey Clark, offered representation to several accused war criminals. "I find it remarkable," Clark said, "that the Department of Justice, which is part of an administration that consistently criticizes Soviet justice, would accept evidence that it's unable to independently examine in a real sense . . . I oppose the idea of regenerating hatreds and pursuits 40 years after the fact." Amnesty

International agreed, deploring the deportation of people to countries with low standards of human rights on eyewitness testimony alone.[28]

In the early 1980s, Pat was contacted by the families of Estonian Karl Linnas and Ukrainian John Demjanjuk. Both men were accused of murdering Jews and faced deportation from the U.S. Their families asked Buchanan to publicize their appeals.[29] They said that their fathers were the victims of mistaken identity. Jewish leaders insisted that the evidence against Linnas and Demjanjuk was overwhelming. Even if either man was innocent of the specific charges against them, they were guilty of lying to get into the country and had participated in the Holocaust by working as camp guards (something neither denied having done). When Pat agreed to take up the cause of Linnas and Demjanjuk, many Jewish commentators presumed—given the weight of evidence against them—that he was motivated by anti-Semitism. The Soviet Union might be a totalitarian state, they said, but its people still deserved justice.[30]

Many Americans of East European descent saw it a different way. Ukrainians and Estonians regarded the charges against Demjanjuk and Linnas as an insult to their entire community, an insult that implied anyone who had happened to live east of the Elbe in the 1940s participated in mass murder. Both men were upstanding members of their community: settled citizens who had built families and careers.[31] The fact that they lied to gain entrance to the USA was a common experience among refugees in the 1940s, and no proof of guilt.[32] These (largely Catholic) ethnics found it particularly galling that U.S. officials would use Soviet evidence to implicate them. It was the USSR, they insisted, whose pact with Hitler made World War II possible and the Holocaust inevitable. In their eyes, Holocaust memory was used by communists to guilt East Europeans into accepting socialism.[33]

Buchanan felt a personal responsibility toward these men because they were Catholics. They asked for his help in a fight and he gave it, just like he had thrown a few punches on behalf of Don Oliver or Richard Nixon. The families of Linnas and Demjanjuk appealed to Pat as a brother in Christ. Anu Linnas wrote Pat handwritten letters detailing her father's physical decline.[34] Pat attended a Mass where the congregation prayed for Linnas's release.[35] Afterward, the East European émigrés crowded around him and shook his hand. They asked, why was the Holocaust so special? Why didn't the U.S. government show as much concern about ex-communists living in America, or demand justice for the victims of the Khmer Rouge or the Ethiopian Red Terror? Was it possible that the OSI had been taken over by Soviet agents? This was what Buchanan meant when he questioned the "singularity" of the Holocaust.[36] I'm not a Nazi, said Pat: just a good friend to two innocent men.

Controversy generated column inches and cash. The further from power Pat was, the freer he was to speak his mind. And the more he said what he thought, the further from power it seemed to put him. Most people presumed that Buchanan was now unemployable anywhere but in the media. Certainly, the Reagan administration was unlikely to offer a job to a lobbyist for accused war criminals.[37]

Ronald Reagan had a benign reputation to safeguard. In 1984, he coasted to reelection on the vague theme of "morning in America." The campaign stressed warm images and patriotic photo ops over new policy. The result was an endorsement of Reagan's administration, a 525–13 electoral vote landslide.[38] But, by avoiding specifics, the President failed to set an agenda for the second term. Suddenly in need of a narrative, Reagan shook up the troika. He eased James Baker out as Chief of Staff and replaced him with a man from the treasury called Don Regan. It was up to Regan to decide what the big message of the second term was to be.[39]

After the election victory, Richard Viguerie drew up a list of dream team New Right appointments by the White House. At the top of the page was Pat Buchanan for the post of Director of Communications.[40] A few days later, Pat got a call from the White House. The new Chief of Staff wanted a conservative on board to shift policy to the right. He asked Pat to serve as the Director of Communications. His predecessor, David R. Gergen, was as surprised by the move as anyone. "Pat has one of the best political minds in Washington," said Gergen. "He is especially good at getting to the heart of a problem and he was a tremendous asset to Richard Nixon. But," he cautioned "the appointment is fraught with potential peril. The question is to what degree this appointment will mean that the administration is more combative and confrontational."[41]

Don Regan was determined to shift policy to the right. Pat's appointment sent as clear a message as if Jimmy Carter had asked Timothy Leary to head up the Drug Enforcement Administration. But the experiment in ideological conservatism would last less than a year.

NINE

Helping Reagan Be Reagan

P at Buchanan's appointment as White House Communications Director caught the media by surprise. The man who wrote Spiro Agnew's best lines was not popular with reporters. At Don Regan's first press conference, it was all they wanted to talk about.

"Why did you appoint him if, in fact, he sees the press as an enemy?" was the first question. Regan denied that Pat was that partisan, but ABC correspondent Sam Donaldson read aloud a column in which Buchanan wrote: "An ideological bulwark of the Democratic Party, polemical and publicity arm of American liberalism, the big media are the strategic reserve of the [Democratic] presidential campaign."

"He didn't say *some* reporters, *some* media," Donaldson complained. "In all of his pieces, Mr. Regan, he lumps under the name 'big media' every one of us."

Regan smiled. He said, "Well, that may mean he's a good communicator and it may not . . . we'll have to see."

But the questions kept coming: Why do you need him and what will you do with him? How can a person who is as clearly identified with one wing or faction within an administration adequately represent the entire administration and the policies of that administration to the American people? How could Buchanan speak for a president he had so often criticized?[1]

Don Regan believed that the 1984 landslide sent a message to Washington.

He said, "The people wanted Reagan to be Reagan. It was my job, as I saw it, to make that happen."[2] Everyone presumed that Pat's appointment meant the administration was veering to the right. It was a fair guess. Regan gave Pat Buchanan the Office of Public Liaison, with a staff of thirty-six and a prominent role in political strategy.[3] He wrote Pat:

> I have directed my staff that I want your personal needs reviewed and acted on as soon as possible. . . . I want space made available for [you] in the West Wing and to provide a suite of offices for you and your staff on the second floor. I want this done even if it means relocating other senior staff because I want to see that your operation is consolidated and benefits from your hands-on coordination and leadership. If we are to "move the needle" it will take all of your considerable skill and personality. . . . I consider your initiative of the highest priority.[4]

(The "suite of offices" put Buchanan in a tiny room without any windows. The press presumed it was an insult, but the location gave Pat better access to the Oval Office and was a running joke among the White House staff.[5] When Pat turned forty-seven in November 1985, the President gave him a framed picture of a window with a false view beyond. When he left the administration, Buchanan put it on display in his house.[6])

Pat made a friend in the First Lady's speechwriter Mona Charen, and the two swapped memos brimming with excitement and possibility. They were going to call the '84 landslide a conservative mandate—and run with it. "We are most successful when we set the agenda and take the offensive," wrote Charen to Pat. It was time to do some of the things that the Republican Party had promised to do, and they would use the President to do it: "The Democrats fear him when he assumes the crusader role as much as the citizens of Hamlin feared the ol' Piper."[7]

These were great days to be a conservative. The economy was hot, inflation was down, and employment up. Enterprise, once scorned as exploitation, was cool. People were making fast money on Wall Street and the stockbroker was king. Not everyone thought greed was good (Pat hated the yuppies). But pocket calculators, junk bonds, and *Dynasty*'s doorway-defying shoulder pads at least represented one in the eye for Seventies socialism.[8] Per capita champagne consumption hit an all-time high in 1984, nearly double what it was in 1979 and 2008. Times were good and people felt it in their wallet. There was no doubt that Reagan's reelection marked a moral victory for the right, a triumph over redistribution and malaise.[9]

The spirit of '85 was on display at a party thrown at the Dawson's Connecticut Avenue Coop. Pat was there as a guest of the Jefferson Educational Foundation, a fine-sounding organization that did PR for the dictator of Zaire, Mobutu Sese Seko. It was a very Eighties affair—champagne, caviar, hair gel, and sequined excess. The event was hosted by wannabe-socialite Jane Dawson, an amateur diplomat. President Mobutu arrived in a limousine, wearing a leopard skin hat and sunglasses. "Are you the richest man in the world?" asked Mrs. Dawson at the door. Mobutu laughed in reply. Unsatisfied, Dawson asked again. Mobutu moved away. A reporter suggested that the question was vulgar. "How else am I going to find out?" said Dawson. "I hear he's only the second-richest anyhow."

People paid good money to meet Mobutu, perhaps offering more for a concession in a cobalt mine or just a week on safari. In Reaganworld, even foreign policy was privatized; the world was up for grabs. The official reason to be there was to lend support to "our African friends in the steadfast fight against communism." Sen. Strom Thurmond, however, was looking more for a good time. "I'm here to see the king," he said.

Mobutu greeted Thurmond by asking, "Do you speak French?"

"No," replied Thurmond.

"Do you speak English?" asked Thurmond.

"No," said Mobutu. They parted in the foyer and Thurmond staggered drunkenly to the oyster bar. Buchanan and the guests hung around at a respectful distance, admiring the imported Louis XV furniture and the diamond chandeliers. Although few people could understand a word Mobutu said, Dawson enjoyed the attention. "Do you like my dining room?" she asked a guest. "I'm going to paint the ceiling gold. I'm really a very gaudy person." And then, "Did you see my hookah room? The one with the red velvet chairs? . . . I do hope you'll mention me in your story," she said to a journalist. "I'm trying to get this party thing off the ground. I really am a Washington hostess, you know. Don't forget to mention me. I really intend to fly with this thing."[10]

In the opinion of the press, the Reagan administration turned nasty in the spring of 1985. Pat Buchanan refused to answer calls from certain newspapers and responded to questions he didn't like with, "No comment. And that's off the record."[11] Style matched substance. Reagan vetoed a farm-aid bill and declared, "I have only one thing to say to the tax increasers. Go ahead and make my day." Administration witnesses on the Hill were encouraged to fight back. Secretary of State George Schultz roasted scientists who questioned the logic of SDI, ridiculed as Star Wars by some in the press. Caspar Weinberger tore apart defense budget ditherers and Clarence Pendleton, chair of the Civil Rights Commission, attacked black leaders who criticized Reagan's civil rights legacy. He called them "racists."[12] Reagan's approval rating dipped when the president told a joke about sales of grain to the Soviet Union at a dinner: "I think we should keep the grain and export the farmers." Buchanan was asked if he wrote the gag. "No comment," he replied. "And that's off the record."[13]

Ronald Reagan was determined to oust the left-wing Sandinista government in Nicaragua.[14] The administration had been prevented from giving direct aid to the opposition Contras by congressional fiat. Regan wanted to get money flowing to the resistance, and so began a series of legislative struggles to overturn the congressional veto.[15] Buchanan drew up a plan of attack that depended on using the President's popularity to guilt or goad legislators into passing his bills.[16] The administration lobbied for a congressional grant of $14 million in humanitarian aid to the Contras, balanced by a pledge to pursue peace.[17] Buchanan saw conspiracy all around him to defeat the bill; he even accused the State Department of working against it.[18]

Pat's hawkishness got him in trouble. National Security Advisor Robert "Bud" McFarlane called him, "Kirkpatrick in long pants," a reference to the aggressive UN ambassador Jeane Kirkpatrick.[19] Pat's number-one enemy was Michael Deaver. Deaver was close to the First Lady, loved like a son by Reagan, and one of the last strong voices in favor of consensus and moderation. Throughout the first administration, he did his best to keep Reagan out of the Nicaragua mess, which he thought could become a second Vietnam. Deaver disliked Pat, disliked his style of politics.[20] On Good Friday 1985, as Reagan headed out to Santa Barbara for a vacation, Deaver read a draft of a radio speech he was scheduled to give the next day. It was a classic piece of Pat: heavy with Easter and Passover themes. Deaver hated it. He called it "a sermon" and a "very preachy kind of thing." Buchanan apparently missed the irony that Reagan would be spending Easter Sunday not in church but partying at his ranch. The address was vetoed. Deaver tried to explain that while Reagan and the conservatives often agreed, their needs diverged.[21]

And so Deaver and the First Lady ruled out many of Pat's suggestions for a propaganda campaign in favor of the Contras. When the humanitarian aid vote came up in May 1985, Pat scheduled a Wagnerian rally in Miami to promote the cause. It would climax in a big bonfire in Little Havana, the President surrounded by thousands of cheering Cubans. But polls showed that tough talk on Nicaragua was unpopular and reminded people of Vietnam. The First Lady rejected Buchanan's schedule on the grounds that it would be a security nightmare. "At least can we have a TV speech laying out the case against the Sandinistas?" Pat asked. Deaver and the moderates in the State Department said no. The President spoke about the federal budget instead. The administration lost the vote in Congress.[22] The next day, Nicaragua's president, Daniel Ortega, visited Moscow.[23]

One of Pat's allies in the White House was a handsome Vietnam veteran called Lt. Col. Oliver "Ollie" North. North cut a romantic figure. He never seemed to sleep, came in on weekends, was a whirlwind of energy and anger. North talked constantly and darkly about his days on special ops in the jungle. For the aged men in the White House, North was a link to the excitement of the battlefield. He helped plan the 1982 invasion of Grenada and handled the destabilization of several Latin American regimes. North was overjoyed to get the Nicaragua brief. A congressman once asked him what the difference was between the wars in Vietnam and Nicaragua. "Ten thousand miles," North said. "In Nicaragua . . . you're talking about something right next door. That's the difference."[24]

Ollie North told Pat Buchanan that he wanted to start a public education program on the Contras. All he needed was some money from wealthy donors to get the scheme up and running.[25] Pat and speechwriter Peggy Noonan agreed to supply a list of conservatives with money.[26] Rich old ladies were invited to the White House, where Ollie North entertained them—riveted to attention, poured into his uniform, and full of stories of derring-do. Pat gave a little speech about the evils of communism and passed around the hat. But not all the money went to tea parties and pro-Contra literature. Unbeknownst to Pat, much of it ended up in the hands of the Contras themselves. Some of those little old ladies donated so much that North's people named helicopters after them.[27] Pat had played a key part in the establishment of back-channel, illegal funds to a foreign army.[28]

North was desperate to get around the boycott imposed by Congress. In 1985, he found a new source of cash. To solicit their help in freeing U.S. hostages held in the Middle East, the administration authorized arms sales to the Islamic republic of Iran. North put a claim in for the profits. He conceived a "neat idea" to use the fundamentalists' money to bankroll the freedom fighters in Nicaragua.[29]

Pat had entered the Reagan administration with high hopes. They were quickly dashed.[30] The Reagan administration was supposed to be the place where the conservative counterrevolution would begin. In practice, life was a day-to-day struggle to get anything done. The problem began at the top. "In the Nixon administration," Pat recalled, "we dealt by memoranda, I mean very candid memoranda. You put all your thoughts and arguments down . . . This administration deals by meetings and verbal communication, even to the point of briefing the president. I used to brief Richard Nixon for news conferences and other public appearances . . . I would send all the questions out that I had devised by reading three weeks of newspapers, news summaries, and the rest of it. I'd ask the agencies and the various shops, they'd get me the material and I rewrote everything. I'd get it to Nixon. He would go into his study for eight hours and study . . . With this president, you go over to the theater and maybe ten of us are sitting there, and he's answering questions thrown up to him. It's totally different."

Buchanan inundated the President with memos in his first few months on the job. Few were read and, as time went on, they shrank in volume and factual content. Weekend reading consisted of three articles, usually one by Pat—key passages underlined. The wording was simple and short. This wasn't a comment on Reagan's intelligence. Pat explained: "I remembered writing memos for Nixon and them showing up in *Harper's* and *The Washington Post,* or whatever. So I would write a memo for Reagan and then say to my secretary, 'Hang on, bring that back.' And I would edit down to nothing so that it wouldn't embarrass anyone if it leaked; down to it being anodyne."[31]

The Reagan White House lacked the intellectual cut and thrust of the Nixon years. Ronald Reagan was a hands-off president who governed by establishing his priorities, setting a mood, and then letting his underlings get on with the job. He could seem distant, even uninterested in policy. Conservatives had to find subtle ways of getting past the wall of moderates surrounding him, of capturing his interest, and getting him to weigh in on their side. One method was to pitch an issue as a joke. It helped if the Soviet Union was the punch line. Pat wanted the President to make a speech decrying sanctions against apartheid South Africa. So he informed Reagan that more black people owned cars in South Africa than whites did in the USSR. "Reagan loved that," Pat remembered. "You could get him on anything if you made your point with an anecdote that he could use. If it was something that made the communists look bad, he *really* went for it."[32]

Buchanan chalked up a few victories. In that first year, he got some exemptions included in the big tax reform measure, giving breaks to stay-at-home moms, charitable fraternities, and disabled veterans.[33] But he suspected that his zeal was but one weapon in the Reaganite arsenal. Everything came back to what was good for the President's sunny image. If circumstances changed, if Pat's usefulness declined, if he became a burden, if his anticommunism started to look reckless and apocalyptic, then Don Regan would drop him like a radioactive isotope.[34]

Within months of his appointment, Pat was in big trouble. The administration had agreed to a presidential trip to West Germany and, as part of the schedule, Reagan was to lay a wreath at the graves of fallen U.S. and

German soldiers from World War II. Bonn requested that the President visit a cemetery in Bitburg. Only a few weeks before the trip did the administration discover that Bitburg contained the bodies of forty-nine members of the Waffen SS.[35]

The Bitburg fiasco paralyzed the White House, shutting down business for weeks. Reagan was determined to keep to the schedule proposed by West German Chancellor Helmut Kohl, if only out of politeness to his host. But the Jewish community was outraged.[36] There was anger from the right, too.[37] Moderate Republican senator Pete Wilson called the visit "inappropriate."[38] A young congressman from Georgia named Newt Gingrich said it was "immoral." He opined that the controversy was "a tactical device of anti-Reagan forces to prevent Jews from seeing who is their natural ally."[39] Jack Kemp called the planned ceremony shameful and complained that the President was being poorly advised.[40]

Telegrams to the White House ran 11,002–2,213 against the Bitburg visit; telephone calls, 9,942–4,483 against; letters, 1,320–95 against.[41] Few placed blame directly on Reagan. He was, they thought, too sweet natured, too patriotic to do something so tactless. Moderate Republicans and Democrats stoked the idea that someone on the White House staff was to blame. Rep. Elizabeth Holtzman of New York made a demand that was picked up by the mainstream press: Buchanan should resign.[42]

Bitburg had nothing to do with Pat Buchanan; the decision to go was made before his appointment. But unfriendly journalists pinned the blame on him and charged Pat with bringing anti-Semitism into the White House. In May 1985, the President met with leaders of the Jewish community to discuss Bitburg. An NBC state department correspondent claimed that he leaned over Buchanan's shoulder and saw him writing that Reagan should resist "succumbing to the pressure of the Jews."[43] In fact Kenneth Bialkin of the Anti-Defamation League had told Reagan to ensure that, whatever decision he took, he not seem to be "succumbing to pressure" from the Jewish community: He wanted the decision to appear to be the President's and not the result of special interest lobbying. Buchanan, who was there purely as a notetaker, was directly quoting the ADL. Bialkin—who was no friend of

Pat's—confirmed this. But he was too late to stop the story becoming popular myth.[44]

Bitburg was Ronald Reagan's fault, or rather the result of letting Reagan be Reagan. He agreed to add a visit to Bergen-Belsen to the schedule, but refused to back down on any other aspect of the trip. At a press conference the President said, "There are 2,000 graves [at Bitburg], and most of those, the average age is about 18. I think that there's nothing wrong with visiting that cemetery where those young men are victims of Nazism also, even though they were fighting in the German uniform, drafted into service to carry out the hateful wishes of the Nazis. They were victims, just as surely as the victims in the concentration camps." The press reported that the "victims" statement was scripted by Pat Buchanan. But it was off-the-cuff. Reagan said it because he believed it.[45] The visit went ahead and was a triumph of damage control. Reagan stayed just eight minutes at the cemetery and delivered a moving eulogy that could offend no one. After a trumpet salute, the two men representing the U.S. Air Force and the German Luftwaffe shook hands.[46]

In a familiar pattern, Reagan survived the scandal because the press preferred to believe that he wasn't clever or mean enough to do evil. It was always his advisors who took the blame.[47] Suddenly, everything Buchanan had ever said about World War II became a press obsession.[48] And it didn't take long for journalists to discover that he was trying to prevent the deportations of his old friends John Demjanjuk and Karl Linnas.[49]

Pat slipped articles into Reagan's reading material about the defendants, but to no avail. He gave an outline of a proposed column on Demjanjuk to Don Regan, and Regan returned it with a demand that a "disclaimer" be attached and some inconsistencies in the defense evidence underlined.[50] However, the emotional Reagan was a sucker for a sob story. Buchanan waited until they were alone one day and brought up Karl Linnas's deportation, which was now before the Supreme Court. We can't hand over an innocent old man to the brutal KGB, Pat said. Put in those terms, Reagan agreed. At that point, Regan entered the room and discussion quickly ceased. But a verbal endorsement of Pat's views from the President was all it took for Linnas's freedom to become a national priority.[51]

Taking his cue from Pat, Attorney General Ed Meese did his best to save

Linnas. Ignoring the Supreme Court's call for immediate extradition, he gave the old man thirty days to find another country.[52] But no other country would take him. Linnas went to Estonia and died in custody, of old age. Demjanjuk was similarly deported to Israel in 1986. He was found guilty in 1988 and sentenced to death. But the charges were overturned on new evidence in 1993. Demjanjuk returned to the U.S. and his citizenship was restored. In 2009, he was extradited by Germany and stood trial on different charges related to the deaths of 27,900 people.[53]

To thousands of German and East European Americans, Pat was a hero.[54] Hundreds of letters landed on his desk, applauding him for his fight for "civil rights, human decency and national self-determination."[55] But many Republicans thought Buchanan's actions were distasteful, obsessive, and proof that he was behind the Bitburg disaster. When, in November 1986, Pat wrote yet another article in a broadsheet newspaper defending a potential war criminal, several White House insiders insisted that he be fired. Who was signing off on these articles? they asked. It was bad enough for a staffer to promote an issue without consultation, but when he chooses such a sensitive matter surely Regan should discipline him?[56] These conservatives didn't want the U.S. to be regarded as a haven for war criminals—a place where men guilty of terrible crimes could flee to in search of a "fair trial." Even if these defendants were not murderers, they had broken the law by lying their way into the country. Buchanan had often called for millions of Hispanics to be deported on that basis, so why not a couple of old Nazis?[57]

"Why do you do it?" a friend asked Pat.

"It does bring me aggravation," Buchanan replied. "I just felt that you have to provide a voice for those who don't have a voice, and these people don't have one. . . . I do have questions about the quality of the Soviet evidence. The Soviets have used forged documents before, and have falsely accused American citizens."[58]

Buchanan did turn away people who approached him for help who were obviously guilty. Dr. Arthur Rudolph got a curt "Sorry, but no"—Rudolph had used slave labor during his time as a Nazi rocket scientist.[59] Yet it was still difficult for many critics to understand why Buchanan would break bread with a man like Rudolph in the first place.

. . .

Reagan's popularity slipped during the 1985 season of meanness. He gave an ill-advised speech in Miami that accused liberals of playing the race card. The Democrats, said Reagan, were, "segmenting America into warring factions—over the years pitting white against black, women against men, young against old." The speech was written by Pat and the White House had to issue a "clarification." Buchanan finally conceded that not speaking to certain journalists was "unrealistic" and started to return their calls.[60] He was fast becoming a symbol for the failure of the "let Reagan be Reagan" strategy.[61] "I hadn't encountered anyone like Pat since I had to deal with the White Citizens' Councils in my days as a Mississippi news editor," recalled Press Secretary Larry Speakes. "That's not to say that Pat was racist, just that he was so blindly reactionary . . . Pat Buchanan caused more trouble in [those first few months] than anyone else who worked closely with Reagan in the first six years." Speakes mourned the hours spent "cutting hardline stuff written by Buchanan's people out of speeches."[62]

Sympathetic conservatives blamed Pat's bad press on the moderates. One insider complained of "a real pitched effort to sabotage Buchanan." They suspected that the Republican establishment wanted the troika back; the good old days when the President limited himself to looking good on a horse and writing letters to his seven-year-old pen pal, Rudolph Hines.[63] Pat's friend, Mona Charen, quit and wrote an account of a White House paralyzed by cowardice. Regan's men, she claimed, were "frightened by ideas—even Ronald Reagan's ideas . . . They treat his approval ratings like a porcelain vase perched on their heads that can be kept safe only by holding very still." Bud McFarlane, she wrote, had defanged Reagan's foreign policy. The only man worth his weight was Pat Buchanan. He was "such an ethereal creature in so many ways that it seems more likely that the plotting and scheming simply passed beneath his notice . . . Buchanan was a happy and prosperous man before Don Regan asked him to be communications director. [Ever] since, he has endured indignities, abuse, foul play, and failure. And all at the hands of people who haven't one-tenth his intellect."[64]

The right celebrated one small victory when Michael Deaver left the White

House in the summer. "Farewell," said Buchanan to the "treacherous 'Lord Chamberpot' in the demonology of the New Right."[65] In the fall, Bud McFarlane stepped down, too.[66] He was tired of Regan's micromanagement, Buchanan's spats, and threats made to the defense budget in order to cut the federal government's growing debt. Pat was pleased to see him go.[67] But his leaving saw no letup in pressure to moderate the President's rhetoric. The year 1985 ended with an unpleasant fight over the next year's State of the Union speech. Buchanan wanted to say something good about Christian families. The moderates preferred a bland focus on nothing-at-all, with a lot of talk about hope and national pride. There was some name calling, reported *The New York Times*, "a lot of tugging and hauling and pushing and shoving." The debate rolled on into the New Year. They were still scuffling over it when tragedy struck.[68]

On the morning of January 28, 1986, the Space Shuttle Challenger launched from Kennedy Space Center in Florida. Viewing figures were unusually high because Christa McAuliffe, America's much-touted first teacher in space, was aboard. At 11:39 a.m., a faulty seal on the right-hand rocket booster failed. Millions watched as the shuttle broke up over the ocean, killing all seven astronauts onboard.

Ronald Reagan was in the Oval Office chatting with an aide when Buchanan walked in unannounced. "Sir, the shuttle blew up," he said. Reagan's eyes went wide and his jaw fell. "Isn't that the one with the teacher on it?" he asked. Bush and the new National Security Advisor John Poindexter joined them and they put the TV on, all of them standing around the President as he watched the news in silence. "It was somber—grim and somber—nobody was saying anything," recalled Buchanan.[69] The men watched as much as they could take and then drifted back to their offices. Secretaries were in tears. The State of the Union address was delayed.[70]

That night, Reagan gave one of the best speeches of his career. It was written by Peggy Noonan. He paid tribute to the astronauts' courage: "We will never forget them, nor the last time we saw them, this morning, as they prepared for their journey and waved goodbye and 'slipped the surly bonds of Earth' to 'touch the face of God.'"[71]

This was what it meant to let Reagan be Reagan: lyrical and human. But for the conservatives that was never enough.

TEN

Iran-Contra

Pat Buchanan saw much to admire in his boss. He marveled at Reagan's wit and charm, his ability to drift through troubles without losing his confidence or spirit. His communications skills were second to none. And the better Pat understood his unique style—the importance of jokes, sad stories, and face time—the better he became at promoting his own agenda. Timing was key. When Secretary of State George Schultz let it be known he wanted a fee put on imported oil, Pat wrote a short memo opposing it. It read: "Mr. President . . . An oil import fee is a tax. And you promised 'no new taxes.'" He put it on Reagan's desk an hour before a meeting to discuss the measure. When the meeting convened, Reagan walked in and said, "George, an oil import fee is a tax. And I promised 'no new taxes.'" The words were obviously fresh in the President's mind.[1]

But while the economy boomed, Pat sensed that a more important culture war was being lost. Sure, there was a revival in televangelism and the capitalist work ethic. But drug addiction, promiscuity, single parenthood, racial division, immigration, and pornography were on the up, too. And the Republicans on the Hill seemed convinced that they could all be solved with a balanced budget. Reagan remained surrounded by an impenetrable wall of pollsters and soft politicians. It was an infuriating business, trying to get right-wing ideas heard. Even in areas where his critics charged Reagan with being ideologically, inhumanly conservative, Pat still found fault, still said that there was more to

do. The message to conservatives: Don't fall in love with a Republican president. He'll only disappoint you.[2]

The fight over the correct way to beat AIDS was instructive. Pat called the
gay rights movement the "revolutionary vanguard" of the 1960s cultural
revolution. Before joining the administration, Buchanan reported from a
gay pride rally in Manhattan with a mix of awe and horror. "There were men
marching naked except for pubic pouches," he wrote, "and floats proclaiming
'Dykes and Tykes.' A giant banner was unfurled on the cathedral steps proclaiming, 'Intolerance and Ignorance Taught Here.' The mockery of Christ,
the Virgin Mary, and the late Cardinal Cooke has been commonplace. Two
years ago, the featured float was a garbage can on wheels with a huge crucifix
inside it."

The idea that gay sex should be protected by law and discrimination against
gays criminalized seemed like the world turned upside down. Tolerance meant
promotion, because to accept that sex was only about fun and consent was to
encourage experimentation. Pat said sin has consequences, so AIDS was the
price that homosexuals paid for defying the natural order. "The sexual revolution has begun to devour its children," wrote Buchanan in one column. "The
poor homosexuals—they have declared war upon nature, and now nature is
exacting an awful retribution."[3]

Ronald Reagan was personally tolerant toward gays and lesbians. Working in Hollywood, he developed friendships with many homosexuals and his
daughter remembered her father telling her as a child that his pal Rock Hudson
preferred the company of men to women. He has been accused of silence and
dispassion during the AIDS crisis. In fact, he answered questions on the subject
as early as 1985 (the disease wasn't properly identified until 1982) and his administration spent billions of dollars on medical research. The lack of understanding about what caused AIDS probably meant that no amount of money
could have found a cure, but the Reagan administration did try.[4]

The debate within the White House was not over whether or not to do something. Pat Buchanan from late 1985 onward agitated for a radio address on the

subject and wrote the lines in the 1986 State of the Union that listed AIDS re-search as one of the administration's top five priorities.[5] The real debate was over the meaning of AIDS, and how to exploit it. There were those—like Surgeon General C. Everett Koop—who saw it as a health crisis and urged condom dis-tribution to stop it. Others—like Pat Buchanan and his ally in the policy de-partment, Tom Gibson—saw it as an opportunity to roll back the cultural revolution.

Buchanan wanted Reagan to treat AIDS as both a medical and a moral crisis.[6] AIDS, he wrote, was a direct consequence of liberalism:

> The real story is that there are several epidemics running loose, not all of them permanently confined to the gay community. They have been largely or solely caused, and perpetuated, by the growing ur-ban population of active gays whose modal form of sexual behav-ior is impersonal, repeated, random and anonymous sex . . . How did gays get led into this mess? Again, very simple: They followed leaders who spouted slogans and clichés about "rights."

The realization of the right to sexual gratification—every bit as wrong as the right to an abortion—led thousands of young men to violate their own nature. Gay rights, Pat concluded, was an artificial, political formulation and AIDS was its end result.

Buchanan and other conservatives felt that condom distribution and sex education were simplistic and counterproductive responses to AIDS. Both of-fered to limit the consequences of easy sex, which would only confirm the prevalent view that sex outside of marriage was okay. Either could promote the kind of cultural attitudes that made epidemics like AIDS more likely: Teach a kid how to have sex safely and they might be more inclined to try it. Conser-vative journalist Joe Sobran quipped that "fighting AIDS with condoms is like fighting lung cancer with filter tips."[7] Meanwhile, sex education reduced the parent's role in the upbringing of their own children. More often than not, said Buchanan, it was actually used to promote alternative lifestyles. Tom Gib-son wrote him a horrified summary of the federal government's anti-AIDS

campaign. It would "feature explicit language describing the physical precon-
ditioning, anatomical features, and the sexual behaviors that transmit AIDS."
In other words, it was a primer on how to have anal sex. Pat and many other
conservatives became convinced that gays and their liberal allies were using
the AIDS crisis to promote homosexuality—by familiarizing the general
public with its mechanics and telling them that the likelihood of infection
could be reduced. What he wanted was the President to use the crisis to
remind America of the benefits of monogamy and marriage. But that's not
what happened.[8]

The administration's response to AIDS satisfied neither its liberal nor its
conservative critics. The volume and tone of correspondence between Buchanan
and other White House conservatives reflects how important they found
the issue—and how bewildered they were by it. But because they didn't like
homosexuality didn't mean that they felt no sympathy for those dying of AIDS.
When the journalist and former editor of *The New Republic,* Andrew Sullivan,
came out as having HIV, Pat sent him a private, handwritten letter of support.
Sullivan found the note "baffling . . . We barely knew each other, and had had
some bruising encounters on television and in print." Moreover, given Buchanan's statements about homosexuality and AIDS, he expected distance
and condemnation. Instead, Pat offered his sympathy and prayers. And Sullivan had to accept them: "I think it would have been perversely churlish not to
recognize [his] good intent, quietly and privately expressed."

What Andrew Sullivan perhaps missed is that Pat hated the sin but loved
the sinner. Privately, he was moved by Sullivan's suffering. Pat's brother Bill died
of cancer and he understood pain and loss. In public, however, Buchanan felt
a responsibility to condemn a sin that led to so many deaths and imperiled
millions more. He saw it as the product of a corrupt values system, and Sullivan as the victim of liberal excess. Tragically, the conservative response to
AIDS led to the stigmatization of homosexuals. But, as Sullivan came to realize when he read Pat's note, "One of the deepest problems of politics in the
culture war is the reflexive imputation of bad motives to the opposition and
the demonization that inevitably follows. The corollary is believing that we
ourselves are capable of nothing but good, and so failing to see where we also
go wrong."[9]

. . .

One issue Pat was happy to go rogue on was the Contras. Before another congressional vote on aid in March 1986, Buchanan wrote a piece for *The Washington Post.* As was increasingly his habit, he didn't bother to okay it with Regan because he knew Regan would have vetoed it. Pat argued, "With the vote on Contra aid, the Democratic Party will reveal whether it stands with Ronald Reagan and the resistance—or Daniel Ortega and the communists." Twenty centrist Democrats complained about Pat's lobbying tactics. Rep. Dan Glickman of Kansas said, "We told [Regan] that he has lost some votes based on the Red-baiting that is going on. It is very, very serious." Nancy Kassenbaum rebuked Buchanan for casting the issue as "a simple choice between good freedom fighters and evil Marxists. I find this simplistic reasoning to be highly offensive."[10] The vote was lost in the House. Charles E. Schumer, a Brooklyn Democrat, said that the Administration might have won fifteen more Democratic votes if it had been "more subtle." In his view, "Pat Buchanan was to blame."[11]

This could have been a firing offense, but for the intervention of the President. Reagan had read the article and loved it. At a press conference, he endorsed everything Pat had written:

> This was not, as some tried to portray it, the usual legislative battle of both having a same goal, but differing on the way to achieve it. Here were two goals and they were separate. And we were trying to call attention to this fact. To vote one way was to continue to fight against the creation or the continuation of this Communist Government. To vote against was, in effect, to simply say that there it was and we weren't going to do anything about it.

Reagan's intervention showed that Buchanan had guessed the President's mood correctly. But the *Post* piece undoubtedly undermined efforts to coordinate administration policy and strategy. It was the action of a tired and frustrated man.[12]

In the summer of 1986, Don Regan moved decisively against the conservative radicals in the administration. In June, he sacked one of the best speechwriters on Pat's staff, Bentley T. Elliot. Elliot was the hardest of the hard-liners: Buchanan described him as "a Green beret in the Reagan Revolution." One of his admirers said, "Elliot was from the movement, and he felt he had to fight every battle." It was a struggle to keep the message pure from compromise, "a constant battle in terms of what we were trying to get into the speeches to preserve the President's policies and what [the moderates] considered Beltway imperatives."[13] Elliot ignored editing; he complained that speeches were returned with nonsensical, unmerited changes from various departments that had nothing to do with the subject at hand. He doubted that the President ever saw his first drafts. Buchanan ignored the sacking and told Bentley to just turn up to work as if nothing had happened. Regan was forced to fire him twice.[14]

Pat was controversial, but his experience and brilliance saved him. In October 1986, Buchanan accompanied the President to the nuclear weapons summit with the Soviets at Reykjavik, Iceland. He saw the Kremlin's old guard up close for the first time since the early 1970s. He was struck by how few of them had changed. Although Reagan matched many of them for age and experience, he looked positively adolescent compared with the communist zombies. The Kremlin men stunk of vodka and cigarettes, their Bolshevik bones cracked as they walked.[15] The talks broke down. Reagan wanted to discuss the elimination of all ballistic missiles, conditional upon allowing the U.S. to continue research into the Strategic Defense Initiative. He proposed sharing SDI technology with the Soviets. It was an extraordinary gamble for peace. The communists countered with a proposal to scrap Intermediate-Range Nuclear Forces in Europe and halve nuclear stockpiles. Their demand was dependent upon the Americans ending research into SDI. Reagan and Gorbachev tussled privately. Negotiations stalled on whether or not SDI research would be confined to the laboratory. Reagan refused, believing he had made an electoral promise to explore its viability to the full. Would Gorbachev pull out of a chance to end the threat of nuclear war over such a small condition, Reagan asked? Gorbachev said yes. The talks ended.[16]

On the way back from Reykjavik, the administration personnel were in a panic. No one quite understood what had just happened. On the one hand, Ronald Reagan—the great Cold Warrior—had just proposed to give up the nukes and share U.S. missile technology. On the other hand, the world had come within a handshake of peace and Reagan threw it all away because of his faith in a weapons system that hadn't even been built yet. Reykjavik had the potential to anger both hawks and doves, and make the President look a little crazy. Pat kept his head and came up with the answer: "Okay. Basically, our story is this: the President made the most sweeping, far-reaching arms control proposal in history. Gorbachev said 'No.' He made a nonnegotiable demand that the President give up SDI and the President said 'No.' The Soviets blew our big chance for peace. Reagan is a man of vision. They are cowards."[17] It was a fine piece of spin, and, when they landed on U.S. soil, that's the line they gave to reporters. Within days, the President's approval rating jumped from 63 percent to 73 percent. It wouldn't stay that high for long.[18]

Pat accompanied Ronald Reagan on Air Force One as he campaigned in the November 1986 midterm elections. Reagan expected to do well. The economy was strong and Reykjavik had solidified his reputation as a world leader. But the elections went against the President. The Democrats took a 55–45 majority in the Senate. It was a blow to the battle for aid to the Contras, and a damning indictment of Regan's bland strategy. Aside from a vague promise to safeguard the recovery, Reagan had offered no positive plan for action. The Reagan revolution had failed to translate into a new Republican majority.[19]

Worse still, some strange stories were breaking in the media. The news trickled out of Lebanon that Bud McFarlane had visited Tehran on a peace mission, dressed as an airline pilot and carrying pistols, a Bible, and a cake. McFarlane had been rebuffed, but not before agreeing to ship a large number of weapons to the fundamentalist regime. On November 6, *The Washington Post* and the *Los Angeles Times* were the first U.S. papers to break one half of the Iran-Contra affair. The arms deals were run to help release hostages, they reported, and they went over the objections of the State Department, which questioned their legality. The trickle of media stories became a deluge: the CIA was involved, the sales saved Iran during the Iran-Iraq War, Israel helped out, other countries used the weapons as an excuse to also sell armaments to Tehran. In the White House, National Security Advisor John Poindexter said that the

President could probably just ride the story out. Buchanan exploded. "What the hell are you talking about?" he shouted. "We can't stand three weeks of this." One thing Pat had learned from Watergate was that you couldn't let a rumor ride. Either confirm it or kill it, but don't expect it to go away.[20]

Buchanan and several others tried to convince Reagan to give a televised speech crushing the rumors of arms sales in exchange for hostages. The President was reluctant but eventually caved in. Pat got the assignment. Ollie North gave him a draft but Buchanan insisted on rewriting it. They sat down and went through every line, fact-checking every statement. An important issue was the size of the shipments, which were apparently delivered on a single C-5 cargo plane. But that didn't square with the rumored size of the goods delivered. "We went over the text and the facts," said Buchanan, "We'd ask him, 'Listen, I know what a C-5 is. Can all these things fit into a C-5?' And they said yes. I told Ollie, 'Tonight, I don't care what he says, the President of the United States' credibility goes on the line. It's all got to be accurate. I don't care what we've said before, or how it's been coppered. It's got to be right.' And they okayed and went over every single line in that thing." North would come to a tricky passage, excuse himself, go through his files, and come back with a negative or a positive. "We didn't have the foggiest idea if it was true or false," Buchanan admitted.[21]

It was false. The speech that night was surprisingly Buchananite in tone, given how often Pat's words had been rewritten. Reagan opened with an unusual dash of vinegar. "I know you've been reading a lot of stories the past several days attributed to Danish sailors, unnamed observers at Italian ports and Spanish harbors, and especially unnamed government officials of my administration. Well now you're going to hear the facts from a White House source— and you know my name." The charges made against him were, said the President, "utterly false. The United States has not made concessions to those who hold our people captive in Lebanon, and we will not. The United States has not swapped boatloads or planeloads of American weapons for the return of American hostages, and we will not." Reagan admitted the shipping of a "small amount" of "defense weapons," but "these modest deliveries, taken together, could easily fit into a single cargo plane." In fact the 2,004 TOWs, 18 HAWKS, and 240 HAWK parts had arrived on eight cargo planes.[22]

Fifty-six percent of the public did not believe Reagan. Even Barry Goldwater, a more cynical and moderate a politician since Watergate, called the deal immoral. Pat went to see Nixon and asked him what they should do. "Get the message out," said the Old Man. "Admit you made a mistake—you tried something, and it turned out badly. But don't cover up." Pat passed this on to Regan and Regan took it to Reagan. He left the meeting looking ashen. The President had rejected Nixon's words out of hand. Ronald Reagan apparently genuinely believed that the arms exchange had never taken place.[23]

Meanwhile, Oliver North started to shred all the evidence before investigators could find it. He pushed so much paper through the shredder he blocked it. His secretary, Fawn Hall, stuffed material into her dress and carried it out of the White House, pregnant with illicit memos.[24] On November 25, Ed Meese announced that money raised in arms sales had been diverted to the Contras. President Reagan fired North and John Poindexter resigned. On December 1, a commission headed by Sen. John Tower opened investigations into the scandal. They interviewed the President on December 2, and this time he admitted authorizing arms sales to Iran. Later he retracted that statement, only to confirm it in his autobiography.

The administration was in crisis and Don Regan wanted it to muddle through with apologies and fudge. One man refused.[25]

On December 4, Regan demanded a "communications plan" from Buchanan. Pat sat down at his typewriter, "smoked through two drafts," and carried an article straight over to *The Washington Post* offices. He knew it would never get past Regan.[26] It was an attack piece on those Republicans on the Hill who were distancing themselves from Reagan. "The whole damn pack had headed for the tall grass," he wrote. "What a classic portrait of ingratitude!" And how stupid, too.

> Do these Republicans truly think the investigative engines of a hostile Congress and the artillery of an Adversary Press are all being wheeled again into position—simply to "get at the truth?" . . . Do they not recognize that the target here is not [Oliver North] but Ronald Reagan—that what liberalism and the left have in mind is the ruination of a second Republican presidency within a generation?[27]

Buchanan broke the chain of command to write the article and Regan went wild. But Pat got word that Reagan enjoyed it—so he carried on.[28]

On December 8, Buchanan flew down to Miami to speak to a crowd of 3,000 people on behalf of the President. Mostly Cuban Americans, they thrilled as Buchanan tore into journalists who dared criticize the Cold War President. "All newsmen should remember that they're Americans first and newsmen second," he said. "All who don't feel that should tell us so. We will know which stations not to watch and which newspapers not to buy."[29] The media coverage was "frenzied, unbalanced, and loaded with innuendoes," representing a "windfall for the Soviets." Most of the administration would agree with that, but Buchanan came closer than anyone else to endorsing North's piracy. "Admiral Poindexter and Colonel North put their careers on the line to protect our country," he told the crowd. "If Colonel North broke any rules, he will stand up and take it as the marine he is. But I say, if Colonel North ripped off the Ayatollah and took some $30 million to give to the contras, God bless Colonel North!"[30]

Suddenly, Pat was all over the press. ABC named him man of the week and the New Right loved it. Paul Weyrich said he received "20 to 30 letters from people saying, 'Why haven't you done what he's doing?'"[31] The press was dumbstruck that men like Buchanan should refuse to regret North's crimes. On CBS's *Face the Nation,* anchor Leslie Stahl asked Buchanan, "Why are you saying it's okay to go out and break the law?" Buchanan insisted that he was just defending North's motives and challenging his critics ("that tribe of pygmies up on the Hill"). But Stahl pressed on. "I'm still asking you how a White House official can go out and break the law?" But Pat would not say sorry.[32]

In December, Pat got a phone call from California. It was Bay. "People are telling me that you've got to run," she said.

"Run for what?" Pat replied.

"Run for president!" Conservatives up and down the country were calling Bay and saying that they liked what Pat was doing on Iran-Contra. They loved the way that he defended conservative principles without moderation or shame.[33] Pat was getting those calls, too, and they were hard to ignore.

The conservative movement was in crisis. Three of their number had announced their candidacies for the presidency, but none had caught fire. Rep. Jack Kemp was popular as a tax cutter, but bad on the stump. Rev. Pat Robertson, an evangelical preacher from Virginia, was far too controversial and sectarian. Al Haig was plain boring.[34] It looked like Vice President Bush was going to cruise to victory, which threw the Reagan crusade into jeopardy, as most of the New Right presumed he was a spineless middle-of-the-roader.[35] Without a cause to whip up interest, various New Right organizations were edging toward bankruptcy. "I think the New Right has a substantial fundraising stake in a hot, populist conservative candidate like Pat," said Kevin Phillips. "He'll get their money moving again."[36] Sure enough, Howard Phillips of the Conservative Caucus rang up Pat and told him he had to run whether he liked it or not—for the sake of the movement.[37] Phyllis Schlafly called, too. "He was the best man around," she said. "Pat was such a good speaker and so charismatic . . . I felt he had no choice but to run."[38]

Howard Phillips went on a tour to promote his man. He visited North Carolina to try to get the backing of the powerful Congressional Club. In 1976, the Club had helped tip the Tar Heel state to Ronald Reagan in the presidential primaries—rescuing his bid and setting him up for the 1980 election. In 1987, the Club was looking for a conservative to back. It had a massive mailing list that made it one of the most powerful political organizations in the country. Club strategists Tom Ellis and Carter Wrenn dropped in on Pat Buchanan at his windowless office in the White House. Pat impressed them. He had charisma, exposure, and intellectual bona fides. Ellis and Wrenn were Protestants, but they sensed that Buchanan's Catholic traditionalism gave them more in common with him than Bush's Episcopalianism. "We should have a meeting at Pat's house," Ellis told Bay.[39]

Phillips's speech at the Congressional Club also impressed a young academic and former priest called Boyd Cathey. Cathey was the son of a Carolinian tobacco planter, a conservative former Democrat whose daddy sent him into the fields to teach him the moral rewards of hard work.[40] After hearing Phillips speak, he wrote Pat: "I have long admired your articulate and forthright exposition and defense of conservative principles. America needs a strong conservative leader to continue and expand the Reagan 'counter-revolution' after 1988 . . . If you decided to run, you would have an extensive reservoir of support here in North Carolina."[41] Cathey and some wealthy southern business-men put together a Draft Buchanan committee. They started a letter-writing campaign and deluged Pat's address with demands that he run. The form letter read:

> We believe you could rally conservatives across the nation and motivate them for the difficult tasks ahead. We do not believe you will "divide the conservative vote." On the contrary, we feel certain you would unite it and engage with it as no one else yet has. There are thousands of activists ready to answer the call of the RIGHT man and the RIGHT cause.[42]

Boyd gave him a personal endorsement in the *Southern Partisan* maga-zine.[43] It was early days yet, but Buchanan had somehow earned the affection of a powerful network of southern heritage enthusiasts. Traditionalists like Boyd were there from the beginning, and they would still be there at the end, trumpeting the lost cause of Pat Buchanan.

On the night of January 14, 1987, the conservative movement gathered in Pat's living room in McLean, Virginia. The meeting was a who's who of the American right: Phyllis Schlafly, Howard Phillips, executive director of the Gun Owners of America Larry Pratt, editor of *Human Events* Tom Winter, and mas-terminds of direct-mail Paul Weyrich and Richard Viguerie. Smoking a big ci-gar in the corner was Carter Wrenn. Shelley dished out cocktails.[44]

Bay was in the chair and she asked for points for and against a run. Kemp was weak, they said. Robertson was unelectable. Tom Ellis spoke up. Pat re-membered what he had to say thus: "He did not know whether we could win or not . . . Hell, he didn't know if America was going to make it or not . . . What he did know was that he had an obligation to his children and his grandchildren to do his damndest to give it the best shot for his country—and, at this time and place, Pat Buchanan represented the best shot. Damn the torpedoes, full speed ahead."

"Let the bloodbath begin!" cried John Lofton, the columnist.[45]

"By the end of the evening we thought Pat was going to run," recalled

Howard Phillips. "He seemed ready, excited. I think he was 99 percent sure he was going to do it. I went home ready for the race."[46]

And the press was delighted. Hunter S. Thompson wrote of "Cruel Crazy Patrick and Big Al [Haig], roaming around Washington like a pair of Foam Frogs in heat, laying 3,000 eggs every night and cranking up a genuinely mean ticket—Haig and Buchanan, Buchanan and Haig. What does it matter? 'We will kill the ones who eat us, and eat the ones we kill . . .' "[47]

Pat locked himself away in his windowless office at the White House. He did what the Old Man did in these situations and took out a yellow legal pad. He wrote the positives of running down one side and the negatives down the other. On the plus side, the movement would be revived, the GOP might move to the right, Buchanan might emerge as the heir to Reagan, and it could be a lot of fun. On the downside, he probably wouldn't win. And if he couldn't win, then all he could do was kick Kemp and divide the movement.[48]

Pat looked out of the fake window on his wall and wondered if he was ready to run. He was a private man who disliked large crowds and strange faces. For years he had been a backstage boy, happy to watch others endure the humiliations of pig judging contests and fancy dress fund-raisers. Richard Viguerie and Pat were driving around Virginia once when they came across a sign advertising a turkey barbecue with a local candidate. "If someone put a gun to my head," said Buchanan, "I wouldn't do that."[49]

Pat rang Ellis and Phillips and broke the bad news: He wasn't going to run. Both were upset. Driving up the George Washington Parkway to home, Buchanan felt a weight lift from his shoulders. Shelley greeted him with a kiss and said she could tell he had made the right choice. And yet, in his sleep Pat was haunted by the refrain of an old hymn: "If you can't stand the cross / Then you can't bear the crown."[50]

In February 1987, Pat announced that he was stepping down from the Reagan administration. There had been one last exhausting fight over the State of the Union address and, again, Pat had lost. But the empty, sunny speech that Reagan delivered summed up the tone for the last two years of the administration.[51] In March, the President went on TV and apologized for Iran-Contra. He denied personal knowledge, but accepted responsibility for the mess. His approval ratings shot back up into the 60s. Pat admired his tenacity. Every bit of mud stuck to Nixon. It slid right off Ronald Reagan.[52]

When Buchanan resigned, Reagan said:

> Pat's communication skills and his commitment to conservative political beliefs have been an important part of my administration for the last two years. I will miss his leadership and his support, but I can count on his voice to remain a beacon for our political agenda.

Insiders said that Pat was unhappy that North had been left to face a jail sentence. Don Regan, worn down by his many failures as Chief of Staff, quit, too.[53]

Pat Buchanan left the Reagan administration with justifiable pride for what he had accomplished. Without him, there might have been no dissenting voice on Iran-Contra and the conservative movement might have retreated in despair. But Pat understood that "the President no longer needed his old pit bull." At a farewell ceremony, the President gave Pat a pair of bronze running shoes in celebration of his service to the White House jogging team. There were tears in Buchanan's eyes. He recalled what he had said of Nixon fourteen years ago: "We rolled the rock all the way up the hill, only to see it roll right back down on top of us."[54]

ELEVEN

New World Order

Leaving the Reagan administration gave Pat an opportunity to stop and think. He retired to the study in his basement to write a memoir. *Right from the Beginning* was about growing up in Washington, D.C., in the 1950s. It was so funny and so pugnacious that reviewers missed its inner sadness. The conservative movement had done a lot of good in the last twenty years, Pat wrote. It put Ronald Reagan in the White House and rescued the country from socialism. But tax cuts and nuclear missiles had done nothing to stop the decline of the culture. Gays and lesbians were out of the closet. A woman's place was no longer at home. No man was guaranteed a job for life with good pay. Drug use was rife, crime was up, respect for elders was gone. Pat didn't feel safe on the streets where he once played war:

> Washington is another city, a city where more than half of pregnancies end in abortions, more than half of all live births are out of wedlock—a city where the "welfare culture" has consolidated its beachhead, and narcotics and crime are always with us.[1]

The Republicans had held the presidency for sixteen out of twenty years since 1968. They had made many people a lot of money. Pat wondered aloud if that was enough.[2]

Right from the Beginning solidified Pat's reputation as one of the leading spokesmen for ideological conservatism. After Jack Kemp's presidential campaign failed to get momentum, Buchanan endorsed Vice President George H. W. Bush in both the primaries and the general election of 1988. He went back to *Crossfire* and *The Washington Times,* and continued to defend the legacy of Ronald Reagan. In 1988 Pat was still an orthodox conservative Republican. But he lived with doubts.[3]

To become President of the United States, George H. W. Bush underwent an image change. He was a preppy, good-looking fellow with plenty of executive experience. But that wasn't enough to win. To capture the Republican nomination, he had to wear his faith on his sleeve and embrace a variety of social conservatism with which he was never entirely comfortable. His conversion was swift and, to some, suspect. But conservatives stuck with Bush because he was electable and he promised to protect their economic legacy.[4] At the 1988 Republican convention in New Orleans, Bush offered the vision of a kinder, gentler Reaganism. He spoke of charities as "a thousand points of light," and pledged support to troubled communities. "The old ideas are new again," he said, "because they are not old, they are timeless: duty, sacrifice, commitment, and a patriotism that finds its expression in taking part and pitching in." He made a promise that he lived to regret: "Read my lips: no new taxes."[5]

Bush sealed the deal with the right by selecting Sen. Dan Quayle of Indiana as his running mate. The Democrats said Quayle was an unqualified idiot. But his malapropisms distracted from Bush's own difficult relationship with the English language, and his voting record helped bring home evangelical voters. Team Bush sent George to visit flag factories, put him in a sweater and baseball cap, filmed him playing with his grandchildren. They called opponent Mike Dukakis a liberal with a revolving door policy on prisons. The public bought it and George H. W. Bush won a 53–46 percent victory.[6]

Eleven months into Bush's presidency, the Berlin Wall fell. After decades of competition and fear, communism crumbled to dust. Its economic system was in ruins and its subjects demanded political reform. In short order, Marxist regimes collapsed in Poland, Hungary, East Germany, Czechoslovakia, and Romania. Bulgaria, Albania, and Yugoslavia followed later and the Soviet

Union disbanded in 1991. Given the near universal demand for democratic capitalism, it seemed as if history itself was at an end.[7]

But what role should America play in a post–Cold War world? Pat Buchanan had a surprising answer: nearly none.[8] The day after the Berlin Wall fell, Pat said on *Crossfire* that the U.S. should offer to remove all troops from Western Europe if the USSR removed theirs from the East. "We are not the Romans," he reminded the audience.[9] Then, in December 1989, he criticized the U.S. invasion of Panama. Dictator General Noriega had ignored election results, roughed up American soldiers, and facilitated drug trafficking. Bush ordered his removal like a police chief ordering a raid on the house of a public nuisance. But America was not the world's policeman, Buchanan argued. Although Noriega was a thug, he posed no threat to vital U.S. interests in the way the Soviets had. Applying the logic of the Catholic Just War theory he had learned at school, Buchanan reached the conclusion that the invasion was unnecessary and an immoral waste of human life.[10]

In early 1990, Pat was invited to participate in a forum in *The National Interest* magazine to discuss post–Cold War foreign policy. This was his first real brush with the neoconservatives.[11] The neocons were recent additions to the conservative family—many were Cold Warriors who defected from the McGovernite Democratic Party, and a significant number were Jewish. Neocons celebrated gender, racial, and social equality and believed that the state could be used to strengthen families and guarantee certain inalienable rights. They also thought that American values were universal and that the U.S. had an almost divine mission to spread them.[12] In *The National Interest* forum, Ben Wattenberg called for a "Pax Americana," or "global hegemony" over a planet unable to resist the "world's last superpower." The U.S. should use its untrammeled influence to bring down dictatorships. In place of anarchy, it must construct a new system of international law and order enforced by American military muscle. Columnist Charles Krauthammer wrote that it should be "our wish and work" to "integrate" America, Europe, and Japan into a "supersovereignty" that would be "economically, culturally, and politically hegemonic in the world." This "new universalism," wrote Krauthammer, "would require the conscious depreciation not only of American sovereignty but of the notion of sovereignty in general. This is not as outrageous as it sounds."[13]

Buchanan begged to differ. He replied:

> America can only lead the world into the twenty-first century if
> she is not saddled down by all the baggage piled up in the twenti-
> eth. For fifty years, the United States has been drained of wealth
> and power by wars, cold and hot. Much of that expenditure of
> blood and treasure was a necessary investment. Much was not. We
> cannot forever defend wealthy nations that refuse to defend them-
> selves; we cannot permit endless transfusions of the life blood of
> American capitalism into the mendicant countries and economic
> corpses of socialism, without bleeding to death.[14]

The debate in *The National Interest* plugged Buchanan into a growing network of conservatives who were thinking seriously about where the movement
should go after the end of communism. Pat's desk piled high with correspondence from like minds testing new ideas.[15] Libertarians lent him the maxim
"War is the Health of the State." Guns and planes cost money. Look at income
tax, they said. Federal income before World War I never exceeded $762 million;
throughout the 1920s it never fell below $3,640 million. Before World War II,
fewer than 15 million citizens had to file an income tax return. By 1945, ap-
proximately 50 million had to do so.[16] Pat saw logic in their argument that
punitive taxation was the result, in part, of a bellicose foreign policy.[17]

Pat rejected the idea that Americans should give their lives so that other
nations might experience democracy. Democracy, he observed, was only one
system of government among many—more appropriate to the United States
than any other, superior probably to most, but no more valid in any given situation than theocracy, fascism, or oligarchy.[18] Buchanan urged Americans to
avoid

> the worship of democracy as a form of governance and the con-
> comitant ambition to see all of mankind embrace it, or explain why
> not. Like all idolatries, democratism substitutes a false god for the
> real, a love of process for a love of country. When we call a country
> "democratic," we say nothing about whether its rulers are wise

or good, or friendly or hostile; we only describe how they were chosen.

You could have a virtuous tyranny and a villainous democracy. What mattered more than popular participation was the quality of each citizen—the state of their soul. A democracy that allowed the mass slaughter of innocents, perversion, the impoverishment of workers, the slander of the Church, or the sexualization of children was worthless. Given the choice, an enlightened despotism might be preferable.[19]

Pat's debate in *The National Interest* was a moment of personal liberation. It freed him from the ties of Republican orthodoxy: He started by trashing one dogma and went on to question the entire religion. By the end of the 1990s, he would no longer be welcome in the Church.

L ike most conservatives, Buchanan was unimpressed with how George H. W. Bush handled the economy. In 1990, the country slipped into a mild recession. Tax receipts fell and payouts to the unemployed went up. The national debt ballooned. At the end of June 1990, President Bush announced a deficit reduction plan would include "tax revenue increases." The *New York Post* ran the headline: "Read My Lips: I Lied." For conservatives, Bush had shown his true colors.[20] The President bungled. He failed to make the case for tax increases and didn't employ any big-name conservatives to defend them. His official statement on the hike was simply posted on the pressroom notice board. George H. W. Bush was not interested in economics. His staff had told him that he could stop worrying about the economy—they had done everything necessary to win reelection. So long as inflation and interest rates were low, jobs and profits would create themselves. In a press conference, the President admitted that he found foreign policy "more enjoyable" than economics.[21]

In September 1990, the administration put a package of cuts and hikes before Congress, including an immediate 5-cent per gallon increase on the federal gasoline tax, and a phased increase of even higher fuel taxes in subsequent years. The House refused to pass it. The government went into shutdown over the long Columbus Day weekend. Finally, President Bush cut a new deal with House Democrats that replaced some of the fuel taxes with a 10 percent surtax on the top income tax bracket, and also included new excise taxes on alcohol and tobacco products, automobiles, and luxury yachts.[22]

The House vote on the new budget took place on September 30. Rep. Chuck Douglas of New Hampshire asked the GOP Minority Leader Bob Michel if he could speak. Michel presumed he was in favor and said yes. Douglas stood up and roasted the President: "The budget we are going to try to pass at the end of the week is the equivalent of the Yalta Summit Agreement after World War II. What it did to Europe, this agreement does to the taxpayers. It sells them out." He charged the administration with colluding with liberals to raise taxes to avoid cuts: "What in this city is called a 'cut' is a limitation on future increases. Where I come from, a cut is a dollar figure that is lower than the one the year before." House conservatives roared with laughter. Douglas concluded, "This outrageous agreement is not in the interests of the economy or the people that sent Members here."[23] Bob Michel told Douglas afterward, "If I had known what you were going to say, I wouldn't have let you speak."[24]

The deal passed the House. It was a victory for sound fiscal management, but Bush's image as an honest man was done irreparable damage.[25] The administration exacted its revenge on Douglas. The Democrats targeted his marginal district and Bush didn't bother to campaign there. Douglas was snubbed by the state GOP and lost his seat. He returned to Concord, New Hampshire, joined a law office, and sat around "twiddling my thumbs." Douglas let it be known that he was prepared to help anyone who wanted to challenge President Bush for the Republican nomination.[26]

Pat Buchanan noticed that there was a growing mood of rebellion in American politics. A series of scandals cast doubt on the honesty of politicians in both parties. From 1985 to 1991, 747 savings and loan associations (S&Ls) collapsed. The sector was bailed out by the taxpayer to the tune of $124.6 billion. In 1989, five senators (including future GOP presidential nominee John McCain) were accused of calling regulators off investigating S&L investor Charles Keating in exchange for $1.3 million in campaign contributions. Keating went to jail for five years but only one of the Keating Five received a reprimand. The S&L crisis was followed by the Congressional Post Office scandal (congressmen were accused of embezzling money through stamps and postal vouchers) and the House Banking Scandal (congressmen were allowed to overdraw money without being penalized). The latter was dubbed Rubbergate for the rubber checks that the politicians bounced around the bars and nightclubs of D.C.[27] Polls showed that it was a tossup between whom voters blamed the most for their woes: the Republican President or the Democratic Congress. Louisianans found an unexpected way to punish both.[28]

In 1989, voters in the 81st District of Louisiana voted for a new state house representative. To everyone's surprise, they gave 33 percent of their votes and first place to a nobody with a Village People moustache called David Duke. Duke was a former Nazi and national director of the Ku Klux Klan. A gangly, awkward youth who wandered around the LSU campus in a Nazi uniform, he tried to professionalize the KKK in the 1970s and turn it into a mainstream right-wing organization. He abandoned the white robes and wore business suits and talked eloquently on TV about being a spokesman for the white middle class. In the 1980s, Duke went one step further. He left the Klan and dropped the talk about the "mongrelization" of the white race. He joined the GOP and called himself a conservative. Rumor had it that he underwent plastic surgery to reduce his nose and strengthen his chin. With a few blond highlights, Duke looked like the boy next door.[29]

As the runoff election loomed, the Louisiana Republican Party, the President, and Ronald Reagan all campaigned against Duke. But the GOP's strategy of intimidation backfired and Duke won.[30] His support came mostly from the poorer parts of the district and he got a majority of votes among those who went for Dukakis in 1988. Duke took various conservative positions (low taxes, prayer in schools), but his signature pledge was to reform Louisiana's welfare system and stop payments to drug users and the sexually promiscuous. Critics felt Duke was exploiting racism by manipulating white assumptions that most people on welfare were black.[31]

To Pat Buchanan, the message of Duke's election was clear: The moderation of the Bush administration threatened to split the conservative vote. Only by getting back to social conservatism could the coalition hold.[32] Given that

Duke had identified some legitimate grievances among middle-class whites, the right should appropriate his agenda minus the implicit racism. "The way to deal" with Duke, he wrote, was "the way the GOP dealt with the far more formidable challenge of George Wallace. Take a hard look at Duke's portfolio of winning issues; and expropriate those not in conflict with GOP principles."[33] One columnist at *The Washington Times* agreed. Sam Francis wrote that Duke seemed to have invented "a new kind of racism that may become a new political creed. The distinguishing feature of that creed might be expressed as the acceptance of race as a biological and social reality." Whites, argued Francis, were beginning to think and vote like a distinct racial group.[34]

In office, Duke was a washout. Isolated from his GOP colleagues, he only authored one successful bill in the state senate. He declared his candidacy for the U.S. Senate shortly after his election—the first of an endless string of attention-seeking campaigns. Because the Democratic incumbent seemed guaranteed election, the official Republican candidate withdrew from the primaries days before the first round of voting. This gave Duke an automatic spot on the ballot. The press was determined to stop Duke from winning. Aside from the fact that he was caught selling Holocaust denial literature from his campaign office, his financial history was an embarrassment. Journalists discovered that Duke had moonlit as an author. In 1976 he wrote the book *Finders-Keepers* under the pseudonym of Dorothy Vanderbilt. The book told women how to "find, attract, and keep the man you want." Chapter 10 advised readers on the best way to pleasure a man in bed. It was far from conservative. Aside from giving advice on how to perform oral and anal sex, it encouraged group activities and swinging. "Do sleep with a married man," advised Ms. Vanderbuilt, "as long as you can accept that nothing too serious will come of it." Duke had hoped that he had a bestseller on his hands that would solve the Klan's financial problems. But it proved "too hard-core for the right-wing and too soft-core for the perverts." Plus, said a former aide, David didn't really know what he was writing about. He lifted most of his professional advice from questionnaires in women's magazines.[35]

Yet Duke did much better than he should have. In the 1990 senate election, he took 44 percent of the vote and won roughly 55 percent among whites. The establishment's assumption that they could guilt people into voting against

Duke was wrong. If anything, people interpreted the attacks on Duke as an attack upon themselves. To quote one supporter on election night: "All over, people say, 'What a bunch of bigots in Louisiana.' I want you to know, I voted for him not because of his background, but in spite of it. We don't want to go back to segregation, we just want equal rights for everyone."[36]

By mid-1990, Buchanan and his conservative friends were furious with Bush. He had lied to them on taxes and, as America sank deeper into recession, he risked handing the country over to the Democrats in '92. Pat Buchanan said, "I don't believe he is a conservative, but every four years he does a passing imitation of one. He campaigns as Ronald Reagan and he governs as Jimmy Carter."[37] But who would rid the movement of this turncoat president? The *Manchester Union-Leader,* the biggest paper in New Hampshire, made a suggestion. Its editor noted that, in twenty years, Pat Buchanan had never fudged a principle or U-turned on a friend. Eloquent and reliable, experienced and recognizable, "Pat Buchanan is the great hope of conservatives." The *Union-Leader* was pleased to announce that Pat was planning a visit to New Hampshire in January 1991.[38]

And then something happened that no one could predict. On August 1, 1990, the Republic of Iraq invaded its tiny neighbor Kuwait. This was the event that the neocons were waiting for. After several months of post–Cold War indecision, they suddenly had a new cause around which to rally: America was to become the great white knight of democracy and national self-determination. Leave Kuwait by New Year 1991, President Bush told Saddam Hussein, or we'll kick you out.[39]

Bush spoke to a joint session of the U.S. Congress regarding the authorization of air and land attacks, laying out four objectives: "Iraq must withdraw from Kuwait completely, immediately, and without condition. Kuwait's legitimate government must be restored. The security and stability of the Persian Gulf must be assured. And American citizens abroad must be protected." He added to this some fateful words that made Pat Buchanan sit up straight: "Out of these troubled times, our fifth objective—a *new world order*—can emerge: a new era—freer from the threat of terror, stronger in the pursuit of justice,

and more secure in the quest for peace." Congress voted to authorize an invasion.[40]

Pat Buchanan denounced Bush's threat and his fantasy of a "New World
Order." In his view, the White House had been occupied by the neocons.[41] This
wasn't true. George H. W. Bush employed neocons on his staff, but they were
outgunned by old-school moderates who preferred a policy of containment. In
dealing with the collapse of the Soviet Union, the President proved a cautious
statesman, willing to live with a whole new generation of tin-pot dictators
and ethnic cleansers. To the chagrin of neocons, the phrase New World Order
turned out to be an empty slogan.[42]

Nevertheless, from Pat's vantage point America was acting like a hired
goon for a Middle East gangster. Kuwait was possibly the richest country in the
world, with $2.8 trillion invested overseas. In the weeks before the Iraqi inva-
sion, Kuwait had tried to bring down the price of oil, because the expansion of
its foreign capital gave it a stake in Western economies hurt by OPEC's greed.
But a falling oil price hit Iraq's economy hard at a moment when it was trying
to rebuild after the devastating Iran-Iraq War. Ergo, Saddam had a genuine
grievance against a state that had all the morality of a junk bond manipulator.
This was, concluded Buchanan, a spat between a dictator and a king that posed
no threat to U.S. interests.[43]

Why, if it made little strategic sense, did the U.S. threaten Iraq with war?
On August 24, 1990, in an edition of TV's *The McLaughlin Group,* Pat gave his
answer: "There are only two groups that are beating the drums right now for
war in the Middle East, and that is the Israeli Defense Ministry and its 'Amen'
corner in the United States."[44] He described Congress as "Israeli occupied territory" and called the Democratic Party "a diapered poodle of the American
Israel Public Affairs Committee."[45] Pat claimed four men were primarily responsible for the anti-Iraq policy—former editor of *The New York Times* A. M.
Rosenthal; former Assistant Secretary of Defense Richard Perle; political strategist Charles Krauthammer; and Henry Kissinger. All were Jewish. Fighting
would be done, noted Buchanan, by "kids with names like McAllister, Murphy,
Gonzales, and Leroy Brown." Some inferred that Buchanan was claiming that
Jews were asking Gentiles to die on their behalf.[46]

Throughout his career, Pat had been a cheerleader for Israel. During the Cold War he saw it as an intrepid democratic ally, surrounded by Soviet-backed Arab dictatorships.[47] But he was shocked by the violence of Israel's occupation of Lebanon in 1982. In the mid-1980s he began to look with sympathy upon the Palestinian demand for an independent state. When Israel lost its strategic significance to the U.S. after 1989, Pat became an open critic. In *The Washington Times*, he wrote:

> Israeli troops have killed hundreds of men, women and children; they have beaten, wounded, maimed some 25,000; they have dynamited homes, and imprisoned, without trial, thousands of Palestinians. Were that the price of holding onto Puerto Rico, most of us, long ago, would have said: Let them go.

Morally, he concluded, the U.S. was on the wrong side:

> What vital interest of ours is advanced by subsidizing a policy that denies to Palestinians that God-given right to a homeland, a flag and a state of their own, that Americans have championed all over the world, all of our lives?[48]

Many Republicans thought Pat had gone crazy. How could he defend a thug like Saddam? How could he question America's historic role as the arsenal of democracy? But some conservatives liked what he had to say.[49] In the summer of 1990, Bay attended the state convention of the California Republican Party. She was surprised to spot a small group of young libertarians handing out "Buchanan for President" literature. They were marshaled by Justin Raimondo, a gay Hispanic-American. Raimondo told Bay that her brother should enter the primaries. He understood that it would be tough—near impossible—to take the Republican nomination away from George Bush. But he had a moral duty to try. "We had to do something," said Raimondo. "We couldn't be silent, not in the face of so much evil—an evil that culminated . . . in thousands of human sacrifices on the altar of Big Oil."

"You guys are great!" said Bay. Raimondo made her promise that she would pass on their message to Pat. Months went by and Raimondo heard nothing. Somehow he got hold of Pat's fax number and published it in his small libertarian magazine. In Buchanan's basement study, letters started to pour out of his fax machine. They spooled out onto the floor and Buchanan scooped them up in his arms and held them up to the light. Every one read: "Run Pat, run!"[50]

TWELVE

Pat Becomes a Paleocon, Runs for President

O n January 17, 1991, Pat flew up to New Hampshire to deliver a speech to the state Republican committee. It was bitterly cold, with icy winds and several inches of thick New England snow. He took a cab to downtown Manchester, where local Republicans gathered to discuss politics. American troops were poised on the Saudi border to invade Kuwait, so Pat, sensing that his audience would expect loyalty to the President, ignored talk about challenging Bush. But he could not resist attacking the mindset that brought the world's last superpower to the defense of a tiny monarchy.

Bush's "New World Order," he said, "is beginning to sound like old world freeloading—Uncle Sam does the fighting and Uncle Sam pays the bill. It is time for a new foreign policy that looks out for America first, and not only America first but also America second and third . . . If Germany and Japan are big enough and tough enough to carry American markets in the world, they are big enough and tough enough to carry their own load in their own defense." And, although he pledged support for U.S. troops during the Gulf conflict, he said, "I see the rape of Kuwait as a vicious mugging on the other side of the world where my family did not live."

Pat was right to play down his isolationism. The crowd sat on their hands when he savaged the wartime president. But things picked up when Buchanan attacked Bush's reversal on his "no new taxes" pledge. "You don't get America out of recession by raising taxes," he said. And it made no sense to provide $15 billion in direct foreign aid while running a $400 billion deficit. Bush was a closet liberal, Pat charged: "Regulation is back with a vengeance . . . We have gone too far in accommodating the tree-hugger . . . There is no doubt that the Republican Party in the last two years has drifted away from the Reaganite principles and Reaganite philosophy. The Republican Party ought to go back to what it believed in, to the philosophy and politics that really captured a whole generation of young people. Pragmatism will lose the young people principle won for us." Pat's eyes drifted to the stars and stripes flying above the hall. "But those are all issues for another day," he said and sat down.

Gov. Judd Gregg took the mic and closed the meeting early. Shortly after 7 p.m., the U.S.-led coalition started bombing Baghdad. The war had begun.[1]

Pat Buchanan was not a lone voice on the antiwar right. Phil Nicolaides, a movement conservative who had run the breakthrough senate campaigns of New York's James Buckley and Texas's Phil Gramm, decided to form a conservative group to oppose the Gulf War. He put the idea to his friend Joe Sobran, an editor at *National Review*. Sobran invited the businessman Jon Utley to contribute. They doubted they would find more than three people to speak out against the war. But Utley, who was going to spend a weekend at a free-market retreat, offered to push a petition. He returned with a surprising number of names: Justin Raimondo, economist Murray Rothbard, Llewellyn H. Rockwell (president of the Ludwig von Mises Institute), Thomas Fleming (editor of the traditionalist *Chronicles* magazine), Judith Bingham (conservative journalist), Henry Regnery (publisher), David Boaz (of the Cato Institute), Philip Collier (a chessmaster), and Rep. Ron Paul of Texas.[2]

The group called themselves the Committee to Avert a Mideast Holocaust. They issued a press release to some conservative mailing lists and got a few thousand back in donations. Sobran hosted a meeting at the National Press Club and the Committee sent a letter to *The Nation* announcing their existence.[3] They were all taking a big risk. On the other side of the debate was stacked the entire conservative movement, the Republican Party, and centrist Democrats like Al Gore. The pro-war Coalition for American Risk spent an estimated $10 million on TV and newspaper advertisements and claimed to field 1,000 media inquiries a day. All that the Committee had was Fran Griffin—a nice Catholic lady with a small PR company.[4]

Jon Utley felt that the war was made possible by an alliance between the military industrial complex, neoconservatives, and the religious right. Each had a tangential relationship to Israel. "They all wanted to refight the Vietnam War and win," said Utley. The money men and the neocons were worried that the collapse of the USSR would result in big spending cuts in defense. A war in the Gulf might expand to a war against the Muslim world, creating a whole new Evil Empire to fight. Meanwhile, the religious right was looking for a fresh moral enemy and was happy to sign up for a war against the Arabs. Many of them thought that the Apocalypse would start in the Holy Land, so they tried to prod Israel into a war with Islam.[5] Utley called this the "Armageddon lobby."[6] Buchanan agreed with his analysis—Pat told Larry King that the "Amen Corner" pushing for war could be found in "Protestant churches. It's a sort of echo chamber."[7] In the view of Utley, these people "weren't just for this war, they were for war period."[8]

The Gulf War had opened a debate between the neoconservatives and an alliance of traditionalists and libertarians that became popularly known as the paleoconservatives (although most of its members hated that term). The paleocons looked upon the social reforms of the previous fifty years with regret and called for a "back-to-basics" variety of Republicanism that demolished the welfare state and promoted Christian ethics.[9] They argued that war had been manipulated since the 1890s to expand government. Liberal administrations in the 1960s and 1970s had then used big government to promote socialism and secularism.[10] The paleocons were a ragtag army of conservative misfits: eccentric professors, rednecks, militiamen, libertarians, ultra-Orthodox Jews, Tridentine Mass–only Catholics, Teamsters, and Civil War reenactors (always on the Confederate side).

One simple way of understanding the differences between conservatives is to see them in terms of competing nostalgias. Cold War conservatives like Pat wanted to take America back to the 1950s, with its nuclear families, wealth, and sense of purpose. Libertarians wanted to return to the late nineteenth century, when capitalism was ascendant and untroubled by regulation. Southern conservatives looked fondly upon the antebellum period, when cotton was king. Many Catholic traditionalists wanted to turn the clock back to the thirteenth century, an age of Christian governance and hierarchical social order.[11]

What made the neocons different was that they were futurists. They posed no challenge to the twentieth century's obsession with equality; quite the opposite. They proposed using conservative means (tax cuts, free enterprise zones) to expand civil rights and democracy. Many neocons rejected the cultural excesses of the postwar era, but they retained a faith that society could be improved. In the opinion of the paleocons, they were hardly conservative at all. War was revolutionary. It divided up families, killed husbands, demoralized the faithful, armed the state.[12] In contrast, paleocons might sound like "neo-isolationists," wrote Pat Buchanan, but in fact "we are not 'neo' anything. We are old church and old right, anti-imperialist and anti-interventionist, disbelievers in Pax Americana. We love the old republic, and when we hear phrases like 'New World Order,' we release the safety catches on our revolvers."[13]

Pat Buchanan never officially joined the Committee to Avert a Mideast Holocaust. But it did impact his life in one important way. Publicity manager Fran Griffin suggested Pat Buchanan meet with Joe Sobran to talk about the war and how to oppose it. She also dropped the name of Sam Francis, the radical conservative who wrote a column for *The Washington Times*. The men met for dinner at the Hunan Noon Chinese restaurant in Alexandria, Virginia. An intense three-way friendship was born. The trio met every month in the same restaurant for the next ten years.[14]

In Pat's opinion, Joe was "perhaps the finest columnist of our generation."[15] Like Buchanan, Sobran's schoolboy Catholicism and sense of history made him a staunch critic of the present. "A century ago, we taught Latin and Greek in prep school," he joked. "Now we teach remedial English at college." He traveled across Europe and developed a love for England. Sobran's favorite party trick was reciting long passages of Shakespeare in the style of various great British actors—Laurence Olivier, Ralph Richardson, or John Gielgud. After some drinks he could bring a restaurant to a standstill with a rendition of

Richard III as played by Laurence Olivier, replete with hunchback and nasal whine. Like many paleocons—all so often charged with xenophobia—Sobran actually admired and even preferred the accomplishments of other cultures. Perhaps the best system of government, he said, was the medieval monarchy of Europe. That at least had a clear sense of limits—no English king ever asked his subjects to give a detailed account of their income every year.[16] He was a nostalgic anarchist:

> Nobody can claim the power to change the moral law or a monopoly of the authority to enforce it. But the state claims the right to do both. It tries to change the moral law by legislation, which is falsely thought to add to the moral duties of its subjects; and it insists that only it may define, outlaw, and punish wrongs. The results of the state's claims include war, tyranny, slavery, and taxation. Human society would be better off without the state.[17]

In 1972, Joe Sobran was plucked from teaching English literature at the University of Eastern Michigan by Bill Buckley and given a job as a writer on the *National Review*. Later he became an editor and eventually won syndication in the *Los Angeles Times*.[18] The power of Sobran's writing lay in his ability to blend humor and traditionalism, simplifying complex ideas in ways that readers could relate to. Take, for instance, his advice on good child rearing:

> Because I write about politics, people are forever asking me the best way to teach children how our system of government works. I tell them that they can give their own children a basic civics course right in their own homes . . . When your child is a little older, you can teach him about our tax system in a way that is easy to grasp. Offer him, say, $10 to mow the lawn. When he has mowed it and asks to be paid, withhold $5 and explain that this is income tax. Give $1 to his younger brother, and tell him that this is "fair." Also, explain that you need the other $4 yourself to cover the administrative costs of dividing the money. When he cries, tell him he is

being "selfish" and "greedy." Later in life he will thank you . . . Every now and then, without warning, slap your child. Then explain that this is defense. Tell him that you must be vigilant at all times to stop any potential enemy before he gets big enough to hurt you. This, too, your child will appreciate, not right at that moment, maybe, but later in life.[19]

Ann Coulter, a big fan, once wrote that "Sobran is the master . . . the only writer whose columns consistently leave me thinking to myself, Why didn't I say that?"[20] Asked shortly before his death to summarize his politics, Joe Sobran replied, "I won't be satisfied until the Church resumes burning for heresy." The remark was typically paleoconservative—funny, offensive, and honest. By confronting his readership with outrageous propositions, Sobran hoped to force them to reevaluate their fashionable assumptions about state and society.[21]

Sobran was a popular columnist at the *National Review* and a friend to Buckley. Buchanan found his dedication to his craft fascinating. He once visited Sobran's house and the lawn was so overgrown that the grass nearly reached his knees. Inside, the property was practically barren but for a chair and piles and piles of books on the floor. Like so many paleocons, he was otherworldly; he preferred to spend money set aside for clothes and furniture on food and fine wines.[22] However, for all his eccentricity, Sobran was still a mainstream columnist. The Gulf War changed all that. Sobran was no pacifist, he insisted. But he had sons who were of fighting age. He was terrified that they might get conscripted to fight a war, as he saw it, in the defense of Israel and Arab oil.[23]

Chatting away with Sam and Joe in the Hunan Noon, Pat found a unique fellowship. All three men were talented writers, all three grasped the realization that the Cold War was over and that conservatism was going to change with it. All three shared a sense of betrayal by their liberal peers. All three loathed the neocons. They were heavy drinkers and big eaters; they came together to laugh, swap jokes, and defend the outrageous at a time when it was becoming harder to do so. All three faced the wrath of the neocon right. Only Pat's career survived.

. . .

Pat Buchanan's predictions of quagmire in Iraq were premature. After an intensive bombing campaign, the allies overran Kuwait in just four days. They found that Saddam's army was ill-equipped and staffed by teenagers. Only 146 Americans lost their lives. The coalition pushed into Iraq and the retreating Iraqis set fire to oil wells, creating fountains of fire that burned for weeks. The allies got within 93 miles of Baghdad and then stopped. They could easily have taken the capital and deposed Saddam but, as the Secretary of Defense Donald Rumsfeld said, "I don't think you could have done all of that without significant additional U.S. casualties . . . And the question in my mind is, how many additional American casualties is Saddam worth? And the answer is, not that damned many." The Iraqis conceded defeat and the U.S. withdrew.[24]

The antiwar movement looked like fools. They had predicted a wider war and perhaps even a nuclear conflict. Instead, the battle lasted less than a week. Bush's approval ratings leaped to over 90 percent. It looked like the collapse of the Soviet Union did not mean the end of the United States's unique role as guarantor of law and order: It enhanced it. "By God," exclaimed the President, "we've kicked the Vietnam syndrome once and for all!"[25]

In March 1991, Bush received a standing ovation by Congress and said:

> Until now, the world we've known has been a world divided—a world of barbed wire and concrete block, conflict and cold war. Now, we can see a new world coming into view. A world in which there is the very real prospect of a new world order. In the words of Winston Churchill, a "world order" in which "the principles of justice and fair play . . . protect the weak against the strong." A world where the United Nations, freed from cold war stalemate, is poised to fulfil the historic vision of its founders. A world in which freedom and respect for human rights find a home among all nations. The Gulf war put this new world to its first test, and, my fellow Americans, we passed that test.[26]

The neocons exacted revenge. In the next couple of years, they purged the paleocons from various journals and organizations. Within weeks of the liberation of Kuwait, Jon Utley was ousted from the board of the conservative Accuracy in Media group. The vote was unanimous. Reed Irvine, the group's chairman, said to Utley, "When we were against the commies you were with us; why aren't you now?" Utley was invited to defend his position but refused. "Reed asked that I resign," he told the press. "I thought it was more honorable to be canned."[27] In retrospect, Utley said, "I was lucky that I had made some money beforehand in real estate. Many people would lose their jobs but I didn't care what they said about me." Much of the membership of the Committee to Avert a Mideast Holocaust would be discredited in one way or another. The most common charge was anti-Semitism.[28]

In December 1991, Bill Buckley wrote an article in *National Review* that definitively spelled out the case against Buchanan. Although criticism of Israel is not proof of racism, Buckley said, given the "obsessive" number of times that he has done it, "I find it impossible to defend Pat Buchanan against the charge that what he did and said during the period under examination amounted to anti-Semitism." He found Sobran guilty of similar crimes and urged him privately to "stop antagonizing the Zionist crowd."[29] Joe was affronted and accused Buckley of libel. One of his last columns as a writer in the *National Review* recommended that *The New York Times* be renamed "The Holocaust Update."[30] In 1993, Buckley sacked Sobran.

Pat's remarks about accused war criminals and "the pressure of the Jews" were revisited on TV and in print.[31] Menachem Z. Rosen—chair of the International Network of Children of Jewish Holocaust Survivors—concluded that:

> Buchanan appeals to the fears and prejudices of white American middle-class voters whose livelihood and security are threatened by the sluggish economy, and who are receptive to diatribes blaming others . . . The difference between him and [an overt anti-Semite] is one of aesthetics and packaging rather than substance . . . It is often forgotten that by the time he became Chancellor of Germany in 1933, Adolf Hitler had distanced himself from the thugs

who roamed Germany beating up Jews. He made a successful effort
to reassure the German establishment by letting them know that he
was really one of them—that he, too, liked children and dogs.[32]

The Jewish economist Murray Rothbard disagreed. He wrote that:

> the only rational definition of an anti-Semite is one who advocates
> political, legal, economic, or social disabilities to be levied against
> Jews . . . Never has Pat Buchanan advocated any such policies,
> whether they be barring Jews from his country club or placing
> maximum quotas on Jews in various occupations . . . let alone legal
> measures against Jews. So . . . it is absurd and a vicious calumny to
> call Pat anti-Semitic.[33]

But Rothbard was an isolated, eccentric voice. Publications like *Commentary, The New York Times,* and *The Washington Post* labeled Pat an anti-Semite
and, for his predictions of disaster in Iraq, a false prophet.[34]

The media and the White House might have distinguished between racist
and nonracist conservatives, but the voters didn't seem to care. In November
1991, Louisianans went to the polls to vote in a new governor. David Duke was
running and running like a mainstream conservative.[35] He wore jeans and a
T-shirt, or else a suit with power-dressing shoulder pads, and a badge shaped
like a fish—a Christian symbol popular with evangelicals. His enemies, he
said, were welfare cheats and liberals, whatever their color. Duke's favorite subject was himself, and the attempt to silence him: "They never accuse me of any
violence toward minorities. They accuse me only of thought crime; of being
politically incorrect; of saying out loud what many say privately."[36] Many white
folks seemed to agree. At a campaign rally shortly before the vote someone
waved a placard behind the candidate that read, "Vote for the White Man, not
the Wong Man."

"What's wrong with being proud to be white?" Tonya McQueen demanded
of a snooty *New York Times* reporter. She had lost her job as a dental hygienist
and was worried about what the future held for her nine-year-old son. Whenever black people got angry, they protested and government listened. Why

shouldn't she get the same treatment, too? Her T-shirt read, "It's a White Thing: You Wouldn't Understand." An oilfield salesman called Chuck Fiorello pointed at his son and said, "Why am I for Duke? Because he's white, he's going to have a harder chance getting into schools, getting jobs. It's not fair."[37]

On election day, Duke took just 39 percent of the vote. But he won 55 percent of whites—68 percent of whites with only a high school level education, 62 percent of white Protestants, 52 percent of white Catholics, 56 percent of whites with an income under $15,000, 63 percent with an income between $15,000 to $29,999, and 60 percent with an income between $30,000 and $49,999. Whites who said that their financial situation had worsened since 1988 voted for Duke by 58 percent. "We won our people," said Duke. And he had.[38]

By the Thanksgiving of 1991, Pat wanted to run for the Republican nomination. He called Bay and let her know. She jumped on a plane to Virginia. They sat down together and Pat put forward his reasons for running. Bay remembered it this way:

> He said that Bush is being called a conservative, but he's not a conservative. And that was bad for the movement. He was basically a moderate and not a very good one at that. But people were calling him a conservative. "He'll break the movement," said Pat. "Everything we've achieved since Reagan will go if people get the idea that he's what conservatism is all about." He started pounding the table. "This is what we've got to get home to people: We're the movement, we're the movement, *we're the movement*! He can't have the conservative mantle. We've got to take it back from him."

Bay was thrilled at the idea of her brother having another crack at the presidency, but she noticed something had changed.

> He kept going on and on about the neoconservatives. I couldn't see how any of it matters, but he was obsessed. [He said] "We've got to show people what real conservatism is. These neocons are not real

conservatives, but they're taking control of Bush and the [Republican] Party. We've got to take it back. We've got to let people understand the difference between us and them."

At first, Bay thought her brother "had gone crazy." As far as she was concerned, a conservative was a conservative, and the difference between "paleo" and "neo" was semantic. So Pat broke it down for her. "He showed me the difference between us and them; how they were trying to steal the movement, how they controlled Bush." Bay took some convincing, but once she saw her brother cared, she was a convert.[39]

Bay put together a meeting at Pat's home similar to the one in 1988. She brought along a young activist called Paul Erickson. Erickson had been the chair of the College Republicans for Ronald Reagan in 1980 and a national officer for the College Republicans for five years. He had a reputation for being "someone with organizational skills." As soon as he heard that Pat was thinking of a run, Paul called Bay to volunteer.

> When Bush signed into law the tax rises, me and many movement
> conservatives were convinced that the only way the Republicans
> could ever control a majority in the Congress and win the presidency
> was to get a leader who would take us back to the Reagan doctrine—
> which Bush campaigned on but didn't believe in. So come 1991, I
> was looking for the largest bluntest object I could find to beat Bush
> around the head with. And that was Pat Buchanan.

Paul's presence at the conference was a case of "virtue by necessity." Barely any professional political consultants would work for Buchanan. No one thought he could win and the Bush administration was busily buying up all the conservative media people. Paul was the best there was at the price Pat could afford. Said Erickson, the meeting at McLean "was the vast right-wing conspiracy . . . the only two people in that room who were not professional writers were Bay and myself."[40] Richard Viguerie suggested the names of two amateur activists in their twenties: Greg Muller and Terry Jeffrey, both of whom went on to become full-time staff. The only established media professional Buchanan put on the payroll was consultant Tony Fabrizio. Fabrizio quit within days of his appointment.[41]

After the McLean meeting, Pat sat down with Paul. Paul had a list of questions.

> There were certain things I needed to know if I was going to organize a presidential campaign. I asked him what his sleeping arrangements were, what kind of pillows he used, how much did he drink? I could tell he didn't like the questions, but they were necessary. I think he saw the campaign in intellectual terms until then. I told him that he was going to give up being a human being. . . . The media would be all over him. He would have no privacy from now on . . . Whatever you've said or done in the past will come back.[42]

When he heard the news that Pat was running, Bill Buckley laughed. "Oh, for an opponent who has written a thousand columns," he said.[43]

Part Two

A Peasant in Revolt

THIRTEEN

The Republican Ho Chi Minh

The first contest between Buchanan and Bush was the February 18 New Hampshire primary. Today, New Hampshire is a wealthy, white-collar state that often votes Democratic—a land of leafy suburbs, high-tech industries, and weekend homes for Brahmins. This was not always the case. In 1992, New Hampshire was in the middle of a painful transition from blue-collar paper mills to middle-class tax havens.[1] Its native population bore the brunt of change. Between 1988 and 1992, the state's five biggest banks closed and the housing market collapsed. One in ten residents fell behind with their mortgage payments. The unemployment rate tripled, the number of personal bankruptcies rose sixfold, and the state lost 10 percent of its jobs.[2] For New Hampshire, the Reagan revolution had come to a bitter end.[3]

Paradoxically, few natives sought salvation in liberalism—the standard go-to for the economically distressed. New Hampshire was as conservative as it was poor, a middle-American state populated by folk who worked hard, played hard, and prayed hard. The state's "Live Free or Die" motto summed up their rough, gung-ho attitude toward life. But the Republican Party had let them down. The state was in economic and moral chaos. On one day in January 1992, the *Manchester Union-Leader* ran with three stories that summed up the mood in New Hampshire. A new high school opened and received over 600 applications for just a handful of teaching positions. Desperate people sent resumes, videotapes, begging letters, and bribes. One applicant sent a hunk of homemade cheese. He didn't get the job.[4] Meanwhile, elderly residents of the Fr. Burns public housing project were in court to protest the court-ordered removal of a crucifix placed in the high-rise's hallway. The state claimed that it violated the First Amendment. The appellants pointed out that since the housing project was named after a priest, it wasn't exactly out of character.[5] In the north of the state, two Girl Scout leaders were also in court—to decide which of them owned a gingerbread float that took first prize in a Christmas parade. The trial ended in a fistfight.

New Hampshire was hungry for change—but its own, peculiar variety of change. In the city of Concord, the *Union-Leader* reported, a small crowd had gathered to welcome a Republican candidate. Its banner read, "Christ and America First! Pat Buchanan: Our Next President."

This was Buchanan country.[6]

Team Buchanan had just one week to go before the candidate officially declared, and ten weeks before the vote. All it had on hand was $50,000 of Pat's own money. That wouldn't even cover his final phone bill.[7] If he was going to avoid total humiliation, Buchanan would have to rely on luck, improvisation, and the kindness of strangers.

Luckily, Pat's reputation went before him. Paul Erickson received a call from Paul Nagy, who lived in Manchester, New Hampshire.[8] Nagy told him that he was a big fan of Pat's and that he never missed an episode of *Crossfire*. An out-of-work computer data processor, he offered his time, money, and a spare room in Manchester from which to run a campaign headquarters.[9] Erickson had never heard of Nagy, but he took the offer.[10] Next, ex-congressman Chuck Douglas called and offered to be a campaign chairman. Douglas wanted payback against Bush, and his endorsement gave Pat a tinge of respectability.[11]

Meanwhile, Bay got on the phone to the *Manchester Union-Leader*. It was the only newspaper with statewide distribution, and Buchanan was an old friend of its previous owner, the eccentric millionaire William S. Loeb III. Loeb was an old-fashioned conservative from the McCarthy era. He believed that American democracy was being perverted by communists who had infiltrated every sphere of civil life—even the Republican Party. Buchanan visited Loeb back in 1968 to try to win his backing for Richard Nixon. He was taken aback by Loeb's stunning 100-acre Tudor estate in Massachusetts, from which he ran the *Union-Leader* by barking orders into the phone. Loeb had cut the tops off all the trees for 1,000 yards, to gain a better view of the hills beyond. He carried a gun in a holster beneath his jacket; his wife, Nackey, kept hers in her purse. Buchanan failed to win the Old Man an endorsement that day, but the Loebs fell in love with Pat.[12]

The *Union-Leader*—inherited by Nackey after her husband's death—called for a Buchanan victory before he even entered the race.[13] It ran an editorial on the front page, with the headline, "Go, Pat, Go!" Nackey's name was on it, but Bay sent it to her and Pat wrote it.[14] Buchanan was a man who "wants to protect Americans from a government that wants to increase our tax burdens and decrease our ability to manage our own affairs." Bush had abandoned conservative principles, "in his quest for some New World Order . . . Bush has continued to place all the blame for our problems on Congress, but it is he with his kindler and gentler approach who has failed to use the power of the presidency to protect us."[15] If that sounded harsh, when Newt Gingrich came to New Hampshire to stump for the President the *Union-Leader* ran with the headline, "Prostitute Sees Problem."[16]

Buchanan spent the first week of December at home, with his feet up in front of the fire, working on his announcement. The joy of staffing for Buchanan, said Paul Erickson, was that he could be trusted to be left alone. Speeches wrote themselves and, since the whole point of his candidacy was that he was a crazy maverick, there was no need to discuss "the right line" to take. So, Paul flew up to New Hampshire and visited the new HQ.[17] Nagy's operations center was an old betting shop on Manchester's main thoroughfare, a tiny room on top of a narrow flight of stairs that could only be climbed single-file. The bookies worked with phones, so there were plenty of lines and sockets. Most staffers shilled for nothing, but those at the top of the campaign pyramid earned the princely sum of $2,000 for two months' work. The fingerprints of the *Union-Leader* were everywhere. The state press officer—Signe McQuaid—was the wife of one of the daily's news editors.[18] Signe was the self-designated "campaign mum." Within days of Buchanan's announcement, college kids turned up at the headquarters from as far away as Florida. Signe found accommodation for most and the rest slept on the floor. She brought casseroles and stew into the office for lunch. It was a children's crusade, populated by fresh-faced kids in baseball jackets and ties. Of course not everybody who turned up was clean-shaven, or sane. One guy drove all the way from California—without a change of clothes or money for the gas back.[19] The first volunteer meeting at the HQ had twelve people. The second had one hundred. Pat called them the Buchanan brigades.[20]

On December 10, Buchanan flew to Manchester to make his announcement. Erickson and he went over his speech in his room at the downtown Holiday Inn. Buchanan was as calm and witty as ever. Erickson was on edge. He had hired out the historic Concord state capitol building and he was worried that no one would show. The campaign and the candidate were untested. It could die there and then. After all, why should anyone have any interest in a guy with no money, no personnel, and no hope of winning? Supremely confident, Pat fired off a couple of the latest Bush jokes he had heard on the plane, put on his coat, and headed for the door. Paul stopped him. He looked him in the eye and asked, "Are you *sure* you really want to do this?"

For the first time in his life, Paul saw a flicker of doubt in Buchanan's eyes. He gazed at the ceiling, lost in thought. Then he shrugged. "Sure," he said, and opened the door.[21]

The announcement at Concord was a riot. Hundreds of supporters packed the antechamber, surrounded by journalists from all over the country. C-SPAN ran it live, showing fans crawling over each other to get to their man, waving banners that read: "Watch Out, George Bush—Pat Buchanan Doesn't Brake for Liberals!"[22] Who these people were, nobody knew. In Pat's campaigns the activists appeared from nowhere.[23]

Nothing was perfect—his microphone broke down. And suddenly, before he had got into his speech, a gay activist shouted, "Act up! Fight AIDS! Fight back!" Buchanan lost his train of thought. He looked for help in the crowd, perhaps half-expecting a TV producer to yell "Cut!" But the demonstration went on. A man out front waved for Pat's attention and shouted, "Mr. Buchanan, I want you to know that I have AIDS and I don't agree with that."

"He ought to listen to you buddy," said Buchanan. The demonstrator was dragged from the hall and Buchanan got it back together. "Be gentle, be gentle," he cooed.[24]

The Buchanan stump speech was eloquent, historical, and angry. He said:

> Today, we call for a new patriotism, where Americans begin to put the needs of Americans first, for a new nationalism where in every negotiation, be it arms control or trade, the American side seeks advantage and victory for the United States.

Buchanan said of President Bush:

> He is yesterday and we are tomorrow. He is a globalist and we are nationalists. He believes in some Pax Universalis; we believe in the Old Republic. He would put America's wealth and power at the service of some vague New World Order; we will put America first.

He asked for the votes of Democrats as well as Republicans. His was not a battle of left vs. right, but of the people vs. the powers that be.[25]

When it was over, Buchanan took a walk down the streets of Concord. "What do I do?" he asked Erickson.

"Just hold out your hand and tell people you're running for president," replied Paul. Buchanan did what he was told. To his surprise, and the surprise of the journalists, he quite enjoyed it.[26] A few men in baseball caps took him by the hand and told him they recognized him off the TV. Many wanted an autograph, some echoed the cry they heard in the hall: "Go Pat, go!"[27] Since it was Concord, there were more politicians and journalists on the streets than voters. Buchanan even bumped into Ralph Nader. But reporters were taken aback by Buchanan's "wide and surprisingly friendly reception," as well as the desperation of the people who crossed the road to say hello.[28]

Later that night, the team settled down in Pat's motel room and opened up a bottle of wine. Pat had brought his family along—Shelley and Bay—and the women were wound up, punchy. Pat's pals Brent Bozell Jr. and Richard Viguerie had flown in especially to offer their experience and expertise. Bozell sat on the edge of the bed and read aloud the fundraising letter that Pat intended to send to supporters.

"What the hell's this?" asked Bozell. The letter was an attack on free trade, a long list of all the industries that had flown to China, Mexico, and Canada. Pat said this was the logical extension of what he had to say about putting America first. If it was time to stop bailing other countries out with arms and aid, then it was time to stop letting them take American jobs, too.[29]

Pat told them a story from when he had run into his uncle Bob and aunt Honey at the 1976 Republican convention. "Why are you supporting this free trade?" Bob had asked. "Don't you know what's happening to the Mon Valley?" Pat had fond memories of the Pennsylvania valley from holidaying there as a child. It was iron and coal country, a land of heroes. Pat had listened for hours to their war stories as they sipped beer in the Charleroi Veteran's Hall. "The Mon Valley is dying," said Uncle Bob. "Imports are killing us." Great men were jobless and broken.[30] Then, in 1987, Pat read that the Japanese industrial giant Toshiba had been caught selling propeller technology to Moscow. Congress voted to ban the import of the company's products.[31] Overnight, lobbyists descended on Washington to plead the corporation's case. Pat knew many of those lobbyists—they were conservatives he had worked with in the White House. What should come first—trade or patriotism?

Bozell and Viguerie listened in shocked silence.

"Pat," said Bozell, "these are conservatives you're going after here in New Hampshire. And conservatives love free trade." Perhaps, he wondered, Buchanan was out of his depth? Viguerie offered to write a new letter.[32] Buchanan was silent. Bay snatched the old letter from Bozell and said, "Pat wrote this. It's what he feels. It's what he wants to send out."

"It won't even raise $7,000," Bozell predicted.

The letter raised $700,000.[33]

Meanwhile, President George H. W. Bush was having problems. On Christmas Day 1991 he went on TV to announce that the hammer and sickle had been lowered above the Kremlin. Communism had fallen in Russia, the Cold War was over.[34] But the economy continued to decline and his poll numbers were poor. Bush didn't get why so many people disliked him, why the talk-show hosts made fun of him, why the newspapers said he had to go. He became withdrawn and grumpy. So internalized were his feelings, and so awkward was he expressing them in front of strangers, that his behavior became surreal. A friend of Buchanan's accompanied Bush on a tour of an insurance firm to discuss the state of American healthcare. Bush sat in silence in the CEO's office, not listening or contributing to the debate. They took him out to meet some of the staff; he stood on a gangway and the workers waited for him to speak. He stared at them queerly, like he had never done this before. Then he said, "Don't cry for me, Argentina. Don't cry for me. I know what you've been hearing. But I'm okay. I'm in good health. Don't cry for me, Argentina." Bush had apparently confused a debate on healthcare with discussion about his own health—all expressed through the medium of song.[35] Bush was disengaged to the point of Zen. "The president seems, at times," wrote *New York* magazine, "like a figment from F. Scott Fitzgerald's imagination."[36]

His advisors said to Bush, "Ignore Buchanan, but don't ignore his issues." If jobs were the problem, and if jobs were going east, then Bush decided that to Japan he would go.[37] So, in January 1992, Bush flew to Japan to open talks on trade.[38] The trip was a public relations disaster. At a banquet at the Japanese prime minister's residence, he fell ill. Fellow diners noticed that his eyelids had begun to flutter and his head lolled to one side. He vomited and collapsed onto the floor, taking much of the table with him. The Japanese prime minister cradled Bush's head in his arms and talked him back to consciousness. After a minute or so, he came to. As white as a sheet, he insisted that he was okay and agents lifted him out of the room. The prime minister led everyone in a round of applause.[39]

An unmanned camera was accidentally running during the meal and journalists snuck the video out and shared it with the world. The Japanese were never going to make any big concessions to begin with, but now that Bush looked too weak even to endure a five-course meal, they were inclined to take every offer off the table.[40] A humiliated Bush slunk back to the U.S. and admitted that "You never get all you want." The trip had been "somewhere between acceptable and a disappointment," confessed a White House insider. It confirmed an image of weakness. The President was sixty-seven, tired, and ill.[41]

. . .

On the campaign trail in those wintry months, Pat never interfered, never complained, never lost his temper.[42] He let his staffers, most of whom were between the ages of eighteen and thirty, decide what to do and when to do it. Team Buchanan began every morning at the breakfast table, reading the newspapers and crafting the day's events. Aides would call up radio stations and offer an interview. Sometimes Buchanan would get up at 5 a.m., put makeup on in the car, and arrive at a TV studio, unannounced and ready to talk about something—anything—on the breakfast show. Bewildered producers let him slip in front of the cameras and launch another tirade against the President, before he got back into the car and drove off to the next event.[43]

Buchanan was a media-savvy candidate, probably the best running that year. His speeches looked spontaneous, but he locked himself away in his hotel room for an hour at a time—writing and rewriting, pacing the floor, getting the words and the delivery exactly right.[44] A decade working in television left him aware of the best camera angle, the best image, and the best sound bite. To accommodate the crews of networks that followed him, Buchanan permanently wore wireless microphones, the transmitters and power packs strapped to his waist like grenades.[45] Access to him was never denied. Anyone, from high school newspaper reporter to Dan Rather, was welcome to ask him a question.[46]

The media strategy was simple: Come up with one outrageous thing to say a day and then find the right moment to pitch it to reporters.[47] The reporters played along. Gun factories were perfect Buchanan events. On a tour of a factory in Newport, Buchanan pointed a .44-caliber pistol at an imaginary George Bush and snickered, "Go ahead, make my day." A journalist (who admitted that, despite her liberal instincts, "I love Pat!") told one of Buchanan's staffers that she was going to ask the candidate if he supported any kind of gun regulation at all. She thought that she might get a better response if Pat knew the question in advance. The staffer passed it on to Buchanan, who smiled and nodded. When they reached the end of the tour, the candidate offered to take questions.

"Do you support any form of gun regulation at all?" asked the reporter.

Buchanan pretended to mull it over.

"In my view," he said, "if it requires a truck to pull it, it should be banned." The remark made the 6 o'clock news.[48]

Buchanan's unequivocal conservatism sounded insensitive. He floated a plan for dealing with the homeless that put them in temporary shelters or jail. "In places like New York, a lot of these homeless folks are stabbing people to death," he told reporters. "I think they shouldn't be wandering the streets frightening women." In any other year, among Republicans, that might have been an applause line. But it wasn't something a politician should have said to an audience staring foreclosure in the face.[49]

Buchanan was discovering the limits of the Reagan economic revolution. He saw textile mills closing down and being shipped wall by wall to Canada. He met people who had been out of work for over a year and who had the blank, downcast stare of the hopeless. He discovered ordinary middle-class workers sleeping on the streets because the bank had reclaimed their home. Sometimes people came up to him when he was campaigning not to ask his views but to ask if he could help them get a job.[50]

For Pat, the trade issue had always been an intellectual conceit. But somewhere down the line, it took on new meaning.[51] It happened on a trip to a paper mill shortly before the Christmas break. Snow began to fall over New Hampshire in late December. It was heavy and thick, as much as six inches in some places. Pat, Shelley, and Paul drove up in a car, watching the land turn white around them. The trip had been planned weeks ago but, in the meantime, the mill hit hard times. When they arrived in Nashua they found that all the workers had been sacked that very morning. They were queuing up to collect their pink slips along with their Christmas turkeys. Buchanan worked the line, approaching each man with his arm outstretched and a cheerful hello. They took his hand, but no one replied. Their eyes were fixed on the ground. They were broken men.

"Hello, sir, I'm Pat Buchanan." he said to one man.

The worker looked him in the eye and whispered, "Save our jobs." That was it. Buchanan reached the end of the line and went back to the car. No jokes this time; no laughs.[52]

They drove back to Manchester in silence. In his rearview mirror, Paul could see Shelley crying. Pat was staring out the window. Paul—a die-hard free trader—looked at his boss and knew that he had lost him for good. "I could tell that Pat had changed from wanting to save jobs in general to wanting to save *those people's jobs* in particular." Buchanan the Republican was dead. Buchanan the populist was born.[53]

Pat had a new phrase that he used on the campaign trail: "vulture capitalism." The problem with America wasn't just its overbearing government; it was the amorality of a free market gone wild. Socialism was dumb, but unfettered capitalism was evil. America needed a new approach to economics that balanced the head *and* the heart. At the center of the family was a gainfully employed father. Cheap goods and offshoring took away his job and tore apart the family. Mothers were forced to work, unattended children ran rampant, healthcare premiums went unpaid, and faith in God was lost. And what, asked Buchanan, was the point of conservatism but to protect the family? Ergo, the Republican Party had a duty to conserve the living of middle-American males.[54]

Pat mellowed. Of course, his friends always knew he was kind and gentle. But now he let the public see this side of him, too.[55] He shifted his position on the homeless. He said society should distinguish between harmless individuals down on their luck and deranged felons who regard vagrancy as a way of life. This latter group was a "tiny minority" of the homeless. Pat said, "If I was miraculously granted an audience with his Royal Highness [President Bush], I would ask him why he is willing to send billions of dollars to the far flung reaches of the world, when people are living and dying in the streets just outside the White House."[56] Before New Hampshire, Buchanan opposed extended benefits to the unemployed. Now, he supported them.[57] "You can't go into those unemployment offices, see those guys about to lose their homes without saying, 'Well, we ought to go ahead with 12 more weeks of unemployment benefits.' "[58]

In early January, Team Buchanan released the "Read My Lips" ad. It featured regular folks from all over the state reciting Bush's pledge. The ad was simple, repetitive, annoying, and brilliant. It captured in one line everything wrong with the Bush administration, all the two-facedness, moderation, and gutlessness. Several staff members hated the ad. It looked cheap and shoddy.

The camera angles were all wrong, and the people in the ad looked too real—ill-dressed and ugly. There was none of the soothing smoothness of ordinary advertising, no star-spangled banners or soft-focus families. And yet, its amateurishness reminded people that Buchanan was the outsider—the maverick running on a shoestring. The campaign got complaints from teachers that children were repeating "Read my lips" in class, that it was becoming common parlance: "Read my lips, two times six equals twelve." "Read my lips, Paris is the capital of France."[59]

It was, admitted one of Bush's men, turning into "the best guerrilla operation since the Vietcong."[60] The Republican Ho Chi Minh began to climb in the polls.[61]

The day after Bush's collapse at the Japanese state dinner, the White House finally sent someone significant to New Hampshire to campaign. Unfortunately, its secret weapon was Dan Quayle. Quayle's term as Vice President had been ridiculed by the national press. His gaffes and malapropisms could fill a book ("Republicans understand the importance of bondage between a mother and child." "We don't want to go back to tomorrow. We want to go forward." "I believe we are on an irreversible trend towards more freedom and democracy. But that could change.").[62] Touching down in snowy Nashua on the morning of January 9, Quayle pledged to "listen to what everyday people have to say." But, in the rush of modern campaigning, the promise proved empty. Wearing a football jacket, he dashed from factory to mall in a series of photo ops at which people cheered and booed him in equal measure. "How does it feel to be the national joke?" shouted a spectator in Plymouth. In a mall in Bedford, the Vice President darted into a Dunkin' Donuts and ordered a chocolate frozen yogurt. The attempt to pump cash into the economy failed when the store's owner refused the payment out of respect for Quayle's office. Thinking that he might have found a sympathizer, the Vice President asked how business was doing. The owner told him that it would do considerably better without Quayle and his Secret Service agents blocking the donut counter. They collected their yogurt and left.[63]

Quayle's advance men arranged for him to visit successful businesses—usually electronics firms that were exporting strongly. Locals were unimpressed.

"It's really just a show," said a guy at a pulping plant. "He ought to be down the street, where they laid off 450 people in the last couple of days." In a barbershop, Quayle got a blunt message for Bush from a thirty-six-year-old machinist. "I think that he should be spending more time on the issues here," grumbled Don St. Pierre. "He should take care of his own before helping other people [abroad]." The atmosphere of the trip was detached, surreal. Thousands were out of work and Quayle only seemed to meet prospering silicon magnates. Quayle spent the night at the house of a popular local doctor. He sipped milk and nibbled chocolate chip cookies by the fire.[64]

In the wake of Quayle's visit, Buchanan's numbers actually went up. And things got a little more personal. Buchanan's response to insult was complex. Insulted by strangers, he laughed. Insulted by friends, he nursed a vendetta. It challenged his code of loyalty and honor. While on the stump, a journalist told Pat that Quayle had said he was "an extremist." What did he think about that? Pat was too hurt to answer. That night he couldn't sleep. The next morning he went on radio and was asked if he would ever attack the Vice President.

"No, I wouldn't," he said. "'Cos I don't want to be accused of child abuse."

A few days later, Buchanan discovered that the journalist had lied. Quayle had never uttered the word "extremist." The incident was one more step along Buchanan's journey into isolation from the press—happy to talk to them about ideas and other people, but not about himself. Embarrassed and cut off from influence, Buchanan never got a chance to apologize to the Vice President. "I regret that," he said many years later—a rare admission of fault from a proud man.[65]

The Quayle hunt aside, behind the scenes, Buchanan was far cooler than his angry rhetoric suggested. It was a family business and Pat's role was the spokesman. If he needed someone to get angry, Bay was the enforcer. If he needed to show compassion, Shelley was there to mother and soothe.[66] Pat never moaned and never refused to do anything his people said was necessary.[67] The flip side of this cool demeanor was that he could appear cold. He never scolded, but he never praised. People wrote speeches and memos, but they would return rewritten, with grammar and style critiqued and corrected, and then he would produce something himself that was "much better."[68] He presumed everyone would always be there for him, ready to perform their duty. There was no time for girlfriends or babies. At the center of the storm was the ever-ready, ever-needy, ever-patient Pat Buchanan. To those who knew him well he was indomitable. But he could break your heart.

Pat never praised Paul Erickson. Except, maybe, once. In late January, all the contenders, Democrat and Republican, were invited to attend a debate at an elementary school. The kids had divided themselves up into teams and designed banners and chants for their chosen candidate. They filled out the sports hall and waited for each man to come forward and make his pitch. Alas, that morning the snow fell harder than ever and the airports shut down. Team Buchanan, desperate for whatever publicity they could get, braved the ice and drove the campaign bus, Asphalt One, to the school. None of the other candidates showed; with one notable exception. Sitting in the far corner of the parking lot was the Clinton bus. Buchanan was thrilled. The chance to debate the Democratic frontrunner one-on-one was too good to be true. Clinton was mortified. One of his staffers spotted Asphalt One pulling up the driveway and told him Pat was on his way. Horrified at the thought of a photograph showing him on an empty platform with a man most pundits regarded as an oddball, Clinton elected to hide in the swimming pool changing rooms. He would wait there until Buchanan had left, and then make his escape.

Someone spotted Clinton slipping away and told Paul. Paul told Buchanan. Buchanan laughed. He entered the sports hall to the cheers of his supporters and called for hush. "What an honor it is to be here this evening," he said. "And what a particular pleasure it is to share the stage with my good friend, the Governor of Arkansas, Bill Clinton." There was a round of gasps. Everyone had been told that Clinton couldn't make it. Buchanan nodded at the Clinton people in the audience, who had been whipped up to a frenzy by an advance man. "The Governor is waiting for you in the swimming pool changing rooms," he said. The girls in the Clinton team went wild, grabbed their banners, and ran out of the room. Buchanan's cruel little laugh echoed down the corridor, the TV cameras following shortly behind.

Downstairs, Clinton got word that he had been found out. One thing worse than being photographed alone with Pat was to be photographed being mauled by a pack of hysterical teenage girls in a changing room. A quick-thinking aide threw open a window and the governor escaped into the snow on his hands and knees. He ran to the bus, jumped in, and sped away.

Mightily pleased with themselves, Team Buchanan got back into Asphalt One and drove off into the night. The candidate was hungry, so they stopped off at a diner. Pat, Shelley, and Bay got out and went inside. The campaign team (Paul and a few others) parked the coach around the back. The parking lot was an arena of ice—thick, slippery, and black. As Paul applied the brakes, he could feel the bus slipping from side to side. When the engine had died, someone spotted the Clinton bus on the other side of the lot. They wanted revenge. The Clinton people were sliding toward Asphalt One, cursing Buchanan and throwing snowballs. Paul and the boys decided to let them have it. Erickson threw open the driver's door and jumped onto the ice below. He slipped about for a bit, then found his grip and landed a punch on an Arkansas staffer. Battle commenced. The parking lot was full of the sounds of battle, gloves against skin, knees against ice, and grown men screaming as they slid around like drunks. Paul spotted his mark: a big ugly liberal sliding toward him in a trapper hat. Paul gave a war cry and launched himself forward. He lashed out, landing a punch on his chin. But Paul couldn't stop. He flew across the ice and landed face forward with a crack. Paul picked himself up and tasted the blood running from his nose. He beat a hasty retreat into the diner.

Inside, Erickson found a restroom and washed the blood off his face. His nose was broken and bent in the middle, like the beak of an eagle. Paul grabbed a handful of paper towels and held them against his nose to staunch the flow. Looking like hell, he limped out of the restroom to find Pat.

The family sat in a cubicle eating steaks. Paul approached the table, nose in hand. Shelley and Bay were horrified and insisted he go to a hospital. Pat continued to eat his steak. He didn't look up.

"What happened?" asked Shelley.

"I got into a fight with one of the Clinton people," replied Paul.

"What does the other guy look like?" asked Pat as he squeezed some ketchup onto his plate.

"Worse," said Paul. "Much worse."

Pat looked up and smiled. He gave him two thumbs up and said, "Well done." Then he went back to his meal.[69]

B y the end of January, the Buchanan campaign was on a roll. Public meetings were impromptu—Buchanan would go wherever he was invited. He gave a speech at a theater, a golf range, and even a Burger King.[70] The people who turned up were a mix of preachers, gun owners, students, housewives, and unemployed men with nothing better to do.[71] Everything Pat said was tinged with humor, and this trickled down to the staff at the HQ. If people rang up and there was no answer, they would hear: "All our staff are now busy with other calls. If you will leave your name, address, and phone number, someone will get back to you as quickly as possible. And remember—volunteers get preferred seating at the Inauguration."[72]

And the money kept rolling in. Within one month, Pat raised $1.7 million. Admittedly that was small fry; the President had $10 million on hand.[73] Nevertheless, Buchanan had scooped $2.5 million by the beginning of February—an astonishing 80 percent of it from single donations of $100 or less. More than 50,000 people contributed and the average sum was just $48. Buchanan threw some $50-a-plate dinner parties and cadged funds off protectionist businessmen, like the United States Business and Industry Council. His demand that America recognize independent—and largely Catholic—Croatia earned him between $100,000 to $150,000 from the Croatian community. But, overall, his campaign was a genuine crusade of the little man: paid for and staffed by ordinary people united in anger at the way things were.[74]

The momentum was going Pat's way.[75] And so finally, on January 15, the globe-trotting Bush came to New Hampshire. A cartoon in the *National Review* summed it up nicely: Bush stood in a café surrounded by angry men in Buchanan buttons. Hands aloft, he said, "On behalf of the American people, I bring greetings to your tiny nation."[76]

The President started the day at the Pease Air Force Base in Portsmouth. About ninety local businessmen shared with him horror stories about the recession. Bush told them that he understood, he was just too well-bred to show it: "I think I've known, look, this economy is in free fall. I hope I've known it. Maybe I haven't conveyed it as well as I should have, but I do understand." But the locals had to look on the bright side, he insisted. He was there to play "Mrs. Rose Scenario" and he shared with them some of his country-and-western philosophy. "I would remind you of another . . . song by the Nitty Gritty Dirt Band: 'If you want to see a rainbow, you've got to stand a little rain,'" he sang.[77]

As the day wore on, Bush started to tire. And he began to sound strange. "I am sick and tired every night hearing one of these carping little liberal Democrats jumping all over my you-know-what," he told workers at a computer parts factory in Rochester. He wasn't going to take any more of "mournful pundits," "egghead academics," and "jacklegs jumping up demanding equal time with some screwy scheme." When someone asked him what he thought about a possible extension of unemployment benefits, Bush replied with almost Eastern inscrutability, "If a frog had wings, he wouldn't hit his tail on the ground." And then, perhaps sensing that he was losing them, he rounded off with, "This ain't the easiest job in the world. Listen, here's the final word. Vote for me. Don't vote for them. Vote for me, okay?"[78]

Bush returned to the White House thinking he had done a good job. His advisors knew better.[79] The crowds were thin and lifeless and the press was beating him up. The only way he could guarantee a big win, they said, was to 1) make some grand concession to the right and 2) shift the blame for everything that had gone wrong onto someone else. It was time to go into damage limitation mode.[80]

Bush decided to use his State of the Union address to get his reelection campaign back on track. It was a strong performance, one of his best. He celebrated the end of the Cold War and berated the isolationists. Next he threw some meat to the right: spending cuts, capital gains cuts, a ninety-day freeze on federal regulations, and a $500 extra tax deduction for each dependent child. Finally, he launched an attack on the liberals in Congress: "I'll tell you, those of you who say, 'Oh, no, someone who's comfortable may benefit from [a tax cut],' you kind of remind me of the old definition of the Puritan who couldn't sleep at night, worrying that somehow, someone somewhere was out having a good time."[81]

Blaming Congress was smart. Polls showed that the public disapproved of the President's handling of his job, but that they *despised* the Democratic Congress.[82] In New Hampshire, Bush's support began to stabilize. He got a rush of local endorsements, spent a lot of money, and sent Quayle back out to reassure conservatives.[83] By early February, the race looked like a cakewalk again. But Bush blew his golden opportunity to take charge. He stayed out of New Hampshire for another two weeks, suggesting that he had lost interest. Then news leaked that the $500 extra tax deduction for each child that he had promised in his State of the Union wasn't going to appear in budget forecasts and may have been an empty promise.[84] Buchanan called it all "a cynical betrayal of the American middle class." Journalists found that New Hampshire voters were repeating his "Read My Lips" pledge without identifying the source—at a subconscious level, Buchanan's annoying ads had done their work.[85]

The weekend before the New Hampshire primary, Bush returned to the state. The reception was even frostier than the last visit. Once again, he started in a hangar. This time the forum was not even half full. Looking lonely and baffled, his voice echoed a plea across the room. "I'm in a tough race," he said. "The stakes are high. I need your help and I'm asking for your support."

George Bush slipped into the presidential limo that held up traffic and blocked the freeway as it crawled off to Goffstown. At midday he stopped at the Fireside Restaurant in the Manchester Holiday Inn to wolf down a cheeseburger and french fries—real people food—before paying with a gold credit card and dashing off to a fishing show down the road. Next he met a handpicked audience at Mountainview Middle School that tossed him softball questions while guest of honor Arnold Schwarzenegger did push-ups for the kids. The crowd preferred the actor to the President. "We want to make sure that when it comes, Tuesday, February 18, will you all go out there and pump up his vote?" shouted Schwarzenegger. Then Arnie broke a previous taboo. He mentioned the enemy by name. "I want you to vote and at the same time send a message to Congress and at the same time send a message to Pat Buchanan: Hasta la vista, baby."[86]

Buchanan held a rally in Manchester the day of Bush's visit and told the crowd: "The Buchanan brigades are going to run head on into the hollow army of King George and cut through it like butter." They joined some blue-collar union people across the street campaigning for Democrat Bob Kerrey in a war chant. "Hey, hey, ho, ho, George Bush has got to go!"[87] They were expressing common anger with the political establishment, but those who gave Bush a frosty reception were still reserved in their support for Buchanan. Marguerite Bylnn, a sixty-six-year-old retiree from Nashua, told reporters that she would definitely vote for Pat. But when asked if she thought he could win, she replied, "Oh, heavens no. That's a frightening thought!"[88]

Monday, February 17, the day before polling, Buchanan boarded a bus for a thirteen-city tour of the state. He was upbeat, giddy. The press said that he didn't have to win to win—they'd take a third of the vote as a repudiation of the President.[89] Pat's media pack rivaled Bill Clinton's or even George Bush's. Better still, they were in on the joke. Buchanan visited a golf range in Windham and smacked a golf ball with Bush's name written on it off into the grass. "There's a chance this could be the pistol shot that is really heard around the world," he quipped and the pundits laughed.[90] "We started a campaign with nothing and all of a sudden we're on the map in New Hampshire and we're on the map nationally," Buchanan said on the steps of Exeter's historical brick town hall. The crowd around him was as small as it always had been—they never really grew. And there were signs of future trouble. Rabbi Avi Weiss of New York was there, dressed as a concentration camp victim with a sign accusing Buchanan of anti-Semitism. But the mass of ordinary voters were disaffected enough to make Buchanan's angry campaign matter. Bay said, "I'm looking to the skies for clouds." Rain, snow, or even just drizzle might discourage apathetic moderates from voting and increase her brother's percentage.

That night, it rained.[91]

FOURTEEN

Leather Daddies and Free Trade

Midday on February 18, 1992, was the first and last time Paul Erickson ever heard Pat Buchanan swear. He went into the Buchanans' hotel room with a copy of a poll that showed Pat and the President were neck and neck.[1] "There's just 4 percent between you," said Paul. "We could win this." Pat sat on the edge of the bed, his typewriter beside him.

"Well, what the fuck do we do now?" he asked.

Pat had only written one speech, an announcement that he was quitting the race. He couldn't stop laughing as he opened up his typewriter, put in a fresh piece of paper, and started work on another. Everyone was in shock. Greg Mueller fielded calls on the phone about the lines building outside polling stations. Paul punched the air. Shelley made coffee. And Pat chuckled as he typed.[2]

The White House was in a state of siege. They got a tip-off from a friend at *The New York Times* that the President and Buchanan were both at 48 percent. The newspaper was preparing the story "New Hampshire Rebukes Bush."[3] Team Bush hit the phones. Local celebrities called voters and gave interviews to journalists. Supporters were bused in from Massachusetts. The phone bank, which was capable of generating up to 5,000 calls per hour, glowed red. Promises of federal money and political appointments were made. President Bush took the news in the Oval Office and looked glum. His staff told him that there was a good chance he might get beat by a TV pundit.[4]

Back at the Buchanan camp, once the speech was written, there was little else to do but drink. Richard Viguerie turned up and they headed off to a restaurant for a steak dinner. Pat moved from table to table, shook hands, and settled down to work their way through several bottles of wine.[5] There was no hurry, there was plenty of time for swapping jokes and Bush impersonations. Paul said that the networks wouldn't start their live election coverage until 10 p.m. So Pat told his guests he didn't have to be on stage until 10:01 p.m.[6]

At 10:01 p.m., Pat and Shelley arrived at a victory party to a crowd of a couple of hundred. They cheered, "God Bless America!" and "God Bless Pat!" Pat climbed the stage and basked in the glory. The polls now showed him at 40 percent and the president at 58 percent. It was an eighteen-point spread, but near enough to be called a moral victory. Pat waited until someone gave him the signal that the networks were cutting to his rally and he then began his speech. It was a victory of the peasants over King George, he said. Something had started in New Hampshire, something that was going to roll down south to Georgia, South Carolina, Louisiana, "and points beyond." He saw the faces of unemployed loggers, Mormon ladies, double-glazing salesmen, hairdressers, cab drivers, libertarians, anarchists, traditionalists, gun lovers, homeschoolers, and he saw his people. "Help me take our party back from those that have walked away from us!" he cried and the brigaders stomped their feet for joy.

It was a significant night. Bill Clinton placed second in the Democratic primary, rescuing his campaign after a sex scandal. And on *Larry King Live,* a Texas billionaire called Ross Perot said that Buchanan's result showed that a lot of angry independents were looking for a leader. Perot had decided to run for president.[7]

Buchanan took 37 percent in New Hampshire. His showing looked better in early returns because he enjoyed a 10 percent lead among unemployed voters who had the spare time to vote. Even *The New York Times* was forced to admit the result meant something. The *Times* expected voters to be angry about the recession, but it was surprised by the "flood of male independent voters" that Pat brought to the polls. Among independents, women favored Bush 54–41 percent. Men favored Buchanan 56–42 percent. Overall, Buchanan carried the independent vote. He failed to win any demographic among registered Republicans except those who felt their economic situation had declined or had lost their job.[8] The *Times* found it shocking how many independents chose to vote for Pat Buchanan rather than Bill Clinton: "His showing will be taken, especially abroad, as a sign of ugly nativism and thinly varnished hostility to minorities." The campaign now moved south. The next primary was Georgia on March 3, followed by South Carolina on March 7, and Super Tuesday on March 10. Super Tuesday included Florida, Louisiana, Massachusetts, Mississippi, Rhode Island, Tennessee, and Texas. The *Times* noted that many of these states were breeding grounds for the kind of white backlash it presumed Pat was riding.[9]

President Bush had to go on the attack and show he was in command of his party. A White House official warned that if the President "goes one or two more states after Georgia and has to put up with a 35 percent, 37 percent showing, he is dead." Team Bush faced a dilemma. It wanted rid of Buchanan but it didn't want to alienate his voters.[10] The loyalty of ordinary conservatives was still up for grabs. The door-knockers, lobbyists, moneymen, and shock jocks of the conservative movement would probably stick with the GOP in good times and bad. But floating right-of-center voters, particularly in the South and Midwest, were a less certain prospect. There was a suspicion that the independents and Democrats who voted Republican in the last three presidential elections did so because times were good and they liked Ronald Reagan. Now that things were tougher and the President looked a lot less like the guy next door, the White House feared that those people might drift back to the Democrats.[11]

They could even lose the South. The GOP had relied on white southern Democratic voters since the 1970s. But Bill Clinton's brand of moderate, Arkansas charm stood a chance of winning them back. And Buchanan's constant attacks on the President upped the odds. One Atlanta reporter went into a bar to gauge the views of voters and was surprised by the anger toward Bush. "I will admit that I voted Republican [in 1988] just because of who the candidate was," said one barfly. "But I won't vote for George Bush again. People are upset with George Bush; they're upset with the state of the economy. Folks don't have jobs." Hoyt Albertson, a man in a baseball cap and overalls, introduced himself as the local "political guru." A retired electrician and self-described "redneck Georgia Democrat," he said, "I'm damn sure not going to vote for Bush. I'm going to vote strictly Democrat. I don't care if it's a damn mangy dog." But what about Bill Clinton's support for the cultural revolution? "Hell," Hoyt said, "when a guy runs around all the time with other women, you know he's not a homosexual."[12]

The President was at risk of losing the conservatives to a philanderer or a TV personality. And so, Team Bush opted for a strategy of dealing with Buchanan that had serious consequences for them and their party. They decided to attack the man but embrace his issues. In a pattern that would repeat itself over the next two decades, a Republican moderate won the battle by slamming his conservative opponent. But he lost the war by aping his ideas.

Buchanan announced that he intended to focus his time and money on Georgia and would then hit South Carolina and "targets of opportunity" on Super Tuesday. Biggest among the opportunities was Louisiana, where David Duke was also running and had stirred up a lot of antiestablishment anger.[13] George Bush hit the road and went negative.[14] In Georgia, he told reporters that Buchanan wanted to privatize Social Security, and that his isolationism was reckless and dumb.[15] The President called Buchanan's foreign policy "naive and defeatist." He lashed out against "the doom and gloom from all these intense talking heads who are happy only when they say something negative." It was good stuff, but useless unless the President could convince people that he was a genuine conservative. And that meant making some concessions.[16]

On February 20, Buchanan launched a tirade against the National Endowment for the Arts. The head of the NEA—businessman and personal friend of the President John Frohnmayer—had taken a "hands-off" approach to art subsidies. He gave millions of federal dollars to controversial artists, without censure or discrimination. Under Frohnmayer's watch, the NEA had funded a publication called *Queer City* that depicted Jesus Christ as a pedophile. It had also underwritten an exhibition that included a crucifix submerged in urine, a photo of a man posing with a bull whip inserted in his anus, a woman smearing herself with chocolate and putting vegetables up her vagina, and a naked man simulating masturbation. Buchanan wanted Frohnmayer gone. Bush apparently liked Frohnmayer and liked his approach. "The Federal Government," said the President in March 1990, "[should not get] into telling every artist what he or she can paint."

That was hardly the point, said Pat in Georgia. The Constitution guaranteed artists' right to free speech, but it did not guarantee them tax dollars. Buchanan told reporters that he would make opposition to the NEA a center-piece of his southern campaign.

On February 21, George Bush fired John Frohnmayer. "We had to wipe away at least one of Pat's points in advance," explained a Bush aide. "Dumping John was craven, but it was just politics."[17] The Frohnmayer U-turn was only the beginning. On February 22, Bush went on radio and made the case for his budget proposals. Included in them was the $500 tax exemption for children. It was back on the agenda, as if it had never gone away.[18] Clearly, Buchanan was dragging his party to the right. He was subverting the party structure and handing power back to the grassroots.[19] Even if Pat went down in flames, his ideas were here to stay.[20]

One night, Georgians saw a new ad on TV. It was shot in a disco, with Donna Summers–type music and strobe lighting. On the dance floor twisted a couple of middle-aged, leather-clad gay men. They romped around suggestively, wiggling their backsides at the camera. A narrator said that this was footage taken from a movie subsidized by the National Endowment for the Arts. It was an example of the kind of "pornographic and blasphemous art" that Bush had used tax dollars to pay for. "This so-called art has glorified homosexuality, exploited children, and perverted the image of Jesus Christ." Whether the leather-daddy ad was silly, racist (several revelers were black), homophobic, or fair comment, it packed a punch.[21] "When I get to be President," said Buchanan of the National Endowment, "we're going to shut that place down, then padlock it and fumigate it."[22]

Did the ad, as many suggested, push the boundaries of good taste? Some in the campaign thought that it might and wanted it pulled. It could seem hypo-critical to voters that Pat's crusade against filth should involve him pumping soft-core porn straight into people's homes. A focus group was needed, but Pat didn't have the time or money to run one. So Bay got on a plane with a copy of the ad and visited her mother's house. She put it in the video machine and waited anxiously as Mom watched. When the ad was over Bay flicked off the TV and asked her what she thought.

"I've seen worse," her mother said. So the ad ran.[23]

The leather-daddy ad helped redefine the campaign and ushered in a wider debate about culture.[24] Up to now, the battle was mostly about economics. But Georgia was not New Hampshire. Unemployment for the country as a whole stood at 6.9 percent in January 1992; in Georgia it was just 3.9 percent. Like much of the rest of the South, Georgia's biggest crisis was one of identity. Since the 1970s, the region had attracted thousands of northern businesses looking for low costs and taxes. Aerospace and electronics industries transformed a largely rural economy into an urban, high-tech one. People quit the countryside and moved into towns. Middle-class families fled the cities in the wake of desegregation—finding shelter in the suburbs with their lily-white private schools. The South was richer than ever before, but its character was changing. Northern migrants followed the jobs and brought with them their cosmopolitan, urbanite ways. Traditional, slow, intensely religious patterns of life eroded. Tobacco sheds stood empty, small towns died. Evangelicalism flourished, but laws regarding public modesty were slowly lifted. Several states chose to plug budget deficits with gambling contracts and state lotteries. Whites were coming to terms with local governments dominated by blacks. Country was going electric.[25]

Social traditionalism and antiestablishment feeling were far more potent issues than trade and jobs.[26] Buchanan knew what buttons to press. At a rally in Atlanta, he reminded his audience that two of his great-grandfathers were "troublemakers and rabid secessionists . . . There's only one candidate in this race who's a conservative and a traditionalist across the board, who believes in lower taxes, in less spending, in traditional values, in standing up for the right to life." Buchanan launched himself into a dizzying round of TV interviews at which he sounded less and less like Huey Long and more and more like David Duke. "Pat is more Southern than many white Southerners when it comes to race," said a local journalist. "I think he's going to play that card hard, and if he doesn't he's a fool."[27]

Buchanan made a pitch for the good ol' boys—Republican and Democrat. He spent a day in Georgia lashing out at the Voting Rights Act of 1965, calling it "an act of regional discrimination against the South." He visited Stone Mountain, into the north face of which was carved a portrait of Robert E. Lee,

Stonewall Jackson, and Jefferson Davis. At dusk, he stood on a platform in
Marietta with former Democratic governor Lester Maddox and future Liber-
tarian presidential candidate Bob Barr. The Stars and Bars fluttered in the wind.
"If you're a conservative Democrat, you only have one choice: me," said Pat to
cheers from the crowd. He finished the day with a moonlit stop at the town of
Perry, where conservative Democratic senator Sam Nunn was born. It was cold
and Buchanan's breath turned to ice in the air. "This is the home of Sam
Nunn?" he asked, as if he had only just realized the significance of the location.
"Why don't you Democrats get a good candidate like Sam Nunn instead of
those five turkeys and run him against me, and we'd do just fine in November."
Many local Democrats agreed.[28]

Family politics came into play, too. On February 26, Pat made a pilgrimage
to Oddfellow Cemetery in Okolona, Mississippi, where at least a dozen Buchanans were buried—many of them former slave owners and casualties of
the Civil War. Pat's fourth cousin greeted him in the pouring rain and he laid
flowers at a monument to his family. Several townsfolk shook his hand and
called him "cousin." These were Pat's people, by blood. Later, at a rally in Tennessee, Buchanan spoke of two relatives who had died at Vicksburg and been
captured during the battle of Jonesboro.

"They both tried to overthrow the government of the United States," he
said. "They didn't. This time we're going to settle accounts for our ancestors in
dealing with the Yankees in Washington, D.C."[29] The southern heritage movement noted Pat's visit to the family grave and wrote up a rave review of the
candidate in *The Confederate Veteran*. His swing across the South was creating valuable pools of support for the future.[30]

Team Bush stuck to the line that Buchanan's message was right, but he was
the wrong messenger.[31] The Bush administration followed the paper trail and
dug up several quotes by Pat that read like extracts from *Mein Kampf*. Women
were "simply not endowed by nature with the same measures of single-minded
ambition and the will to succeed in the fiercely competitive world of Western
Capitalism." Feminists were "harridans." Homophobia was a "normal and natural bias in favor of sound morality." The voters were morally corrupt and "if
the people are corrupt, the more democracy, the worse the government." Most
controversially, in June 1990 Buchanan had written: "The Negroes of the 50's

became the blacks of the 60's; now the African-Americans of the 90's demand racial quotas and set-asides, as the Democrats eagerly assent and a pandering GOP prepare to go along. Who speaks for the Euro-Americans who founded the United States?"[32] There was worse. "The racial hazing of a black cadet . . . is played up as big," he wrote in 1988 after such a case hit the headlines. "Little mention is found, however, of the rapes of white coeds by black criminals."[33]

Buchanan laughed it all off and much of the press pack laughed along with him.[34] Among journalists, Buchanan was fast turning into the best assignment. With his "one piece of outrage a day" policy, he guaranteed them something to write about. They didn't even mind following him out into the wilds of northern Georgia, so long as the beer and the banter continued to flow. One reporter noted that, "There are two Pat Buchanans currently crisscrossing Georgia. One is the archconservative populist candidate who rouses rural crowds with his relentless bashing of the Washington establishment. The other is the television commentator who climbs onto the press bus afterward to analyze his own performance." So unusually self-aware was Pat that he would say something shocking at one stop, get back on the bus and chat with journalists about why he said it, how well it went down, and how they should write it up. He gave tips on good bylines. Some reporters felt guilty about how much they enjoyed the company of a man who discussed Japanese trade policy in faux-broken English. But then he delivered such excellent quotes: "I may not look natural up here, but I look better than George would," he said when he climbed onto a tractor at Joel "Bubba" Goolsby's peanut farm in Terrell County.[35]

Buchanan did look good. He had been denied a place on the South Dakota ballot, but 31 percent of voters in the February 25 primary voted for an uncommitted slate.[36] He also picked up his first significant establishment endorsement—Louisiana GOP chair William Nungesser, who warned "If we don't stand behind Pat Buchanan, we will lose the true conservative legacy of Ronald Reagan."[37] Then Buchanan scored his biggest goal yet. Bush conducted an interview with *The Atlanta Journal* in which he apologized for the 1990 tax increase. "I did it," he said, "and I regret it." He regretted it not for economic reasons—Bush still refused to admit the country was in recession!—but rather for all the "political flak" he was getting. He, of course, blamed the Congress. "I thought this one compromise, and it was a compromise, would result in no more tax increases ... And now we see Congress talking about raising taxes again." But for all these qualifications, nobody could deny that Bush had finally apologized.[38]

The President visited Georgia the weekend before the primary. He was a different candidate from the one who had trudged wearily through the snows of New Hampshire. Here the economic news was on his side and he was more open about his opponent's flaws. In Savannah, he attacked opponents who would "run from the new realities, seek refuge in a world of protectionism, or high taxes, or even bigger government." In Atlanta he smeared "those talking heads out there, the folks who don't seem to feel good unless they find something bad to say about the country."[39] It was probably working, but Bush's strategy was paradoxical. On the one hand he attacked Buchanan personally. On the other, he stole his best lines and ideas.[40] Across the South he talked about replacing welfare and aid to cities with a bipartisan effort to shore up the American family.[41] The crowds were big and friendly—12,000 came out to see him in Savannah.[42] In a play for humility, George and Barbara took dinner on Saturday night at the home of Georgia campaign manager Fred Cooper. The Secret Service personnel sat in the next room eating pizza while George cooked steaks in the kitchen. Fred Cooper excitedly told the press that the President "preferred regular sour cream for his potato to the low-cal brand," and that there were raspberries for dessert. Bush talked football with Cooper's kids until 9 p.m. Then, in a classic act of Bush oddness, he insisted on saying thank you and good-bye in the street, from inside his limo with the use of a microphone. Neighbors peered through their windows as the Coopers gathered around the car and listened to a disembodied voice thanking them for the raspberries. Then Bush sped way to a five-star hotel.[43]

On election day, Buchanan took one last whirlwind tour of the state aboard Asphalt One. The TV was showing a new commercial that accused the President of promoting affirmative action. An all-white crowd responded angrily to his 1991 Civil Rights Act while a doom-laden voice said, "George Bush has broken many promises, but the one that hurts the most is the one that steals hope and fairness from our children." News leaked out that there had been a massive increase in requests for Republican absentee ballots and registrations—particularly in the parts of the state that Buchanan had visited. "We had people call up and ask, 'If I vote Republican [today], do I have to vote Republican in November?' " said Billie Davis, a Catoosa County election official. "We tell them no and they say, 'OK, I think I'm going to vote Republican.' "[44]

The brigaders were in an Atlanta airport hotel when news came through of the result. Bush 64 percent, Buchanan 36 percent. A single point behind the New Hampshire result and big enough to show it wasn't a one-off. A Sousa march filled the air as people chanted, "Read our lips, no second term!"

"We're here tonight for the theater," said Fitzhugh Opie, a retail store manager from Decatur. "Pat's got the street fighters with him."

Paul Quarles of Elijay went wild when he heard Buchanan had carried his county. The retired business owner's wife said, "I thank God for Pat Buchanan; this campaign got my husband out of the house."

Pat came onstage and took the applause, his face beaming, wallowing in the frenzy. He compared his campaign to the Confederacy, promising, "The truth crushed to earth shall rise again . . . The battle of Georgia is now over, and it is won. The battle of the South now begins."[45]

For the second time, the press reported that Pat had thrown together a unique coalition. The Buchanan vote relied heavily on Democratic crossovers in rural parts of the state.[46] He won again among independents—by 58–42 percent.[47] Arguably, of all the elections he ever ran in, Georgia was Buchanan's finest hour. So big was his pull on independents and Democrats that, for the first time in history, more Georgians voted in the Republican presidential primary than in the Democratic one. There was a moderate southern Democrat running that year. But rather than protest the economic downturn by voting for Bill Clinton, many rural Democrats changed their party registration and voted for Buchanan instead. Buchanan even won Houston, home to Sam Nunn. Only conservative governor Zell Miller's endorsement of Clinton prevented a total sweep of the northern counties.[48]

Once again, Pat won without winning. The same day, Bill Clinton reemerged as the Democratic frontrunner by easily carrying Georgia. By showing he had a lock on Dixie he guaranteed that he would sweep the southern states on Super Tuesday and lead in delegates. In Colorado, maverick liberal Jerry

Brown eked out a surprise victory that proved he was a first-tier candidate. But Buchanan dominated the press. By replicating his New Hampshire vote he demonstrated that he had the capacity to embarrass the President all the way to the convention.[49]

South Carolina was next; Pat didn't make much of an effort there. He still outshone David Duke's flailing candidacy. On Friday, March 6, David Duke arrived in the state by commercial jet. He was greeted by a handful of admirers and barely a dozen journalists. Duke looked upbeat but resigned. He had been eclipsed by Pat. Most of his personnel had quit to work for Buchanan and he had just $58,000 in the bank. His organization consisted of people in other states with the money to pay for his air ticket to come visit.[50]

Local supporter Daphne Haught said Buchanan had "taken all Duke's ideas, and he doesn't have the stigma Duke has." Many racial nationalists liked Buchanan. "In one sense, Pat Buchanan can be viewed as a clean Duke," wrote the editor of *Instauration*. "Two Dukes are better than one." The anti-Semitic magazine *The Truth at Last* opined that Buchanan "could well become the leader who eventually leads the struggle to save America from Zionist domination." Duke supporter Sam Dickson told *The New York Times*, "I think they're appealing to the same fundamental concerns of the Euro-American majority, the concern about reverse discrimination, the concern about runaway tax and government, the concern about the changing demographics of the country."

But to some on the right, Buchanan was nothing more than a "shill" for the Jewish establishment. One Grand Wizard of the KKK said that the damage Pat did to Duke's campaign looked like a Jewish put-up job. Other white nationalists surmised that Pat was an instinctive racist but didn't realize it. They complained that he damaged the supremacist movement by appropriating its issues and stealing its votes but failing to identify the Jews as the real enemy. He was a distraction. The conclusion most on the racist right drew—given Duke's slide into obscurity—was that it wasn't worth identifying with either candidate.[51] "We're not supporting anybody," said Carl Franklin on behalf of the white supremacist group Aryan Nations. "They're all establishment; they're all basically anti-Christ."[52]

Many white supremacists voted for Buchanan. In 1996, some campaigned openly for him. But they didn't love him. Pat was too Catholic, too Republican, too clever. They would have preferred to stick with Duke, who had been with them from the beginning. But he was a busted flush. He had aimed too high too soon and now looked like an opportunist. Kenneth Knight, a former New Orleans police officer who coordinated volunteers in Duke's gubernatorial race, said, "I will always be a David Duke supporter, but come election day I'm going to cast my ballot for Pat Buchanan. Pat Buchanan has a better chance of winning than David Duke. Let's face it, David Duke is not going to the White House."[53]

The South Carolina primary was held on Saturday, March 7. Pat was wise to stay away: Bush took 67 percent to Buchanan's 26 percent. Duke took just 7 percent.[54] The press ignored the result but Pat Buchanan was understandably proud of what he did to David Duke. He felt Duke was a racist, that he gave conservatism and Republicanism a bad name. Thousands of people voted for David, Pat rationalized, because no one else addressed the problems that he addressed. But they never agreed with the racist logic behind his solutions. By offering an intelligent alternative, Buchanan brought those people back into the mainstream. Extremism often flourishes when conservatives shift to the center. Marginalization results when people feel ignored. By stealing his vote, Pat Buchanan made the Republican Party and orthodox conservatism relevant once again to the Deep South.[55]

As Super Tuesday approached, Buchanan leapfrogged from state to state. On the bus or on the plane, Pat sat with his typewriter on his knees bashing out the next speech for the next stop. He went wherever anyone would have him, the visits arranged last minute and through local fans. Bay had final word as to where they went.[56] One man who labored above and beyond the call of duty—and won a visit to his home state as a result—was Charlie Cipollini. Cipollini was a fifty-year-old math teacher from Massachusetts who drove up to New Hampshire every day throughout the primary to campaign for his man. He held aloft a big red and yellow homemade sign that read "Buchanan for President." The sign made it onto the cover of *Time* and *Newsweek*. "For hard core, you got Charlie," said field director Pat Mancuso. "Charlie is the essence of . . .

this campaign—the empowerment of the people who felt disenfranchised from the system." Cipollini was the eldest son of his first-generation Italian American parents, who taught him the value of "doing for himself." A teacher for twenty-seven years, the only person he admired above Buchanan was his mother: "She taught me everything. I know how to cook, I know how to sew, I know how to garden because of her." They lived together, independent of the state, surviving against the odds through sheer effort. And from that experience had come his philosophy: "If not him, why not everybody?"

Charlie wore a straw boater and a vague smile that belied a terrifying fanaticism. Campaign workers spoke in awe of his performance on New Hampshire primary day, when he spent twelve hours in the snow brandishing his sign. The wind chill temperature was below 30. "My hands were swollen for a week," he admitted. "And then I came down with pneumonia." But still he carried on. He got out of bed and arranged a rally in his home town of Fall River, Massachusetts. He threw it together himself; put up the bunting, did the advertising, went out of pocket to make sure people had transportation. When he got a call to say that Buchanan was fogged in somewhere in Mississippi and wouldn't be coming, Cipollini lost his cool. He rang up Mancuso and screamed into the phone. "I thought he was crazy," recalled Mancuso. "He said things to me that you wouldn't want to print." Charlie got on the phone and stayed on the phone, tearing a piece out of Mancuso every time he picked up. When he realized that Cipollini wasn't going to go away, Mancuso surrendered and put Pat on a plane up to Fall River. It turned out to be one of the best rallies they ever had, and Mancuso watched Cipollini in awe as he stood before the TV cameras and "lost 30 pounds just sweating, just sick as a dog, holding up that damned sign."[57]

But the enthusiasm of folks like Charlie couldn't overcome the mounting odds. In Georgia, Pat Buchanan picked up 40 percent of the vote of evangelical Christians. This was an impressive showing for a Catholic. But the organized religious right was committed to supporting the President. A week before Super Tuesday, Bush gave a good performance at the fiftieth anniversary meeting of the National Association of Evangelicals, a group that represented 4.6 million conservative Protestants from seventy-five denominations. He then sent out a letter to voters with an endorsement from Pat Robertson. The leadership of the religious right was not prepared to give up its influence in the White House for a candidate who most commentators said could not win.[58]

Running against growing odds, Pat hopped between Rhode Island, Mississippi, Tennessee, and Louisiana. The White House let it be known that it was prepared to concede Louisiana and Mississippi.[59] Bush was improving his performance on the stump. He swung through the South in a weeklong jaunt that culminated in a fishing trip to Alabama on the weekend. He took Gulf War hero General Schwarzkopf with him to beef up the patriotic theme.[60] His language—usually faux-folksy and inarticulate—was better scripted and full of conservative imagery:

> I learned a great deal when I was young from the greatest teachers I ever had, and that was my parents. And in church and in dinner and in political talks of my mom and dad, I learned that life means nothing without fidelity to principles. It's what I believed as a Navy pilot in World War II, as a businessman, and now as your President.[61]

Bush took his shirt off in the sweaty heat of southern Florida and got hoots of appreciation from the reporters. Next, he met the families of servicemen at a naval museum and posed in a torpedo bomber named after him. He swiped at isolationists and military budget-cutters. When it came to defense, he warned, "the next challenge may not come from abroad at all. The next threat may be a sneak attack by some congressional subcommittee."[62]

On Super Tuesday 1992, Pat Buchanan garnered roughly one third of the vote. His biggest totals were in Florida and Rhode Island (32 percent), his worst in Mississippi (17 percent). In Louisiana, presumed his best chance for first place, Bush took 62 percent and Buchanan 27 percent. Combined with Duke's total, the protest vote in Louisiana was a creditable 36 percent. But it was still far from a victory. Bill Clinton swept the Democratic primaries and looked set to win the nomination, although Jerry Brown wouldn't go away. Pat gave his response to the vote to a sparse crowd in Michigan.

> My friends, I know what the returns are saying tonight. But consider what we have accomplished in just three weeks. We have torn away one third of the Republican Party from the national establishment for good.

That was his dilemma. Pat was running too badly to win but too well to quit.[63]

FIFTEEN

The Message from MARs

S ome commentators called Pat the white man's Jesse Jackson. It was said in jest, but had a ring of truth. Buchanan was now a spokesman for conservative white males everywhere—Republican, independent, even Democrat. Pat looked at the returns from the polling stations and dreamed of building a new coalition of cultural traditionalists and economic populists, an alliance of nostalgiacs.[1] The brigaders wanted to go back to the world before Toshiba, Jane Fonda, and Lee Harvey Oswald. They wanted to bathe in the warmth of a perpetual summer of '63.[2]

But by the middle of March 1992, Buchanan was no longer the preferred champion of the little man. He had gone as far as he could in a contest that was stacked against him. Now, businessman Henry Ross Perot became the nation's leading revolutionary. Perot had made millions out of government contracts for his electronics business and moonlit as a problem solver. He helped put Texas's educational system in order and campaigned for the release of POWs in Vietnam.[3] In 1992 he agreed to be the front man for a "good government" ticket.[4] Perot went on *Larry King Live* and, in a move that captured the spirit of his campaign, refused to run unless people put him on the ballot themselves. "If you feel so strongly about it," he said, "register me in fifty states. If it's forty-nine, forget it. If you want to do fifty states, you care that much, fine, then I don't belong to anyone but you." The fact that he actually came off rather badly on TV (a dwarf with jug ears and a motor mouth) only played to his advantage.[5]

The national media ignored the King interview. The *Los Angeles Times* buried it in a three-page paragraph on page 18. *The New York Times* didn't mention it for three weeks. But to a growing mass of independent voters, the establishment's blessing was worthless. People wanted integrity—someone unblemished by power who could offer simple solutions to complex problems. Eccentricity wasn't a problem so long as you could put on a good show: This was the generation that got its views off *Donahue* and *Oprah*.[6] The day after his appearance on *Larry King,* Perot's phone system was overwhelmed with positive responses. He set up a toll-free number with thirty lines.[7] A few days later this was extended to one hundred, with voicemail for overflow. Perot gave a speech at the National Press Club and fleshed out his program. Stealing some of Buchanan's ideas, he offered political reform, a swift reduction of the deficit, and protectionism. The speech drew 70,000 mail and 2,000 phone requests for transcripts. He followed it with more appearances on *Donahue, 60 Minutes,* and *Larry King Live.* Still the newspapers ignored him. By May, they were finally forced to put his photograph on their front pages. A poll for *Time* magazine showed that Ross Perot led Bush and Clinton in the presidential race, by 33–28–24 percent respectively.[8]

What was going on? Pat Buchanan took credit. "I think our campaign in New Hampshire and the result . . . engendered the protest vote nationwide, certainly in the Republican Party," he told reporters. "It gave it shape and voice and direction and, secondly, it exposed the vulnerability of George Bush and the extent to which he had lost touch with his own party." Buchanan people showed up at Perot rallies. They sported Perot badges on the front of their cowboy hats and Buchanan badges on the back.[9]

Pat's friends said that he didn't represent a point of view so much as a social force. This force had been around for a long time; railing against immigration at the hair salon or throwing empty beer cans at the TV every time Ted Kennedy tried to socialize something. But it was Pat who brought these people to the polls, and it was a small body of intellectuals that tried to define what they felt and thought about the great crapshoot of American politics. Pat started to refer to this marriage of anger and ideas as the "Middle American Revolution."[10]

O f all Pat's buddies, the one most excited by his campaigns was columnist Sam Francis. Francis was a Protestant southerner who had worked for North Carolina senator John East before landing a job with *The Washington Times*. Physically, he was a fearsome toad. The journalist John Judis observed that, "he was so fat he had trouble getting through doors." He ate and drank the wrong things and the only sport he indulged in was chess.[11] The mercurial, funny, curious Francis was an unlikely populist. But he was ahead of the curve when it came to Pat's insurgency. Back in the 1980s, Francis had predicted an uprising against the liberal elite that governed America.[12] The only people who would break their stranglehold were the ordinary folks who made up the ranks of the "Middle American Radicals," or MARs. Mr. MARs was Mr. Average. He was either from the South or a European ethnic family in the Midwest, earned an unsatisfactory salary doing skilled or semiskilled blue-collar work, and probably hadn't been to college. He was neither wealthy, nor poor, living on the thin line between comfort and poverty. All it took to ruin him was a broken limb or an IRS audit.

But Francis argued that the Middle American Radicals were defined less by income than by attitude. To quote Francis, they saw "the government as favoring both the rich and the poor simultaneously . . . MARs are distinct in the depth of their feeling that the middle class has been seriously neglected. If there is one single summation of the MAR perspective, it is reflected in a statement: . . . The rich give in to the demands of the poor, and the middle income people have to pay the bill." Preferring self-reliance to welfare feudalism, the MARs were puritans. They felt that the U.S. government had been taken captive by a band of rich liberals who used their taxes to bankroll the indolent poor and finance the cultural revolution of the 1960s. The MARs were a social force rather than an ideological movement, an attitude shaped by the joys and humiliations of middle-class life in postwar America. Any politician that could appeal to that social force could remake politics in their own image.[13]

Two things made the MARs different from mainstream conservatives (and libertarians). First, not being rich, they were skeptical of wealthy lobbies. They hated big business as much as they hated big government.[14] They opposed bailing out firms like Chrysler, or letting multinational companies export jobs overseas. They were especially critical of businesses that profited from smut, gambling, and alcohol. Although free market in instinct, they did appreciate government intervention on *their* behalf. They would never turn down benefits like Social Security or Medicare.[15]

Second, the MARs were more revolutionary than previous generations of conservatives. Conservatives ordinarily try to defend power that they already control. But the MARs were out of power, so they had to seize it back. This was why conservatives like Buchanan behaved like Bolsheviks. "We must understand," wrote Francis, "that the dominant authorities in . . . the major foundations, the media, the schools, the universities, and most of the system of organized culture, including the arts and entertainment—not only do nothing to conserve what most of us regard as our traditional way of life, but actually seek its destruction or are indifferent to its survival. If our culture is going to be conserved, then we need to dethrone the dominant authorities that threaten it."

Buchanan agreed. He wrote, reflecting on Francis's words: "We traditionalists who love the culture and country we grew up in are going to have to deal with this question: Do we simply conserve the remnant, or do we try to take the culture back? Are we conservatives, or must we also become counter-revolutionaries and overthrow the dominant culture?" He concluded the latter.[16]

The populist counterrevolution that Francis proposed was not explicitly racial. In theory, Hispanic or black industrial workers were just as threatened by economic change and high taxes as their white coworkers. And the cultural values of Hispanic Catholics and black Pentecostals were just as challenged by liberalism as those of their white brethren.[17] But in Francis's view, these two ethnic groups had become clients of the liberal state. Their interests contradicted those of the Americans of European descent. Only political correctness—argued Francis—prevented whites from admitting this and organizing themselves into their own ethnic interest group. In this worldview, the Democrats gave handouts to African Americans in exchange for votes. Hispanics were brought in from Mexico to lower wages and break unions, providing cheap domestic labor for the ruling class and maximizing corporate profits. The only people without friends in high places were the middle-class white majority.[18]

Buchanan and Francis disagreed over this point. Like any paleocon, Pat was concerned about the decline of Western civilization.[19] But he never saw Western society in explicitly racial terms. He opposed both welfare and mass immigration, but he thought they hurt blacks and Hispanics as much as whites. There was a tension within paleoconservatism between the southerners and the Catholics, who worked from different reading lists. The Catholics looked to Plato and St. Augustine for authority; the southerners to Robert E. Lee and Strom Thurmond. Francis believed that human characteristics—including intelligence—were shaped by race. Defending the unique character of America depended on maintaining the white majority.[20]

Sam Francis said that Pat's candidacy had awoken the revolutionary spirit of the Middle American Radicals. But what was odd about this populist campaign was the amount of legwork that was done by intellectuals. One volunteer in the March 17 Michigan primary was the philosopher Russell Kirk. Kirk lived in his ancestral home of Piety Hill in Mecosta, Michigan—a tiny village that his industrious family built and owned. He wrote books in an old toy factory that had been converted into a mammoth library. Kirk was a genius. The author of thirty-two monographs and hundreds of essays and short stories, he was the intellectual godfather of the conservative movement. Russell Kirk married New Yorker Annette Yvonne Cecile Courtemanche in 1963. He was forty-two and she was seventeen. Together they had four daughters— Monica, Cecilia, Felicia, and Andrea—and became exquisite hosts at Piety Hill. They welcomed East European refugees, African kings, Republican statesmen, wandering philosophers, and vagabonds. Summer afternoons were spent playing croquet with Malcolm Muggeridge, Robert Graves, or Richard Weaver. Kirk greeted them all in his trademark three-piece suit and fob watch; coffee and cake in the garden, Schubert in the drawing room, tea and honey in the kitchen. At dusk, Russell told ghost stories.[21]

One day in 1992, Russell Kirk came home and told his wife that he had decided to become the Michigan state chair for the Buchanan for President campaign. Annette wasn't overjoyed: "I knew it meant I would do all the work." Because Russell lived independently of a university, he had to supplement his income with tours and speeches. Much of the week, he wasn't at home. So Russell became the state chair in name and Annette in person. A brilliant, fast-talking New Yorker, Annette loved the role. The kitchen at Piety Hill became campaign headquarters and "half my time was spent trying to keep weirdos out." Like everywhere else, they had no money and no organization. But unlike in New Hampshire and Georgia, they had no Pat Buchanan, either. In Michigan, the campaign took on a life of its own.[22]

Annette shared her workload with another academic—economist Harry Veryser. Donnish, monkish, and fiercely right-wing, Veryser was a powerhouse in radical conservative politics. He knew and loved the Middle American Radicals like family. The Michigan GOP was split between the industrialized East and the suburban West. The two worlds hated each other and Veryser, a traditional Catholic, was king of the East. Many of the GOP activists out East were members of the United Auto Workers union. These were ethnic Catholics who worked with their hands. George Bush represented the socially decadent world of the West—big money people who voted Republican for the tax breaks, but who wouldn't turn down a toke at a pool party.[23]

Pat Buchanan's Michigan campaign was run out of a philosopher's kitchen by an economist with an army of Catholic trade unionists. It was an extraordinary alliance between scholars and workers, but it reflected the spirit of Buchanan's paradoxical campaign. Pat thought he might win Michigan. Sam Francis fed his ambition. It looked like MARs territory, Francis said. The state was poor and getting poorer. Once an industrial metropolis, Detroit was a ghost town. Overregulation, bad management, and foreign competition were killing the motor industry. Across the state, unemployment was high—at 9 percent, well above the national average. A return to the economic nationalism of New Hampshire had the potential to score a hit.[24] Cars became the theme of the contest. Bush offered to veto fuel efficiency and environmental legislation that affected the cost of producing new automobiles. Buchanan accused Germany and Japan of "stealing America's markets." They were both "dinky little countries." Japan was just a "pile of rocks."[25]

During the primary, Harry Veryser arranged a meeting between himself, Buchanan, Francis, and Kirk. Of all the men at the dinner table, Kirk was by far the most intellectually respected. And yet, Pat ignored him. Buchanan and Francis behaved as if no one else was there, and Pat sat in rapt silence listening to his friend expand upon the coming revolution. It was an intellectual romance, said Veryser. Harry was embarrassed, Kirk was furious that he wasn't paid the attention he deserved. Both concluded that Buchanan was in love with Francis's mind, that he truly believed that the two men could remake the world.[26] The paleocons were always realists. But Francis was a true believer, and his zeal infected Pat. He gave to Buchanan's peculiar rebellion the theoretical structure of a popular revolution.[27]

Buchanan ran an ad that detailed the administration's cozy relationship with Japanese business interests. "Senior advisers to the Bush campaign work for auto concerns," it said as the names of officials Charles Black and James Lake were flashed across the screen. "No wonder Michigan has lost 73,000 jobs." Lake was a founding partner of a lobbying firm representing Japan Auto Parts Industry Association. Black was part of a team that lobbied on behalf of a Japanese seafood processing business. The Bush campaign was "beginning to emerge as a wholly owned subsidiary of Japan Inc."[28] Veryser's hard hats working on the ground loved language like that. As an economist, Veryser was skeptical about Pat's ideas on free trade. But he was pleased to see an isolationist message being sold effectively to men who flew the stars and stripes on their front lawns.[29]

The Michigan campaign was a return home for Shelley, too. Shelley was quiet and dignified on the trail—a throwback to an earlier age. She extended the logic of her private life into the campaign. At home, she was Pat's partner—she did the work and the research while he conveyed it all on camera. The media misunderstood this division of labor. Some presumed Pat was a Neanderthal sexist who wouldn't let his wife speak in public. Others thought that she hated politics and her silence was a protest. Women like Hillary Clinton and Barbara Bush had assumed political personas of their own. Whether assets or liabilities, the media expected them to talk openly and constantly about how great their husbands were. When Shelley refused to play ball, the press turned nasty. *The New York Times* said: "At rallies she sits demurely by her husband's side, her round face frozen in a smile, waiting for the cue that will give her her only public role in the campaign." The *Detroit Free Press,* which requested an interview and were insulted when she declined, wrote that she stood, "woodenly at her husband's side, smiling stoically, her hair frozen in time, her face set in marble, reminiscent of Pat Nixon, circa 1968."[30]

In fact Shelley was Pat's barometer of success. If he gave a speech that went well, she lavished praise. If he gave a speech that bombed, she would say, "That was lovely." It was all part of a subtle game the two played: Shelley was the only one who could tell Buchanan to his face if something had gone wrong, but she was always careful to protect her husband's ego. She understood how much it would hurt a man like Pat if his wife laid into him. So Buchanan would have to spend the rest of the day teasing the errors out of her, all of which she rehearsed in the nicest possible way: "Well, honey, you might have sounded a little bit too angry," or "You could have been a bit nicer about the Vice President."[31] When it came to questioning strategy, Shelley directed her comments to Bay. Bay then passed them off as her own to Pat.[32] That way the campaign was protected, but so was the marriage. In a manner more subtle than the press understood, the Buchanans really were the anti-Clintons.

Shelley was responsible for one gaffe. Team Bush discovered that Buchanan owned a Mercedes. In Michigan, owning a foreign car was tantamount to treason. "While our auto industry suffers, Pat Buchanan chooses to buy a foreign car," one Bush ad growled. It superimposed a Mercedes logo over a picture of Buchanan. "It's America first in his political speeches, but a foreign-made car in his driveway . . . Michigan has too much at stake to trust Pat Buchanan." In fact, the Mercedes belonged to Shelley; Pat drove a Cadillac.[33] Conceding that the gaffe had hurt him, Buchanan joked about it at a rally in Holland, Michigan. He introduced his wife to the crowd and said that she "has a used Mercedes to sell if anyone is interested."[34]

In Michigan, Buchanan discovered the limits of his populist message and the MARs revolt. Carried away by his success among blue-collar audiences, he wanted to concentrate on union halls and factories. Because many of his most fervent supporters were members of the UAW, he thought he had the union on side. Veryser told him he was wrong. Maybe twenty years ago the union halls would have welcomed Pat with open arms. But since then they had moved with the times and embraced affirmative action, gender equality, and even gay rights.[35] The UAW's membership might have been conservative and Catholic, but the bureaucracy was fashionably liberal.

Buchanan wasted time zipping from one end of the state to the other, talking to hostile or tiny audiences. He did barely any TV or radio. Pat should have hit Macomb County, a poor but conservative district of Detroit rich in votes. Instead, he tried to use a shutdown General Motors facility as a backdrop for his message of industrial decline. The local UAW branch refused to let him in. They heckled him, called him names as he stood in the snow shouting at them to "come out and talk to me." The workers were emotional and bewildered. The last thing they wanted was to discuss tax breaks with a wealthy TV commentator who owned a foreign car.[36]

There was another problem. Other candidates were turning on to Buchanan's message. Democrat Jerry Brown, the former governor of California, stole it wholesale. Brown was an eccentric politician who, after two terms as governor, had gone to India to discover himself. He returned preaching a new gospel of popular democracy. He entered the 1992 Democratic primaries calling for limits on campaign donations, pollution clean-up, and a flat tax. At face value he was a hippie in a suit. But Brown was also a Catholic and an ex-seminarian who shared much of Buchanan's conservative philosophy. He believed that America was living beyond its means, and that it required a spiritual reawakening to get it moving again.[37] Brown's religion might have been Vishnu and yoga, but he shared Buchanan's abhorrence for materialism and despised the "go for growth" politics of Clinton. Buchanan and Brown often met at the end of the day in TV studios. Paul Erickson bemoaned the fact that when they got talking, he couldn't stop them. "Pat and Jerry saw eye to eye on a lot of things," he sighed. Trade became one of them.[38]

Brown went to Macomb and addressed parents and pupils at an all-white school. He told the blue-collar audience that Clinton favored giving the President "a blank check, quasi-dictatorial authority, to go down to Mexico in secret with a lot of paid lobbyists and negotiate the export of American jobs, Michigan jobs." He said he opposed such trade negotiations and said they could cost "an additional 400,000 good-paying jobs." Brown's state organizer said, "The class issue—the fear that you'll be next, the hatred of the system—is overcoming the social issues." To make sure no one missed the point, Michigan's attorney general, Frank Kelley, an old-line Irish politician, stood behind the candidate, along with Art Blackwell, the president of the Wayne County Commissioners, who was black. "It's a nightmare, this state," said an observer, "and Jerry Brown can really draw the lightning. He's a pure protest candidate, a Democratic Pat Buchanan. He appeals to people who are mad at the rich guys."[39]

Stripped of the racism and ticking all the cultural boxes that modern Democrats needed to tick, Brown soaked up the labor vote. Buchanan sunk in the polls. There was a glimpse of how it might have been in Illinois, which held its primary the same day. Pat had written off the state and scheduled just one half-day visit.[40] The *Chicago Tribune* gave him a grand welcome. "Patrick Buchanan is not an alternative but a disgrace," it editorialized. "[He is] a loathsome boil on the body politic. Illinois Republicans would do their party and the nation a service by lancing the boil, rejecting Buchanan and his intolerance and isolationism."[41]

The reception he received was stunning.[42] Blue-collar Eastern Europeans remembered his uncompromising anticommunism and his call for the independence of Soviet satellites, and they loved him for it. He went to a Lithuanian national hall and attacked Bush for being too cozy with Mikhail Gorbachev. "I was ashamed that time of the behavior of my government and the leaders of my party," he said. The crowd, surprisingly big, roared with approval. Then he dropped in on a 400-strong Croatian gathering on the Northwest Side and slammed Bush's lack of support for an independent Croatia. The mob went wild and threw $10 bills at him. Somewhat dazed, Buchanan finally drove to an Irish pub on the South Side. The red-faced construction workers inside cheered him and pounded their fists in the air.

These were the people who Buchanan advised Nixon to go after in 1972. They were the men (and they were mostly men) who went for Reagan in 1980 and 1984. Anticommunist and religiously conservative, they were also under economic threat. Jobs were no longer for life. Their kids went to college now and trained to become accountants and lawyers, not fitters and machinists. The shops were full of foreign-made crap. Hucksters on Wall Street in fancy foreign cars made millions of dollars manipulating takeovers, while they tried to make an honest buck in a shrinking market. They had been undone by the Japanese, the liberals, and the vulture capitalists. Thrilled by their response to him, Buchanan returned to his people in Chicago on Saturday. He drew an overflow crowd at the Ukrainian Cultural Center. He attacked the death sentence that had been handed out to John Demjanjuk, the man accused of killing thousands of Jews at Treblinka. Bush should tell the Israelis to release "this innocent American citizen," he argued. Down in Illinois, Buchanan exploited ethnic divisions in a way that organized labor just wouldn't allow in Michigan.[43]

Bush walked the Illinois and Michigan primaries. In Illinois, he won 76–22 percent. In Michigan, he won 67–25 percent. Pat put the blame on Jerry Brown and said that he had siphoned off his votes. Certainly Brown commanded an unusual coalition that probably dented Buchanan's performance: He took a third of voters with union membership and a third of those with a postdoctoral qualification, giving him 28 percent to Clinton's 48 percent.[44] Buchanan had some good news. In Michigan, 71 percent of his voters said they liked him and 42 percent said that they could not vote for Bush in the general election. Buchanan's vote was narrowing, but it was more committed and this gave him leverage come the convention. Even though Pat was losing, the President still needed his endorsement to sew up independent and Republican conservatives.[45] So Buchanan would not stop.[46]

A fter Michigan and Illinois, Pat received a phone call from Richard Nixon's office. The Old Man wanted to see him. "I don't doubt that Nixon loved what Pat was doing," said one of Nixon's friends. "He loved to see someone stick it to the establishment."[47] The Old Man shared some of Buchanan's views on foreign policy, too.[48] Privately, he told a friend of Pat's that he didn't appreciate "some of the fatuous assessments of the New World Order emanating from many of the foreign policy experts who live in the Washington Beltway—the modern version of Plato's Cave . . . I feel strongly that the United States as the only complete superpower in the world today should play a positive role on the world scene. On the other hand, we have to bear in mind Frederick the Great's admonition—'He who tries to defend everywhere, defends nothing.'"[49]

The Old Man greeted his loyal boy at his home in New Jersey. Nixon had aged physically, but his mind was still young. "He was full of questions and jokes," remembered Buchanan. They talked for an hour, Nixon pumping Pat for gossip and opinion on the political situation. He played that old fugue again: "How is it on the campaign trail? What does Bush think of you? Will Clinton win the Democratic nomination on the first ballot? Will Perot run in November?" Everything was discussed, except the most important issue of all. Then Nixon fell silent. His aide, Monica Crowley, said, "It's probably time for you get out of the race. From now on, you can't win and you can only hurt Bush." Nixon smiled.

"I'm not getting out," said Buchanan. "I owe it to my people to carry on going." Nixon interrupted and changed the subject. "And that," concluded Pat, "was how he told me to quit the race."[50]

Afterward, Nixon basked in the attention of reporters and offered this: "I agree with [Pat] on some things and disagree on others, as was the case when we worked together. There's only one thing worse in politics than being wrong, and that's being dull. And Pat Buchanan is far from dull." Perhaps, after his years of service to a man with nothing left to lose, Pat could have expected more than an ironic compliment. But if you loved Richard Nixon, you had to learn to live with hurt.[51]

Team Buchanan decided to focus on North Carolina (May 5) and California (June 2). Bay had roots in California's ultraconservative Orange County and polls showed that local conservatives were unhappy with the Bush presidency. The campaign got a small boost when movie star Mel Gibson was asked about his politics in a TV interview and replied, "I'm a Pat Buchanan Republican." This came as no surprise to Bay. Like Pat, Gibson had a strict Catholic upbringing and was a critic of the modern Church. His father, besides being the 1968 *Jeopardy!* grand champion, was also self-publisher of the conservative periodical *Is the Pope a Catholic?* Bay remembered Mel's involvement this way: "I knew Gibson and his father liked Pat, and someone gave me a phone number . . . I left it with local people. I can't comment on whether or not he did anything." But two national campaign workers insist that he threw a fundraiser.[52]

With or without Mel Gibson's money, California proved too big to purchase much media in. So North Carolina looked like a better investment.[53] Pat thought he might find more of the MARs to stir up among the Tar Heelers. The decline of the textile industry meant that plenty of working-class Democrats and Republicans were hurting.[54] Plus he had some personal connections to the state. Both Sam Francis and campaign press spokesman Jerry Woodruff worked in the late senator Jim East's office.[55] One afternoon, Pat swung down south and hosted a fund-raising event in Raleigh. After the national press had left, conservative senator Jesse Helms and his wife appeared from nowhere. A lone local reporter caught the scene as Pat and Jesse said hello, Jesse embracing Pat with obvious warmth. This was not an endorsement, he said. But that wasn't how it was reported.[56] It was, wrote local journalists, "interpreted by many as giving a green light to North Carolina conservatives to support the insurgent Republican's campaign."[57] And many did. In two weeks, Tar Heelers gave Buchanan $30,000.[58]

The Confederate heritage people loved Buchanan. North Carolinian Boyd Cathey wrote Pat in November 1991 to pledge the support of his friends in the Sons of Confederate Veterans. He added, "as a traditionalist 'America First' conservative and a 'pre-Vatican II' Catholic, I take special interest in a Buchanan effort. Let us know what we can do, Pat. . . . My prayers are with you and Shelley. May the Lord and St. Patrick be of special assistance to you."[59] Bay Buchanan asked Boyd Cathey to serve as Pat's state coordinator.[60] Cathey was a little-known but influential player in Tar Heel politics. As editor of the *Southern Partisan*, the magazine of choice for Confederate standard bearers, he was able to give what amounted to an endorsement. He called Pat "the current leader of the conservative movement in America."[61] A former chair of the state Young Republicans and of the 1988 Pat Robertson campaign, he had plenty of contacts to call upon. But he also had history. Boyd called up Bay and said that there was something she needed to know. Boyd was once a member of the advisory board of the Institute for Historical Review. The IHR specialized in Holocaust denial and was widely regarded as an anti-Semitic hate group. Bay said nothing, so Boyd continued. The IHR contacted him in the late 1980s, he said, when they were searching for mainstream historians to give them some legitimacy. To lure unsuspecting academics, their letter of introduction failed to mention the Holocaust and focused instead on their revisionist views on the

Spinning Jenny and the Mongolian Empire. They also offered a dozen free books in return for a signature. Boyd, who was a sucker for freebies, signed up. He never went to a single conference and quit the organization when he discovered the truth.[62]

"If that's your story, I believe you," said Bay. And that was that. Boyd stayed on as state coordinator and his association with the IHR was never mentioned again.[63] Bay's behavior was typical of the Buchanans—loyal and trusting. And reckless. In 1992, they got away with it in large part because the media ignored North Carolina. In 1996, the campaign's willingness to turn a blind eye to the sins of its activists nearly killed it.[64]

Boyd helped Pat exploit a split in North Carolina's politics similar to the one in Michigan.[65] Conservative Democrats and Republicans disliked Bush and lapped up the challenger's populism.[66] So Pat picked up support from the old 1988 Pat Robertson organization, the state Christian Coalition, Concerned Charlotteans (with a mailing list of 10,000), and about 150 members of the powerful Congressional Club.[67] Noel Garrett—a former field representative for Helms in 1990—was appointed political director of the state campaign.[68] "This is a battle for the future of the Republican Party," Boyd told a local newspaper.[69] It was a battle between "Big Government vs. Old Right small (and responsive) government"; a campaign to force the Republicans to think about "the burdens of a tax and economic system upon the middle class, the lack of accountability, and the need for principled leadership for the future."[70] The Bush people gave as good as they got. State GOP leaders told Boyd he would lose his job if he worked for Pat. Helms had to step in to save him.[71]

North Carolina turned out to be a disappointment. The Congressional Club wouldn't give up its lists and Bay found the state too expensive to spend any significant amount of time in. It was forgotten in the dizzying first three months and when Pat finally turned up, the media no longer cared. But the press ignored the Buchanan effort at its peril. For a start, Buchanan was starting to hone a fresh message. He sent out to the mailing lists a leaflet describing a coming "Culture War," along with a taped speech. It was pure Sam Francis. Rich liberals in both parties were intent on destroying the livelihood and culture of ordinary Americans, he said. That's why, from now on, he was going to emphasize "hot-button" issues within the conflict: affirmative action, arts fund-ing, and immigration.[72]

The slower pace of campaigning gave Pat a chance to think more clearly about his message. It also gave him a chance to build a relationship with the men and women who would, in years ahead, become his loyal soldiers. He trav-eled the country, speaking to various right-wing groups, establishing himself as the effective leader of the conservative movement.[73] In April, Boyd put to-gether a big bash in Raleigh. The audience was full of good ol' boys in ten-gallon hats smoking $10 cigars. There was a lot of money in the heritage movement, in the pockets of the businessman patricians who spent their weekends hoisting flags and tending the graves of the war dead. They might not see Pat as a winner, but they appreciated the things he had said in Mississippi. They also appreciated his masculine wit. A glass of chardonnay in hand, he said that Ted Kennedy had been less than kind in his description of Pat's no-hoper campaign. "But I respect him," he confessed with a wicked grin. "I respect any fifty-nine-year-old man who still goes to Florida for Spring Break."[74]

It was all over when Jesse Helms became honorary chair of the Bush cam-paign. That signaled that the state's conservatives were falling in line behind the President.[75] On May 5, Buchanan barely polled 20 percent in the North Carolina primary.[76] Few people noticed the result. The press's attention was moving beyond the primaries and toward the general election. On the Demo-cratic side, Jerry Brown pulled off a surprise win in Connecticut in March and looked set to derail Clinton in the New York primary.[77] Then he said that he would consider picking Jesse Jackson to be his running mate. Jackson had once referred to New York as "Hymietown." Clinton swept the primary and looked set to walk the June primary in California.[78] But Brown had done plenty of damage to Clinton, who as the Democratic candidate would ordinarily inherit the antiestablishment vote. He forced Clinton to appeal to the party base and made him and his wife look sleazy. He played on claims that Bill had funneled contracts and money to Hillary's law firm while governor of Arkansas.[79] Ross Perot was still ahead of Bush and Clinton in the polls.

After North Carolina, Pat joined a one-mile "fun run" in Ridgewood, New Jersey. The reporter trailing him from *The New York Times* was cynical. The campaign was over, but Pat wouldn't stop running.

He dismisses last Tuesday's primaries in Arkansas and Idaho, in which Mr. Bush beat him, again, better than five to one. He chooses to ignore polls that indicate that in the contests on Tuesday, especially the much-watched California primary, he may fare even worse, given all the political attention now being focused on Ross Perot . . . He seems unconcerned that, of late, some Buchanan rallies have drawn as few as a dozen supporters and no reporters.

Pat would have nothing of it. "Not the point, not the point," he said. "I sent them a message." And he wasn't going to stop sending it. His people were already printing "Buchanan for President 1996" T-shirts. "More than anything else, my candidacy, my historic candidacy, has been aimed at moving our party back to the right, back to its roots." It was correct to say that he had forced Bush to rethink his economic policy and to reach out to cultural conservatives. But the long-term impact of his campaign upon the GOP wouldn't become obvious for a couple of years; nor would his claims that liberals were also stealing some of his language.

On the fun run, the reporter noted with pleasure that Buchanan "started last and finished last." But before he vanished, Buchanan said that "he *deliberately* started last and finished last because the news cameras were positioned at the back of the pack." It worked. Buchanan made the evening news and the morning papers.[80]

Pat wasn't through yet. A riot in California in April put his culture war back on the agenda.

SIXTEEN

The Culture War

On April 29, 1992, a mob of 300 people gathered outside a courthouse in Simi Valley, Los Angeles. Inside, four LAPD officers were cleared of assault against Rodney King, a young black man who, a year earlier, had been beaten while resisting arrest. When the officers left the court, the mob threw stones and punched and kicked the accused. News of the acquittal spread quickly. In South Central, young men threw rocks at cars. They dragged the drivers out and beat them on the street. The police were told to retreat for their own safety. The rioters set fire to South Central. The media flew helicopters over the smoking buildings to record the violence. They caught on camera a white trucker called Reginald Denny as he was pulled from his truck and beaten with blocks of concrete. A few streets away Fidel Lopez, a Guatemalan immigrant, was taken from his vehicle and his head smashed open with a car stereo. The crowd spray-painted his chest, torso, and genitals black. Lopez was rescued by a black minister who put himself between Lopez and the mob and said, "Kill him and you have to kill me, too."

The horror spread out to Westwood, where shops were burned and looted. The pack wandered downtown as the sky turned purple. They flipped a police car over outside City Hall and set fire to it. The ammo in its trunk crackled like fireworks. On the morning of the second day, the rioters turned their attention to Korean-owned shops. Without any police protection, the residents of Koreatown handed out guns and built blockades. There were open gun battles on the streets of Los Angeles—black vs. Korean and Hispanic vs. black. People hid in their homes. The power went off and the mail stopped. They kept the blinds shut and prayed for the mob to pass. A tearful Rodney King appeared on TV and said, "Can we all get along?" Finally, the mayor declared a curfew and troopers were airlifted in. President Bush denounced the "anarchy" in the streets. Four thousand National Guard troops entered the city on the third day. Bush told a TV audience that the "brutality of the mob" would not be tolerated. The riot was quickly suppressed and by day five was over. Fifty-three people had died. Nearly $1 billion was lost in property damage.[1]

Pat Buchanan visited Los Angeles shortly after the National Guard had restored order. "It was just terrible," he recalled. "There were upturned cars and broken windows. It looked like a different country." Pat said that the African American rioters should go to jail, but that Mexican immigrants also had to take responsibility for "coming into this country illegally and helping to burn down one of the greatest cities in America." His solution was to build a massive wall along the border to keep them out.[2] Some liberal commentators said Pat had a point. This was an interethnic war for jobs and money. Half the residents of downtown L.A. were born abroad and 40 percent spoke Spanish at home, while nearly half of all black youths were unemployed. Pat found that the black working class of Los Angeles was just as mad about the economy as the white Middle American Radicals up in New Hampshire.[3]

No one denied that the cause of the rioters' anger was police brutality and joblessness. But a debate raged over why they chose to riot rather than demonstrate peacefully. Local congresswoman Maxine Waters justified the riots as an "insurrection." It was the only way that poor people could get noticed.[4] But this explanation was unacceptable. The graphic nature of the violence, the targeting of Koreans—none of this horror could be satisfactorily explained as legitimate protest. It was vicious and criminal. The anger behind the riots was caused by economics. But, some politicians said, the riots themselves reflected a failure of values. They were the inevitable consequence of the cultural revolution of the 1960s.[5] Pat's culture war speech at the 1992 convention was the most famous example of this analysis, and it earned him bogeyman status on the left. But Buchanan only turned into poetry what many were already saying in prose.

On May 9, President Bush visited L.A. and gave a speech in South Central. He acknowledged that poverty and racism existed in America. But he denied that these justified the "purely criminal" acts during the riots. Nor was higher welfare spending the answer; nearly $3 trillion had been spent on fighting poverty since the Great Society. Instead, he argued, welfare had sapped the entrepreneurial spirit and tempted single moms to stay single lest their benefits be cut. The social experiments of the 1960s had encouraged nihilism and moral collapse.[6]

At the Commonwealth Club in San Francisco, Dan Quayle seconded the President's view that the riots were criminal acts. He said, "I believe the lawless social anarchy which we saw is directly related to the breakdown of family structure, personal responsibility, and social order in too many areas of our society." The problem partly lay with "a welfare system that encourages dependency and subsidizes broken families." But he also blamed the media for promoting 1960s values that ran counter to the social good. "I know it is not fashionable to talk about moral values, but we need to do it. Even though our cultural leaders in Hollywood, network TV, the national newspapers routinely jeer at them, I think that most of us . . . know that some things are good, and other things are wrong." He singled out a TV show called *Murphy Brown* in which a female character had chosen to raise a child alone. "It doesn't help," he said, "when primetime TV has Murphy Brown—a character who supposedly epitomizes today's intelligent, highly paid, professional woman—mocking the importance of fathers, by bearing a child alone, and calling it just another 'lifestyle choice.'"[7]

Some cried that this was a typical conservative response—blame the victim. But in the smoky after-light of the Rodney King riots, many Democrats agreed.[8] Presumptive nominee Bill Clinton said that while poverty was to blame for the anger of rioters, nothing justified their behavior. They looted because, "They do not share our values, and their children are growing up in a culture alien from ours, without family, without neighborhood, without church, without support." He, too, promised welfare reform that would put an emphasis upon punishing absent fathers and fostering work.[9] He said that government programs should "demand more responsibility from the poor."[10] In the middle of May, a rapper called Sister Souljah was asked to comment on the causes of the L.A. riots by *The Washington Post*. Imagining the thought process of young black men, she said, "If Black people kill Black people every day, why not have a week and kill White people?"[11] A few days later, at a dinner hosted by Jesse Jackson, Bill Clinton dropped the quote. Before the stunned audience, he said, "Her comments . . . were filled with a kind of hatred that you do not honor . . . If you took the words 'white' and 'black,' and you reversed them, you might think David Duke was giving that speech." Jackson was furious but Clinton went up in the polls.[12]

In the summer of 1992, there was a moment of consensus in America over the decline of the culture. Pat Buchanan's speech at the Republican convention in August brought it to an end. Buchanan and Clinton agreed that families were hurting, that kids weren't being raised right. But they disagreed on one key point: People like Pat blamed people like Bill for creating the problem in the first place.

In the June 2 California primary, Clinton knocked out Brown and Bush knocked out Buchanan. However, it was Buchanan who was celebrating, not Bush. Pat pledged to start afresh in November and fight for the 1996 nomination. Bush, he said, had won the battle "but not the war." The torch had been passed to Ross Perot. "We took on Mr. Bush first, showed them how it is to be done. Mr. Perot is saying we have to phase out foreign aid, and Japan and Germany maybe better start spending more on their own defense. It sounds familiar." The Bush people agreed. One insider said, "Pat made it legitimate to stand up and voice frustration . . . As he began to demonstrate that he couldn't beat Bush, the people he was energizing began to look elsewhere. They found Perot."[13]

Both Bush and Clinton looked at a California exit poll and shuddered. If Perot had been on the Republican ballot, Bush and he would have run even. If Perot had been on the Democratic ballot, Perot would have edged Clinton out. In the Ohio Democratic primary, held on the same day, Perot held a theoretical lead over Clinton of 46–35 percent. The L.A. riot had played a part in stoking voter anger. Among Democrats, six out of ten blamed the administration for the violence, seven out of ten wanted stricter gun control, and six out of ten wanted wider use of the death penalty.[14] And who were the Perot people? According to polls they were independent white males—the group that tended to favor Buchanan (and to a lesser extent, Brown) in the primaries. They were Republicans protesting Bush's economics and Democrats protesting Clinton's social liberalism.[15] Bush's people concluded that they were floating conservatives. They thought that they might win the Perot voters over with a fulsome endorsement from Buchanan.[16]

The strategy didn't run smoothly. The day after conceding the race, Pat dashed into a hospital for elective heart surgery. The announcement came as a big surprise. Pat had refused to share medical information with the press and kept his staff in the dark. He was suffering with angina. Pat didn't feel any of the symptoms and was advised that he could wait until the primaries were over. But the surgery was long and complex. He had his aortic valve replaced with an artificial valve at the Washington Hospital Center.[17] The week-long stay disabled him through to July. This put Bay in charge of negotiations.

When the primaries ended, Bay accepted a role as a pundit for *Good Morning America*. She reported live from the Democratic National Convention in early July. Bay witnessed the revival of the Democratic Party.[18] Clinton kept controversial speakers off the podium and focused on economics, while touting his moderate, New Democrat image. Clinton accepted his nomination "in the name of all those who do the work and pay the taxes, raise the kids, and play by the rules, in the name of the hardworking Americans." He talked about his difficult journey from the town of Hope, Arkansas—son of a single parent, son of the South. He extolled the virtues of hard work. He promised to crack down on men who abandoned their children: "Take responsibility for your children or we will force you to do so. Because governments don't raise children; parents do. And you should."[19]

The convention signaled that Clinton would focus on the economy in the fall election and open himself up to cultural conservatives. To emphasize the point, he invited moderate Tennessee senator Al Gore to be his running mate. Real conservatives screamed that the ticket was still pro-choice and pro-gay, but Gore's dull, southern, all-American image made it seem less so. Clinton might have dodged the draft, but Gore served a tour of duty in Vietnam.[20] At the end of the convention, Ross Perot withdrew his candidacy. He said that Clinton had cleaned the Democrats up and given voters a real alternative to Bush.[21] Suddenly the independent vote was back up for grabs. For the moment, it swung to Clinton. Bush wanted a piece of it, too.

While she was at the convention, Bay got a call from Bush's advisors to ask if they could meet to discuss Pat. Charlie Black and Jim Lake flew up to New York and they talked turkey. The polls showed that Bush needed Buchanan's endorsement. What was Pat's price? "We want a primetime speech," she said. And Bay was very specific about what primetime meant. Television coverage of the conventions had shrunk to one hour live a night. Given that one night would be the President's speech, one night the Vice President's, and one night the keynote (Jack Kemp, who didn't want to share the limelight), that left just one hour on the opening night. Two speeches of thirty minutes each would be crammed into that hour—so Pat was competing with many, many statesmen for a tiny slot of time. Nonetheless, Bay stuck to her guns. "We want a primetime speech," she said. Frustrated, the men left without a deal.

A couple of days later, Team Bush arranged another meeting with Bay at the RNC offices in D.C. Black and Lake put Bay in a room and asked her again what she wanted. "A primetime speech," she said. They disappeared into an adjoining room, made a phone call, came back, and said no. What about before Kemp, just before primetime? But Bay wouldn't shift. So they went back into the room and emerged once again. The higher powers still said no. But Bay wasn't moved by this mysterious display of clout. "We want a primetime speech," she repeated. And they sent her on her way.

Finally, Black and Lake called her back in late July. One of them sat Bay down and said, "Ronald Reagan's speaking on Monday night. Would Pat agree to speak before Ronald Reagan, in primetime?"

Bay thought, *Are they really* asking *me this?* She tried to look serious and said, "That sounds reasonable." She shook everybody's hand, doing her best not to laugh or shout with joy, and excused herself. She drove like a madwoman over to Pat's house and burst into the kitchen with the news. "You are not going to believe this!" she cried.

The deal was that Pat would give an unequivocal endorsement, praise the Reagan legacy, and attack Clinton. When the news broke, there was joy throughout the GOP. Said pollster Dick Bennett, "Buchanan will help win back that part of the protest vote made up of Republicans and more conservative Democrats that went first to Buchanan and then to Perot." Said pundit Lyn Nofziger, "Conservatives will read Buchanan's speaking at the convention as a sign that George Bush is beginning to recognize that conservatives exist and are of some value to the GOP. It's a major step in the right direction."[22]

The administration helped out with polls and tips on the right buttons to push. In that sense, the speech was written to order. But then, when they arrived at the convention, Charlie Black and Jim Lake asked to see a copy.

Pat refused. He was terrified of leaks, so much so that when he did a practice run-through at the Houston Astrodome, he didn't put it on the teleprompter and banned anyone from listening.[23] When he came to deliver it, aide Terry Jeffrey typed the speech in personally to make sure no one else read it. Finally Pat relented. He, Shelley, Bay, Greg Mueller, and Terry Jeffrey went over to the Bush trailer, parked behind the Astrodome, and handed it off to Jim Lake. Lake and some policy people worked over it in front of them. They made just one change. Lake called it "brilliant stuff." Later, when Jeffrey was alone in the trailer with the Bush advisors, he saw one of them putting the speech into a fax machine. Jeffrey demanded to know what he was doing. The man said he was sending it to President Bush. It came back with the words "Thumbs up!" written on it.[24] "The White House saw that speech," recalled Greg Mueller. "And they loved it."[25]

In the months that followed, as the convention started to look like a vote loser, Team Bush revised its opinion. White House advisors briefed reporters that Pat Buchanan had been allowed to "kidnap" the convention because they were so desperate for one man's endorsement.[26] Charlie Black said that he knew the speech was "too red meat" but that Buchanan's jealous guarding of it denied them the opportunity to edit. "Pat Buchanan was popular with about 30 percent of the country," he calculated. "But about 50 percent did not like him, particularly many independents and women." By having him speak, Pat brought home the conservatives and alienated the moderates.[27] But that's not what Bush's people thought, or said they thought, at the time.

· · ·

Houston in August was forbidding. According to Michael Kennedy of the *Los Angeles Times:*

> Most days here in the heat of August, thunderclouds roll in from the North. Lightning flashes. Rain pummels the ground. Then heat shimmers from the Earth. The feeling here in late summer—the heart of the hurricane season—is a mixture of sluggishness and unease. It is an unsettling time of the year. Now come the Republicans to renominate George Bush, and they may have unwittingly picked the perfect town to reflect their own mood.[28]

The Buchanan brigades waited for Pat in the lobby of his motel, along with TV cameras and amused journalists. Chip Cipollini was there with his sign, scanning the road anxiously, looking for the candidate. "I've been a supporter since the draft-Buchanan movement in November," he was saying when suddenly the car pulled into view. There was a mad dash for the man, reporters and delegates tripping over each other to reach him. They scrummed around.

"No speech until Monday," Pat said. He pushed his way inside, shook a few hands, and disappeared. Cipollini was left out on the road, still holding that sign, looking forlorn. He didn't even get a handshake.

"This was never just a campaign," an earnest young man told a reporter. "This was a movement. This was a middle class revolution."[29] He handed over a card with Pat's new phone number: 713-923-1996.[30]

The speech on Monday night was apocalyptic. Pat laid into the Clintons and their fellow travelers—the feminist, gay liberation, pro-choice people who made up the rank and file of the Democratic Party. "There is," he said, "a religious war going on in our country for the soul of America. It is a cultural war, as critical to the kind of nation we will one day be as was the Cold War itself." It was a tough message, but it did exactly what Pat had promised. It raised doubts about Clinton and rallied the conservatives. Before the convention, Clinton led Bush 52–35 percent. After the convention, Clinton led by just 45–42 percent.

The President led among men by 47–41 percent. The leap came the day after Buchanan's speech, and before Bush's.[31]

The first TV reviews were ecstatic. David Brinkley: "It was an astoundingly good speech." Hal Bruno: "I've never seen a better first night." Sander Vanocur: "Viewed in terms of classic raw rhetoric, that was the most skillful attempt to remind the party faithful of the role that ideas have played in American politics since Eugene McCarthy nominated Adlai Stevenson at the 1960 Democratic convention." Ted Koppel: "They walked out of [the convention] tonight enthusiastic, they walked out of here with something the Republicans have not had for quite a few months, a sense of optimism."[32]

The Bushes seemed to like the speech. The mood in the box, where Shelley sat next to Barbara, alongside the President's son, George, was electric.[33] At a party afterward, the President was happier than he had been for many months. He congratulated Buchanan and thanked him for all his work. And while Pat's rhetoric stood out in eloquence and tone, its message was far from unique.[34] Pat Robertson said Hillary Clinton was out to "destroy the American family." Dan and Marilyn Quayle agreed. At the podium, Marilyn contrasted herself with Hillary Clinton. She said of the 1960s: "I came of age in a time of turbulent social change. Some of it was good, such as civil rights, much of it was questionable. But remember, not everyone joined the counterculture. Not everyone concluded that American society was so bad it had to be remade by social revolution."[35] Even President Bush joined in when he asked for an America that looks a lot more "like the Waltons and a lot less like the Simpsons."[36]

But Bay sensed that the party moderates were uncomfortable with the tone, and that they were plotting to fight back. "It started as a squeak and ended as a roar . . . The media brought all the moderates onto TV and asked them what they thought of Pat's speech. Of course, they hated it. And a speech that saved the administration suddenly hurt it."[37] While Pat and George were sipping cocktails and congratulating each other, disgruntled Republicans lined up outside the network boxes for interviews.[38] They kept good company. Rumor had it that even Ronald Reagan was upset with the speech, that he particularly didn't like the gay bashing.[39] Barry Goldwater said the platform positions on abortion were wrong. Pro-choice people wandered the floor in search of cameras, wearing "Barry's Right" buttons.[40]

The next day, conservative columnist George Will wrote:

> The crazies are in charge. The fringe has taken over. The social is-
> sues were a source of strength to the Republicans when they
> seemed to be supporting the mainstream moral concerns of most
> Americans . . . But morally concerned Americans do not want the
> AIDS menace to go unchecked while Pat Buchanan calls it the ho-
> mosexuals' punishment . . . These are not people who read the
> Book of Revelation as condemning the New World Order. They are
> not wild-eyed figures from the fringe that Mr. Bush is now reduced
> to courting. No wonder the Republicans must beg people to come
> into their shrinking tent. The fringe on that tent's entrance is for-
> bidding, and the tent is becoming mainly fringe.

In just twenty-four hours, Pat went from the voice of the people to right-
wing nut.[41]

The story of Houston was turned on its head.[42] At the beginning of
the convention, Pat was the hero who brought the conservatives home to
Bush. By the end of the week, he was a prowling Nazi ape who had set back race
relations in America by thirty years. In the general election, Clinton used Buchanan to bash Bush. He said that while America was hurting, the Republicans
were obsessing about helpless minorities. Pat's speech was run and rerun by the
media throughout the fall, with unflattering close-ups to his arm chopping the
air and his mouth curling into an angry "O."[43] The press decided that it had
enough of beating up on Clinton and gave him a free pass through to election
day. It overcompensated after the inauguration.

Bush lost in a 43–38 percent defeat. Ross Perot, who dropped in and out of
the race, reentered at the last minute and took an impressive 19 percent. Some
Republicans blamed the result on Pat. Pat blamed the Republicans.[44] "America
was still basically conservative and Clinton was too liberal," he said years later.
"Bush went up in the polls when he hit Clinton on his past and on the social
issues."[45] The President's tax hikes had lost the GOP the vote of anyone worried

about the economy. But, said Buchanan, there was still a middle-American majority out there that distrusted the Democrats and that could be mobilized by issues like abortion and gay rights. The biggest problem was Perot.[46]

"Perot's voters were really our people," said one of Pat's workers. "They were independent conservatives who Bush lost when he raised taxes. Put the Perot and the Bush vote together and you've got a majority . . . The challenge was to win back Perot's people. And that required a new message . . . I don't think the Republican Party was quite ready for it though."[47]

SEVENTEEN

Hunting the Clintons

A t fifty-five, Pat Buchanan was finally a statesman in his own right. All his life he had played wingman to great men; now he was the master of his own destiny. The responsibility liberated him in some ways; there was no need to compromise, or nurse the vanities of another man. But life at the top could be lonely. He lacked a team of equals to kid around with, to share the burden of defeat and the indignities of modern politics. His family was smaller in number. Brother Bill died of cancer in 1986. Pop passed away in 1988. Bay, who had divorced her husband and raised two kids single-handedly, moved their mother to a nearby home so that she could care for her. Ma passed away in 1995. The funeral was held at the Blessed Sacrament in Washington. The church had changed dramatically since the 1950s, when Pop had taken Pat there to pray for all those terrible sins committed in the night. There were fewer Irish, more Hispanics and African Americans; posters on the walls promoted peace groups and gay rights; and the priest told journalists that the parish was considerably more "progressive" than it had been in Buchanan's day. Pat took one look at the tiny, elderly prayer group who had come to mourn his mother, and he broke down in tears. "All these people I've known over the years," he said. "A lot of people accuse me of living in the past, but if you'd been there, you'd understand." Shelley held him.[1]

There were still plenty of siblings to drink a beer with, and to recall those

golden summers of the postwar years. Hammering Hank was now an accountant, Kathleen the secretary to columnist Robert Novak. "But the family was
very compartmentalized," remembered a friend. "They didn't like to impose
themselves on each other."[2] The Buchanans had no children. "I think it's probably the great, unspoken tragedy of Pat's life," said another friend. "He would
have made such a wonderful father." She once asked Pat why he never adopted.
He quoted C. S. Lewis in response: "You play the hand God dealt."[3] The 1996
presidential campaign became the Buchanans' family, and the young people
who surrounded them their children. To Greg Mueller, "Pat was a sort of adopted father. He and Shelley were so kind and gentle . . . He taught me a great
deal, about how to write and how to get a point across. He was incredibly patient and never got angry. And he was always there for us."[4]

After the presidential election, Pat threw himself into his work—talking,
campaigning, writing, speechifying, electrifying the right with his magnificent wit. And with Clinton in the White House, he had plenty of material. It
took just one month for the public to turn against the new president. The press
unearthed a land deal called Whitewater, and whispers slipped from the White
House that the Clintons were renting out the Lincoln bedroom in exchange
for campaign donations. Tabloid headlines screamed "thief" and "adulterer."
Nothing in the Clinton epoch seemed sacred; nothing was beyond exposure
and destruction.[5] At his home in New Jersey, Richard Nixon dictated a jeremiad to Bill Safire. It is the age of the "non-incumbent," he said. "People want
change. Clinton asked for it; now the country is going to demand it."[6]

Clinton's first U-turn was on tax cuts. In the campaign, Clinton had promised a middle-class tax cut but, in office, forecasts showed that reducing the
budget deficit was more important. The legislation he sent to Congress contained
just one ambitious social program (a national service corps for young people)
and a hefty tax rise. The new Republican Minority Leader in the House—Newt
Gingrich—called it a liberal, big government budget. Pat Buchanan hated it so
much that he threatened to sue the administration for earnings lost.[7] It only
passed the House by two votes. In the Senate, Vice President Al Gore had to
cast the deciding vote. The battle over the budget left an enduring image of
incompetence and broken promises.[8]

President Clinton also set up a task force, headed by his wife, on the subject of healthcare reform. It produced a proposal that was 1,000 pages long, naive, and bureaucratic. After a sustained attack funded by the healthcare lobby it died in Congress.[9] The fiscal conservatism of the budget and the liberalism of the healthcare plan confused voters. Clinton's brains trust tried to keep him on both sides of every issue, reaching for the center ground. But it seemed cynical, and Clinton's failure to pull it off made him look inept.[10] "All my life I had but one prayer," said Buchanan quoting Voltaire. "That God might make my enemies look ridiculous—and God granted it. The Clintons' problem today is not just that they look venal, but that they look ridiculous. . . . They are the Jim and Tammy Faye Bakker of American liberalism."[11]

Pat opposed the Clinton healthcare plan. But he didn't feel it was the biggest issue facing the nation.[12] While the GOP leadership chose to attack Clinton's "big government agenda," Pat allied himself with disaffected liberals to challenge the one area of policy in which the Republican leadership agreed with the White House: free trade.

The Clinton years are popularly remembered as an era of remarkable economic growth. But they were also a period of difficult transition. With the end of the Cold War, things were going global. It became cheaper for companies to make goods overseas in countries with low wages and taxes, package them there, and sell them off in the West. "Offshoring" was great for business. It shrank costs and increased profits. The American consumer benefited from lower prices and took out loans to buy more.[13] The market became awash with cheap, shoddy goods—many of them sold in faceless malls that sprung up on the outskirts of towns and cities. Family merchants all but disappeared. Walmart was king—offering aisle upon aisle of plastic necessities.[14] The stock market soared. And Clinton fed the beast with free trade deals, tearing away the last remaining barriers to disinvestment from the U.S. economy. American industry was auctioned off, piece by piece.[15]

The theory was that while the developing world would make things, a well-educated American workforce would design and sell them. Many new jobs were created, but they tended to be underpaid or full-time equivalent. Benefits were minimal and much of the service economy involved wiping tables and mopping floors. The Clinton administration changed the way the Department of Labor calculated employment figures to count part-time jobs as full-time work. The massaging of figures hid a human cost. Given increases in taxes, college fees, and medical bills, people were actually working harder for less.

America had been hemorrhaging manufacturing jobs since the 1970s. Free trade deals sped the decline. Factories shut down and went south to Mexico, where wages were cheaper. Lumberyards and paper mills closed and went north to Canada, where the tax and regulatory burden was lighter. Places became ghost towns as people moved out to find better work. Those left behind got little in the way of welfare thanks to declining tax receipts. Crime and drug use soared.[16]

In California, one in three aircraft engineers were fired in the 1990s. Forty-seven-year-old Robert Muse told a journalist that he used to make planes for $20 per hour. Now he worked half the time for half the pay as a maintenance engineer for the state—cutting tree branches and unclogging toilets. His union hall was empty; his workshop was gone. He used to get medical benefits and a generous pension. Then a kid half his age in a suit walked into his office and announced that they were moving production overseas. "Even if you work for nothing," he said, "you're still too expensive." Now Robert Muse got certificates for good attendance at work and a free transistor radio. He used to be one of the blue-collar elite, a craftsman. "The cellophane on a cigarette pack is four times thicker than the margin for error on some airplane parts," he recalled with pride. "There was a feeling of, 'I'm doing my job, and I'm doing a good job. So why should it ever go away?'" But now he spent his free days watching daytime TV and drinking cold beers, dreaming of an America that had slipped through his fingers.[17]

A buy American craze swept the country in the early 1990s. Walmart covered its stores in stars-and-stripes motifs and "Made in the USA" signs. The signs were placed in several instances over imported products, but that wasn't the point. A book called *The Patriotic Consumer: How to Buy American* became a bestseller. It offered a guide to every room in the house, with charts detailing the origins of several hundred products. Crafted with Pride, a patriotic textile promoter, enjoyed a $15 million advertising budget and the Made in the USA foundation had 50,000 individual members.[18]

Fears about free trade created an unusual, bipartisan alliance. Shortly after his inauguration, Clinton made it clear that he intended to send a slightly modified version of the North American Free Trade Agreement to the House. NAFTA, which had been originally negotiated by President Bush, would eliminate more than one half of import restrictions on goods coming from Mexico, and one third on goods going the other way.[19] Within ten years, all tariffs would be eliminated, except on agricultural products. Liberal Democrats were furious. Activists like Jesse Jackson and Ralph Nader called for the House to reject NAFTA and free trade agreements on principle.[20] In the House, Democratic Majority Whip David E. Bonior declared he would fight against it. Bonior was from a deprived part of Michigan. He had watched enough American jobs go south of the border under Bush and Reagan. He wasn't about to sacrifice yet more.[21]

An irate Ross Perot went back on the talk show circuit. On NBC's *Tonight Show* he showed a photograph of Mexicans living in cardboard shacks and said that was what America would look like in five years' time. He said 5.9 million jobs would be lost if NAFTA was signed and they would all hear a "great sucking sound" as they went south.[22] A few nights later, Al Gore and Ross Perot went head-to-head on *Larry King Live* to debate the treaty. Things got ugly. Perot charged that the agreement was the work of high-paid foreign lobbyists "wrecking this whole thing." Gore called him a hypocrite. The Vice President said Perot had tried to get the House Ways and Means Committee to approve a tax break for his own business in the 1970s. By the end of the night, it looked like Gore had won. He stayed on message about America's ability to compete in a changing world. Perot was flustered and personal. The Brylcreemed, preppy Gore represented the future. Perot spoke up for the past.[23]

The coalition of labor, Perot, and Pat Buchanan was unexpected.[24] Pat loved the idea of a nonpartisan alliance and described it romantically as a coalition "of blue-collar workers and America-Firsters, of black laborers and small businesses, of populists and Perotistas."[25] Covering a "comical and portentous" anti-NAFTA rally, a *Wall Street Journal* writer reported:

> An unemployed Perot sympathizer passed out the "Special NAFTA Issue" of *The Spotlight,* published by the paranoid Liberty Lobby.

Another Ross backer who works for Federal Express . . . told me he opposes the treaty because it is a "step toward One World," under the Trilateral Commission. A third was toting one of the AFL-CIO's "Don't Send My Job to Mexico" placards though he owns a non-union construction company . . . The augury was that . . . trade fears bond Americans who share nothing more than a dread that their country is not itself anymore. Unionists have felt this way for years . . . but to their numbers have been added a wide swath of white-collar America. Now this new mass, or perhaps new majority, is pitted against what it sees as a corrupt elite presiding over the ruin of their land.

"Exactly," Buchanan replied. He argued that free trade had turned liberals into sovereignty-conscious conservatives and conservatives into compassionate human beings.

The men at the rally were instinctively right: It is about losing America, the country we grew up in, the country we love, where the first duty of government was to look out for Americans, not just those with the skills (technical, financial, and lingual) to prosper in the new economy. Behind the rising spirit of rebellion in this land is a gathering consensus that the nation's elites do not give a damn about the old republic.[26]

On August 26, Buchanan held a press conference to denounce NAFTA. He assailed labor and environmental side agreements as infringements on American sovereignty and bribes to the Mexican government. He had a point. The U.S. government committed $6 billion to clean up the Mexican side of the border, where factories operated without pollution regulations. "Why should the American people be responsible for the cleaning up of the pigpen that the Mexicans have made?" Buchanan asked. It was an unusual first shot in the coming presidential race: Pat opened with a plug for labor and an attack on the Republicans in Congress. Facing union resistance to the treaty, Clinton was counting on bipartisan support from the GOP. It was working. Jack Kemp and Senate Minority leader Bob Dole came out in favor of NAFTA.[27]

Buchanan's criticism of free trade went further than ever before. He attacked the materialism of modern conservatism, its heartlessness: "To some on the right, economics seems the be-all and end-all of existence. If in their econometric studies of jobs lost and jobs gained, NAFTA comes out of the computer a net winner for the U.S., then it ought to be approved—and where is the argument?" He quoted, as an alternative, from *A Humane Economy* by the European Christian democrat Wilhelm Röpke:

> The market economy is not everything. It must find its place in a higher order of things which is not ruled by supply and demand, free prices and competition. It must be firmly contained in an all-embracing order of society in which the imperfections and harshness of economic freedom are corrected by law and in which man is not denied conditions of life appropriate to his nature.

"This is a sentiment of the paleoconservatives fighting NAFTA," said Buchanan. "It would seem more consonant with Christian tradition."[28]

On the night of the NAFTA vote, lobbyists from both sides descended on Washington. The lobbyists in favor of passage took over a room on the first floor of the Capitol building, an elevator ride away from the House debate. Weighty quotations ("We Defend and We Build a Way of Life Not for America Alone, but for All Mankind") were inscribed above every door. A television was installed. Cellular telephones were everywhere—not clunky low-rent models, but the teeny ones that folded to the size of lemons. People carried about gift neckties with buttons attached, reading "Don't tie the economy in knots." By contrast, according to one reporter, the lobbyists against passage squatted in "the spectacularly ugly Rayburn House Office Building, in a barren hearing room of the Education and Labor Committee. It was two elevators, a subway and a long walk from the House debate. The dress was union-label, inexpensive suits and nylon jackets inscribed with numbers and insignias of various locals. There was one telephone, decidedly not portable, and basic black. That fit the mood."

The debate was passionate and close—far too close considering that the President's party enjoyed a comfortable majority. The fracas hit its low point at 7 p.m., when Greenpeace activists entered the lobby and threw faux-$50 bills down on the representatives. "The only thing free about NAFTA is the amount of money passed around Washington to pass it," said Democratic representative James Traficant of Youngstown, Ohio. It finally passed by a vote of 234–200. The ayes included 132 Republicans and 102 Democrats. Democrat Marcy Kaptur, an opponent from Ohio, wept as the result was read out. Republican Robert H. Michel joked, "Think of the three most famous nonelected opponents of NAFTA: Ross Perot, Pat Buchanan, and Ralph Nader—the Groucho, Chico, and Harpo of NAFTA opposition."[29] But the coalition for the bill was just as unusual as those against it. It wouldn't have passed without the support of Newt Gingrich and Bob Dole.[30]

Buchanan wrote:

> In the end, they had to buy it. In the end they won the bidding war, not the battle for hearts and minds. All week long we were witness to an astonishing spectacle—the open selling of America by men and women entrusted with her governance. For 72 hours Congress was like the "pit" in the Chicago commodities market when word hits that the corn harvest will be 20 percent smaller than expected. It will be a long time before the stench of bribery leaves the Capitol building.[31]

The vote tally indicated that Clinton had exhausted the goodwill of party liberals. But Pat also found significant splits in the Republican ranks.[32] Polls showed that support for free trade fell among Republican voters during the row over its passage. Perot had lost the debate against Gore, but many conservatives thought he had won the argument. The champion of middle-class populism gave Buchanan's own position legitimacy within the Republican base.[33] There was a generational change taking place. Older Republicans were steeped in the Cold War internationalism of the 1940s and 1950s. Younger Republicans were more worried about jobs. Only 22 percent of House Republicans over the age of forty voted against NAFTA. But 42 percent of Republicans aged forty and under did so. The politics of trade was infecting the Republican ranks.[34]

In 1993, Pat Buchanan founded a group called The American Cause to act as a front for a second presidential campaign. Bay served as president, Shelley as vice president, and the staff comprised regulars from the 1992 campaign.[35] The Cause was designed to publicize Pat and enlarge his list of donors. But he also tried to use it to stir up debate about America's cultural decline. Although the press ridiculed him as a philistine, Buchanan's campaigns were remarkably literate. The Cause's first big meeting brought together "some of America's finest writers, artists, scholars, and grassroots activists" to discuss "ways and means of 'Winning the Culture War.'"[36] One of America's greatest living sculptors—Frederick Hart, who contributed to the Vietnam War Memorial—gave a talk on the failings of postmodernism. The meeting pushed the message that all Americans—black, white, rich, and poor—suffered when culture declined. There was Michael Medved, a Jewish critic of Hollywood; a woman who served as a school board president in Queens, New York; and Ezola Foster, an African American teacher who had been raised on welfare.[37] Sitting in the audience, Sam Francis "grumbled all day" about Pat's newfound "inclusiveness." He whispered to philosopher Paul Gottfried, "I'll bet they eat this up at *The Washington Times*."[38]

The American Cause's goal was about protecting middle-American jobs and culture. Sam Francis reasoned that the two were linked, that people who worked with their hands were God-fearing patriots, too. The success of Perot in 1992 showed there was a new coalition of people under assault by the careless capitalism of the liberal elite.[39] Pat agreed. It was time, he said, for a "new conservatism . . . not about any ideology or paradigm of empowerment. It is about old things, the permanent things—about a moral vision of man rooted in the Judeo-Christian revelation and 2,000 years of Western history."[40]

Pat's activities on foreign policy, trade, and culture caught Nixon's attention. The Old Man would still call him for gossip from time to time. Buchanan recalled: "Even though he was not in that battle at all, he was very interested in it . . . because there was something going on in society and politics. I've never seen someone who was more consumed with—with politics and issues and ideas and personality and gossip. He loved gossip. 'Tell me about this, Buchanan. What is—what's happening? What do you hear there?' "

In early 1994, Pat hadn't heard from the Old Man in a while, so he called his house in New Jersey and suggested they meet. "And he said, 'Well, look, I'm coming down to the square'—over in Washington Square, this little hotel. And he would call me up and I would go in there and be in there for an hour or ninety minutes, and he would come in and he would exhaust all the information you had about what's going on in the White House, who's up, who's down. 'What—what are they doing here? What do the conservatives think?' And I called him up there, and he said, 'Let's do it again. I'm gonna be down soon, I think in about a month.' And it was either that day or the next day that I heard he had a stroke."[41]

The Old Man passed away on April 22, 1994. Even at his funeral, politics came first. Bob Dole won the chance to deliver the big eulogy. The media reported that he looked and sounded like the frontrunner in the coming presidential nomination race. Pat wore a "Nixon Now" badge. Clinton, Bush, Reagan, Carter, and Ford were there, along with several Watergate celebrities. It was a crowd only Richard Nixon could pull: a queer mix of presidents and ex-cons.[42]

P at Buchanan's American Cause was a joke to the Republican leadership. They read the public mood differently. In the 1992 election, they said, the GOP had become the nasty party. That a reprobate like Clinton could beat a war hero like Bush showed that voters were far more concerned with money than morals. Christianity was now a vote loser.[43]

Moderates started a fight back against the conservatives.[44] The chair of the Oregon GOP threatened to form an independent state branch free from the religious right. "I can't tell you how many people deserted this party in the last election," griped Craig L. Berkman. "We have simply got to take the party back from the mean-spirited, intolerant people who want to interject big government into people's personal lives." He was thinking of an effort by the Oregon GOP to pass a ballot measure to classify homosexuality as "abnormal and perverse." A similar battle raged in nearby Washington, where the Republican governor took on a state GOP that wanted to ban witchcraft and yoga.[45]

It was a question of where the GOP should place its emphasis—on tax cuts or moral values.[46] The departing Republican national chair, Richard N. Bond, gave a startling speech that set the tone for the battle to come. In front of an audience of party moderates, he said that Republicans should end their opposition to abortion and "not cling to zealotry masquerading as principle." They gave him a standing ovation. He singled out Buchanan as an example of where the party went wrong in 1992. He regretted his failure to stop him from getting primetime coverage at the convention, repeating a myth often invoked by moderates that Pat had somehow hijacked the convention. "America is getting more diverse, not more alike," he said. "And our job is to recognize this change and offer platforms and candidates and policies that reflect changing times."[47]

Republican moderates said that the GOP was a broad coalition of groups that benefited from smaller government. They might disagree on how they wished to live their lives, but their mutual taste for lower taxes and balanced budgets ought to hold them together. They saw the Republican Party as a "Big Tent." Gay or straight, all decent Americans who wanted safer streets and lower taxes were welcome within. Even pro-choice Republicans like Massachusetts governor William Weld were celebrated as vote getters among the Democrats. "I have a hard time taking people like Pat Buchanan seriously," Weld said, "when he talks about spreading individual freedom abroad but is seemingly contemptuous of it here at home."[48]

The Big Tent Republicans took their lead from Bill Clinton. Clinton might have made a mistake when he tried to lift the ban on gays in the military, but he wasn't the libertine conservatives expected. He launched a campaign against teenage pregnancy that stressed personal responsibility, and he conceded that "It is certainly true that this country would be better off if our babies were born into two-parent families." Clinton tried to redefine family values for the 1990s. This new moral structure was all about old-fashioned concepts like responsibility, respect, and self-sacrifice, but updated to suit post-1960s attitudes toward sex, gender roles, and child rearing. It was better for a child to be raised by two parents, but they didn't have to be a man and a woman. Children should be protected from pornography and taught self-discipline, but sex was no longer a sacramental act limited to a husband and wife. This reorientation of family values for *The Simpsons* generation was probably more in tune with popular opinion than Buchanan's *Leave It to Beaver* moralism. Clinton was in touch with the spirit of the Caring Nineties. The GOP's leadership saw that and tried to ape him. Pat Buchanan, they said, was living in the past.[49]

Regardless of what went on inside the Big Tent, politics in the first term became ever more partisan. In October 1993, the Republicans elected a new Minority Leader. Newt Gingrich had little in common with Buchanan. Pat called him a "Big Rock Candy Mountain conservative" who believed that social ills could be cured by tax cuts and technological innovation.[50] Although he represented a district in Georgia, Gingrich was an immigrant to the South and a supporter of Civil Rights. The minority leader felt little commitment to the blue-collar, rural idyll of yesteryear.[51] Pat and Newt differed on policy and priorities. Yet Newt understood the power of populism.[52]

As the midterm elections approached, the media presumed there would be just a small swing against the President's party. In September 1994, unemployment dipped below 6 percent for the first time in years and the economy produced 250,000 new jobs each month. The estimated deficit for 1995 fell from $284 billion to $171 billion. A British newspaper said that, "The joke on Wall Street is that Clinton is the first conservative Republican president in the White House." But Clinton struggled to get an approval rating above 50 percent, and his party felt the lash of public anger. Whitewater was the rallying cry for the furious. "What threatens this president seems to be much larger than mere partisanship," reflected one journalist. "There is a level of mistrust and even dislike of him that is almost visceral in its intensity."[53] Gingrich grasped that anger at Clinton was anger at politics-as-usual, that Ross Perot was onto something.[54] He put together a ten-point plan for reform called the "Contract with America." It embraced several popular ideas (cutting the budget, welfare reform, anti-crime initiatives) and a few specifics that were designed to bring conservatives to the polls (incentives for adoption and no to allowing U.S. service personnel to fight under the UN flag).[55]

Pat's views on the Contract with America were complex. At the time he expressed support, and he felt that Gingrich had stolen some of his best ideas.[56] But many years later he said:

> The Contract with America was one of the most overrated things in politics. During that campaign in '94, people weren't out there cheering about the Contract. But after the election they said, "That was it! That's what won for us!" The Republicans ought to get off this idea of putting together programs or ideas that divide our coalition . . . Putting out a great big program is a silly idea. That's a stationary position. It leaves you open to attack . . . The idea of getting yourself into a fortress and defending ideas that some of your own party don't agree on, that is what the press says you need to do. It is not.[57]

Pat stumped hard in the 1994 midterm elections. To earn his stripes as a party loyalist, he toured the country speaking up for conservative candidates.[58] On election day the Republicans added 54 seats in the House and 8 in the Senate. This was the first time the GOP controlled the House since 1954. They also picked up 12 governorships and 472 legislative seats, giving them control of 20 state houses. Gingrich was elected Speaker of the House, Bob Dole Senate Majority Leader. The press, the President, and even the Republicans were stunned. Clinton looked beatable.[59]

Pat said that the Republican Revolution was really about a backlash among cultural traditionalists.[60] "Social conservatism," he said "is in vogue."[61] The fury among gun owners suggested he might have been right.[62] Clinton had signed into law the Brady Handgun Violence Prevention Act, which required state officials to carry out background checks into the criminal record of anyone trying to purchase a firearm. The administration thought the bill was a vote winner because a majority of people polled supported it. But conservatives, who called it unconstitutional, understood differently. According to antigovernment activist Grover Norquist, "The White House thought they had a majority issue because a majority of people agreed with them. What the Clinton people didn't get was that anti-gun people don't actually vote on anti-gun issues. But the pro-gun minority do . . . So in 1994, Clinton was on the publicly popular side of the issue but when the anti-gun people didn't show up at the polls and pro-gun people did, the Democrats went down."[63] When Clinton also backed an assault weapons ban, he sealed the fate of several members of Congress and tipped the balance in favor of the GOP.[64]

Buchanan concluded that the real story of 1994 was the big turnout of cultural and religious conservatives during a low turnout year. Only 45 percent of the public voted in 1994, but 22 percent of those voters were regular church attendees.[65] One of the new congressmen agreed with Pat: Joe Scarborough from Florida's 1st District. Nobody thought Scarborough could win; the district had been Democrat since Reconstruction. But Scarborough sensed that Pat tempted a lot of conservative Democrats over to the dark side:

> These were conservatives who felt that there was something wrong with the Democrats, but who never felt the pull toward the GOP. Pat changed that. He brought up issues that these people cared about and gave them a voice in the Republican Party. Immigration, trade, abortion . . . Yeah, basically my voters were social and fiscal conservatives, kind of populists. They weren't middle ground Republicans. They liked Pat.

Scarborough won with 61 percent of the vote.[66]

One issue that didn't make it into the Contract was free trade. In November 1994, Dole, Gingrich, and Clinton worked together to pass through Congress America's membership in the new World Trade Organization. The WTO was to be a supranational body that set tariffs and trade regulations. For economic populists it looked like one more step toward the New World Order.[67] Nader, Perot, and Buchanan were against it. It would erode the sovereignty of the United States and violate consumer and environmental laws. It was a battle, according to Nader, between the conservatives and the "corporatists"—between those who wanted to protect the integrity and prosperity of Main Street against those whose votes were bought by Wall Street. The American Cause spent several hundred thousand dollars running ads against the WTO, buying commercial time on radio stations in twenty-five states.[68]

Sen. Bob Dole liked the WTO. Dole was a classic Cold War Republican free trader. But many of the Republicans who had just been elected were not. Joe Scarborough defied Dole and Gingrich in every trade vote: "I believed in fair trade, not necessarily free trade. And it drove the leadership crazy." The new intake was home-orientated in its thinking—fixated on cutting the budget and making life easier for middle-class constituents. In Scarborough's opinion, they did not necessarily subscribe to the view that "what was good for Merrill Lynch or the Bank of China was good for Joe Six Pack."[69] So, rather than test the nationalism of the Republicans, Dole agreed to ram membership of the WTO through the lame duck Democrat Congress.[70] It was a cynical move and Buchanan called him out on it. "Money talks," he said. "All the big money in the Republican Party is [pro-WTO], and all the populists are against it. The party went with the big money, and stiffed the populists, to pay its campaign debts." Membership in the WTO passed easily and Bob Dole got some good publicity. Coming off the back of his brilliant performance at Richard Nixon's funeral, Dole looked like a shoo-in for the 1996 presidential nomination.[71]

For Pat, the WTO vote was frustrating. The message of 1994 was that Clinton was beatable and that there was a powerful coalition of cultural conservatives and economic populists waiting to be exploited. But the GOP just didn't get it. They were stuck on appealing to big business and cosmopolitan liberals. So, once more into the arena he went.

In the spring of 1995, Pat declared his second run for the presidency. On March 20, 200 activists gathered in New Hampshire to hear him lay into taxes, free trade, gay rights, and "leap-year conservatives" like Bob Dole. Signs in the crowd read "New Hampshire Right to Life" and "New Hampshire Gun Owners for Buchanan." "I will use the bully pulpit of the Presidency of the United States," he said, "to defend American traditions and the values of faith, family, and country from any and all directions. And together, we will chase the purveyors of sex and violence back beneath the rocks whence they came."

Then, inevitably, four young protestors burst onto the podium and called the candidate a racist. They were bundled from the hall by brigaders and kicked down the steps into the street outside. The charge of anti-Semitism was back. "My friends," said Pat trying to calm the crowd, "now you know what we're fighting against in this country."[72]

EIGHTEEN

Weighing Up the Opposition

Pat Buchanan's biggest opponent, Sen. Bob Dole, kicked off his presidential campaign on April 11, 1995. He came home to Kansas and the locals greeted him like a returning war hero. They covered the Landon Arena in Topeka with signs that read: "We love you, Uncle Bob!" and "Dole, Heartland Hero, 1996!" Foul weather forced everything inside, where the convention center steamed up like a sauna and the signs crimpled in the heat. Rain grounded a squadron of vintage World War II airplanes that were due to fly overhead in a tribute to Dole's war record. The man himself looked like a matinee idol greeting his public—not a bit the seventy-three-year-old legislator—but as youthful and as dynamic as he was when he first walked down Main Street and asked the folks to send him to the state house.

Bob Dole leaned forward on the podium, redistributing across his body some of the pain he still felt from the injuries he sustained in World War II. "I have been tested and tested and tested in many ways," he said. "I am not afraid to lead, and I know the way." When he spoke like this, there was a hush in the crowd. Dole rarely talked directly about what happened in Italy in 1945. He didn't have to. People knew. They had read in the newspapers how doctors had put him back together piece by piece, how he carried a pen in his right hand to signal that no one should try to shake it—it was atrophied and useless, and the source of constant pain. Bob Dole was a survivor.[1]

Bob Dole was born in Russell, Kansas, in 1923. His father ran a small creamery and when the Depression hit, the family moved into the basement of their house and rented out the rest to make ends meet. Crippled by machine-gun fire during World War II, Dole was awarded two Purple Hearts and a Bronze Star. After the war, he made some money in law and was sent to the Senate in 1968. He was elected leader of the Senate Republicans in 1985 and ran for the presidency twice, in 1980 and 1988. There was a feeling that Dole's time had come. The dynamics were right, too. Clinton was unpopular, and looked shallow and incompetent. Bob Dole had the experience to get things done. A safe pair of hands—a devil people knew well. "Everything old is new again," said his former speechwriter. "It seems like he's been around forever, but there is a resilience to him, a refusal to surrender to the forces of fashion . . . In a political culture that burns out and uses up and tosses away leaders, he's still here—longer than any figure in any television series ever."[2]

Bob Dole wasn't Bob Dole the man; he was Bob Dole the trademark. So much so that he referred to himself in the third person. "People have confidence in Bob Dole," he said at a fund-raiser in New Hampshire. "They know I'm not going to take you over the edge. I'm a stabilizing force. I'm not a polarizer. You have to work with people in this business. Yes, with Democrats, yes, with independents and, yes, with Republicans. The American people want us to get things done—get things done." Having made their protest in 1994, Dole presumed that voters now wanted someone in the White House who could implement the Contract.[3]

Dole's reputation as a Mr. Fix-It was nonideological and out of touch with the revolutionary spirit of the times.[4] Bob Dole was happy to make concessions and meet liberals somewhere near the center-ground. Red-meat conservatives called that treachery.[5] Buchanan pointed out that the senator was an architect of budget-balancing tax rises in the 1980s and 1990s: "Until Bill Clinton took office, Bob Dole never met a tax increase he didn't like . . . Bob Dole taking a pledge not to raise taxes is a little bit like Madonna taking a vow of chastity."[6] Larry Pratt, head of the Gun Owners of America, plain hated him. Dole had lifted a Republican filibuster on the Brady Bill. Pratt said that the moderate Republicans "Saw the gun issue as a liability . . . when in fact 1994 proved that it was a vote winner. They had a touch of Stockholm Syndrome. The Democrats took them hostage when they called them child killers, or whatever, and they started to believe it."[7]

Gingrich's Republican Revolution, the Perot revolt, Clinton's slide in the polls—all these things told the conservatives that there was no need to go with a vacillating technocrat like Bob Dole. And for those who hated Bill Clinton (really, really *hated* him), Bob Dole's softly, softly approach was an insult. They wanted a candidate who would speak truth to power—who would call Clinton out as a crook, a liar, and a liberal.[8] Bob Dole refused to do that. When he spoke about morality in politics, he seemed awkward. His Chief of Staff, Sheila Burke, felt that he never understood the fury of the right. She said that people of Dole's generation, "attached almost a moral significance to living within your means . . . that healthy skepticism about government extended to what now are social issues, but were then personal issues that you didn't really talk about . . . a discretion which is based on self-respect and respect for others."[9]

Bob Dole had tons of money and a lot of endorsements, but his team was split on how to win. They understood that the attractiveness of the Dole brand might suffer if a younger, fresher alternative came on the market. They also appreciated that a firebrand might steal the votes of grassroots conservatives.[10] Some on the staff—old friends like Bill Lacy and Sheila Burke—wanted to let Bob Dole be Bob Dole. They told him to talk about his legislative accomplishments and emphasize his war record. Others—like newbie Scott Reed—felt that he should reinvent himself as a right-wing maverick. The debate was never resolved and Dole swerved from left to right.[11] One day it was Beltway Bob, the next it was Elmer Gantry. And the staff could never stay on top of his idiosyncrasies. Dole was a "meddler" who wasn't about to hand the most important race of his life over to a bunch of professionals. The people behind the scenes spent months working out a strategy, and then he went ahead and did what the hell he liked anyway.[12]

Bob Dole didn't do soaring rhetoric. In the middle of a speech, he would wrap up a thought with "Whatever." In New Hampshire, he said, "This election is about people who paid their taxes and always tried to make certain the next generation had it a little better. Your kids had it better than your parents. You had it better than your parents—whatever."

"Whatever" said that Bob Dole had come to the end of a point; Bob Dole was done speaking. Bob Dole had better things to do.[13]

Bob Dole was still head and shoulders above his competition. Texas senator Phil Gramm looked like the biggest beast among the conservatives. He enjoyed the support of some of Buchanan's old friends, including Phyllis Schlafly.[14] Gramm was an ugly duckling. His wife, Dr. Wendy Lee Gramm, recalled that when she first met him her reaction was "Yuck!" Tall, "with the round, wizened face of a snapping turtle," Gramm made a pass while trying to recruit her to work at Texas A&M University. "As a single member of the faculty," he said in his tin-whistle voice, "I'd be very interested in having you come to Texas A&M." Wendy turned him down the first two times Phil asked her to marry him.[15]

To conservatives, Gramm looked like a safe bet. He had all the right views and a record as a winner. Coming from Texas, he knew lots of oil men, too. The night before he declared, Gramm hosted an event in Dallas where he took in $4.1 million in contributions—the biggest sum at a single event to that point in history. Then he said something silly: "Thanks to you, I have the most reliable friend you can have in American politics, and that is ready money." The press seized on the quote as if it were Gramm's only case for the nomination. It sounded trashy. The senator declared his candidacy on February 24, 1995, at Texas A&M in an event that could have been broadcast live from Tiananmen Square. Gramm arrived onstage by walking through raised sabers and took a salute from hundreds of uniformed cadets. The event closed with the roar of cannons. Given that Gramm deferred his way out of serving in Vietnam, a Dole insider joyously quipped that he may as well have put a sign over his head saying, "I never served."[16] Still, said the press, if he could place second or third in Iowa, skip New Hampshire, and sweep the South on Super Tuesday, he might win.[17]

Four days later, the former governor of Tennessee, Lamar Alexander, declared, too. Preppy, strawberry blond, Alexander was a credible non-Washington candidate. His big pitch was that everything should be sent back to the states— education, welfare, gun control, even abortion. By answering every question on policy by saying it was none of the President's business, he was able to avoid saying what he really thought. Conservatives guessed that he wanted the state to wither away. Moderates thought it was sneaking social tolerance in through the backdoor (presumably he would leave liberal state governments to legislate as they wished). The presidency should be used as a bully pulpit to encourage voluntarism and charity, he said—to set an example for others to follow.[18]

Alexander sounded and looked like a monogamous Bill Clinton—a baby boomer conservative who knew the Bible back to front and seemed at home in a pair of jeans. He was pitched perfectly. The Alexander campaign was upbeat, colorful, and homey. Wearing his trademark plaid shirt, he launched himself with a "walking tour" and pledged to cover the entirety of New Hampshire by foot. Then he leaped up onto a stage and played the theme song from *Rocky* on an upright piano.[19] Posters appeared overnight—bold colors covered with the single word "Lamar!" It was a name you couldn't forget, a name that people had to put a face to. That the face was pretty and tanned was a pleasant surprise. The Lamar campaign was pure hokum. He closed every rally by playing ragtime on his traveling piano. Who else could do that? Who else, but Lamar![20]

Some liberals and libertarians coalesced around Arlen Specter, a Jewish senator from Pennsylvania. Specter sold himself as the Big Tent guy, a pro-choice Republican. But he was a curiosity, not a candidate. Specter announced from the Lincoln Memorial to emphasize his personal commitment to "equality and opportunity." "When Pat Buchanan says there is no constitutional doctrine of separation of church and state, I say he is wrong," Specter said to scattered applause from the tiny crowd.[21] Perhaps a nicer, more patient man would have lasted longer in the race. Said a Pennsylvania newspaper editor, "Everyone thinks Arlen's a genius and all the same people think he's a jerk. It's his personality—if you don't have your intellectual jockstrap on, you're going to walk away from him crying."[22]

These were the big hitters, but a couple of other also-rans popped up to cause trouble. Indiana senator Dick Lugar tried to run a distinctly "positive" and "clean" campaign, and so was largely ignored by the voters. Maurice "Morry" Taylor, a tire magnate from Michigan, wanted to be the Ross Perot of 1996. He offered to manage the U.S. like a business and poured $6.5 million into his eccentric candidacy. He turned up to events with a phalanx of blonde actresses in leather. They rode from state to state on motorbikes, like a soft-core parody of a campaign. Morry was nicknamed "The Gritz" on Wall Street for his notorious temper. "I'm abrasive because I want to get the job done," he told reporters. "The politicians—they all want you to like them. I don't care if people like me. I just want them to say, 'I respect that guy because he got the job done.'"[23] But despite handing out free televisions at campaign rallies, the only permanent reporter he got was the humorist Dave Barry. "The Gritz has a very direct style of speech," Barry wrote. "He sounds a little like a Quentin Tarantino movie gangster who has somehow developed an intense interest in the US trade deficit."[24]

Also making his debut on the presidential campaign circuit was former UN ambassador Alan Keyes. Keyes was a rarity—a black conservative. He ran twice for the Senate from Maryland and was beaten badly both times. On his second go, he blamed his 29 percent on racism. The local party blamed *him*.[25] An Alan Keyes speech was like a revivalist sermon, peppered with references to the black freedom struggle. Every line was delivered with the sped-up zeal of a preacher trying to cram a whole sermon into a thirty-second response. "Alan Keyes has probably the best delivery of any speaker you will ever hear," admitted a Buchanan backer. "He makes Jesse Jackson sound like he stutters."

Buchanan and Keyes should have been good friends. Both were grassroots, conservative Catholics. But even if Keyes agreed with Buchanan on a lot, he felt that his emphasis upon immigration and trade betrayed a racist message. Buchanan in turn got sick of being called a bigot. There was something inflexible, even cold about Keyes's conservatism. Buchananism was all about family, class, time, and region. It was about belonging. Keyes was a man who didn't belong anywhere—a black conservative who found it hard to make friends. Alan Keyes was born to martyrdom, and it came easily.[26]

One candidate who did have a sense of humor was Bob Dornan, an ex-navy pilot and House representative. Show business was in his blood. His uncle was Jack Haley, who played the Tin Man in *The Wizard of Oz,* and his mother was a red-haired Follies showgirl. Bara Dornan was maimed in a car accident and became a reclusive insomniac devoted to reading political biographies. Bob doted on his mother and frequently mentioned her in speeches. "She was gorgeous and she was smart," he gushed.

Elected to Congress from Orange County, California, he campaigned against a primary challenger by warning that "Every lesbian spear-chucker in this country is hoping I get defeated." Once in office he displayed his notorious "courage to be flamboyant," which usually meant heaping personal insults on those who dared cross his path. Bill Clinton was "a sleaze ball who can't keep his pants on" and a "draft-dodging adulterer." He called a Soviet propagandist a "betraying little Jew" (he meant to say Judas but got carried away in the heat of the moment). He outed a fellow Republican from Wisconsin in a House debate over gay rights. Accusing the congressman of voting in a way that enhanced his secret sex life, Dornan said Steve Gunderson had "a revolving door on his closet."[27]

Dornan was hated but also adored—by friends, rivals, and the Secret Service agents who passed on gossip to him about life in the Clinton White House. "Bob's a willing participant in the image he takes such pleasure in," explained Gov. Thomas R. Carper of Delaware, a close chum. "He's a patriot, loves our country, and he has a sense of humor about himself." When Dornan arrived in Delaware to announce his candidacy by train, he was greeted by Carper. The governor had been rehearsing a political lampoon show and was dressed as a woman. He stood on the platform with padding under his skirt to look pregnant. Carper held up a sign that read, "Dornan's the One." The candidate didn't get off the train. He just gave Carper a black look from his carriage window until eventually the governor got the message and went on board to say hello. Dornan did not like quips about his manhood. "Homophobia?" he said in an interview. "I'm not afraid of homosexuals. I love them, just as I love people with a lot of other problems. Remember, I grew up in New York and Beverly Hills," he said darkly. Apparently Dornan was regularly harassed while hitchhiking to his Jesuit high school in West Los Angeles. "Oh, I've been hit on," he said wearily. "And always the same ridiculous line: 'Boy, you have nice thighs.'"[28]

"Come with me," Dornan said at his campaign launch. "I'm going to enjoy myself."[29]

Bob Dole, Phil Gramm, Arlen Specter, Dick Lugar, Morry Taylor, Bob Dornan, and Pat Buchanan. In July 1995, liberal journalist Maureen Dowd observed the Republican talent pool at a New Hampshire picnic and was not impressed. Neither was Buchanan. "You know what I say?" Pat said onstage,

"Any race that's got Phil Gramm and Bob Dole in it, I come off as warm and fuzzy. And any race with Bob Dornan in it, I come off as a progressive."

"The only decent smile in the bunch belongs to Pat Buchanan," wrote Dowd. "And that one has a disturbing Jack Nicholson edge."[30]

Once in a while, Pat would let one of the journalists who followed him around into his Winnebago for a one-on-one chat. One afternoon a reporter from the *Village Voice* knocked on the door. He did not look like Pat's type. "He had hair down to his navel, jeans, and a T-shirt," recalled Bay. "Pat thought he might have been a homosexual."[31] The young man sat down and Pat eyed him suspiciously, waiting to be called a woman-hater or a racist. But instead the boy said, in the nicest, politest voice, "Mr. Buchanan, I've been waiting my whole life for someone running for president to talk about the Fortune 500 as the enemy. And when I finally get my wish, it turns out to be you."

"Thank you," said Pat.

And later, the journalist wrote up that while he thought most of Buchanan's supporters were toothless simpletons, he had to admit that "To a progressive's ear, a great deal of Buchanan's conglomerate bashing has a familiar, disconcertingly alluring ring—the kind that's capable of bringing out the old socialist firehouse-dog slumbering in many of us."[32]

Pat was working to a different game plan from 1992. Back then he could count on the vote of every Republican who hated President Bush. Now he had to make a case for himself in a big field filled with men selling similar messages. But he had two things he didn't have the first go: money and time. According to *The Nation,* he clung on to $937,272 from the 1992 campaign and put most of his staff on The American Cause payroll.[33] Greg Mueller, Terry Jeffrey, and new staffer Connie Mackey helped build up organizations in the states. Dollars rolled in through the mailing lists.[34] Bay started with about 20,000 names and that was enough to pay for the office and staff. Every month she tried a new source—borrowed a Civil War reenactment list or a Catholic prolife list—and added 1,000 or so names to the original file. By late 1995 she had roughly 40,000 names of people happy to donate money. "But you couldn't just sit on your hands," Bay explained. "You have to keep churning it up so that people want to give." Just like back in 1992, Pat had to come up every week with a new line that would get him back in the press.[35] And every six weeks, he had to go to an event and win it.

In Iowa, Buchanan hit the road with his wife and Connie Mackey. Their Winnebago had a bumper sticker that read: "Caution: Future President Aboard." The message everywhere he went was the same: economic nationalism. Japan and Germany, he argued, "are countries out to win industrial supremacy, which leads to economic supremacy, which then leads to military and geopolitical supremacy. If we don't put America first, who will? You think the Prime Minister over in Japan will? No way." There was not an import that Buchanan would not tax. Japan would get 10 percent on all products to help pay down the budget deficit; China, 20 percent to teach it a lesson about imprisoning dissidents. Mexico would get a "social tariff" to "insulate us from un-American competition with workers making seventy-five cents or a dollar an hour." NAFTA and the WTO would go and there would be no American participation in UN peacekeeping exercises in Bosnia or Rwanda, or "anyplace else where we have no national interest." Immigration would be banned for five years until U.S. salaries rose to an acceptable level. He would build a wall along the border. Buchanan was the first presidential candidate ever to promise that.

Of course, big business would hate all of Pat's ideas. But, "if the corporate chieftains don't care about the USA," he said, "I don't care about them." Buchanan once saw public enemy number one as the socialists in Washington. Now it was the corporations on Wall Street. "I think it's corporations who have gone global, who have lost all loyalty to America," he said in Iowa. Their loyalty "is to the bottom line on a corporate balance sheet."[36]

Pat wasn't as out of step with conservative voters as pundits presumed. Clinton economics was based upon big business, free trade rationalism. Republican opposition was rooted in small business parochialism. The GOP screamed daily about "corporate welfare," attacking the handouts and welfare net that made life so easy for the big people but so costly for the little. Small businesses could not afford new healthcare costs or tougher environmental regulations, and they didn't like competing with foreign producers. The millions of Americans who had been laid off and turned into involuntary entrepreneurs since the late 1980s saw few business interests in Hanoi or Bogota. They ran garages, computer shops, florists, poodle parlors, and language schools and their markets rarely extended beyond three or four blocks. All they wanted was a tax cut.[37]

And these people were culturally conservative—decent, hardworking folks who went to church every Sunday and always put a little profit aside for the collection plate. Big business, in contrast, was amoral. It sold cigarettes to kids and encouraged young girls to aspire after drug-taking rock chicks with loose morals.[38] The *Wall Street Journal* wrote a scathing editorial about the lead singer of the Grateful Dead, calling him "the drugged up knock-off of a social experiment that went sour." Numerous conservatives and liberals wrote in to point out the contradiction in the *Journal*'s free market moralism. If millions of fans bought the records and went to the concerts then, by the law of the market, he must have been a good musician. "The market proved it," wrote one conservative critic. "That is if you believe in markets."[39]

Buchanan was pitching for the Perot voters, creating a new alliance of economic populists and religious social conservatives. Phil Gramm warned Iowans that such antitrade talk would damage agricultural exports and turn the state into "a dust bowl." Fine: Buchanan conceded support among farmers. His views "go over better in New Hampshire," he said. But still the candidate drew bigger and bigger crowds. "When I raise my hand to take the oath of office," he cried, "this whole New World Order is coming crashing down."[40]

That phrase—New World Order—meant a lot. To some in the media it was a Masonic handshake with the neo-Nazi far right. And the far right were wound up and ready to explode. In February 1993, federal agents stormed the compound of the Branch Davidian cult in Waco, Texas. A fire broke out and seventy-six Davidians—including twenty children—were killed. Waco came on the back of a similar incident in Ruby Ridge, Idaho, where federal agents attempted to arrest Randy Weaver for selling illegal shot guns. In the standoff, Weaver's son and wife were killed. Both were shot with their backs turned while retreating, possibly unarmed.[41]

To men like Gun Owners of America (GOA) chief Larry Pratt, Waco and Weaver were signs that the federal behemoth was getting out of control. Guns were the last line of defense. Pratt was a soft-spoken, gray-haired gentleman who looked less like an urban guerilla than an accountant. He grew up in a New Jersey suburb and only touched a gun once in his youth, on a duck hunt. Pratt bought a firearm when he moved to Washington, D.C., and riots broke out in the summer of 1968. A political science major, he got a job with the Gun Owners of America, which had splintered from the "moderate" National Rifle Association. By 1976 Pratt was president of the organization, which had a political influence disproportionate to its membership of 150,000.[42]

Larry Pratt wrote a book called *Armed People Victorious* that examined the success of popular militias in Guatemala and the Philippines against drug warlords and oppressive governments. He also made sure that the GOA gave money to relatives of the Davidians killed at Waco seeking legal redress. The only way to prevent future massacres, he said, was to establish militias all over the country: "The government behaves as a beast. It did in Waco, and we have somebody, whoever it might have been, whatever group it might have been, assuming they can't rely on the Lord to take vengeance."[43] Pratt met Buchanan one afternoon while recording an episode of *The McLaughlin Group*. He liked the sound of his views on guns and offered to help if he ran for the presidency again. In 1994, Larry Pratt became a co-chair of the Buchanan for President Campaign. The decision would haunt them both.[44]

Pratt's organization was composed mostly of gun enthusiasts. But groups like the GOA were also being infiltrated by militiamen and white nationalists looking for influence. They believed that there were Russian tanks parked at the Canadian border ready to overrun the U.S. They said that Clinton wanted to ban all guns, black helicopters were used to stalk anti-Zionists through the Idaho countryside, there were biological weapons hidden in Ohio salt mines, and that the federal government had constructed slaughterhouses and crematoriums to massacre thousands of patriots in four different states.[45] In Coralville, Iowa, Pat attacked the New World Order and Ralph Clements translated for a *Newsweek* reporter: "It's the international conspiracy. It's the bankers who want to establish a one world government." Buchanan said hello to Ralph and Ralph's wife Frieda told him that they had changed their registration to vote for him. "The Democrats left us," she said sadly, "especially on social issues."

Then Ralph asked Pat, "What do you think about these black helicopters and Russian tanks in the U.S. we keep hearing about?" Pat replied that he hadn't seen any "hard" evidence for either, but he would look into it.[46]

The concept of a New World Order didn't just appeal to crazies. Many Middle Americans understood it to mean government by cosmopolitan, liberal snobs. The phrase was bandied around the religious right and Pat enjoyed high levels of support among evangelicals. In September 1995, a poll of the Christian Coalition found a shocking level of sympathy for Pat. The Christian Coalition suppressed the results. The group's supremo, Ralph Reed, said he had seen them and that Dole, Gramm, and Buchanan were running even on 20–30 percent of the vote. He conceded that Dole's support was soft.[47] Pat's ability to reach out to these people helped immeasurably. Since 1988, Christian Coalition people had infiltrated the GOP and now dominated in several states. The Iowa Christian Coalition flexed its muscle when, in early 1995, they won a titanic battle to drive a longtime member off the Des Moines school board after he came out as gay.[48]

Many Buchanan brigaders saw Bob Dole as a patsy for the New World Order. But Pat didn't waste too much time talking about him. His early target was Phil Gramm, whose presence in the race threatened to split the conservative vote.[49] This dovetailed nicely with Dole's strategy. Team Dole looked at the polls and saw that the only candidate coming close to their man was Gramm. If Gramm could convince people Bob Dole was a closet liberal, he might sew up the conservative majority and win the primaries. If Gramm and Buchanan could get into a fight and split the conservative vote, Dole could keep his lead. Better still, if Pat emerged as the candidate of the right then they thought they could walk the primaries. And so there emerged a bizarre, unofficial alliance between Buchanan and Dole to cripple Gramm. For Dole it proved to be a mistake. He created a monster.[50]

In August 1995, the angry middle class flexed its muscles once again at a convention in Dallas. Three thousand supporters of Ross Perot's United We Stand America gathered in the steamy city to hear a parade of big-name politicians bid for their votes. Buchanan was there, along with Gingrich, Dole, and all the other Republican candidates. So, too, was White House counselor

Thomas F. McLarty III, who said that while there were "areas of honest and honorable disagreement between the President and Ross Perot," the administration was still committed to a balanced budget and lobbying reform. Buchanan got a warm reception for a speech that bashed government-to-government handouts, including a recent bailout of Mexico: "For whose benefit was that $50 billion bailout of Mexico City? It wasn't the workers of Main Street, it was the bankers of Wall Street. Citibank, Chase Manhattan, JP Morgan and Goldman Sachs all got off, and they put us on. If I'm elected, you have my word: I will cancel foreign aid, and there will be no more $50 billion bailouts of socialist regimes anywhere in the world!" Jesse Jackson and Pat Buchanan shook hands. Perot declared that he and Jackson had been separated at birth, and that their parents had given Ross up because they couldn't afford him.[51]

A poll following the convention reflected the rebellious mood of the country. Fifty-five percent of Americans wanted a third party. Fifty-nine percent said there was not a single elected official today who they admired. Seventy-nine percent, the highest figure in recorded history, said that government was run by a few big interests looking out for themselves. A third-party candidacy had legs, depending upon who was the candidate. In a three-way race, Perot could get 23 percent, Jackson 11 percent, and Buchanan 8 percent.[52]

A couple of weeks later came the first real test of the candidates' strength—the Iowa Straw Poll. It was as much a show of money as it was of popularity. Residency in Iowa was optional; anyone with a $25 ticket could vote. Campaigns used buses, trains, motor homes, and airplanes to bring in supporters. Car plates hailed from as far afield as Nebraska, Minnesota, and even Florida. Lamar Alexander airmailed friends in on two chartered 727s.[53] Dole ran coaches from across the Midwest and hired a single-engine plane to buzz ahead with a banner that read, "Go with a Winner—Vote Dole." Gramm spent a small fortune: Iowans received as many as half-a-dozen glossy brochures urging them to attend. His wife, Wendy, sat on the board of a local meatpacking company called IBP, Inc. She used her clout to arrange buses to pick up workers from eight plants around the state and bring them to the event. The *Wall Street Journal* reported that IBP was threatening workers with the sack if they didn't show. When the sullen-faced meatpackers arrived in Ames, they were greeted by a hog-roast and a clay shoot. Gramm walked around saying hello with his friend Charlton Heston by his side. It was, said Arlen Specter's campaign manager, "a vote-buying scam." Dole spent something like $75,000; Gramm, anything between $200,000 and half a million. An estimated 40 percent of voters came from outside the state.[54]

But something went wrong. Dole's local organizer, Tom Synhorst, bought 3,000 tickets. He calculated that 90 percent of those ticketholders would turn up, giving the candidate a comfortable victory with 33 percent of the vote—anything more would raise expectations too high ahead of the January caucus. He was told that the ideal result would be Dole first, Pat second, and Gramm third. When he started calling up registered Republicans, he found 300 people who said they were for Buchanan. Desperate to hurt Gramm, Synhorst gave their names to Bay. The problem was that he presumed Dole was still on top and that the real battle was for second place. It wasn't.

On the day, Tom Synhorst visited the convention and panicked. Buchanan's tent was full of thousands of people eating hamburgers. Gramm had thousands of people wearing blue "Vote Gramm" T-shirts. But the Dole tent was practically empty. A few dozen people hung around the oyster bar in silence. Synhorst got hold of the Dole staff and told them something was wrong.

Bob Dole could feel it, too. He and his wife, Elizabeth, flew in on a commercial flight and were disappointed at the low turnout at a welcome rally. "Something's wrong," he said. "It's not happening here." He walked out on the stage at the convention and there was polite applause. He looked beneath him and saw a sea of Gramm and Buchanan supporters. Both candidates had bought up all the tables near the stage so they could intimidate opponents. Dole burst backstage in a fury. What had gone wrong? The audience actually sat on their hands during his speech! Pat talked about the coming Armageddon and they gave him a standing ovation.

"Fuck, fuck, fuck," said Synhorst. He hadn't counted on the religious types turning up to vote. "It was so different to organize against people who prayed, the Christian right. They had an intensity, behaving and talking as if they were on a mission, as if they *had* to be there that night because it was a calling." Dole's campaign manager told him straight that there was a chance he might lose.[55]

Out on the floor, Bay was feeling good. She asked Brian Kennedy, the state chair, how they could be sure that there would be no double voting. He showed her an indelible stamp that they put on everyone's hand after they cast their vote. That put her mind at rest. As long as they played it fair, she sensed it was tight between Buchanan and Gramm with Dole in third place.[56] But then Shelley asked her for a word—quietly so as not to panic Pat. She had voted and gone to the bathroom afterward. When she washed her hands, the stamp rubbed right off.[57]

Bay was furious. She suspected it was a scam. But still, she reasoned, the turnout was so obviously on their side that they couldn't let Dole win. At the very least they would place Gramm first, then Buchanan, then Dole. A second place would do. Counting took place behind closed doors and the campaigns were told they were allowed to send in witnesses. But the Buchanan witness was turned away. Bay went wild. She found Kennedy and demanded to know what the hell was going on. Technical difficulties, he said. They were going to count the votes without anyone present.

"They stole it," Bay insisted. "They couldn't win it, so they stole it."[58]

Whether Bay was right or not, the result was very close. Dole and Gramm tied exactly, both candidates taking 2,582 voters, or 24 percent. Pat got 18 percent. Bay believed they had cut a deal. She hypothesized that Buchanan narrowly came first, Gramm second, and Dole last. Worried that the press would say Pat won and anoint him the leader of the conservatives, Bay said Gramm had maybe agreed with Dole to accept a face-saving tie and put Buchanan back in his place.[59] Even if that fiction was agreed upon, it didn't work.

Dole's people walked around in a funk and admitted defeat. "This is a reality check," said a senior aide. Gramm's first place was outshone by Buchanan's second—most pundits predicted he would come in fifth or sixth. Everyone sensed that something had gone wrong in Iowa that night. The establishment was losing control.[60]

In Bay's estimation, the result saved Pat's candidacy. The Buchanans were happy under the radar. She said:

> We knew what we were doing. When you have a campaign where you're not the frontrunner and you don't have the money to be frontrunner, you don't want to show up at everything placing third

or fourth every time. You want to turn up at the odd thing, make a big splash and disappear ... What you need is credibility. You need loyalty. You need a base. You need some supporters. You need to keep doing stuff every so often so that you can send a message in your direct mail that you just [placed second] in a straw poll. [The readers] don't know that there were several straw polls in states prior to that ... And they don't expect you to start winning all of them, you're coming from behind. That's [the vibe] you want to create: you're coming from behind, these guys are the establish-ment, they have the money ... But we've got the issues. We've got the people. It's a grassroots campaign.

So while the press talked about Dole and Gramm, the message local orga-nizations received was that, against the odds, Buchanan was getting their voice heard. "We created a strategy where we could come from behind and surprise them," said Bay. And that's what they did.[61]

NINETEEN

Coming from Behind

In September 1995, Pat opened a full-time office in Manchester, New Hampshire. All the people who had worked for him in 1992 drifted back. Signe McQuaid mothered a skeleton staff of fanatics. Above the outside of the office was a sign advertising "Spooky World: America's Horror Theme Park." Just next to the picture of a grinning Pat Buchanan was a huge cartoon skull with a speech bubble that read: "Open Nightly In October!"[1]

That fall, the media searched around for someone other than Buchanan to beat Dole. Gramm was too shrill and right wing. For a few weeks they pushed Gen. Colin Powell. The son of Jamaican immigrants, Powell was a four-star general and former Chairman of the Joint Chiefs of Staff. Both parties had tried to get him on the ticket in 1992, but he declined. Powell was a thoughtful, moderate man—not easily defined as left or right. He was fiscally conservative but backed abortion rights and affirmative action. Although he was an unusual breed of Republican, he was still popular in the ranks. Without his declaring, one October poll put Powell way out in front in both Iowa and New Hampshire.[2]

Powell made a big show of hemming and hawing. He wrote a book and did some TV. Conservatives seethed. If a pro-choice, pro-affirmative action candidate won the nomination, they would lose the GOP. In turn, if the conservatives walked away from the GOP then Powell would probably lose and take the entire Republican Party down with him. Conservatives dominated donations and grassroots activism. Their power might have been disproportionate to their numbers, but without them the GOP would wither.[3] Conservatives called Powell every name in the big book of right-wing hate: liberal, baby killer, affirmative-action baby, snob, wet, elitist, socialist.[4] Buchanan warned viewers of ABC's *This Week* that Powell would split the party: "You'd have people walking out of the convention." Pat would be one of them.[5]

Powell dropped out, citing personal reasons. He didn't have the fire in his belly. The Big Tent guys wanted him to be a poster boy for something he wasn't—a last hurrah for liberal Republicanism.[6] Privately, everyone was relieved. Pat said he was looking forward to debating him, but had he won the nomination then Buchanan would have been forced into a third-party bid. Bob Dole, of course, was thrilled. He wondered aloud if Powell might consider the vice presidential slot. The race settled back down and Dole rode out in front.[7]

Then, on September 15, everything changed. For months, multimillionaire Steve Forbes had badgered his friend Jack Kemp to enter the race and make the case for tax cuts. Kemp went to see Gingrich to ask him what he thought. Gingrich told him he had swung so far to the left that no conservative would vote for him. Kemp ruled himself out.[8] Frustrated, Forbes decided to enter his own name. His announcement at the National Press Club, said one GOP insider, was "the equivalent of throwing a stick of dynamite into the mix."[9]

Steve's dad was Malcolm Forbes, an eccentric tycoon who ballooned, yachted, motorcycled, and collected Fabergé eggs. The *Washington Post* pointed out that the Forbes Sr. and Forbes Jr. relationship defied stereotypes. While Senior was a Dionysian adventurer, Junior was a stay-at-home prude.[10] Toward the end of his life, Senior divorced his wife and explored a late-blooming sexuality with characteristic battiness. According to *The New York Times*, "he was seen regularly roaring up on his motorcycle in tight black leather to Manhattan nightclubs and, according to current and former workers at *Forbes*, pursuing some of his young male employees." Steve never discussed this with his father. "Compassion," he said, "is not the same as approval."[11]

Steve Forbes was a respected commentator, but surely not presidential material. He was uncharismatic—gray haired, with a soft pudgy face and two tiny eyes that were magnified to absurdity by spectacles. Nor did he have the common touch. Why, asked journalists, did he want to become President of the United States when he already owned his own country? Laucala (pronounced La-tha-la) was a seven-square-mile island, located about 2,600 miles southwest of Hawaii. Before Forbes Sr. bought it in 1972 for $1 million, Laucala was populated by cannibals. Forbes sacked the chief man-eater and rebuilt the island in his own image. He forced the locals to diversify into goat-herding and constructed a store, a workshop, a worker's dormitory, and a refrigeration plant. For himself, he built an airstrip, roads, a nineteenth-century-style plantation house, and a plot of bungalows for paying guests. Laucala practiced a kind of trickle-down economics, attracting large numbers of immigrants to work as coconut farmers, porters, and busboys. When Senior died, Junior kept the tax-free tradition going. Holidaymakers, who paid $2,100 per week per person, were flown to and from Fiji on a jet emblazoned, "Capitalist Tool."[12]

Steve Forbes—who had never even stood for the school board before—hit the ground running. He hired a bunch of conservative strategists, like Carter Wrenn and Tom Ellis, Pat's old friends from North Carolina, to tell him what to do.[13] They flooded the airwaves with ads.[14] Between September and December 1995, Forbes spent $7 million on promoting his candidacy.[15] It worked. He bought relevance. In New York, a state with candidate registration rules that were fixed to favor big-name candidates, Dole, Forbes, and Buchanan were the only contenders that made it onto the ballot. Buchanan ran a grassroots campaign in upstate New York and got 30,000 signatures—letting him field delegates outside of the titular city. Forbes spent $1 million to buy 55,000 signatures and so got on the ballot everywhere.[16]

But what to run on? Steve Forbes for President wasn't enough: on the doorstep he looked like he had come to fix your computer. So Forbes floated a vote-winning idea. If elected, he would abolish all personal taxes and replace them with a single-rate flat tax—at just 17 percent. It was bold, simple, and easy to remember. Of course, Forbes stood to gain a lot of money out of it. But that didn't dim its appeal to voters disappointed with the field and looking for the next big idea. Forbes was like the Music Man. He came into town at the head of a big parade, offering a simple solution to everyone's troubles. The flat tax was a once-in-a-lifetime special offer, an all-singing-all-dancing magic mountain of an idea. With a wave of the wand, *"puff!"* all your worries disappeared in a cloud of smoke![17]

Pat Buchanan didn't buy the Forbes hokum. It was tax cutting, which was good, but it lacked an empathy for the poor and let the rich off the hook.[18] "Under Mr. Forbes's plan," he said, "the middle class loses all deductions for home mortgage interest and church contributions; the federal budget would be thrown scores of billions of dollars deeper into deficit, and lounge lizards in Palm Beach pay a lower tax rate than steelworkers in Youngstown."[19] The difference between Buchanan and Forbes was that while Pat raised money with $50-a-plate barbecues in someone's backyard, Forbes threw $1,000-a-glass champagne receptions at the Waldorf Astoria. In one evening, he entertained the chairman of Bear Stearns and the chief executive of Estée Lauder. Joan Rivers told jokes.[20] When Forbes couldn't make it to a New Hampshire debate because of a snowstorm that left him stuck at his estate, Buchanan cracked, "A couple of the polo ponies got sick."

But when Pat attacked Steve he was poking fun at more than his background. He was actually questioning the Reagan Revolution itself.[21] The Reaganite flat tax was a panacea, a liberating force—a fantasy of Big Rock Candy Mountain Republicanism. Forbes thought "economics is the answer to everything," Pat sighed. "You've got violence in the cities: Cut taxes and put enterprise zones in there and everything's going to be fine, and it's not. There's a much broader dimension to America's crises: It's moral, it's social, it's economic, it's spiritual."[22]

Forbes's entrance changed the dynamics of the race.[23] His team decided to make their mark by attacking Dole. They ran a series of ads across the country calling him out of touch, a big spender, and too old for the job. Dole's support fell dramatically, while the flat tax pushed Forbes up in the polls.[24] He was fast establishing himself as the Ross Perot of 1996. And as the politics of the Beltway became more bitter and confused in the last months of 1995, Forbes's tagline was a winner: "Steve Forbes . . . Not Washington."[25]

In November 1995, negotiations between Clinton and the Republican-controlled Congress on the next federal budget broke down. Dole and Gingrich demanded bigger cuts in social spending than Clinton wanted to balance the books. To keep the government running in times of deficit it was necessary to increase the limit of debt that the Treasury Department was authorized to accrue. Gingrich told Clinton that if he didn't accept his proposed budget cuts he would refuse to raise the limit and so put the country into default.[26] The President called his bluff. On November 14 the federal government shut down. Nearly 800,000 public employees went home.[27]

Voters weren't sure whether the Republicans were being mean or the President stubborn. Gingrich made up their minds for them. The next morning he said in a press conference that he had sent a tougher budget bill to the White House because Clinton had refused to talk to him and Dole on a flight back from the funeral of Yitzhak Rabin. "It's petty but I think it's human," he said. "You've been on the plane for twenty-five hours and nobody talked to you and they ask you to get off the plane by the back ramp. . . . You just wonder, where is their sense of manners? Where is their sense of courtesy?" The New York *Daily News* ran the headline "Cry Baby" next to a picture of Gingrich in a diaper.[28] That afternoon the White House published a photograph of Clinton and Gingrich talking on the plane. With one throwaway remark Gingrich made the Republicans look irresponsible and vindictive.[29]

Dole's people thought that the budget negotiations would help their man. It would make him look statesmanlike and affirm his central importance to the Republican Revolution.[30] But the government shutdown was not popular and those who did support the GOP's militant position suspected Bob Dole was the weak link. The strains of the negotiations meant he could not make his case to the public.[31] By the end of the year, Dole had dropped ten points in the polls and Forbes was now in second place. He was running close to even in Iowa, New Hampshire, and Arizona.[32]

The Dole people didn't get it. It angered the senator that his years of experience and hard work could be eclipsed so easily by a spoiled brat with his own island. "When Forbes has a fund-raiser," he growled, "he just takes his wife to dinner and writes a check."[33] But Forbes's endless round of attacks on Bob Dole worked. This was bad for Dole but great for Buchanan. So long as all attention was focused on Dole and Forbes, Bay's beneath-the-radar strategy could still work. And then, at the year's end, Bob Dole helped make Pat Buchanan front-page news again.

. . .

In late 1995, Buchanan spotted an opening down south. Louisiana had decided to hold its caucus before Iowa, breaking with tradition and upsetting
a lot of Iowans. Gramm jumped in, and Pat Buchanan and Alan Keyes quietly
joined him. Everyone else stayed out. Gramm presumed the caucus would
be a cakewalk, a way of launching him into Iowa. His people helped write the
rules. They made it a caucus to keep turnout to a minimum, and scattered the
forty-two polling sites in obscure places across the state.[34] They kept their fingers crossed that Louisianans were unfamiliar with the recent revelation that
the senator had once invested in the production of a porno movie. (It was
called *Beauty Queens*—the senator said that he thought it was a documentary
about beauty pageants.) Gramm put his name on the ballot but kept visits to a
minimum.[35]

Pat's people realized that Gramm was being lazy and stupid, putting all his
eggs into one basket. So Pat started to work the state in December 1995. He
crashed a Christmas musical in Lafayette to denounce, "The tragedy and atrocity of the systematic slaughter of the life of unborn children across America."
Surrounded by confused children dressed as shepherds and sheep, Buchanan
slashed the air with his hand and lashed out at bureaucrats "in sandals and
beads" who wanted to replace the Bible with *Playboy* in public schools. "We are
going to put back into its rightful place the true God of the Bible," he said to
cries of "Amen, brother!" Gone, with a slash of the hand, was pornography.
Gone was homosexual marriage. Gone was "secular humanism." "Easter's
gone," he cried. "Now it's Earth Day. We can all go out and worship dirt!"

Buchanan pushed his anti–free trade message just as hard.[36] "There's no
doubt there is an inherent contradiction between conservatism and unfettered
capitalism," he said in New Orleans. "Conservatives ought to be worshipping at
a higher altar than the bottom line on a balance sheet. What in heaven's name
is it that we conservatives want to conserve if not social stability and family
unity?" Free trade advocacy trashed these values by putting profit before
people. "For what? So that I can get 37 varieties of shirts? I mean, what is it all
about? I've gone around this country, and I've seen what happens when company towns become ghost towns. These working people, who agree with us on

so many cultural and social issues, they're wondering why we're selling them down the river."[37]

We should not forget, said Pat, that the free market has no soul. Take gambling. In the early 1990s, a number of southern states lifted restrictions on gambling to plug holes in their state budgets. Schools were subsidized by lotteries and revenue was raised from casino licenses. To conservatives like Gramm, this was the free market in action. Buchanan thought it was "a deal with the devil."[38] Pointing out that both Dole and Gramm had received money from gambling interests, he said "organized gambling is a destructive and ruinous social force that leads to political corruption." He also tied it to prostitution and drugs. "I intend to make it an issue," he said. That was a smart move. Louisiana had just elected Gov. Mike Foster on the strength of his anti-gambling credentials. The previous governor had opened up steamboat casinos and grown rich on kickbacks. He was now facing jail time. The public was sick of this kind of corruption and Gramm's "ready-money" vibe was all wrong for the state.[39]

There were other signs of a synergy between Foster and Buchanan. Foster's gubernatorial campaign manager, Roy Fletcher, joined as a senior advisor to Team Buchanan.[40] Next, Foster himself announced that he would vote for Buchanan. For those who cared to notice, it was all very suspicious.[41]

Dole was behind it. He wanted Buchanan to win Louisiana. This would drive Gramm out of the race. With Gramm gone, Dole presumed that conservatives would group around him to beat the unknown Steve Forbes. Team Dole persuaded Foster to endorse Buchanan in exchange for a big profile at the convention, maybe even the vice presidential nomination. Nobody knew what was really going on, not even Buchanan. He thought Mike Foster actually liked him.[42]

Returning to Louisiana, Pat risked running into David Duke. Since 1992, Duke had reinvented himself as an amateur powerbroker. Whenever there was an election, the ex-Klansman endorsed the strongest candidate and, afterward, told the press that "my people" had swung the result. He was all over Buchanan '96. Duke wrote to his supporters, "Buchanan doesn't share my racial viewpoint, but on most other issues, he's very close to me." Come out for Buchanan, Duke told his people—and many of them did. Several Buchanan delegate-nominees were ex-Duke activists. "He supports me," said Buchanan sourly. "I don't support him."[43]

Duke went to every Buchanan event possible, angling for a photograph of him shaking Buchanan's hand. The media would leap on any image that confirmed the two were buddies, so it was guaranteed front-page coverage. On one occasion, Buchanan was plunging through a crowd when Duke suddenly appeared and thrust his hand forward.

"Hi, Pat," he said.

"Good-bye David," said Buchanan. He turned around and walked away. They met again at a picnic. Buchanan was working a long table, shaking hands with each voter. At the end of the table he spotted Duke in a suit with a big smile. Pat got to within two chairs and then said out loud, "I think that's enough for today," and left the table. He got a thrill in knowing that he had denied the publicity-hungry Duke his front page.[44]

Duke was there at a 2,000-strong party convention in New Orleans in January 1996, and he got plenty of applause, too. He shook hands with a black delegate, Ronald Bookman, and quickly pointed out his good deed to the press. "[Bookman] might not share my racial viewpoint," Duke said, "but he respects me as a party leader. Listen to all the Republican candidates and they sound like David Duke. My words coming out of their mouths. Something, huh?"

Phil Gramm threw a private party—catfish and sticky T-bone steaks—and waded through the crowd cooing, "Howyou? Howyou? Howyou?" Occasionally, the senator would kiss a lady on the hand. Most approved of the gallantry, although it came out of the blue. One woman was so stunned, she left the room staring at her hand, and walked straight into the cash bar. With the men, Gramm was less familiar. "That's a great tie," he'd say, staring at their collar. "What a pretty tie. Good tie. Where'd you get it?" Someone thought he said, "What's the time?" and replied, "Half past four." Phil Gramm was out of his comfort zone.[45]

Pat, meanwhile, wowed the delegates. In his speech, he lashed out at abortion, immigration, free trade, military adventurism, affirmative action, and secular humanism. Then he turned his attention to the President, who was drifting to

the right and telling everyone that he wanted a balanced budget. "Can you believe Bill Clinton's State of the Union address?" he asked. "I'm gonna sue that fella
for copyright violation." But for all the flimflam, Republicans had to take the boy
from Hope seriously. "Let's face it, he's an effective communicator," said Buchanan. "If we're going to beat this man, and we've got to beat him for the good
of this country, we're going to have to put up against him someone who can put
him in the crossfire and take this fellow apart!"[46]

Two men rode with Buchanan's motorcade through New Orleans whose
stories said it all. Vincent Bruno was a retired cop, a tough-looking man with a
master's degree in theology. Angry at the state of America, he volunteered for
Duke back in 1991. Riding alongside him was Gus Payne, a journalist who kept
an ACLU membership card in his wallet. An investigator and proud troublemaker, he fought for Jesse Jackson back in 1988. "I'm a liberal and I can't
imagine supporting someone like this," said Payne, "but here Pat is, saying
everything I believe in. Term limits for federal judges, no free trade, stop giving
away American jobs. And so I end up sitting with a guy like this—a right wing,
born again, gun nut."

Bruno nodded and said, "We're all worried about the same things—layoffs,
downsizing, incomes going down, jobs disappearing. Some of us think there's
a conspiracy of the moneyed people, the international bankers. Rush Limbaugh doesn't think it's a conspiracy, but what else can it be?"[47]

Pat took a break from stumping in Louisiana to visit Alaska. It proved to be
a brilliant move. At the end of January 1996, Alaska held a three-day straw
poll—one week before Louisiana's caucus. The state was uninviting—dark,
snowbound, and difficult to traverse. Pat had some people up there who were
doing a great job by themselves with little support. But Bay said they should do
more. The coming-from-behind strategy had left Team Buchanan without a
substantial showing since Iowa back in August. They needed a lift going into
Louisiana and Iowa—something to show that Pat was a winner. Given that
none of the other candidates seemed to notice Alaska was happening, it looked
like a good bet.[48]

Over on the opposite side of the country, in New Hampshire, Bay set up a shift system on the telephones. When the people calling Iowans and New Hampshirites were done for the day, they were replaced by a team who called residents in Alaska. The time difference meant that the office could go on working until 2 a.m.[49] Meanwhile, Connie Mackey's team in Iowa booked into hotels that offered free national calls. They took over whole floors and—at Holiday Inn's expense—rang Alaska night and day. It was cheap and nobody noticed, except the hotels.[50] In the last week of January, Pat visited Alaska and took a dogsled ride in Fairbanks. He also spent about $80,000 on TV advertising, much of it during the Super Bowl. Beneath the radar, people started to drift to the campaign. Churches liked his antiabortion stance. Local trade unions liked his position on NAFTA. The old Buchanan coalition was resurfacing—angry white, blue-collar men of every partisan persuasion.[51]

Alaska offered a rare treat: a Christian Coalition local that came out for Pat. Nationally, Ralph Reed sat on his hands and refused to endorse anyone. "Dole was going to win," he explained. "But we liked Pat and all the other candidates, so we were just nice to everyone."[52] But the Alaskan Christian Coalition liked Pat too much to stay quiet. They premiered him at the Abbott Loop Community Church one Saturday night. He started by ridiculing recent efforts to rename Custer National Battlefield to stop offending Native Americans. "I know the Indians don't like Custer," he laughed. "That's why they shot him full of arrows." He said that the World Bank's loans to Vietnam dishonored veterans' sacrifices. The UN was trying to set up a New World Order. The Education Department should be shut down. Clinton was an enemy of life and liberty. Pro-choice Arlen Specter was pathetic: "He's at 1 percent in the polls, with a 3 percent margin of error—he might not even exist!" Pat finished with a plea to Christians. "In Alaska, efforts to keep religion out of schools and to revise history texts are evidence that special interests are at war with traditional American culture and values. We've got to make this God's country again." It earned him a standing ovation. Local Christian Coalition president Art Mathias gave the candidate a gold pan, in appreciation.[53]

Buchanan said that his big issue was the federal land in Alaska. He was going to give it back to Alaskans. Of course, most of the protected lands were areas of outstanding national beauty that sat atop a potential reservoir of oil. State politicians dreamed of becoming a North Pole emirate, using the black gold to bankroll tax cuts and lavish public services.[54] Alaskans are frontier people. The trappings of civilization are little protection against the snows, bears, and oppressive blackness of the tundra. It's a land of rigid self-sufficiency and rugged individualism, of cowboys on snowmobiles. They don't like being told what they can and cannot do; especially if it stops them making money.

Buchanan visited the Alaska Gun Collectors Association fall gun show at the Egan Center and his people were out in force. Some tables showed off black powder pistols and muskets. Others boasted heavy-duty modern hardware, including Buck Rogers–style guns that melted metallic silhouettes. Customers were getting around the Brady Bill five-day waiting period by faxing checks there and then through to the Alaska State Troopers, who zipped through digitized criminal records and faxed back a yes or no within ten minutes. "I feel it's no business of the government if I own guns or not," sighed one shopper. "But the law's the law." This was Walt Hargis, fifty-four, who was pleased to see Buchanan on display. But then Hargis was an old-fashioned guy. Beneath a Stetson, he wore a gray handlebar mustache, a gold pocket watch, plaid shirt, and cowboy boots. "I should've been born one hundred years ago," he said, getting an autograph from Buchanan. Above them, an NRA banner read: "It's more than guns. It's about FREEDOM."[55]

Other candidates caught on. Dole claimed that he was disinterested, but made sure he got the endorsements of Alaska's governor and both its senators. His wife, Elizabeth, toured the state. Minimizing expectations, Gramm nevertheless spent $30,000 on radio. But it was Forbes who flooded the airwaves with flat tax advertising and telephone calls plugging his candidacy. Fearing that his millions might help overtake them, Team Buchanan decided to go on the attack. "We did some research," said Bay. "Forbes said he was pro-life but we found on paper some comments that suggested otherwise . . . With pro-life people there's no compromise and as soon as someone says, 'I'm personally antiabortion but—,' you know you've got a fraud." Bay also knew that the one group of Alaskans guaranteed to vote was the pro-lifers. "In early January the nights go on forever, there's no light, it's bitterly cold, and you have to wait in line for hours to vote. Only pro-life people would put up with that." She waited until the morning of the first day of voting to start the attack, so Forbes wouldn't have time to respond.[56] Dozens of people in New Hampshire rang up thousands of people in Alaska and said this: "Steve Forbes believes in abortion on demand, virtually, till the sixth month of pregnancy. Pat Buchanan's pro-life all the way."[57]

Over the polling weekend, turnout was high. In Fairbanks, the temperature sank to 30 below zero. But 320 people showed up to vote, well above the average of 60–80. "The word is 'overwhelmed,'" said the local party chair. "When they first proposed this, I thought, 'It's going to be 40 below and three people will show up.'" A total of 263 people voted in the district east of Fairbanks. In Ketchikan, 225 voters turned out—three times the normal rate.[58] In total, nearly 10,000 people participated: an all-time high that's never been matched.[59] At Dimond High School, Anchorage, there was no parking for a square mile. Inside, a line of voters curled through a large lunchroom and down a narrow hallway to the front door. Along the way to the ballot box, people passed tables covered in literature and bumper stickers. A television at one table showed Buchanan warning against Big Brother. "He's not part of the system," said a fan in the line. "Dole, Gramm, they're so ingrained. He's not bought and paid for."[60]

On January 30, the votes were counted and Pat Buchanan came in first with 33 percent. Forbes was a strong second with 31 percent; Dole 17 percent; Gramm got a disappointing 9 percent. Buchanan was thrilled. "I think it gives our campaign the kind of momentum it's looking for," he said on CNN. "Energy, fire, and enthusiasm." He was right.[61] "We were the only ones who could beat Forbes' awesome checkbook," he laughed in a telephone interview. "God's hand might be in this."[62]

Joking aside, Pat had found Forbes's Achilles heel. No pro-choice candidate could expect to win the Republican nomination thanks to the importance in the process of small, conservative caucus states like Alaska. Now Pat looked forward to the chance to blow out Gramm in Louisiana.[63]

Alaska made the front pages and Pat suddenly had momentum. He flew back down to Louisiana to wrap up what he called his "grudge match" with Gramm. He visited a Fruit of the Loom factory that used to make underwear, before offshoring to Mexico and killing hundreds of jobs. He also drew attention to the collapse of the crawfish industry thanks to "irradiated Chinese crawfish" imports produced by "slave laborers." The crowd was boisterous. Some called Clinton a communist; one man suggested they draw a target on his back and send him to Bosnia. "I'm a Huey Long for the '90s," said Buchanan.[64]

Pat and Gramm met up at a picnic thrown by the NRA. Gramm was a life-long hunter and appeared on that month's NRA magazine front cover comparing calibers with his good friend Charlton "cold-dead-hand" Heston. Mama Gramm had a trophy for pistol shooting and Phil sent a message to criminals everywhere. Don't break into his mother's home, he told the crowd, because "Mama's got a thirty-eight Special and she knows how to use it." In place of gun regulations, Gramm promised tough new criminal laws that would mean felons got ten years if they committed a crime with a gun in hand, twenty years if they fired it, and the electric chair if they killed anyone with it. "We've got to stop building federal prisons like Holiday Inns," he said. He'd take out the TV, the porn, the downtime, and even the air conditioning.

Buchanan, by contrast, was a faux-enthusiast. He wasn't a member of the NRA and certainly wasn't on first-name terms with Charlton Heston. In fact Pat only once shot a gun, on a hunt when he was a boy. He so hated taking the life of a little animal that he never fired a shot again. But Pat still stole the crowd. Guns weren't all fun and games, he said. They symbolized the self-reliance that America was built upon. He reminded the audience of the American colonists' stand against the British at Lexington and Concord. "What were the British soldiers going for? They were going for the colonists' muskets," Buchanan said. "Once they took their guns, they could impose their will on them. That's what this is about. It isn't about shooting ducks and clay pigeons. It's about defending your wife, your family, and your community." The crowd loved that. But they also loved it when he went on to talk about NAFTA and jobs. Those people were gun lovers, true, but they were also factory workers and small businesspeople. Gramm treated voters like special interest groups that could be bought with promises. Pat treated them like human beings, with material and spiritual problems that they could solve together.[65]

On February 6, Buchanan won the Louisiana caucus. His margin was small (44–42 percent) and turnout was just 4.9 percent of registered Republicans. But what mattered was that no one saw it coming. Not even the Dole people who made it possible. And it was great TV. The tiny turnout was concentrated in just forty-two voting sites. One official said that the voting at his station was "like a third world country. It's been a zoo." The lines stretched around the block, sometimes nearly doubled by the cameramen who trickled in as they sensed a story about to break.[66] One resident was asked if his town ever saw such an array of TV cameras and journalists before. "Well, yes," he said. "We have a rabbit festival the third Saturday of every March. We get people coming here from all over."[67]

Pat's support came from a mixture of Christian Coalition members and people earning less than $30,000 per year. He won easily among the elderly, folks on welfare, French-speaking Cajuns, and Catholics. Buchanan was delighted. He told CBS that he had done "tremendously well" among "the working people that we need to bring back to our party to defeat Bill Clinton." Among a narrow sample, he was right.[68] Perhaps these results were unsurprising given the lack of alternative candidates, but Buchanan still managed to fashion a message that he was gathering the votes of Reagan Democrats. And the media bought it.[69] More important, Gramm was mortally wounded. Moderate Louisiana daily *The Times-Picayune* noted a couple of days after the contest that the race was much closer than the networks reported. But that wasn't the point. "If Gramm had won, it would have been dog bites man," said the newspaper. With this result, it became "man bites dog."[70]

After the results were counted, Pat flew to Iowa. At the airport he gave a cheery press conference. He said:

> The argument we're going to make for the rest of this campaign here in Iowa is this: Pat Buchanan is the conservative who can win this race . . . We're going to ask Democrats and independents to come out and help us out in the Iowa caucuses, and join this new coalition we're trying to build—of traditional social conservatives, economic conservatives, and populists, the Perot folks, the Reagan Democrats, and the Republicans.[71]

The Dole people should have listened. But they were still too busy worrying about Steve Forbes's millions.

TWENTY

Winning Without Winning

Twenty to 40 percent of Iowans said they didn't know who to vote for. The *Los Angeles Times* visited the Hair Receiver and Tanning Salon in the town of Dike to gauge the mood. "I just don't like the mudslinging," said stylist Karen Grant. "I think everything can be done in a positive mood." The salon was busy, prom was approaching, and the tanning beds were full of roasting blondes. Anne Kersten, who engineered a recent appearance by Steve Forbes in the town, popped in for a bottle of Fat Cat hair volumizer and admitted that nobody's perfect. Her man had thrown around a lot of mud recently. But, she said, he at least had one good new idea. The women of Dike were unhappy with the President, worried about their jobs, bored of the rhetoric, unimpressed by the candidates, and cynical about the electoral process. They wanted something different. "All old stories," said Mr. Ashland, a professional artist undergoing a trim. One of the girls did his nails as he flicked through a copy of *Vogue*. Mr. Ashland was going to a Buchanan rally that afternoon to see what he had to say for himself. Many ladies were for Forbes because they knew his more exciting father Malcolm. He raced air balloons over Iowa cornfields and was "common as an old rag" (a compliment in this state). But Steve Forbes's wife was too frumpy. She needed to do something about her hair. Sister Eugene corrected them from beneath the dryer. The little old nun taught politics and government at the local high school and had a good sense of history. Eleanor Roosevelt was plain, she reminded them, and she was the best First Lady they ever had. Everyone agreed with that.[1]

Team Dole was tearing its hair out over Forbes. They knew that they had to do something about the flat tax proposal, to hang it like an albatross around Forbes's neck. The problem was that every attack they made came across as the establishment pulling rank.[2] Dole brought in Gingrich to say that the House Republicans were against it. Appearing in Washington before the American Association of Retired Persons, Gingrich said Forbes was trying to buy the election. But it wouldn't fly because the flat tax idea was "nonsense." Dole agreed, telling a rotary club luncheon in New Hampshire that he was for a "flatter, fairer, simpler tax," but not for Forbes's bizarre idea. "And we've got to be very, very careful. Why don't we do it the right way? Why don't we have hearings on it?" Here was the problem with Bob Dole. He didn't like silver bullet solutions, but conservatives do. Sensible though Dole was, he just didn't get it. He was out of touch with the populist spirit of the times. He saw everything in process terms. He was boring. "It's got to pass the Congress," he said. "It can't happen by edict. And if Congress sees $180 billion, $200 billion [in projected deficit increases], it's not going to happen . . . You'd think with experience somebody would know you ought to see how the American people react to it, bring in the experts and then see what happens?"[3]

Forbes bashing did good business. In the grand Iowa caucus debate, everyone piled in. Gramm said that Forbes wasn't committed to a balanced budget (Dole joined in with a counterattack on Gramm, pointing out that he had failed three grades at school). Lamar Alexander punched out one-liners, saying that the flat tax was a "truly nutty idea" and it was "going up there like the Great Pumpkin—it's going to solve every problem that we have."[4] He got personal and said to Forbes, "The only thing you've ever run is a magazine you inherited, and you raised the price of your magazine."

"Yeah," laughed Bob Dole. "Maybe the government could borrow money from Steve Forbes."

Forbes was boxed into a corner, with little constructive to say about any other issue. Asked how he would mend America's racial divisions, he said he would build "a vibrant and strong economy which we can only achieve with a flat tax that is also a tax cut."

Buchanan chuckled. He said the flat tax idea "looks like one that was worked up by the boys at the yacht basin."[5]

They gave their closing statements. Dornan ran on his fecundity. "I have more progeny than all the rest put together," he declared.

Buchanan said his opponents were confusing conservatism with free market economics. "What this campaign is going to decide is what conservatism means in America in the post-Cold War era," he said.

Bob Dole trotted out old favorites. "I'm from Kansas, I'm a neighbor. In 1988, the Iowa people said Bob Dole is one of us, and I don't think anything's changed . . . Bob Dole is not a polarizer. Bob Dole provides leadership, Bob Dole delivers. Bob Dole tries to get things done."

Whatever.[6]

But in his effort to oust Forbes, Dole did engage in a little polarizing.[7] Alaska showed that Forbes could be beaten on moral issues. Forbes was personally religious, but his obsession with the flat tax and his failure to come up with clear positions on sex, drugs, and crime gave the impression of libertarianism. His father's homosexuality didn't help much, either.[8] Someone started to make anonymous phone calls to Iowans. The caller would say that Forbes was for abortion on demand and gays in the military and then hang up. The National Right to Life Committee did not confirm or deny that it was them. But its director, David O'Steen, did angrily say that trying to get a straightforward abortion stance from Forbes was "like trying to nail a jellyfish to a wall." Someone pointed out that the Forbes family owned a photograph by the gay artist Robert Mapplethorpe. Wasn't that evidence that the Forbes millions supported homosexual porn? Unwisely, a paranoid Forbes denounced the Christian Coalition for trying to fix the election. That confirmed everything.[9]

Forbes's support among social conservatives fell from 20 percent to 1 percent.[10] A Des Moines Register poll put Dole at 28 percent, Forbes at 16 percent, Buchanan at 11 percent, and Alexander at 10 percent. Forbes lost his geeky cool and lashed out at Dole, Buchanan, and the Christian crowd. Buchanan's response was straight from the streets of Georgetown. "He's like a little kid who got hit back after he's been throwing rocks at people," he said. "Somebody knocked his glasses off and he's whining and crying." Dole went a little bit further to the right. He met with a Christian Coalition group in Ottumwa and said that Forbes thought "people of faith have no place in politics, but [he's] wrong. Today, America's greatest challenges are moral and cultural."[11] Only the other day, said Dole, he had received a phone call from Mother Teresa to thank him for helping to pass a ban on partial-birth abortion in the Senate. And Bob Dole was not for sodomy, either. The Christian Coalition threw a rally for heterosexual marriage in Des Moines and Dole sent a letter apologizing for not being there but saying that, in his opinion, the Coalition didn't go far enough on this issue: "Not only does Government have a duty to protect the foundation of marriage, it has the duty to promote it."[12]

Buchanan was at the rally, shaking hands with his kind of people. One preacher said it was time to send sodomy "back to Satan where it came from!"[13] Pat offered some friendly advice for anyone struggling with same-sex attraction: "While you may not be able to determine your orientation, you can determine your behavior. There are many individuals who have proclivities to various kinds of . . . vices who've contained and controlled them by willpower and by training and by constant, repeated denial."[14] Pat drove his Winnebago to the Knights of Columbus hall in Carroll and spoke to a German and Irish crowd of Catholics about abortion. "If we split our votes we're going to lose it all. We could lose it to Steve Forbes. And there it all goes; everything we fought for, everything we've worked for."[15] But, he added, he wasn't running on hate. He reminded the audience of the Catholic Church's teachings on the duty of wealth creators to the poor. Workers had a "moral right" to a "living wage."[16]

Poor old Gramm was campaigning harder than ever before—doing seven or eight stops a day—and pushing a new Dirty Harry image. He videotaped a commercial in front of the Café Di Vang that began, "Hi, I'm Phil Gramm, live from the site of a gang murder right here in Des Moines. Don't you think that it's time we grabbed violent criminals by the throat, and not let 'em go to get a better grip?" He closed with his zinger of the season. "I want death when somebody kills our neighbor, and *I want to stop building prisons like Holiday Inns*." On Friday night, he watched a televised debate that he had chosen not to attend. When a questioner in the audience asked what the candidates would do about violent crime, Gramm yelled at the TV, "I'm gonna stop building prisons like Holiday Inns, lady!"

(Gramm should have stayed a night in a Holiday Inn. He would quickly discover that they weren't that high a benchmark.[17])

Bob Dole was no more visionary. He was buttoned down, repressed. He wore a crisp dark suit, starched white shirt and, pinned to his lapel, a Purple Heart. There was no kissing babies, no empty promises, no attempt to feel people's pain, just experience and good sense. When he sustained a burst blood vessel in his eye, he looked for a moment like Bela Lugosi contemplating a fresh victim.[18] "Why do you want to be President?" asked a college professor. *What a dumb question,* Dole thought. He answered, "I think sometimes it might be easier dealing there than dealing with, I'd say, 100 prima donnas in the Senate, counting myself. So, you wouldn't have that many in the White House." Dole was asked the question again in South Carolina during a speakerphone conference. "Because of Elizabeth!" he replied this time. "She made me do it!"[19]

It was a pre-bought campaign by numbers. And in his obsession with Forbes, Dole was in danger of forgetting two other candidates. One was Lamar! The abdication of the center ground opened up space for the great plaid shirt.[20] People unhappy with Dole's bitterness, and repulsed by Buchanan, could vote for a conservative with a nice smile and anti-Washington credentials. Alexander was getting better, too. Speeches became standing room only and television crews appeared from nowhere, uncertain of who to cover now that the race was opening up. Alexander was a blank canvas; people saw in him what they wished. Dole had a past, Forbes was a bore, and Buchanan was half-crazy, he said. But Alexander was a gospel singing, piano playing, clockwork toy who could say anything to order.[21] "I am better prepared than Mister Forbes," he said at every stop in Iowa, "and I have fresher ideas than Senator Dole. And remember your ABC's. Alexander Beats Clinton!"[22]

But the other candidate Dole forgot about turned out to be the bigger problem. Pat Buchanan was gathering steam.

In the precious week between Louisiana and Iowa, Bay Buchanan blanketed supporters with news of Pat's wins. Iowa residents received a mock newspaper that headlined his victories in Alaska and Louisiana. The message: Pat is now the candidate of the right. He hit the phones. New computer technology allowed him to conference call one hundred people at a time. "Folks," he said, "there's only one candidate in the Republican Party who can bring home the Perot voters because there's only one candidate who stood with them on NAFTA, who stood with them on [the WTO], and who stands with them on campaign finance reform."[23]

Buchanan played the media like a violin. He spent every morning with a long list of local radio stations, calling in to ask if the host wanted to speak to him. Sometimes he knocked on the door of the local TV station to offer a breakfast chat. It was pulled off like a covert op. "We do the TV—what we call our hits—on countless stations," he explained. "We'll show up there before dawn, and we now know how to get in all these places. You go around to the back door . . . Most of them are very friendly. They all know you—'Here he comes again!'" While other candidates wasted hours crossing Iowa in buses and airplanes, Buchanan's voice— urgent, cajoling, amused—blanketed the state. "That's how we get the message out," he confided. "You know, it's what we did for a living. All that *McLaughlin Group, Crossfire, Capital Gang*—the training was not for naught." He even invited TV cameras to film him filming a TV commercial.[24]

The candidates gathered for a dinner followed by another debate. Each man brought along a table of supporters to ensure a healthy round of applause when he spoke. A reporter from *The New Republic* caught up with a Gramm supporter and his wife. They had defected to the Forbes table. A couple of weeks before, Gramm had showed up at the couple's house for an orchestrated "impromptu" question-and-answer session. The journalist asked the wife if she had noticed that Gramm spent the entire interview staring at her breasts. She did; it was the thing she noticed most about him. Her husband looked shocked. "I didn't want to tell you," she said pushing a spoon through her soup.

The liberal journalist sat down at the Buchanan table. The snobbery of his reportage was typical of how the brigaders were treated by the press:

> Unlike the Forbes people, who are clearly wearing what they do every night, the Buchanan supporters look as if they have dressed up for the first time in years. The more you look at it, the more the Buchanan section reminds you of some morality play waiting to take the stage. In addition to the jowly red-faced old men, the sec-

tion contains a real live minister in a collar and a young woman who is a dead ringer for Brooke Shields. The young woman has no interest whatsoever in the priest or the speeches; indeed she works at cross purposes with them. She is busy winning the competition with them for the attention of the Republican mind.

Suddenly Alan Keyes stormed the table, shaking hands with every Buchananite, willing them to switch. The journalist told him that he was from *The New Republic* and that he would write a piece about him in exchange for a year's subscription to the magazine. Rightly insulted, Keyes said, "You are easily bribed." Then Pat's press director, Mike Biundo, asked Keyes—for a laugh—what it would take to get him to endorse Buchanan. Wrote the journalist: "All hell broke loose."

A week before, Pat had told a joke in a speech that Keyes found offensive. Buchanan recalled that when John Dean was sent to trial over Watergate, he plea-bargained to continue his charitable work with the Hopi Indians. John Mitchell's lawyer followed suit. But before he did, Mitchell leaned across and, in a whisper loud enough for everyone to hear, said, "If they offer you the Indians, turn them down."

Back in the present, Keyes screamed "Why is this funny?" The entire room turned its attention on the Buchanan table. "Will someone please explain to me why this is funny?"

The journalist almost felt sorry for Biundo:

> He is sitting there with a kind of nervous nausea on his face, staring up at a black man raving on like a lunatic about the importance of Indians to the Republican Party. If you saw this scene unfold on the street you would cross over to avoid the man who is shouting and wonder why they ever let those people out of the mental institutions in the first place.

The news cameras gathered around as Biundo melted into his seat, thinking, *I'm going to be remembered as the guy who hates Indians.* Keyes repeated his question once more—"Would someone please explain to me why this is funny?"—then turned to the cameras and did it all over again for CNN. Keyes said he had met Native Americans who wept when they thought of babies killed in the womb. But they would not join the GOP because racists like Buchanan made them feel uncomfortable. Was it all an act? Did Keyes really think he could win the Republican nomination by riding a wave of political correctness?

The journalist spotted Buchanan looking oblivious at the other end of the room and ran over for a comment. "What have you got against Native Americans?" he asked. Pat didn't know what he was talking about. The journalist broke down Keyes's critique. Buchanan dimly remembered, then fully remembered his speech.

"Oh, Christ!" he said. "That wasn't a joke. It happened. Mitchell actually said that!" Could he clarify the remark, asked the journalist? Pat started; then stopped. He saw Keyes raging in front of an ABC camera.

"There's no point going over this," he said, and turned away.[25]

The Iowa caucus was held on February 12. Team Dole felt confident. Their polls showed that Forbes's social tolerance and constant negativism had damaged him. The $4 million he spent on ads had dragged Dole down, but not far enough to kill him.[26] Forbes knew that, too. He downplayed expectations by spending the afternoon reading *The Little Engine That Could* to school children in Coon Rapids. The book was about a train loaded with toys that struggled to get over the mountain. Forbes closed the book sadly and said to the kids, "After tonight, they're going to say some of our engines aren't moving." The flat tax would have to wait its turn.[27] An exit poll taken at 7 p.m. showed a clear victory for Dole in the mid-30s. The senator had 35 percent and, to everyone's surprise, Buchanan had a strong second-place showing of 19 percent. The Doles relaxed. Elizabeth gave Bob a big kiss and they settled down in their hotel room to watch the results.

Then Bill Lacy rang through to say that the percentage had slipped to 33 percent and could go lower. A few minutes later it lowered to 29 percent, then 28 percent, and Pat was rising to 20 percent, then 21 percent. Bob Dole's face fell. He started flipping channels. He found Lamar Alexander looking pleased with his third-place showing. Dole switched the TV off. Someone told him that he was down to 27 percent. Pat was at 23 percent. But a win is a win, said Elizabeth. Silent, Dole collected his thank-you speech and went down to the party below. In the ballroom they played "You'll Never Walk Alone," the music he listened to a thousand times when recovering from his war wounds.

"Thank you Iowa," he said.[28]

Buchanan's celebration party was an alcoholic frenzy. A six-piece Dixieland band revved up the crowd with "California Here I Come!," "Happy Days Are Here Again!," and "Dixie!" Buchanan staggered onto the stage, giddy with excitement.

"Go Pat, go!" the people shouted.

"We're going!" he replied. "Let me tell you, Pat is going right on to the Republican nomination!" He acknowledged all the Christian voters who had stuck with him ("The religious right are great people. And I'm one, too!"), and he thanked the people of Iowa for taking a risk on him. It was straight on to New Hampshire from here. Remember, Republicans: "There is only one conservative in this race who can win." But remember, also, Democrats: He was the only candidate who spoke for the little people—the steel workers, the textile workers, the car makers whose jobs were disappearing fast.[29] "This is a victory for a new idea in the Republican Party and in national politics, a new, spirited conservatism of the heart."[30]

Backstage, Terry Jeffrey and Connie Mackey were watching the returns. There were now just 3,000 votes between Buchanan and Dole, and the heavily Catholic county of Dubuque hadn't yet declared. When the result finally came, the media tally gave the county to Pat; the state GOP gave it to Dole. It was a small discrepancy but if a similar error had occurred across the state, then the media was calling Iowa for the wrong man.[31] Connie thought it was a put-up job. "They've taken our first place away from us," she said.

"Never mind," consoled Terry. "Two out of three ain't bad." And the polls in New Hampshire looked even better.[32]

Pat Buchanan won the Iowa caucus without winning. Dole took 26 percent and Buchanan 23 percent. Alexander took 18 percent and Forbes came in fourth with a disappointing 10 percent. Gramm dropped out.[33] Iowa had done its job and the GOP had found its field. It was Buchanan vs. Dole. And Buchanan was ahead.[34]

TWENTY-ONE

The Peasants' Revolt

Pat flew to New Hampshire to a fiery reception. A thousand people met him in a tiny room in Manchester. The stage was too low to see their man, so they screamed at the TV cameras to get out of the way. Buchanan gave 'em Hell, sulfur bubbling from his mouth. "Bob Dole's got no vision . . . no agenda . . . No convictions, beliefs. T. S. Eliot's Hollow Men. We've got heart, we've got soul." Remember 1992? Remember how they laughed at Pat Buchanan then?

"They ain't laughing now, Pat!" shouted someone in the crowd.

"They're shaking in their boots," yelled another.

"Yes! The establishment in Washington is quaking in its boots!" Buchanan screamed. "We shocked them in Alaska! Stunned them in Louisiana! Stunned them in Iowa! They are in terminal panic. They hear the shouts of the peasants from over the hill! All the knights and barons will be riding into the castle pulling up the drawbridge in a minute. All the peasants are coming with pitchforks."[1] When Buchanan takes the oath, the bureaucrats will race out of Washington in "covered wagons. Like immigrants! So I can have more room for my limousine!" He laughed.

"This is too much fun!"[2]

Bob Dole didn't think so. On the plane to New Hampshire, he instructed his staff to give him something to say about free trade. The voters wanted populism, so he would give them populism.[3] The next day he visited the State

House in Concord and spoke to the legislature. Looking tired, tight-lipped, and depressed, Dole halfheartedly spelled out a new campaign theme. "Corporate profits are setting records and so are corporate layoffs," he muttered. "The bond market finished a spectacular year. But the real average hourly wage is 5 percent lower than it was a decade ago. Two years ago, family earnings were hit with the largest tax increase in the history of America."[4] There was no "Bob Dole does this" or "Bob Dole thinks that," just a couple of dispassionate U-turns. He finished abruptly with an assault upon the UN. A small clique in the gallery went wild, but the state legislators looked confused. This wasn't what they expected Bob Dole to say.[5]

Later, Dole set himself a gutsy challenge: "Whoever wins next Tuesday in New Hampshire, will probably be the Republican nominee." The polls said: Dole 23 percent, Buchanan 20 percent, Alexander 18 percent.[6]

Perhaps Pat Buchanan was onto something with all his talk about free trade? New Hampshire threw a Republican costume party. All the other candidates showed up in their standard suit and tie. Pat came dressed as P. T. Barnum. One man who shook his hand was Ron Mitchell, an electrician. Ron told Pat that he was making the same salary as he was thirteen years ago, while prices were shooting up. He had to send his wife out to work at an oatmeal factory, leaving the kids at home to raise themselves. The Mitchells ate sparingly and kept the thermostat below 55 degrees, "walking around the house like Indians in blankets." Ron worked for Dick Gephardt's Democratic presidential candidacy in 1988. But he couldn't stomach Bill Clinton and none of the Republicans had anything to say about the wage problem. There was one exception; and that's why he had driven miles to come and meet Pat Buchanan. Mitchell said he was impressed. He didn't quite understand how Pat was going to bring the 1950s back, but he seemed to understand his problems. Pat felt his pain.[7]

On Valentine's Day, Pat visited a company in Madbury that grew roses. He bought a dozen for Shelley and laid into free trade. By lowering tariffs on South American flowers, he said, America was "killing one flower grower after another after another after another." He called Dole "the biggest taxer in the modern history of the Republican Party . . . Mr. NAFTA, Mr. [WTO], and Mr. Mexican bailout . . . Mr. Dole put the interest of the big banks—Citibank, Chase Manhattan, Goldman Sachs—ahead of the American people."[8]

There was a huge crowd waiting for him in Manchester later that evening, bigger than ever before. "Look what's going on in our country, my friends," he rasped. "When AT&T lops off 40,000 jobs, the executioner that does it, he's a big hero on the cover of one of these magazines and AT&T stock soars. We've got to have a new conservatism of the heart that looks upon all Americans as brothers and sisters. We've got to be concerned about all of our folks." He reserved a drip of bile for President Clinton, who he sincerely believed was stealing his agenda by embracing the goal of a balanced budget. "Next week he'll be up here with the gun owners of New Hampshire," he laughed, "holding an assault weapon over his head, wearing one of those camouflage outfits, saying, 'Don't try to take mah fah-arms away from me.'" Then, after comparing Dole to Rip Van Winkle, he finished with a candid discussion of strategy that stretched back thirty years to his time with Richard Nixon. "We talked together about Roosevelt's New Deal coalition, about how we could pull apart pieces of it and put together a new majority coalition. That's what we're building. This is an open movement."[9]

Next day, at a breakfast in Goffston, Dole shrugged off Buchanan's assaults. "We left [Iowa] ahead—and in our head, that's important, too. But this is the big one now. This is the one that really counts. This is the shot that's going to be heard around the world, and around America." Twenty-four out of thirty-one of the nation's Republican governors came to New Hampshire to stump for Dole. He signed a pledge never to raise taxes—a huge risk, but a sign that he was putting all his money on a convincing win.[10] Was he stealing some of Pat's positions in an effort to hold on to his lead, journalists asked? Dole winced. No, he said, Bob Dole was just letting Buchanan's voters know that he understood their anger.

Incredibly, for all Pat's success, the people behind Dole still refused to take him seriously. He had peaked in Iowa, they said, and could go no further. Scott Reed and Bill Lacy looked at the numbers and decided that Lamar Alexander—who had not won a single contest—was the real man to beat. If they let him go on getting good press there was a risk that he could emerge as the electable alternative to Dole and Buchanan. So they told Dole to cool the attacks on Pat and focus on Alexander.[11]

Admittedly Lamar! ("a bionically unauthentic man," according to Richard Cohen of *The Washington Post*[12]) looked pretty good in a plaid shirt, walking across the state saying "Hi!" to school children and seniors.[13] He ran off a string of airy radical ideas that were loosely budgeted. Alexander would create a new army for patrolling the border. How much would it cost? "I don't have any idea," he admitted. "But I do think it's one of the things we have to do." He was also going to abolish federal welfare and let taxpayers decide which local charities should get their money. Of course there was the problem that poorer counties would have a smaller tax income to redistribute—and that single mothers would be overlooked in favor of the local dog home—but that wasn't the point. It was new, Lamar was new, and, by implication, everything he did and said was infinitely preferable to Bob Dole.[14]

New Hampshire experienced something akin to "Lamarmania" (the candidate's own words). People were drawn like moths to the flame: cold, depressed voters to the warm hub of television cameras that surrounded him wherever he went. Alexander welcomed them with his piano rendition of "Alexander's Ragtime Band." He told audiences that—in his eyes—they were just swell and he was going to entrust them with a lot more power.[15] Alexander went where the Republican Party seemed unwilling to go—the center. This was a smart move as moderates were looking for a candidate. So far, the race had ignored them.

Elizabeth Hager, a former state legislator and unsuccessful candidate for the gubernatorial nomination, planned to be out of town on polling day. She sent off a blank absentee ballot. "It's hurtful," she said, "but I am really cross." There was no one in the race prepared even to smudge their position on abortion, or to talk about wider social, racial, and environmental problems. Their solutions didn't have to be liberal, but the 40 percent of New Hampshire Republicans who called themselves moderate deserved a voice. Hager and her group, Republicans for Responsible Conservation, ran a bipartisan environmental forum in the weeks before the primary. Al Gore came, but the only Republicans to show were Keyes and Dornan. "The candidates don't realize how strongly New

Hampshire feels about a clean environment," Hager moaned. Although she endorsed and campaigned for Dole in 1988, this year she wasn't even approached. "I think they must have made a calculated decision that they didn't want prominent moderates."[16]

N o humiliation the Tea Party endured in 2010 could match the things that were said about Pat Buchanan in New Hampshire, 1996. To the press he was one part Hitler, one part Marx brother; a slobbering shouting fool, as likely to deny the Holocaust as he was to slip up on a banana. *The New York Times* editorialized: "He has the appeal of the hard-nosed police chief, the take-no-prisoners military man, the town tough given to dressing up and rallying the good old boys on marches or maneuvers. All he needs is a sidearm and an armband."[17] His rallies were "Yankee versions of the kind of Dixie rallies Mr. Wallace introduced to national campaigns. These crowds are more redolent of the trailer park and the bowling alley than the country club. Some of the folks arrive in cars with rusted-out fenders. Sometimes when Mr. Buchanan warns them to 'calm down' it is because he recognizes that a few of the potbellied boys in the back would be happy to throw a punch just for the recreation of it."[18]

Conservatives were some of the harshest critics.[19] Antitax activist Grover Norquist said, "Pat Buchanan is Ronald Reagan with Dick Gephardt stapled to his head."[20] George Will said the brigades were full of "victims and crybabies," presumably referring to the unemployed.

> Buchanan, whose candidacy gives a patina of validity to media caricatures of conservatism, says, "We are taking our party back." From whom? From virtually everyone with conservative credentials. From the spirit of Ronald Reagan, champion of free trade. From William F. Buckley who has judged some Buchanan statements anti-Semitic . . . From Newt Gingrich, a student of history who surely recognizes in Buchanan's brew of nativism and protectionism a recipe concocted by the European right—statism in the service of xenophobic nationalism.

He called Pat a Holocaust denier.[21]

Will confronted Buchanan on ABC's *This Week*. He accused him of fascism and of flirting with the worst excesses of the Christian right. Reporter Sam Donaldson piled in and asked if Buchanan accepted the Creationist view that the world was created in six days and, if he did, what was he going to do about it? He probably expected an equivocation or denial. If so, he didn't know Pat. "God did it according to the Bible," Buchanan said. "You may believe that you are descended from monkeys. I don't believe it . . . The New Testament is literally the word of God and the Old Testament is the inspired word of God. I believe that children should not be forced to believe the Bible, but I think that every child should know what is in the Old and New Testament." He would scrap the Department of Education and ensure that every parent "have a right to insist that godless evolution not be taught to their children or their children not be indoctrinated in it." Will looked stunned. The next day, at an overflow rally, Buchanan said, "Will was yapping at me like a little poodle, and I had to take a newspaper and roll it up and hit him with it." Even though he had a chance of victory, Buchanan refused to change his opinions or mute his answers.[22]

But then a story broke that threatened to stop the campaign in its tracks. The week of the New Hampshire primary, the Center for Public Integrity published a report that said that one of the Buchanan campaign's co-chairs was a Nazi sympathizer. The press had discovered Larry Pratt.[23]

Back in October 1992, Larry Pratt attended a meeting at Estes Park in Colorado to discuss gun rights.[24] Unbeknownst to Pratt, the event was run by a mix of Christian militiamen and neo-Nazis. Louis Beam, a Texas Klansman and a leader of Aryan Nations, was there. So, too, was Aryan Nations chief Richard Butler, who told the group, "I have to confess to you, I am a bigot." Pratt had been invited under false pretenses. He had no idea that these people would be present or that he would share a platform with them. But he had a policy that he had no place judging the politics of the people who reached out to him for help—so long as they didn't violate the law. Pratt privately told the organizers he was disgusted with the views of the people present. But he gave his speech anyway.[25]

Public Integrity's revelation that Pat's co-chair had shared a platform with racists was old news—*Rolling Stone* exposed Pratt's attendance at Estes months before. Nor was Pratt the fringe figure that he was painted as. For good or ill, he was a part of the conservative movement mainstream. The Gun Owners of America contributed to nineteen GOP House and Senate campaigns in 1994. House Majority Leader Dick Armey even turned up on the letterhead of a Pratt-run religious-right subsidiary called Committee to Protect the Family. Pratt also sat on the conservative Council for National Policy. Its membership included Dick Armey, Tom DeLay, and Jesse Helms. Whether Pratt could be labeled an extremist or not, if Pat was guilty by association with him then so, too, was the Republican congressional leadership.[26]

But the Pratt scandal let the press go back to calling Buchanan a bigot. For a couple of days, the media had been forced to take his economic agenda seriously. Now they dug up an interview from 1992 in which Pat complained that he walked through Washington, D.C., one day and saw "these guys . . . sitting on the corner playing bongo drums. I mean, this is the town I grew up in." Rhetoric that was once treated as a joke was now dissected as Hitlerian prose.

Journalists made the troubling discovery that Pat's southern campaign was riddled with ex-Duke activists. He sacked a campaign county chair in Florida who was revealed to be a leader of David Duke's National Association for the Advancement of White People. She took his demand to resign with good grace. "I will do so," she sighed. "I will do anything I can to help Pat Buchanan's campaign." Then he was forced to oust a member of his South Carolina steering committee—William Carter. It turned out that Carter ran David Duke's 1992 presidential campaign in the state. Carter claimed he was recruited by Buchanan's people.[27] David Duke wouldn't go away, either. Over in Louisiana, he held a rally in Baton Rouge against affirmative action. It was only about 175 strong (compared with a counter-demonstration of 7,000) but it still got attention. Did Duke mind that Buchanan had sacked two of his people? Not at all, said Duke: "I think that Pat Buchanan is the best candidate for President. I'll support him."[28]

"Are you anti-Semitic?" a radio host asked Pat. "Oh, for heaven's sakes!" he replied. "We've got rabbis on the board of our campaign. We've had Jewish friends our whole lives . . . Many of the editors that edited [my] columns were

Jewish folks. Do you really think that they would put in their papers something they believed was like that? It's absurd." Anti-Semitism, he moaned, had
become "the cuss word of modern politics."[29]

(The one rabbi on the campaign committee was Yehuda Levin. Levin faced
ridicule in his community for campaigning for Pat, but did so because he saw
Buchanan as an ally in the culture war. The rabbi was shocked by the advent of
gay rights in the 1970s and felt he could not keep silent. "To lose one's own soul
and go to Hell is bad enough," he explained. "But to deny that something is
wrong, and thereby to encourage others to do it, is to sin twice and take two
people to Hell." Levin's presence on the committee might have persuaded some
that Pat wasn't anti-Semitic, but Levin came with baggage. In his protest against
Israel's tolerance of alternative lifestyles, he notoriously renamed the Holy Land
the Homo Land. And of Pat Buchanan, Levin could only say, "Is he an anti-
Semite? I do not know." For the purposes of saving souls, he did not care.)[30]

Phil Gramm endorsed Bob Dole, and joined in the Pat-bashing. He said Buchanan's people handed out racist literature during the Louisiana caucus. "In
the party of Bob Dole and Phil Gramm, there is no room for racism," he said.
Someone asked what he thought about the background of Buchanan's staff and
supporters. "A famous philosopher once said, in no way can you get a keener
insight into a leader than by looking at the people he surrounds himself with."
Gramm waved a hand. "You don't see David Duke standing up here with us."[31]

P at was furious about the Pratt scandal. Not because he was angry with
Pratt or because it threatened to derail him, but because he felt the press
was picking on an innocent man. Buchanan knew Larry and believed he was
no racist. His wife was from Guatemala and he spoke fluent Spanish at home.
He and Bay were fans of Mexican cuisine, and Pratt would interrogate the chef
in every restaurant about how it was cooked. If he spoke to militiamen, Pat
reasoned, he did so because it was his job. They were members of his organization and he had a duty to represent them and stand up for their constitutional
right to carry a gun.[32] Now the press were camping outside Larry's door and
Pat hated the thought that his friend was getting slandered for a crime he did
not commit.[33]

The rest of the team was unsure what to do. Greg Mueller called Bay from the headquarters in Manchester and said, "There are media people here crammed into the building. Their noses are pressed up against the glass outside. They all want to talk about Pratt. Bay, we have to dump him." Mueller could almost taste victory. Why allow one man to squander four years' work?[34] Bay called Larry and asked him to tell her the whole story of Estes. He said he was innocent and she believed him. Her political instincts said Greg was right and Larry should go. But her moral instincts said he should stay. It was up to Bay to broach it with Pat. The final decision lay with him and, as always, only Bay could elicit it. What do you want to do, she asked her brother? There wasn't a moment's hesitation in Pat's reply: Back Larry. "We stick by our friends," he said. "Larry was there for us, so we'll be there for Larry." And rather than run away from it, Pat decided to confront the issue head on. He would turn a debate over race into a debate over character.[35]

That night's New Hampshire debate was a farce. The tone was set by Alexander. Seconds into his opening statement, he tried to set himself apart by accusing Bob Dole of picking on him. He turned to Dole and said, "You're better than negative ads. Why don't you pull them?" Dole shot back, "I didn't know about negative advertising until I saw you do it [first]." The floodgates opened. Gunning for the top spot, Buchanan took on Dole. Thinking long-term, Dole attacked Forbes. Hoping to be the new number two, Alexander went for Dole. Also wanting to place second, Forbes lashed out at Alexander. Buchanan asked Dole why he was running ads accusing him of extremism. "If I am extremist, why are you pirating my ideas and parroting my rhetoric?"

Dole bitched back: "Pat's really gotten carried away tonight. I don't know what happened. Did you have a bad day or something?"

Forbes was asked why he was slipping in the polls. He said that he regretted that "I spent too much time discussing my opponents."

"Too much *money*," corrected Bob Dole.

Struggling for attention, Forbes called Alexander a crook. He said that Lamar! had used his influence as governor of Tennessee to get sweetheart deals for companies that he owned stock in. Bob Dole got bored by all of this and played his trump card. He interrupted Forbes to say that if he insisted upon making negative ads about him, then he might at least use more flattering photographs. He leaned over Robert Dornan to pass on a photo of Dole with his wife and pet dog. "That's Elizabeth on the right," he said, as if there could be confusion.[36]

Dornan, not to be outdone, whooped, "Wow, the senator gave me my opportunity!" He whipped out an enlarged photograph of himself with his latest grandchild. The point: Dornan could breed.[37]

It came to the closing statements. Everyone said their piece about the economy, the budget, Clinton, and negativity. But Buchanan did something different. Pat looked directly into the camera and said Larry Pratt wasn't a racist. Pat wouldn't sack him. "I don't dump people over the side the way they do in Washington and wipe my hands of him and say good-bye," Pat said. "He's got a right to defend himself. And when he gives me his word as a brother Christian, I take him at his word."[38]

It is hard to think of any other politician who would have chosen to stand by someone so controversial, so close to victory.[39] Perhaps it is why many people stuck with Buchanan and pulled the lever for him. The *Washington Post* wandered through a gun-and-sports store in Nashua and found almost unanimous support.[40] Angry people were leaning to Buchanan; angry people looking for a bit of honesty. "I don't think it's true that he's a racist," said Laura Gustafson, a twenty-six-year-old mental health worker. "He just says what he thinks. He's very honest. He's not like a politician." James Carbonaro concurred. "It's not a time for moderation," he said. "Everyone says he's a right-wing nut, and I'm hoping they're right."[41]

After the debate, Bay spoke to Pat privately in his hotel room. He had done the right thing standing by Larry, she said. But the press and the other candidates were shouting so loudly that he was a fascist that his good ideas could no longer get heard. The independents were lost, the undecideds a write-off. Bay urged him to make an appeal to the people who had voted for him in 1992. "Tell them to stick with us. Ask them to be as loyal to you as you have been to Larry." [42]

They cut an ad wherein Pat said "I'm asking you to stand by me." It was a pitch aimed at the Christian conservatives, particularly those without a job.

Pat had never run away from the pro-life issue, he reminded them. And it was he and he alone who fought for tariffs to protect people's jobs. For four years since 1992 he had supported them. Could they not do the same for him? He appealed to the ordinary Joes. "We're going to make the Republican Party working class," he said later that day in a TV interview. "We are revolutionaries."[43]

Some people "respected" Dole and "leaned toward" Alexander. But Buchanan's people "believed" in him. He said it as it was, laid down the line, tore things up. "What are they trying to do to us?" he demanded at a Christian Coalition rally in Manchester. "They" were the liberals in Congress, the businessmen on Wall Street, the globalists in the UN, the European Union. What one supporter called "the creeping crud"—that strange, indefinable sense that the world was going to hell in a handcart. People turning up to the Buchanan headquarters included, "Two tiny identical twin old ladies wearing Buchanan buttons. A Florida couple on their honeymoon. A woman carrying a white Maltese bedecked in barrettes. And a Connecticut man who left his job and drove up in a bullet-riddled truck outfitted with deer headlights."[44] They were mean, tough people these Buchanan folks. An Alexander supporter gave an eighty-four-year-old woman $50 to put one of his signs on her house during a Buchanan rally across the street. The woman, Lillian Giberson, took the money and dumped the sign in a trash can. She went to see Pat at a rally and stuffed the $50 into his pocket. "This is taking from Lamar to pay Pat," she said. "I told God he better win." Lillian Giberson let reporters know that she had spent her whole life working for a Maine Democratic officeholder. Pat was the first, and only, Republican she had ever liked.[45]

It was the day before voting and four polls were held. Two showed Dole and Buchanan even. One showed Dole ahead; one showed Buchanan ahead.[46] All they had to do, Bay repeated, was hold their 1992 vote and they would win. It was a test of loyalty.[47] Journalist Bob Woodward found Pat in his hotel room doing telephone interviews with radio stations. He had been there all day, stretched out on the bed in shirt and tie. He did the morning shows when people were driving off to work, the mid-morning shows when people were on their break, the afternoon shows when people were at lunch, and the late-afternoon shows when people were driving home. While Bob Dole hung around shopping malls shaking hands with two or three people, Pat reached thousands through radio. He said on the phone, "They're afraid of me. Ha! Ha! I can win. It's a dead heat. That's why it's imperative every conservative traditionalist and populist realize this thing could be decided by twenty votes. Come on out to those polls! Get on out there! Bring a friend!"

Greg Mueller came in and reported that a local poll put Pat at 26 percent, Dole at 25. Between calls, Woodward asked what Pat thought Nixon would have made of this? What would the Old Man have said?

"He would have loved it!" said Pat, joy flooding his face. Greg gave him the phone for the twenty-eighth interview.

"How are you doing?" said Buchanan into the receiver. "Ha! Ha! Ha! Ha! Listen, I do hear this thing is dead even . . ."[48]

Forbes was flailing. He held a meeting in a gymnasium in Daniel Webster College in Nashua. He wanted to give a formal, thirty-minute speech but there weren't enough supporters present to pack the bleachers behind him. So aides corralled students. "They asked us to come sit behind him because they needed more people," one told a journalist. "And to pretend that we support him." Forbes was followed everywhere by Vermin Supreme, a street performer from Boston who had some point or other to make about dental plaque. He invaded photo shoots, standing at the back in a Viking costume wielding a giant toothbrush. A French TV reporter asked him what his point was and Vermin lost his cool. Forbes had been dodging his questions about gum decay all week. "I'm frankly fascist!" he shouted and then turned on the candidate. "What are you going to do about the weather?" he demanded.

Forbes answered, "Even a politician can't control that."[49]

Things were worse for trucking millionaire Morry Taylor, who didn't appear in most polls. He slipped off the radar and was spotted drunk and dripping wet on the dance floor of a New Hampshire hotel.[50] Asked what happened, Taylor said the next morning that he had "boogied" (his word) the night away and hadn't even been to bed yet. The press pack was not impressed. Dick Lugar and Alan Keyes were getting squeezed out. Keyes got rock star treatment at the Presidential Bisquick Pancake Flipping Contest. But when the picnic was polled, he came in fifth with 9 percent.[51] The absent Buchanan won with 37 percent. Steve Forbes arrived late, flipped a pancake, and it disintegrated. He joked that he didn't flip-flop like the other candidates. Dornan said he could do better. He flipped a pancake and it went right over his head and off the stage.[52]

On election day, Bob Dole made a remarkable statement. Speaking to more than 300 workers crammed into the cafeteria of Cabletron Systems in Rochester, he said, "We didn't plan it this way. I didn't realize that jobs and trade and what makes America work would become a big issue in the last few days of this campaign."

Buchanan was apoplectic. "Where has he been? Where has he been?" he exploded in his hotel bedroom. "This is a pristine example of an attitude or outlook in Washington—of a Washington, D.C., that is totally out of touch with America. How they could go through an entire campaign of a year and not be aware of this, I do not really know." Pat spent the day at a failing lumberyard and promised the moon to men with rough hands and sad eyes.[53] A reporter, before he could ask a question, introduced himself as an Israeli. Buchanan stopped him in his tracks. "Let's get some Americans up here," he said with a smile.[54]

Buchanan won with 27 percent of the vote. Dole took 26 percent, Alexander 23 percent, and Forbes 12 percent.

At the Buchanan office in Manchester, there was a riot. The media turned up from nowhere and tried to break in. They pushed their way up the narrow staircase, squeezing against the walls, waving boom mics and tape recorders at a terrified Signe McQuaid. At the front was Larry King, shouting, "Where's Pat? Where's Pat?"[55] Pat arrived out back, leaping out a car in a "USA" baseball cap. He spotted a voter and said hello. The press pack ran around. "From across the street," wrote one journalist, "it looked as if Buchanan had suddenly gone berserk, seized a hostage and was being followed by a SWAT team." Pat was world news. He made the front page in London, Tokyo, and Moscow.[56]

Things were just as crazy at camp Lamar!. A TV cameraman trying to catch a shot of the candidate kicked over a tripod. It hit a woman in the face and knocked her unconscious. Alexander climbed the stage and played the piano. In a few hours, Alexander said, he had leaped from "relative obscurity" to central player in "a battle for the soul of our party and its future." Reporters gathered around and he said, "We had to have a big debate with Dole. Now we have to have a big debate with Pat Buchanan."[57]

Bob and Elizabeth Dole were stunned. They drove to the Holiday Inn in Manchester that night in silence. Elizabeth leaned over to her husband and said, "Bob, after all you've done for your party, and your lifetime of public service, if the voters want to turn their backs on you, it doesn't matter." He had done enough—run the Senate, ran for Vice President, ran for President three times. If this was where his career ended, then so be it. "You're head and shoulders above them all," she said. Bob Dole didn't speak.

The ballroom of the hotel was full of local officials nursing martinis; looking confused, nervous. Dole read a speech. He stumbled over the words, obviously reading them for the first time. This was the party of Lincoln, he said; no place for a man like Buchanan. There would now be a "battle for the heart and soul of the Republican Party. In the next month we will decide if we are the party of fear or hope, if we are a party that keeps people out or brings people in. And if we are angry about the present or optimistic about the future."[58]

When Buchanan climbed the stage on election night, they were singing "God Bless America" down on the floor. They began low and grew loud. Buchanan joined in. His voice was raw and broken. The crowd lifted him up and up and up. "We're going to recapture the lost sovereignty of our country," he said, "and we're going to bring it home." Those people down there in the audience were the real people—the "legitimate and rightful heirs of the Founding Fathers." Oh, the aristocracy was quaking in its boots now! "All the forces of the old order are going to rally against us. The establishment is coming together. You can hear them. The fax machines and the phones are buzzing in Washington, D.C." What do we do now? What next? We need "more troops!" he shouted. "Do not wait for orders from headquarters. Mount up and ride to the sound of the guns!"[59] Buchanan was on a roll—rolling, rolling toward the White House.

> They call me names. [He laughed.] Somebody the other night called
> me a socialist. They call me the right. They can't figure out where we

are—left, right, New Deal. Where is that fella? Some strange creature from the '30s, no he's '60s, the 1700s. We don't know where
he's from! [A prophet slighted in his home, that's what Buchanan
was.] We've got to buckle down and we've got to move forward.
We've got to move forward with strength and courage and conviction and take what they're going to deliver to us. We know what
they're going to do to us, coming at us every way. But you stay with
me. Say your prayers about this cause and campaign. I promise
you, I will lead as long as I can and as hard as I can and as far as I
can, until we drop the torch and someone else picks it up!

The crowd went mad. Some jumped, some shouted, some danced. Alan
and Ann Horlick did the Twist right there in the middle of the pit, pink arms
sweating and waving, fingers clicking, red lips hollering. "This is the beginning
of a great movement!" Horlick shouted at a camera. "We old folks feel it. This is
going to be a revolution!"[60]

Pat asked his people to stick with him, and they did. The exit polls showed
that his voters were the poorest and the most likely to be unemployed. They
were more likely to attend church once a week than any other candidate's voters. They were pro-life, pro-gun, and pro-protectionism. And they were more
likely to have previously been registered Democrat. This was the high tide of
the Middle American Revolution.[61]

TWENTY-TWO

Losing

Buchanan took two hours of sleep and ten cups of coffee and flew to Mount Rushmore. How things had changed! Last time Pat came to South Dakota, he and Shelley showed up with a couple of photographers at somewhere called "the Pig Arena." Now 400 supporters and 200 journalists stood before Mount Rushmore; Greg and Terry talked on their cell phones trying to find motel beds for the 35-strong staff. Buchanan waved at Washington, Jefferson, Roosevelt, and Lincoln and said, "All four of these men agreed with me!" Roosevelt had once opined: "In this country, pernicious indulgence in the doctrine of free trade seems inevitably to produce fatty degeneration of the moral fiber." Perhaps, someday, the candidate speculated, they might carve out a spot for Pat Buchanan up there: "Somewhere to the right of Lincoln."[1]

As a sign that he had made it, Clinton gave Pat a Secret Service detail. They had their work cut out for them. When they arrived at Mount Rushmore they were greeted by a guy sitting on the hood of his car with a semiautomatic. They presumed he was a lunatic, disarmed him, and threw him into the back of a truck. It took an hour to work out that Mr. Art Oakes was actually there to introduce Buchanan. He was the candidate's western South Dakota coordinator. Oakes explained that he came armed because he was worried Buchanan might get assassinated by agents of the New World Order. He said no more because he didn't want his words to be misinterpreted by the press. "I will not be part of the lynch mentality that is out to get Pat Buchanan," he told reporters.[2]

In a couple of days, there was the Delaware primary. In one week's time, South Dakota, North Dakota, and Arizona would vote. South Carolina was the week after that. Pat had avoided campaigning in Delaware because New Hampshirites complained that it was holding its primary too soon after theirs, trying to steal their thunder. And he wrote off the Dakotas as farming states loyal to Dole's brand of prairie conservatism. They both relied on exports to survive.[3] Pat decided that he had to win Arizona, the land of Barry Goldwater. A victory there would propel him into South Carolina, and a strong enough showing in South Carolina would give him a shot at winning southern states on Junior and Super Tuesdays.

Polls in Arizona showed Buchanan was the clear favorite.[4] Republican governor Fife Symington said he had it in the bag.[5] Buchanan was now a serious candidate for the presidency of the United States. According to a national poll, more Republicans had an "unfavorable" view of Pat than a "favorable" one (35–29 percent). But his New Hampshire victory was making voters look again. Unlike in 1992, the vast majority of his backers thought they were voting for a future president; 69 percent believed he could beat Clinton in November. Only 35 percent of Dole supporters felt the same about their candidate. Among all Republicans, 51 percent thought Buchanan had the necessary skills to be president. Since January, Buchanan had tripled his support. Nationwide, Dole was first choice among 39 percent of Republicans, Buchanan 25 percent, Alexander 12 percent, and Forbes 5 percent.[6]

On February 25, Pat Buchanan met a wild, angry crowd at a gun rally in Phoenix. They were enthusiastic and heavily armed, an intimidating gang with mullets and mustaches, Levi jeans, and big-wheel trucks. Buchanan, in a business suit, French cuffs, and Venetian silk tie took his jacket off and picked up a rifle with the price tag still attached.

"What do you have to say to the other candidates who are criticizing you?" asked a journalist.

Buchanan swung the gun behind his back and stretched his shoulder blades. "Take a couple of Prozacs, guys," he said. He turned his attention to the crowd.

"Join my crusade for America," he cried. "We're taking back our country, restoring our country to the traditions and ideals upon which it was founded."

"Yeah!" they shouted back. "Amen!" And then came the "Go Pat, go! Go Pat, go!" that had become his battle song, building up to a crescendo of noise that sounded like a native war cry. Buchanan put on a big black cowboy hat. It clashed with the colors of his Brooks Brothers tie, so someone asked if he would prefer a gray one.

"No," he replied with a cartoon snarl. "I'm the bad guy."[7]

To some it felt like Weimar Germany, 1933.[8] Leo Ribuffo, a liberal historian, called Pat Buchanan "the Irish Catholic George Wallace, although he's less anti-black and more anti-Jewish than Wallace." Neoconservative David Frum said Buchanan's "real message is inseparable from his sly Jew-baiting and his not-so-sly queer bashing, from his old record as a segregationist, and his current maunderings about immigrants and the Japanese." The late-night funnies were harsh. On the *Late Show* David Letterman said that Buchanan was "going to take a couple of days off after the New Hampshire primary and then invade Poland." Jay Leno on *The Tonight Show* congratulated Buchanan's campaign on generating so much heat: "It's mostly from burning books and crosses, but it's heat."[9]

The press leaped on the fact that Pat won an unsolicited endorsement from the Russian nationalist Vladimir Zhirinovsky. Zhirinovsky had done surprisingly well in the recent presidential elections by promising every voter a bottle of vodka and a pair of underpants. The Russian suggested that he and Buchanan could work out a bilateral deal to deport their countries' Jews.[10] *Newsweek* ran with a front cover that showed Buchanan's face lit up to make him look like Dracula. The headline: "Preaching Fear." Syndicated conservative radio host Jay Severin took an avalanche of calls angry about the media's attacks. "We're honest people," one caller said. "We pay our taxes. And for the elite media to continually tell me and my husband that we're right-wing extremists, when we used to be considered the normal Americans twenty years ago . . . They try to belittle us, shame us, ridicule us in every way, and they do it proudly. They're treating us like we're children, poor little peasants."

Severin nodded along and concluded, "Most of my callers feel betrayed. They feel with the certainty that the sun will rise tomorrow that there is a demonstrable liberal bias in the gathering and presentation of the news. They feel the system is corrupt." Even conservative media outlets felt the heat. Radio host Rush Limbaugh got a handful of death threats for not backing Buchanan.[11] He told how one listener, "threatened me, and said if you succeed in taking Buchanan down and destroying this country in the process, then I think you should know what we're going to do . . . We will take the country back by force. Lock and load!"[12]

Washington was bewildered, bits of it were panicking.[13] Parts were contemptuous—especially the neoconservative parts. "Someone needs to stand up and defend the Establishment," wrote Bill Kristol. "In the last couple of weeks, there's been too much pseudo-populism, almost too much concern and attention for, quote, the people—that is, the people's will, their prejudices and their foolish opinions. And in a certain sense, we're all paying the price for that now . . . After all, we conservatives are on the side of the lords and barons."[14] Jack Kemp called Buchanan's positions "too pessimistic, too negative, and too exclusionary." Mayor of New York Rudy Giuliani said "I would like to see Mr. Buchanan defeated by the largest margin possible in the state of New York."[15] Colin Powell told ABC's *Prime Time Live* that he could not support Buchanan if he was nominated: "Pat gives out a message of intolerance, which I think is very unfortunate. This is not the time for intolerance. This is the time for inclusion."[16]

The problem the establishment faced was deciding which moderate candidate to rally around. Alexander had proven himself as a vote getter, but he wasn't even on the ballot in Pennsylvania and New York. There was a move to coalesce around Dole, but he was dull and attracted no enthusiastic support. For his part, Dole decided to run with the "mainstream vs. the extreme" theme he raised on the night of the New Hampshire vote. He told a crowd in North Dakota, "It's a race between hope . . . and fear. It's about freedom and it's about intolerance . . . It's about maintaining the Republican Congress. This is deadly serious business."[17] Commonly used words were "fear, intolerant, divide, and fringe." In Colorado, he pointed out that Buchanan was nothing but an upstart celebrity. "I may not be a good talk show host, but I'm a good leader," said the senator. "I've been in the real crossfire. It wasn't on television; it was over in Italy somewhere, a long time ago."[18]

Calling Buchanan an extremist led to a backlash among some movement conservatives, particularly evangelicals. The tone was critical at that week's Conservative Political Action Conference in Washington, D.C. Ralph Reed told the gathering, "It is strategically unwise and politically shortsighted to label Buchanan or his supporters as, ipso facto, extremists or intolerant. That is the language of the left and the epithets of the Democrats. Using those kinds of terms will only drive more religious conservatives toward Buchanan and potentially propel him to the nomination." Besides, said several speakers, don't we share many of Buchanan's views? Dole's language tarred them as much as it did Buchanan, and his people were mostly well intentioned. The head of CPAC, David Keene, called Dole's strategy, "very troubling . . . It seems to be geared not to taking on Pat Buchanan's ideas, which should be taken on, but rather to co-opting some of the worst of those ideas and then criticizing conservatives generically."[19]

The Delaware primary came and went with little press attention. Team Dole thought they could count on this northeastern state to deliver, but they didn't realize how much Forbes was spending on ads there. Initial exit polls showed them coming in third and Bob Dole hit the roof. Finally it evened out to Forbes on 33 percent, Dole 27 percent, and Buchanan 19 percent.[20] Dole laughed it off. "Forbes spent $15 million against me," he said. "I hope he goes broke."[21] But behind the scenes, he demanded a shake-up. Advertising was bad and the candidate wasn't getting speeches long enough in advance to learn them. His private polls were way off and Dole put all his effort into the wrong areas because of them. To protect his own position, Scott Reed took command and convinced Dole to sack old hand Bill Lacy.[22]

A miserable Dole took a pilgrimage to Paradise Valley, Arizona. His bus drove through the shadows of the McDowell Meetings to a ranch where much of this had started. Sitting by a log fire, frail old Barry Goldwater gave Bob

Dole his blessing. "He is the heir," croaked Goldwater, "to the Barry Goldwater, Ronald Reagan legacy of conservatism."

"Was Buchanan not an heir, too?" asked a reporter. Definitely not, scowled Goldwater. He called Buchanan's message "fearful and divisive." Then, going off script, Bob Dole sighed, "Barry and I—we've sort of become the liberals."

Goldwater liked that and laughed. "We're the new liberals of the Republican Party," he said. "Can you imagine that?"[23]

Pat started to get it into his head that he might actually win Arizona. He was way behind in money and endorsements, but ahead in volunteers and charisma. Phil Gramm's people gave Dole a plush, Phoenix office, along with John McCain's endorsement. It was a rocket-age setup; the operations room looked like the inside of ground control—flashing lights, TV screens, and row upon row of telephones.[24] A couple of miles away, Buchanan's campaign was shaking to life in a suburb called Mesa. Karen Johnson, a mother of eleven, put her furniture into storage so that she could transform her modest tract home into a headquarters. The kitchen and bedrooms were crammed with folding tables and telephones staffed by volunteers. There was a line of people to collect a lawn sign. It looked like a garage sale. "This is flying by a wing and a prayer, but I think Pat's going to win," said Johnson. "It's crazy how this had just kind of mushroomed." Bob Wolff was in charge of motivating volunteers. He had driven seventy miles to make telephone calls from Johnson's kitchen. He was angry that the federal government controlled 70 percent of the state's land in parks or reserves. Buchanan would give it all back. "I'm telling you, the federal government should only control ten square miles around Washington, D.C.," Wolff said between calls. "The truth is, I think this is unconstitutional."[25]

It was a wild ride. One campaign day started at an Arizona Right to Life breakfast. Pat promised an end to the "evil empire" of abortion and said in cases of rape, "we should execute the rapist and let the unborn child live." Next, he drove down to Gila Bend, a predominantly Hispanic town, and spoke out against immigration. He was interrupted continuously by a student, Marciano Murillo.

Murillo shouted, "Why are you talking against Mexicans when they're coming here for a better life for their families? They come here to work. They help this economy."

"I know they work hard," Buchanan replied. "But they've got no right to break our laws and break into our country and go on welfare, and some of them commit crimes."

"Why do you only say Mexicans are on welfare?" Murillo asked. "When you have millions of African-Americans and Caucasians on welfare . . . Let me tell you something—"

But Buchanan had enough. "Let me finish, friend," he sneered. "I've got the microphone."[26]

Buchanan events were like a revival meeting; a polyphonic chorus of Pat shouting and the crowd shouting back. When Buchanan denounced the Mexican bailout in Denver, someone at a rally yelled: "That's our money!" When Buchanan declared in Gila Bend, Arizona, that American soldiers "didn't take an oath to the United Nations—they took an oath to you and me," people shouted out "Yes!" and "Amen!" and jumped out of their chairs in excitement. One old boy at a school rally hoisted a Confederate flag every time Buchanan hit a high note, shouting out: "Liberty or death! Liberty or death!"

At face value, these were just ordinary folks down on their luck. But actually, many had a long list of well-established grievances. At a Denver rally, Albert Bolton, forty-two, worked in his first-ever campaign as a volunteer. He signed people up wearing a T-shirt that read, "As a former fetus, I oppose abortion." Eric V. Field, president of the Jewish Republican Coalition of Colorado, circulated a petition against affirmative action. June Fish, a lady in her seventies, was there because a friend told her Buchanan was addressing the issue that had concerned her since the UN Charter was ratified in 1945: "The threat of a world government." George Allen, a rancher from San Luis Valley, wearing a cowboy hat and sipping a beer, described himself as a "guy who gets up at 5:30 in the morning" and was tired of paying taxes for social programs. "I'm the guy who is footing the bill," he drawled, "and I'm sick of it."[27]

The militias liked Pat. He was one of them—a man who saw the patterns in supposedly unrelated events, who connected the dots, who called out the New

World Order. Bob Fletcher, a militiaman and radio host in West Los Angeles, said, "Pat's general program is absolutely verbatim with those things that we've been talking about." The New World Order, the slaughter of innocents in Waco, the liberal conspiracy to reduce the native population. "Everything he says, it looks like I wrote his platform. The powers that be will do everything to stop him. Even if that means sending him to Dallas, Texas, to take a ride in an open convertible." Russell Smith, head of the Texas Constitutional Militia, was a volunteer. "My wife and I are working hard for him," he said. "We're educating people, talking to people, passing out fliers. Any place we see people, any place, we strike up a conversation. At gun rallies. At gun shows. And we're getting a pretty good reception."[28]

The candidates piled in on Buchanan at a debate in Arizona. "Pat, I'm not going to let you hijack my party," said Alexander. "We need a strong America, not a divided, pessimistic America."

"When you put politicians in charge of trade, you lose," said Forbes. "Tariffs are one more form of taxes. I believe in free trade."

Buchanan loved it. Any other candidate might have withered under such attacks; Buchanan blossomed. "Lamar, welcome to *Crossfire*," he joked. This election, he said, "is a battle for the heart and soul of our party" that would determine whether the GOP would defend "working men and women of this country [who have been] betrayed by trade deals . . . I'm only asking the GOP, please keep the door open, I will bring these good people home." Alexander tried to put Buchanan down by quoting his own governmental and business experience. He did it so often that it began to attract groans from the audience. "Lamar, we're not electing a resume," Buchanan interjected and the audience laughed.[29]

But on the ground, Buchanan's staff was running into a problem. Greg Mueller met "hundreds" of people who told him that they loved Pat and were thrilled by his victory in New Hampshire. But they had already voted. Arizonans could apply for a postal ballot. In late 1995, when he was riding high in the polls, Forbes sent out ballot applications to thousands of voters, followed by a $4 million TV campaign introducing him as the only conservative who could beat Dole. Before Iowa and New Hampshire and the revelations about Forbes's past views on abortion, this had the ring of truth. Roughly one-third of Arizonans voted long before Pat became competitive. The campaign hadn't even started and Forbes had already won.[30]

Yet all Pat and Bay could see were the huge lines outside the polling booths. Touring the state, they felt sure they had a landslide on their hands. Governor Symington called Bay to offer his congratulations. He could see a line forming down the street and outside his own office, covered in "Go Pat, go!" signs. But then Bay got calls from activists saying that they had been turned away from voting stations. According to local brigaders, for two hours at lunchtime, the Maricopa county station was shut down without explanation.[31] Bay believed it was a conspiracy: "They wanted to suppress the vote. They knew our people would be headed there during their lunch hours. By closing it, they cost us a crucial few hundred votes."[32]

Exit polls looked good: Buchanan seemingly placed first, followed by Forbes and Dole. Dole comfortably won North and South Dakota, but no one was watching those states. On ABC, Ted Koppel pronounced Pat the winner of Arizona and Dole effectively out of the race. "The candidate is not looking well, politically speaking," he said of the senator. "Yes, he won North and South Dakota tonight, but that was not the prize of this primary election day. The prize was Arizona, with its thirty-nine delegates, winner take all. Bob Dole did not win in Arizona: he came third." On behalf of the media, Koppel offered Pat an apology. "We've all been so wrong about the Buchanan candidacy. And now there is the smell of genuine electric excitement about it."[33]

But when voters woke up the next day, the result was: Forbes 33 percent, Dole 30 percent, Buchanan 27 percent. The early postal voting gave Forbes an edge, hid Dole's inbuilt strength, and took support away from Pat. The exit polls were right: Pat won the vote that night; but not by enough to win the entire primary.[34] Ignoring everything they knew about Forbes's strength in postal ballots, the brigaders preferred to believe that Dole had stolen it. Connie Mackey said, "The establishment couldn't let us win. A lot of strange things went on . . . I wouldn't be surprised if they cheated." Pat was deflated. He looked confused. Typically, he chatted about the changing dynamics of the race with reporters—the political analyst in him appreciating the drama. "It's fascinating, isn't it?" he commented to a journalist. "It's hard to figure what army to strike."[35]

. . .

Sam Francis offered Pat encouragement. It wasn't over yet. Sam wrote in
Chronicles magazine:

> For those on the right who only want to oust the incumbent resi-
> dent of the White House or impress their friends with invitations
> to the court soirees of the next Republican successor to the presi-
> dential purple, winning [Arizona] is all that matters . . . But the
> courtiers and professional partisans miss the larger victory the
> Buchanan campaign is on the eve of winning . . . The reason Bu-
> chanan has not been submerged is that the torch he carries illumi-
> nates new social forces that only now are forming a common
> political consciousness . . . Those forces consist, of course, of the
> broad social and cultural spectrum of Middle America.[36]

South Carolina was next and Sam said that it looked like fertile ground for
the Middle American Revolution.[37] Said one of Pat's local fans: "The people
coming together under the campaign for Pat Buchanan are the same people
who came together for Ronald Reagan in 1980 . . . This is the coalition that can
win the nomination and it is the only coalition that can beat Bill Clinton."[38]
Traditionalists were enraged by recent attempts to lower the Confederate battle
flag from the state capitol building and to allow women to study at the all-male
military academy, the Citadel. The leadership of the local Christian Coalition
was largely behind Dole, but its membership liked Pat.[39] On Pat's campaign
board now sat Gramm's former chair state representative Terry Haskins, Reagan's 1980 state co-chairman Ambassador Weston Adams, Rick Daniels of the
NRA, Ellie Lits of the Christian Coalition, and Holly Gatling of South Carolina
Citizens for Life.[40]

Pat also hoped to pick up support among those affected by layoffs in the
textile industry. South Carolina textile jobs fell from 162,000 in 1984 to 126,000
in 1996. Textile imports to the U.S. exceeded exports by $32.2 billion in 1995.[41]
But the picture was more complicated than Pat's speeches suggested. Take the
town of Iva, population 1,200. On the edge of town sat the silent, empty Jack-

son Mills plant. The plant spent the last decade swimming against a tide of cheap imports. When the Far East moved in on the cotton-textile market, the plant adjusted to produce rayon and flax fibers. But then companies in India and Pakistan began competing in rayon. After a year of cutbacks, the plant closed. Four hundred lost their jobs. Next door apparel maker Iva Manufacturing Co. saw its output and employment drop by 80 percent in the same period. The culprit was NAFTA, said the president of Jackson Mills. "The great fault in our national policy is we don't have a manufacturing policy. If we are chosen to be phased out, something should be done to slow down and smooth out the process . . . I'm pleased that at least Mr. Buchanan has brought this issue up."

But for every loser in free trade, its supporters claimed a winner. David Lewis, who ran the Texaco on the edge of Iva, worried aloud that trade barriers would slow exports. "If we stop letting other countries sell stuff to us, they're going to stop letting us sell stuff to them. That only makes sense."[42] And for an economy that increasingly relied on external investment, this was a big worry. Since 1990, exports from South Carolina doubled. Foreign makers of cars rushed to invest in a state with low taxes, low wages, and a lot of skilled workers looking for a job. The week of the primary, BMW announced a $200 million expansion of a local plant, creating 1,700 new jobs.[43] Doug Woodward, an economist at the University of South Carolina, said that Buchanan's views on abortion would help him, but that his position on trade was a vote loser. "It's going to sound odd," he said, "when Buchanan says, 'Foreigners are the problem.' They're going to say, 'Wait, I work for them.'"[44]

Dole had to win South Carolina, and win big. The media and his team built it up so that a loss would kill his campaign, but a victory would guarantee him the nomination.[45] Dole decided to use the trade issue, to turn South Carolina into a referendum on Pat's economics.[46] He told voters that Pat's protectionism would turn away foreign investors.[47] "Pat is thinking of a South that he saw when he campaigned with Richard Nixon in the 1960s, when there used to be a lot of sweatshops with a lot of manual labor," said Dole's senior southern consultant. "The South is changing and our economies are diversified and we have brought ourselves to the level where we are able to compete globally."[48] The senator developed a more nuanced approach to the issue, an approach that would become Republican policy in November. His slogan was "Fair Trade, not Free Trade." There would be no reversal of free trade agreements, but President Dole would strictly enforce those clauses that were supposed to protect the American worker. He said, "Illegal shipments must stop. Trade cheating must stop. Surrender at the negotiating table must stop."[49]

The message was backed up by an all-star team of South Carolina politicians. Aside from most of the state's GOP leadership, Dole was joined on the campaign trail by Gov. David Beasley and Sen. Strom Thurmond. Both were nervous about the growth of the Christian Coalition and didn't want the party machine to lose its grip. Secretary of State Jim Miles let reporters know that if Dole lost, he would challenge the aging Thurmond in the senatorial primaries.[50] It was a test of nerve for the establishment. They poured manpower and money into the Dole campaign. Dole received $172,202 in one week from local donors; Buchanan got just $59,520, most of it from a textile manufacturer.[51]

The press rallied, too, and Dole won the endorsement of every major local paper. Said *The State*:

> Pat Buchanan rose to prominence shouting at people on television.
> He is still shouting, trying to frighten us into voting for him. He
> exploits our fear for our jobs, our fear of free enterprise, our fear of
> those different from ourselves. Bob Dole isn't afraid of foreigners.
> He's faced the worst they can dish out. Pat Buchanan, who (like
> Bill Clinton) never served in uniform, talks tough about running
> "to the sound of the guns." Bob Dole doesn't talk like that because
> he's heard those guns too closely.

Republican news outlets evoked a quiet conservatism that was different from Buchanan's populism. South Carolinians liked to think of themselves as gentlemen farmers, not revolting peasants. The city of Charleston had the air of an English seaside town, not Paris at the barricades.[52]

On paper, South Carolina was a good test site for the Buchanan coalition and the Middle American Revolution. But, in practice, the locals were too conservative to pull the lever for a revolution of any stripe. A national poll showed that Pat was gaining ground among the public at large, but at the expense of alienating traditional Republicans. His rating was now 45 percent favorable and 44 percent unfavorable. His support was highest among the poor and lowest among the rich: 52 percent of college graduates and 53 percent of those who earned $75,000 a year or more disliked his campaign.[53] Pat's pitch to the blue-collar voter was increasingly alienating him from Republican voters. Outside a closed textile factory, he said, "I know there are Democrats that agree with me, and there are independents that agree with me. Go ahead and join the party of greed for a day, and then resign after that!"[54]

The day before the vote, there was a noontime debate in Columbia. Alan Keyes was excluded because of his single-digit poll numbers and announced that he was going on a hunger strike in protest.[55] The debate got nasty. The candidates were asked to criticize their opponents' ads and defend their own. Forbes's claim that Alexander got rich by using his political connections as Tennessee governor came under fire. "Steve, you haven't learned a single thing in your whole campaign—you know that's not true," said Alexander. He told Forbes, "You should be ashamed of yourself—smearing me, smearing the other candidates."

Forbes replied: "That was a charitable ad—that ad did not talk about some of those cozy business deals you did as governor."

Alexander exploded: "You just wait a minute! My ethics have never been questioned . . . You should go practice your dirty business on a race for the school board before you try for the Presidency of the United States of America."

Buchanan agreed that things had turned mean. He didn't like Dole's ads that called him "Too extreme" to be the nominee. "I think that displays the hollowness of your campaign," he barked at the senator.

"Yeah!" said Alexander. "Why don't you tell us where you want to take the country instead of calling Pat Buchanan names and distorting my record? While I was keeping taxes low, you raised taxes."

"Amen to Alexander," said Pat.[56]

Pat spent the afternoon at the Citadel military school. He spoke to the boys through the iron bars of the school gate. In the pouring rain, he declared that, if elected, he would have the Justice Department lawyers protect the school from admitting women. "As of today, you are changing sides," Buchanan would tell them. "You are on the side of the Citadel, or you are going back to

Berkeley!" He got a rousing round of applause.[57] That night, all four candidates showed up at the Christian Coalition God and Country meeting in Columbia. The Embassy Suites ballroom was so full that police had to turn people away. Pat spoke first and was the clear favorite. He struggled to be heard above cries of "Go Pat, go!" Then Dole spoke to lesser applause, then Alexander to a smattering, and then Forbes to none. By the time Forbes took questions at 10:20 p.m. the hall was half empty. Dole went back to Washington, D.C., for a vote. Pat boarded a plane for a rally in Charleston. A reporter beckoned him over to ask more questions. Buchanan cupped his hands to his mouth and shouted, "Use the stuff I said at the Citadel!" He laughed and skipped up the gangway. At midnight, Alan Keyes ended his fast.[58]

The next day, the result was Dole 45 percent, Buchanan 29 percent, Alexander 13 percent, and Forbes 10 percent. It was over.

The trade issue reached its limit. Half the voters said American trade policies had created more jobs for South Carolina. Dole won the support of half of those voters; Buchanan only one-fifth. Half of the voters said Pat was too extreme, and Dole won two-thirds of them.[59] Money and influence helped the result, but Bob Dole had found his message, too. With Buchanan and the rest out of the way, he was free to say what he wanted. And finally he spoke of the kind of conservatism that the Greatest Generation understood: humble, decent, charitable, human. In Hartford, Connecticut, while waiting for the results, he talked to some friends at the statehouse. What he said made people cry:

> You show up to these things and some people think you're born in a blue suit and a necktie. That's not the case. That's not the case. Let me tell you just a little about Bob Dole, just so you'll understand who I am and where I'm from . . . Like everyone else my age—and I see some out here—we went off to war, in World War II, and like some, I got tied up in Italy somewhere.
>
> I ended up being wounded like a lot of young men were, and I spent 39 months in hospitals. And that taught me a lot, a lot about people, and a lot about being sensitive, a lot about being caring. I couldn't feed myself. I couldn't dress myself. I couldn't walk. I still use a buttonhook every day.

But I learned a lot about Bob Dole, too. I learned a lot about myself. At first I didn't think it was fair. Then I looked around in the next bed, and they were taking somebody away who had passed away or somebody who had lost both legs or done something else, so I didn't feel so sorry for myself.

But I want you to know, I understand America. I understand America. I understand people who have problems. I understand there are people who need help from our government. I've never said that government is bad. I say we ought to downsize it, it could be better, it could be more efficient, and we could save money. But the Government does a lot of good things.[60]

He never said "whatever" once.

TWENTY-THREE

Triumph of the Big Tent

In the weeks after South Carolina, Buchanan continued to poll well. Three days later, on Junior Tuesday, he sped through Georgia and New England in search of votes. On the Georgia-Alabama border, he stood on the back of a bunting-covered truck and tore into members of Congress and their pensions, into Boeing for opening a plant in China, and into corporations whose officers, he said, "Get their big mugs on magazine covers for chopping jobs . . . We're going to go up to that big Republican country club and demand admission. We're going to use the swimming pool and everything." Afterward, as he scooped up pancakes and coffee in Atlanta, a journalist pointed out that a poll showed he had run better among Democrats and independents in South Carolina than he did Republicans. Pat laughed. "Got to do something about that," he said.

Ever the analyst, Pat couldn't hold off from letting his feelings show. One minute he'd be up on top of the truck smashing "Beltway Bob." The next he'd be counting on his fingers the coulda-shoulda-beens. "If we'd have won Arizona," he said, "click, click, click, everything would have fallen into place. But the absentee ballots saved Bob Dole, and Steve Forbes spent $4 million. If we had more time, I could beat all these guys. If I had more money, I'd kill them. If they didn't have the Governor and the former Governor and Strom Thurmond in South Carolina, we'd have won there." He looked lonely in the middle of nowhere, talking on his cell to Bay in D.C., asking where she wanted him to go next. When he caught the press looking sympathetic, he said, "Polls are irrelevant. Focus groups are irrelevant, consultants, advance men, too. Just a lot of additional baggage to drag around."[1]

At a debate in Atlanta, Alexander laid into Buchanan's support for tariffs. Pat corrected him on the facts then commented, "I'm surprised you didn't study this up at Princeton or that little prep school you went to." Alan Keyes was denied the right to participate again. This time, he tried to rush the security people and was dragged off to jail.[2]

Georgia was Pat's best showing on Junior Tuesday, March 5. He took 29 percent to Dole's 41 percent. Elsewhere, he scored 25 percent in Massachusetts, 24 percent in Maine, and 21 percent in Maryland. All respectable tallies, but the anti-Dole vote was split and he swept all eight contested states with pluralities of 40 percent or more.[3] Richard Lugar and Lamar Alexander bailed out and endorsed Dole. On March 7, New York voted. Steve Forbes received a last minute fillip with an endorsement by Jack Kemp. Dole was insulted; he had courted Kemp all year. Scott Reed rang the congressman and begged him not to do it. It would damage his relationship with the GOP, Reed said. Kemp shrugged his shoulders. The love affair was already over. Pat's strong showing suggested Kemp was too centrist for the modern Republican Party.[4] Kemp backed Forbes and Forbes lost 30 percent to Dole's 55 percent. Forbes quit, along with Morry Taylor.[5]

There was a flash of hope in Missouri, a hint of what could have been. The Missouri GOP was in the middle of civil war over abortion, and its caucuses on March 9 divided not on candidates but on the life issue. Pat's campaign was run by the wife of a county commissioner and a passionate Christian. As a teacher, she said that she often used Pat's columns in class as examples of good grammar or religious instruction.[6] Pat also got help from Phyllis Schlafly, the dainty little antifeminist who had raised six children and beaten the Equal Rights Amendment. Schlafly held a rally in Westport, greeting a large pro-life crowd with the cry, "Welcome peasants!" She laid into Bob Dole and his greedy, fat-cat friends and set out the logic for a Buchanan nomination: He at least would have something to debate about with Bill Clinton. Dole had compromised, or threatened compromise, on the issues of NAFTA, Bosnia, and abortion. "God's hand is in Pat's campaign," said local businessman Frank Kellam.[7]

The caucus was unpleasant. Buchanan's people turned up in big numbers, many of them new and militant. Moments before the meeting began at the second congressional district in St. Louis, Committeewoman Jan Klarich glanced around the room and decided "It's going to be a fiasco. The Buchanan people are motivated by passion. The Dole people, we're the organizers. We're the type that tend not to be passionate." The leader of the brigaders was Eric Enlow, a twenty-three-year-old radio producer. He won a 533–373 vote on who should be chair. The Dole people objected and tried to get the room to accept a proportional, rather than a winner-takes-all, distribution of delegates. The brigaders chanted "No, no, no!" and voted it down. Next the Dole people tried to get the vote thrown out because there were known Democrats in the room voting for Buchanan. Someone spotted Norman Champ, a Clayton Township Democratic committeeman. When Dole's people announced from the podium that Champ was sitting with the Buchananites, the brigaders roared their approval. That's when half the Dole people walked out. In a last-ditch effort, Dole activist Loretto Wagner took to the podium and accused Buchanan of distorting Dole's position on life. The brigaders shouted her down and she gave up. At least, pleaded another Dole person, let this convention pledge support for the Republican nominee, whoever that might eventually be? Eric Enlow threw that motion out. He couldn't vote for anyone but Pat. "Buchanan is the only vision of conservatism that is making any effort to cross ideological lines," he said. Lisa Linn, twenty-six, of Maryland Heights, agreed: "I'm a Christian, and I'm totally pro-life—no exceptions." Her four-year-old daughter ran around the gym waving a poster, shouting "Go Pat, go!"[8]

Buchanan won the March 9 Missouri caucus with 35 percent to Dole's 30 percent.[9] He pledged to fight on for the sake of the unborn: "If Bob Dole is able to win this, if the people around him in the establishment win it, they will sell out the right-to-life movement in the flicker of an eyelash," he said. "I would urge the right-to-life movement right now, if you really care about this cause as I think you know I do, join and unite behind me now. We need you."[10] On March 12, Pat took roughly a quarter of the vote in the Super Tuesday primaries.[11] His last decent showing was Michigan on March 17, where he took 34–51 percent. "After that, it all went quiet," remembered Signe McQuaid. "The phones stopped ringing."[12]

. . .

The culture war was back. Pat wrote to supporters to say that victory in the primaries was now unlikely. But that didn't mean that they had to concede the battle of ideas. "No, my friend, we've come too far in this campaign to give up now. I intend to go to the Republican National Convention in San Diego and fight with all the fervor I have for a conservative platform." He warned that "liberal Republicans" were readying themselves to take over the GOP with pro-choice and pro-gay planks. He pledged instead to fight for the abolition of the Department of Education, prayer in schools, an end to "taxpayer subsidies of public television, which often glorifies in the homosexual lifestyle," and for a Human Life amendment to the Constitution. "Don't let the moderate establishment hijack our party and produce another electoral disaster," he warned.[13]

The Dole people presumed that Pat would now drop out and endorse their man. Dole wanted it, and not just because he needed it. Dole admired Buchanan. "I like his wit and I like that smile he has," he told Scott Reed. "And he kind of laughs at himself, you know, that little laugh. Beltway Bob!" he repeated. "Busboy for corporate America! You've got to admire a guy like that. I mean, it doesn't irritate me. If somebody else would say that, I'd be all upset, but when Buchanan does it I think, boy, that guy's smart."[14] But Pat let it be known that not only was he staying in right up to the convention, but that he couldn't guarantee an endorsement.[15] Confused, Scott Reed called Bay. He had worked with her before and they had a good relationship. He always thought of her as a levelheaded, party loyal operative. He was shocked. "She went nuts and yelled, 'We're going third party. Pat's not there, but I am. What you've done is outrageous.' The personal assault on Pat in the negative Dole ads had been out of bounds, she said, the worst thing in American politics in twenty-five years." Bay refused even to meet to talk about it. Reed felt she was "psycho" and that Buchanan "was on a jihad."[16]

The conversation was more revealing than Scott Reed realized. Bay had concluded that there wasn't room in the GOP for Pat. His conservative message was too hot and the establishment hated him too much. Besides, he was chasing votes outside the party—among the independents and Democrats.[17]

Bay got that, but Pat didn't like the implications. In his defining speech at the 1992 Republican convention, he had told the brigades: "The [GOP] is our home; this party is where we belong. And don't let anyone tell you any different." That meant something back then, although he wasn't so sure now. A new dynamic opened up in the relationship between brother and sister. From thereon in, Bay became bolder and more radical.[18]

N ow that he was the winner, Bob Dole went about reerecting the Big Tent. Step One: Pat Buchanan was banned from speaking at the convention. Step Two: Colin Powell and several other moderates were given primetime slots instead. "You look at the lineup for opening night—Colin Powell, President Ford, Nancy Reagan," said the leader of the gay Log Cabin Republicans group. "With those types out there, moderate Republicans are feeling very good about the convention." As the summer wore on, they began to sense movement on the social issues. Bob Dole sent a signal that he was prepared to negotiate on some of the cultural stuff Republicans took for granted.[19] The platform committee met in the first week of August to discuss the party's plank calling for a constitutional ban on abortion. Of the platform delegates, forty-one told *USA Today* that they wanted to keep it, thirty-one to scrap it, and twenty-five refused to say.[20] "The Dole people certainly wanted to get rid of the abortion plank," opined Phyllis Schlafly. "At the very least, they wanted to water it down . . . But the Republican Party was nothing if it wasn't about abortion. We had been pro-life since 1980."[21] Diana Banister was a native Californian and in charge of putting together the Buchanan effort at the convention in San Diego. She said, "What they wanted to do was terrible, to wipe away twenty years of activism. It convinced many of our people that Dole was basically a liberal."[22]

In fact, all Bob Dole wanted was a "tolerance clause" in the platform. It read: "While our party remains steadfast in its commitment to advancing its historic principles and ideals, we also recognize that members of our party have deeply held and sometimes differing views." But it was offensive enough to bring together the Coalition to Keep the Republican Party Pro-Life, whose membership included Schlafly, Buchanan, and Ralph Reed. If Dole messed with the platform, they said, he would lose the brigaders. At a press conference, Reed pointed out that Dole was only attracting 50–60 percent of the evangelical vote. "He has to get between 75 and 80 percent of that vote, and he is not going to do that unless he sends a strong [pro-life] call."

"If you look at the polls now," said Pat, "one of the things Bob Dole has to do in the next few weeks is bring his base back home. This is the only way to do it."[23]

"We were never going to be anything other than pro-life," insisted Scott Reed. "Bob Dole had been visibly pro-life for forty years. This was about trying to show that the conservatives still controlled the party even though Pat lost. And there was no need. They did."[24] Ralph Reed flexed his muscles and threatened to put in a high-tech whipping operation.[25] "We spent a ton of money," he said. "We've got a war room two blocks from here, we've got a communications command center, we went to Motorola and had them develop software specifically for this convention." Then Bob Dole announced a compromise: The tolerance language would only feature as part of a minority report. The call for a constitutional ban would stay. Reed looked disappointed. His Motorola antiabortion action center would go to waste. "I think that it is now unlikely that the system will have to be deployed for anything," he said with a pout.[26]

Bay tried to get Pat a slot at the convention, but Dole said no. Pat was insulted. It seemed that the GOP was stealing his best ideas, but distancing itself from him.[27] The new party platform was a list of brigade demands: fair trade not free trade, a call for protection of American sovereignty, and a "defense of American borders." The brigades were essential to victory in November, admitted some in the establishment. The delegate chair from Iowa, Brian Kennedy, told *The Washington Post* that the GOP in his state had gone from trailing registered Democrats by 100,000 voters in 1994 to leading them by 15,000 now. That, said Kennedy, was thanks to Pat Buchanan.[28] But if Pat played too big a role in the convention, memories of 1992 might resurface. "It was a hateful speech," said the chair of the Connecticut delegates, remembering Pat's culture war pitch four years ago. "It was crazy. It was very difficult to be at that convention." Dole made sure it never happened again.[29]

. . .

T he day before the 1996 convention, Pat threw a big rally in San Diego. The mood was ugly. It was a hot, dry afternoon and the rumor was that Buchanan was going to endorse Dole. After four years of fighting, after coming so close to toppling the kings in their castles, the peasants weren't ready to accept that. Connie Mackey was worried for Pat's safety. There were people in that crowd with hunting rifles. She and the other staff tried to persuade him to not give the endorsement onstage. But Buchanan had never been anything but square with his people, and he intended to tell them truth. Oliver North warmed up the crowd.[30]

An argument broke out, captured on TV. Ruby Ingram, wearing seersucker shorts and red, white, and blue earrings was screaming "The Truth" at the top of her voice. She was interrupted by Don (surname withheld), clad in jeans, an unbuttoned vest, and a single silver hoop earring. Don was a gay schoolteacher who had been thrown out of the military after they found a letter to his lover.

"Why don't you want me to share my life with who I choose?" he said to cries of "Pervert!"

"What's your relationship with Jesus?" Ruby demanded.

"It doesn't matter," replied Don. "In this country there's freedom of religion."

"You have to accept Jesus as your savior, or you're going to Hell," she said.

"You're making our lives Hell here on Earth," he screamed.

A Baptist minister jumped between the two to protect Ruby. "Why don't you get your lover and go reproduce someplace?" he said to Don. "Just stay away from my kids and leave me alone!"[31]

Pat walked out onstage. The crowd erupted. It seemed they would have done anything he asked at that moment. If he had told them to, they would have stormed the convention and taken Bob Dole hostage. Pat kept them high as he talked about the New World Order and how they shook them to their eyeteeth. Then he brought them down as he ticked off those obsessive coulda-beens: "Had Lamar just run second in New Hampshire, instead of third," he said, "we now know Senator Dole would have quit the race." There were some boos at the mention of Dole. But Pat predicted that someday the Republican

Party would become a "Buchanan Party." If that day did not come, then perhaps a third party might be necessary. The crowd rose to their feet and chanted, "Go Pat, go! Go Pat, go!" He waved them down. But not now, he said. In 1996, there was only one place for conservatives. And that's why he was endorsing Bob Dole for president.[32] And then—*amazingly!*—the crowd turned on Pat. Connie thought they might jump up on the stage and throttle him. Pat walked off to boos. To her astonishment, he was laughing. "He loved it," she said. "He respected them, respected the brigaders. He understood that it wasn't about him, it was about the ideas. Pat was so pure in his thinking that he could see he didn't matter to them really. They were believers, dreamers, not followers. You don't get enough of that nowadays."[33]

B ob Dole was nominated without a challenge. He chose Jack Kemp as his running mate. Dole had what he wanted, but to get it he had muddied his image. To secure Pat's endorsement, he moved to the right and spoke out on immigration and abortion. To win over moderates, he moved to the left and froze out the conservatives. And although Buchanan's endorsement slashed Clinton's lead by ten points, the convention itself recorded no bounce at all. The Big Tent, hastily erected at the last minute, was empty of ideas. Maureen Dowd said, "The Republican convention was so gauzy and feminized, with treacly videos and speeches featuring women, kids and a rainbow of ethnic groups, it made the Olympics look like Al Bundy territory." The cover of *Time* magazine featured a photo of Dole and Kemp clasping hands, above a headline for a space story: "Life on Mars."[34]

The momentum was with Bill Clinton, who had spent two years flooding the airwaves with ads promoting his policies and bashing the Republicans. He was a better president now, more in touch with the public mood. In 1995, a homegrown right-wing terrorist blew up the Alfred P. Murrah Federal Building in Oklahoma City. The blast killed 168 people, including 19 children under the age of 6. What was intended as a retaliatory attack after Waco galvanized public anger against the far right. Radical appeals became harder to swallow.[35] Clinton delivered a moving eulogy. "That was the moment when he really became president," observed Pat. "It defined him as a man of the center . . . of healing. He became harder to beat. Or at least, it would take something excep-tional."[36]

Whatever "it" was, Bob Dole didn't have it. His tepid embrace of "fair trade" failed to stop Ross Perot entering the race a second time. Bill Clinton's centrist strategy brought home the independent vote and he cruised to victory with a plurality of 49.2 percent. Bob Dole took 40.7 percent, Ross Perot 8.4 percent.[37]

Pat was disengaged. He was thinking about 2000.

TWENTY-FOUR

Threatening Third Party

Bill Clinton's reelection in 1996 was a liberal victory in the culture conflict. A Democratic playboy beat a Republican war hero. It represented, in part, a triumph of baby boomer values. That same year, United Artists released *The Birdcage*, a timely remake of the French feature *La Cage aux Folles*. It was a surprise hit and grossed more money than any other LGBT-themed movie ever made. The film is set in a drag club on Florida's South Beach where Jewish owner Armand Goldman (Robin Williams) lives with the star performer, Albert (Nathan Lane). There the lovers raise their straight son, Val, who was abandoned by his biological mother. Calamity falls when Val announces that he is going to marry a girl called Barbara. Barbara's father, Kevin Keeley, is a conservative Republican senator from Ohio and the founder of the Coalition for Moral Order. Fearing their reaction if they learn the truth about Val's background, Barbara tells her parents that Armand is a cultural attaché to Greece, and that Albert is both a woman and a housewife. She also changes the family name from Goldman to Coleman to hide their Jewish background.

Most reviewers commented that Gene Hackman played Senator Keeley "as a buffoonish Pat Buchanan," a whiskey-slugging class warrior.[1] Keeley is a champion for moral values at a time when morality is on the move. Keeley is told that the cofounder of Coalition for Moral Order has been found dead in the bed of an underage black prostitute. He and his wife speed down to South Beach in the hope that a quick wedding to a "traditional, wholesome," all-American family will rescue his career. To disguise the fact that the Goldmans are a less-than nuclear unit, Albert drags up and pretends to be Armand's wife. The best scenes in the movie come when the Buchanan-substitute Senator Keeley meets "Mrs. Coleman" and instantly likes her. The two develop a strange chemistry, whereby Albert enjoys playing the Republican housewife and Keeley is delighted to meet someone living up to the codes of the Moral Order. "Maybe I'm just an old-fashioned girl," says Albert, "but I pity the woman who is just too busy to stay at home and look after her man."

"Hear, hear!" says Keeley. "It's so nice to meet people like you!"

The movie ends in chaos. Albert is unmasked and Keeley goes into shock, unable to comprehend that the woman he admired is really a man. Before the film ends, Albert makes a plea for a new kind of family values. Throughout the evening "Mrs. Coleman" agrees with everything Buchanan/Keeley has to say about the death penalty, monogamy, and abortion. When he has been de-wigged, Albert tells Keeley, "I don't know if this helps but I meant every word I said about a return to family values and a stricter moral code . . . It's still me; with one tiny difference. Well, not *tiny* . . ."

The Birdcage made a plea for a new moral order, or a transgressive version of the old one. It was a manifesto for the age of Clinton, a marriage of civil rights and family values. Modern families come in all shapes and sizes, said the Clintons, but that doesn't mean they can't live by old-fashioned standards of civility, respect, and duty. The moral cretins of the movie were the hypocritical politician who went to bed with an underage prostitute and the hippie mother who abandoned Val.[2]

Clinton signed legislation that forced fathers to take responsibility for their kids, and for public schools to be allowed to require their students to wear uniforms. He championed the new V-chip system that let parents monitor what their children were watching on TV.[3] Meanwhile, mainstream media broadcast the message that all gays wanted were the freedom to marry and raise kids like good heterosexuals. Beyond a minor reinterpretation of the Old Testament, they posed no threat to Judeo-Christian morality. And many of them were rich. In 1997, American Express invested $250,000 in researching the gay and lesbian market. They found that homosexuals are informed and loyal consumers, more likely to buy from service providers who pitch to them. Suddenly, big business had a stake in gay rights. The pink dollar was born.[4]

The sense of loss—that America was slipping through their fingers—only made conservatives madder. South Carolina's Attorney General, Charlie Condon, gave pride of place on his office wall to a framed photo of Pat Buchanan. The inscription read: "To Charlie Condon, who is saving lives while others prattle on about the rights of drug addicts." Condon was a Catholic and an ex-Democrat, and came to office as a conservative populist. He had found an unusual way to reopen the debate on abortion. Condon prosecuted pregnant crack addicts for child abuse and manslaughter. The implication: If a mother could commit manslaughter against a fetus then that fetus must be classed in law as a human being with constitutional rights. Condon first brought a prosecution against a woman whose baby had been born with traces of cocaine in its blood. "You don't have the right to have a drug-impaired child," said Condon. "The child comes from God. We think we're in line with how most people feel in this country. We recognize the fetus as a fellow South Carolinian. And the right to privacy does not overcome the right to life." In October 1997, the state supreme court upheld the verdict. The U.S. Supreme Court later rejected it. Condon helped secure the Citadel's male-only status and refused to swear in an atheist justice of the peace. To speed up executions, he suggested the electric chair be replaced with an "electric sofa."[5]

But Condon's confrontational style was probably not what a majority of Americans wanted in their politics. Old-time religion was losing its grip. After 1996, the Christian Coalition's membership plummeted and it spiraled into debt. Pat Buchanan still spoke for a solid demographic, but its numbers were shrinking.[6]

After the elections, Pat returned to *Crossfire* in time for its fifteenth anniversary. Birthday congratulations arrived from Al Gore and Jack Kemp, and Larry King did a retrospective on his show. Tom Braden had long since retired, but was adequately replaced by a string of liberal mouthpieces. Said one reviewer:

Members of the *Crossfire* quartet play stock roles reminiscent of those cherished old feature actors who won our hearts by doing the same number in movie after movie . . . Viewers are never strained to figure out whose side they are on; whatever the ostensible issue, you're either on Pat's side or on [the liberal's] side, never mind the details. In a complicated world, this is a nightly comfort.[7]

Pat may have been the show's lead conservative, but he spent more time attacking the Republicans than the Democrats. In the summer of 1997, there was an attempted coup against Gingrich in the House. It came to nothing—Dick Armey tipped Newt off in time and he was able to rally his supporters. "The coup de farce intended to topple Speaker Newt, in which faithful lieutenants betrayed him, only to re-embrace their beloved leader, has the makings of a Broadway comedy," wrote Pat, back in his role as a columnist. "Unfortunately, the farce is also a tragedy. A great party, for whose principles good people have worked their whole lives, has been abused by those accorded its highest honors. The House leaders have done what Bill Clinton could not do. They have made the party of Ronald Reagan look ridiculous."[8]

Pat started a major new writing project covering the things that he had learned from his 1996 campaign. It was so long that his agent told him to cut it in two. Part one—*The Great Betrayal*—was an analysis of the impact of free trade upon America. No one of comparable stature had published such a comprehensive piece and it remains a testimony of Nineties angst. Buchanan wrote:

We are losing the country we grew up in. America is no longer one nation indivisible. We are now the "two nations" predicted by Kerner Commission [on Civil Disorders] thirty years ago. Only the dividing line is no longer just race; it is class. On the one side is the new class, Third Wave America—the bankers, lawyers, diplomats, investors, lobbyists, academics, journalists, executives, professionals, high-tech entrepreneurs—prospering beyond their dreams . . . On the other side of the national divide is Second Wave America, the forgotten Americans left behind. White collar and blue collar, they work for someone else, many with hands, tools, and machines, in factories soon to be hoisted onto the chopping block of some corporate downsizer in some distant city or foreign country.[9]

This was the first time that Pat was able to communicate his feelings about economics with nuance. The most effective—and, for the conservative movement, most radical—parts of the book dealt with the relationship between traditional values and money. He wrote:

> A nation is organic, alive; it has a beating heart. The people of a na-
> tion are a moral community who must share values higher than
> economic interest, or their nation will not endure . . . Man does
> not live by bread alone. In a true nation many things are placed on
> a higher altar than maximum efficiency or a maximum variety of
> consumer goods. Once, conservatives understood that.[10]

The Great Betrayal was received by most conservative critics as an overdue letter of resignation from the Republican right. The National Review wrote:

> Buchanan almost never talks about cutting government any more,
> certainly not about ending specific programs or programs that ben-
> efit the middle class. It is true that most Republicans these days share
> this reticence. But only Buchanan says that advocates of the flat tax
> have spent too much time with "the boys down at the yacht basin."
> Not even liberal Democrats bash corporations with his gusto, de-
> ploring as he does their greed, questioning their loyalty, and second-
> guessing their decisions . . . This is not the conservatism of Ronald
> Reagan, or Barry Goldwater, or William F. Buckley Jr.[11]

Pat was invited to testify before a House committee on free trade. Rep. Tom DeLay said he sounded "Marxist," that he was talking more like AFL-CIO boss John Sweeney than like Adam Smith.[12] Pat replied:

Well, Tom, if I sound like Sweeney on the issue of protecting the wages of our workers and keeping manufacturing at home, it is because, on this issue, I agree with the AFL-CIO leader. And in the Republican era from Abraham Lincoln ("Give us a protective tariff, and we will have the greatest country on Earth") to Theodore Roosevelt ("Thank God I am not a free trader"), all Republicans believed that. In that GOP era, U.S. economic growth averaged 4 percent a year—for 50 years. That's why I'm standing with Sweeney. Now, you tell me, Tom, what you're doing standing with Bill and Al, *The Washington Post,* the Council on Foreign Relations, Strobe Talbott and the Trilateral Commission. What are you guys forming up there—the New World Order Conservative Club?[13]

Pat was working ten- or eleven-hour days on his books and columns, buried in his basement study, hidden away from friends and relatives. The Clintons continued to make excellent subjects. On January 26, 1998, Bill Clinton held a press conference at the White House to deny claims that he had an affair with a White House intern called Monica Lewinsky.[14] Standing next to Hillary, he said, "I want to say one thing to the American people. I want you to listen to me. I'm going to say this again: I did not have sexual relations with that woman, Miss Lewinsky. I never told anybody to lie, not a single time; never. These allegations are false." The next night, the First Lady appeared on NBC and, defending her husband, said, "The great story here for anybody willing to find it and write about it and explain it is this vast right-wing conspiracy that has been conspiring against my husband since the day he announced for president."[15] The last great battle of the Clinton-era culture war had begun.

Zippergate inflamed partisan tempers.[16] Leaders within the GOP and the religious right demanded the President resign or be forced from office. No one was more scathing than the paleocons. For them, Clinton was the Sixties president, an exemplar of baby boomer self-indulgence. Joe Sobran wrote:

Clinton has been trying to define his "legacy"; well, here it is. He's the sex president. That's his essence, and that will be his reputation

for all time. It goes deeper than mere "womanizing." He's both advocate and exemplar of the sexual revolution. He has used the presidency to promote everything from gay rights to late-term abortion.
The notion that he has been a "non-ideological" president is nonsense; his ideology is a fusion of Hugh Hefner and Gloria Steinem . . .
His party almost universally favors the half-covert revolt against
the Creator.[17]

But for all the outrage on the right, the Democrats actually picked up seats
in the 1998 midterm elections. Pat spotted a contradiction that many on the
right missed: As Clinton's approval ratings soared, polls showed that public
trust in him fell.[18] Buchanan wrote in his column:

> The essence of Clinton's success has been to persuade America that
> this scandal is about human weakness, not crime, and that at its
> core is not a string of felonies but a sin familiar to all—adultery.
> Clinton knows that while Americans may consider adultery a seri-
> ous matter, a breach of faith and a betrayal of trust, they also be-
> lieve it to be a private matter between husband and wife, priest
> and penitent, not a federal issue . . . Also, unlike those generals and
> admirals who pop up on Page One, charged with adultery, Bill and
> Hillary are, well, family. Like J. R. Ewing and his long-suffering
> wife, Sue Ellen, of *Dallas*, they have starred in our national soap
> opera for six years. All America has heard stories of lamps thrown
> and curses traded. So there is an aspect of the burlesque to this, as
> well as the stuff of high crimes.[19]

The lame-duck House impeached President Clinton on December 19, 1998.
The trial was held in the Senate; Clinton was found not guilty on February 12,
1999. Many conservatives fell into despair. The great test case of American
values was lost.[20] But while some counseled retreat, Buchanan upped the ante:

> We cannot quit. We can no more walk away from the culture war
> than we could walk away from the Cold War. For the culture war is

at its heart a religious war about whether God or man shall be exalted, whose moral beliefs shall be enshrined in law, and what children shall be taught to value and abhor. With those stakes, to walk away is to abandon your post in time of war.

The Senate vote confirmed the betrayal of ordinary Americans by their elites, much as the Catholic hierarchy had betrayed the laity and the Republicans had betrayed the conservatives. In defense of tradition, there must be revolution. Buchanan noted:

> What is needed today is the same awareness that finally hit the conservative men of America in the early 1770s. Loyal to their king, they had rejected the counsel of Sam Adams to rebel against him and fight. Finally, it dawned on these conservatives that they had to become radicals; they had to overthrow the king's rule to keep what they had. And they found in George Washington a conservative leader with the perseverance to take us to victory over an enemy superior in every way but courage and character.

But it wasn't George Washington that the Republican Party wanted. It was George W. Bush.[21]

In the summer of 1999, Bay and Pat were invited to lunch with Rep. Chris Cannon of Utah. "We think it's great you're going to run," Bay remembered him saying on behalf of the House Republicans. "But in no way must you go after George W. Bush." George Bush was the governor of Texas, and the son of Pat's old enemy from '92. "He's going to be the nominee," said Cannon. The GOP establishment had lined up all the money and necessary endorsements. They had a timetable for victory in the primaries and they intended to dictate media access, coverage, and message.

"Do you know where he stands on the issues?" asked Bay.

"We don't care," Cannon replied. "When he's elected, Congress will control policy. We'll just send him the bills to sign."[22]

Gov. George Bush was a logical choice. He was a proven vote-getter, winning a surprise election over a popular Democrat in 1994. His public image was the opposite of Clinton's—a born-again Christian and family man who overcame a long battle with alcohol. Bush was associated enough with the evangelical right to guarantee a big block of votes, but he was more moderate than his liberal critics thought. As governor, he increased funds for education and learned Spanish so that he could reach out to Hispanic voters. Just as Buchanan called for a conservatism of the heart, Bush called himself a compassionate conservative. The poor needed the moral support of the rest of society, he argued. Unlike Buchanan, Bush saw government activism as the answer. Welfare reform, standards-based schooling, and foreign aid were new priorities. Bush's religious temperament was well tuned to the ethics of the Caring Nineties.[23]

The GOP was looking for a winner. Conservatives loved Pat, but he didn't fit the bill.[24] When he picked up the phone and called in favors in early 1999, Pat found that many of his staff and friends had already signed on elsewhere. Some, like Greg Mueller, Richard Viguerie, and Harry Veryser, had been plucked by Steve Forbes. Forbes had spent the years since 1996 building links to the religious right, hoping to establish himself as the conservative candidate with money. He formed a PAC called Americans for Hope, Growth, and Opportunity. In a news release posted on its Web site, Forbes opined that "Life begins at conception and ends at natural death" and "Partial birth abortion is a euphemism for infanticide, and it has no place in a civilized society." The rumor mill said that even Pat Robertson now looked on Forbes with favor. Robertson had been dismissed by Forbes in 1996 as a "toothy flake."[25]

Why, some asked, was Pat even thinking of running? He had been beaten twice already and there was no evidence to suggest that his chances of winning had improved between 1996 and 2000. Many left him because they felt exhausted.[26] Others argued that he was a victim of his own prophesies. He foresaw that free trade would change America and destroy the industrial working class, and it did. So who was left to vote for him?[27] Take New Hampshire. In the past, Pat could rely on a warm reception in a land of lumber mills and churches. But since 1996, the state had become more diverse, more affluent, and more moderate in its politics. Unemployment was just beneath 3 percent and home prices were back to their Reagan-era high. More than 60 percent of residents were born outside of the state and, on average, they were far wealthier than those who moved away in search of work. High-tech industry had all but replaced manufacturing as the economic base; where there were once pulping plants there were now robotics firms and Amazon.com. In 1996, the state elected its first Democratic governor for two decades. In 2000, according to polls, the hottest issue in the state was not taxes but education. People moving in expected more public services and lacked the natives' resolve to "live free or die." The state had even imposed its first-ever state income tax in 1999 to pay for everything a middle-class consumer had come to expect—environmental clean-up, therapeutic social services, computer training, old-age benefits, and millions of dollars in support for dyslexic children. New Hampshire, once a conservative state, was now a bastion of bourgeois liberalism. It was Buchanan country no more; without it, there was no guaranteed good start to the primaries that was necessary to matter, let alone win.[28]

But the Buchanan campaign continued, propelled forward by the Buchanans themselves. Their minds were full of "what ifs" and "if onlys": What if they had come first in Iowa and pushed Dole out of the race by beating him twice? If only they had placed first or second in Arizona, Pat might have come closer in South Carolina and maybe won the South. Tom Piatak, a journalist friend who stayed with Pat through thick and thin, said, "We came so close that we thought, 'With a little bit more money and a few more votes, next time we might do it.' And we thought Dole had stolen it, too. The establishment won because they cheated. This time we knew what we were up against and thought we could beat them."[29]

Besides, Pat had a base to speak up for. Without him in the race, those people had no representation; so Buchanan felt a duty to run.[30] And then there are the little vanities that a politician can't admit to in an interview. Perhaps he had become used to running; perhaps he couldn't imagine life without a primary or a debate to prep for. Maybe he saw George Bush waffling malapropisms ("I know the human being and fish can exist peacefully") and felt, "That should be me up there." Whatever the cause, the 2000 campaign was Buchanan's most representative. It was built on a mountain of passion and logic. But it was also foolhardy and hopeless. Someone should have told Pat not to do it, but they would have had to get past Bay first.[31]

The Republican primaries were crowded with conservatives in 2000. Aside from Buchanan, Bush, and Forbes, there was Alan Keyes (the second of what was to be three tries), Gary Bauer, and Bob Smith. Family values activist Gary Bauer looked like a schoolboy, standing at five foot two, with floppy blond hair and big bulging eyes. "I'm not delusional," he said. "I don't look like a president. I don't sound like a president. It is possible for me to walk into a room without anyone noticing." Bauer was religious but economically populist, so much so that he ruled out privatizing Social Security and praised Medicare. He raised $22 million out of small donations in just one year.[32]

Bringing up the rear was New Hampshire senator Bob Smith—the last of the big beast northeast conservatives. Certainly, he was big. According to one journalist, he was six foot six, 280 pounds, with "a mountain ridge of a nose." He had a black comb-over and a body that "calls to mind a duckpin with legs." His Republicanism had taken a Messianic bent in recent years. He voted down a $20 million road building project for New Hampshire because it smelled of pork. He promised to throw money at defeating GOP moderates. "Anyone who wants to run against these RINOs"—Republicans in Name Only—"I'll help you," he told a barbecue. "We should defeat every one of them—then make them watch a partial-birth abortion." Smith hated partial-birth abortion and was one of the first to campaign against it in the Senate. He attacked a plastic doll with a pair of scissors in session, to show how painful it could be.

The folks who gravitated to Smith were even more fringe than Buchanan's people. They regarded Buchanan's employment at CNN as an act of betrayal because CNN was owned by environmentalist Ted Turner. It was the sort of thing that Bob Smith would never do, if only because no right-minded TV producer would ever employ him. Sure, he had a soft side: Bob Smith wanted NASA shut down because it used Russian monkeys on test flights into space. But otherwise he served up traditional red meat. Asked about rich and poor public schools, he replied, "Everyone can't make a million dollars, and everyone can't drive a Cadillac. To try to equalize is socialism and it's not America." Could he reconcile his pro-life and pro–death penalty beliefs? Of course. "Capital punishment certainly existed in Christ's time. He was a victim of it." At a garden party, he talked about Chinese spies selling nuclear technology to the Iranians and the Libyans. "We executed the Rosenbergs for less," he noted. At this, an intense young man jumped to his feet and asked, "Senator Smith, when will Clinton be executed? This is a serious question—"

"I have to leave," said Smith. It was the only controversial issue he ever avoided.[33]

Buchanan, Forbes, Keyes, Bauer, and Smith showed there was life on the right. But donors weren't interested in giving to lost causes. The right had lost its romantic edge. The battles with Clinton had made it more cynical, more determined to win. George Bush, his opponents pointed out, was soft on immigration and in favor of more federal spending on education. He was pro-life but fuzzy, opposing a constitutional right-to-life amendment. Yet when Bauer and Forbes called him out on it, Pat Robertson went on TV to defend him. A Bush operative summed up the problems facing Buchanan et al nicely. "We understand that guys stuck at 2 percent in the polls have to hurl a rock and try to hurt somebody," he said. But with the endorsement of leading conservatives, "that kind of attack is badly undercut. Bush can do a mail dropping in Iowa with [Robertson's friendly] quotes, and then where do they go?"[34]

Observers expected that the candidate who would pose the biggest threat to Bush would be Elizabeth Dole. Pretty, accomplished, and full of southern charm, she was the first woman to run a viable candidacy for the presidency. She drew big crowds and delivered speeches about morals in a precise, homely manner. "While we worked to eliminate the Federal deficit," she liked to say, "we have done little to eliminate the deficit that exists in our basic American values: honesty, integrity, personal responsibility, civility and respect for our fellow man." But she had nothing to offer that trumped Bush and she found the right-wing money was all dried up. By the summer of 1999, she was second in opinion polls to Bush. But that was no comfort. Bush led her 62–16 percent. The others were in single digits.[35]

With all these conservatives running, the media was desperate to find a liberal to write about. Vice President Al Gore seemed to have the Democratic nomination sewn up. His opponent, Sen. Bill Bradley, was doing well in New Hampshire but badly everywhere else. Both men were basically centrists; neither had much personality. Bradley defined himself as the candidate of the left, coming out for greater gun control, campaign finance reform, and national health insurance. But his campaign never caught fire.[36] Lacking a story, the press fished around for a maverick.

In March 1999, NATO forces bombed Yugoslavia in response to an alleged attempt by the Yugoslav state to ethnically cleanse the province of Kosovo. Supporters of the action talked about the first humanitarian war. Coupled with the arrest of Augusto Pinochet, the former dictator of Chile, while visiting Britain, it seemed like the New World Order was starting to do some good.[37] Paleocons were predictably outraged. Clinton claimed that upward of 500,000 Kosovars had been murdered by the Serbs. When local reports found evidence of just 2,108 dead, Buchanan and company said their Serbian murderers were the patsy for the creation of a new American empire.[38]

One conservative who backed Clinton enthusiastically was Sen. John Mc-Cain of Arizona. McCain had intended to declare his presidential candidacy in April 1999, but suspended his campaign to make the moral case for the war in Congress and on TV. He gained attention by advocating the use of ground troops. His motto, "We are in it, now we must win it," turned him overnight into a leading voice among Senate Republicans, and a lifelong bête noir for the antiwar right.[39] On paper, McCain was the ideal conservative candidate. He was a war hero who suffered torture as a POW in Vietnam. He was respected by fiscal conservatives as an enemy of pork-barrel spending and had a straight-down-the-line pro-life voting record. But he also took stands on individual issues that appealed to independents. He said the tax cuts George Bush proposed were too weighted toward the rich; he would help the poor and spend the budget surplus on Social Security and Medicare first. He made campaign finance reform his signature issue, coming out for transparency and against soft money.[40] McCain traveled everywhere on a bus called "The Straight Talk Express." Onboard, his staff handed out booze and burgers to journalists, keeping them tipsy and sweet. The senator was always available to reporters and he spoke at such length and with such freedom that he gained a reputation as a nice guy and a rebel. The press censored anything he said that he shouldn't have. McCain gave a ten-minute speech about campaign reform at each town he went to; then stayed until he had answered every question in the house. They called his growing army of fans "McCainiacs."[41]

P at and Bay Buchanan thought that the Bush vs. McCain fight was "window dressing." Bay said, "Eight months before the New Hampshire primary and the Republican bosses had already decided that they wanted Bush. Everything else was done so that they could say, 'Hey, look what a vibrant party we are.' But it was fixed . . . And I said to Pat, 'We just can't run in these primaries and honestly tell our contributors that you can win. It's fixed. We'd be lying—it'd be like fraud.' "[42]

Bay hadn't forgotten the threat they made in 1996 to go independent. She pointed out that Perot's performance in 1996 had earned his Reform Party $12.6 million in guaranteed federal funds for the 2000 general election. Perot said he didn't want to run again, so the party's nomination seemed wide open. Take the money, the argument went, combine Reform's poll numbers with Pat's, get into the debates, and Buchanan could gain traction.[43] In a hypothetical race, Bush was on 39 percent, Gore 35 percent, and Pat 16 percent. Those kind of figures meant that Buchanan was guaranteed a place in the debate.[44] And if Pat was good at anything, it was debating. One supporter said, "Everything—*everything*—hinged on getting Pat into the debates. Gore and Bush were such bad speakers that we thought Pat could get another ten points tearing them apart . . . He couldn't get the platform he needed in the Republican primaries, so Reform looked like a way of getting him into those debates by the backdoor."[45]

R eform itself seemed open to the idea. Perot's 1996 running mate, the protectionist economist Pat Choate, was a big fan of Pat's. Choate did his best to woo Buchanan, telling him that the nomination was his for the taking and that he could guarantee the support of the party establishment.[46] Given that Choate was Perot's man, this sounded like an endorsement from Perot himself.[47] Choate called Bay Buchanan every day for six weeks and said the same thing every time—"When's Pat going to declare?" The charm offensive had its effect. It managed to convince Bay that Reform meant business.[48]

But what Perot personally thought of Pat was a mystery. Perot governed Reform like a god on a mountaintop, occasionally sending down prophets to impart his wisdom. He never personally said "yes" or "no" to anything and only allowed his thinking to be revealed by the trusted few. In the summer of 1999, Russell J. Verney asked for a meeting with Bay. Verney was as close to Perot as a man could get. He served as his spokesman and chief advisor in 1992, director of the 1996 campaign, and coordinator of United We Stand America. Choate put the meeting together in secret. Verney asked Bay directly if Pat would run on the Reform ticket. Understandably, Bay took this to mean that Perot wanted Pat to be the nominee. That's what she reported to Pat, and he believed her.[49]

The reason why Pat Buchanan ran in 2000 on the Reform ticket was Bay. With people like Greg Mueller and Terry Jeffrey gone, and Pat stuck down in his basement writing books, Bay was in total command of strategy. The Buchanan family structure was tough and resilient, but also impervious to good advice. There are those who thought Bay's influence was bad and when they heard that she had got the Reform bug, they finally came forward to tell Pat to find a new manager. She had made too many mistakes, they argued, and this looked like another. One big donor dropped out because she failed to provide receipts or pay people. Some even whispered that she needed Pat to run—on any ticket—to keep the donor money rolling in. Pat Buchanan was more than a man. He was a business empire of books, mailing lists, donations, and campaign paraphernalia.[50]

In fact, Pat Buchanan was nothing without Bay. She gave him the courage to run. She understood what made Pat, Pat; she shaped every campaign to reflect that. Any mistakes she made were inevitable given the flea-circus nature of every Buchanan candidacy—cash starved and staffed by volunteers, some of them half-mad. Without Bay, Pat might have taken the advice of men like Viguerie and Bozell and stuck to running on taxes in 1992. There would have been no protectionism, no culture war, no riding to the sound of the guns—and probably no first place in New Hampshire in 1996. But Bay was blinded by a mix of love and faith in the cause. Everyone else had gone, but, lacking the objectivity of a friend, her belief in Pat endured.

So Bay said Pat should go independent. He was skeptical. Pat was suffering from stomach problems and was in occasional bouts of pain. But he did what he was told. It is ironic, given Pat Buchanan's reputation among liberals as a chauvinist pig, that he made the biggest mistake of his political life because he couldn't say no to his sister.[51]

The last test of Pat's support in the Republican Party primaries was the August 1999 Iowa Straw Poll. Pat had seen the GOP establishment fix a poll before, but he still hoped that a decent showing could cement his status as leader of the conservatives. A good speech could get him some airtime, at least. In an interview before the poll, Buchanan scoffed at talk of him leaving the GOP as a trick to reduce his support. But he confessed to frustration at the party's stance on abortion and trade. "I'm going to follow those ideas and ideals straight down the road," he said. "If the Republican Party veers off the road, that's their business. My first commitment is to my ideals and convictions. As Jack Kennedy once said, 'Sometimes party loyalty asks too much,' but right now I'm going down the road as a Republican."[52]

At Buchanan's headquarters in downtown Des Moines, there was a quiet, sulky air. Activist Tim Haley sighed, "It's tough. Last time, we could bus 'em in from out of state." But new rules saying that voters had to prove their residency in Iowa made that impossible. Haley pointed at a campaign worker. "This fellow over here, he brought up a bus from Alabama [in 1996]. This time, it's all Iowa people. We can't hire the multimillion-dollar talent. We've got a '50s band from Clive, Iowa. We're selling our candidate, Pat Buchanan." On the phones were Diana Haas from North Carolina and Dottie Watson from New Orleans. They worked the lists of gun people, truckers, and pro-life activists. "We're finding a lot of people upset with the Republican Party," said Watson. "We'd like to see it become a Bush-Buchanan battle." But Pat was running a dime-store operation. Watson ran outside to help unload several hundred boxes of Maurice's Barbeque Sauce from a truck. The Bush people would be offering oysters and champagne. The Buchanan brigade was getting ready for a church picnic.[53]

On the day of the poll, Forbes spent close to $2 million and Bush $750,000. Forbes's army arrived early, paid for and even dressed by the billionaire. They wore bright-orange shirts and snaked for the equivalent of more than a city block, queuing for breakfast. Bush's people turned up in the afternoon; many of his 100-plus buses got caught in the huge traffic jams on the roads around Ames. Forbes bought 7,711 tickets and handed out 7,500 in the street. Bush bought more than 10,000. Bush not only offered lunch, but dinner for those staying late into the evening. Buchanan couldn't compete with that, but there was some joy when the Iowa Teamsters Union announced that it had bought 500 tickets. Mike Mathis, the union's legislative director, said "our people will be informed" that Buchanan was the only candidate opposed to NAFTA. But, on the eve of voting, Buchanan conceded defeat. On Fox News with Sean Hannity, he predicted that "five or six fellas may never survive" the vote. Then Hannity asked him if he was thinking about the Reform Party. Buchanan joked, "Let me admit, Father Hannity, I have engaged in impure thoughts about possibly running for another party." He added, "But no one has consummated any act, Father."[54]

The speech Buchanan gave at the poll was one of his best. He said that if he took the oath as the nation's "chief law enforcement officer," he would turn to Clinton on the inaugural stand and say, "Sir, you have the right to remain silent . . ." and the audience erupted into laughter and applause. At the end, he spoke directly to his supporters. "I see the storm coming," he said. "If there's a place and a part for me, I believe I'm ready." Next, Bush got up to speak. He delivered a longwinded bore, read off a scrap of paper with the kind of dislocation that suggested he had only just been handed it. Pat Buchanan, who had served great speakers like Nixon and Reagan and who understood and revered the art of rhetoric, was disgusted. Bush was either lazy or incompetent. Either way, it was an insult to the audience. And an insult to Buchanan, who already knew that Bush had bought an early victory. That night, Bush came first with 31 percent. Forbes took 21 percent, Dole 14 percent, Bauer 9 percent. Pat pulled just 7 percent.[55]

On Fox News, he looked tired and forlorn. It hurt to get beaten by an illiterate. George Bush, he said, was "altogether unexceptional" but "they are hungry for a winner." Pat shrugged his shoulders. The party was over.[56]

TWENTY-FIVE

The Reform Nightmare

I n late September 1999, Pat strolled into the green room at CNN and shook hands with Skip Smith, the makeup guy. "Skipper," Pat said, "I'm in trouble again." He was there to defend the second part of his grand Jeremiad, which had just hit the shelves.[1] *A Republic, Not an Empire: Reclaiming America's Destiny* charted a long history of conservative opposition to military adventurism. What Buchanan had to say about the Second World War was strong stuff. Pat argued that Hitler did not want war with Britain and France in 1939, that the Allies made war inevitable by guaranteeing Poland—a country they could not defend. He said that the Soviet Union was as much an aggressor toward the Poles as the Third Reich and, if they wanted to protect Poland, the Allies should have declared war on the USSR, too. Pat claimed that Roosevelt forced war with Japan by starving her of oil. America entered the war in Europe at a point when the Nazi empire was clearly in decline, trapped between the RAF and the Russian winter. It was, he wrote, an unnecessary, bloodthirsty gamble.

Pat Buchanan defended the isolationists of the 1930s as patriots against globalism. Their "struggle with FDR was over one issue: Should we follow the counsel of [George] Washington and stay out of European wars, or the example of [Woodrow] Wilson and go in? By the fall of 1941, the two great combatants were Nazi Germany and Stalinist Russia. Most Americans did not believe their husbands, fathers, or sons should die for either one."[2] But, asked the critics, did

Buchanan not feel that it was worth dying to save the millions of Jews, gypsies, homosexuals, leftists, Christians, and liberals that Hitler murdered?

After recording his interview with CNN, Pat returned to his office and dictated a press release for his officials. He had the TV on with the sound turned off. Out of the corner of his eye he noticed that the CNN special he had just done was playing. He saw images of himself fade away to goose-stepping soldiers, and then the liberation of Dachau. "Oh, my goodness," he whispered, "they've got Hitler's guys here, and Stalin. My goodness, they've got this huge thing on all the camps and stuff." Shelley rang. She was upset and Pat soothed her over the phone. "We're getting hammered," he said, "but I think we can do it if we hang in there." It was "a hatchet job," he decided and, to prove it, CNN called and apologized. They offered him the right to reply but he put the phone down on them. He went on MSNBC instead, where he got into a shouting match with historian Stephen Ambrose.[3] The Reform nightmare had begun.

Had Pat not written *A Republic, Not an Empire*, the Reform campaign might have turned out differently. But the book revived the old charge of anti-Semitism. And Pat could hardly claim victimization. He must have understood the inflammatory nature of his remarks. Norman Podhoretz wrote a much-read review in *The Wall Street Journal* that called him "as soft on Hitler as, conversely, the revisionist historians of the Cold War were once (rightly) accused of being on Stalin."[4] John McCain used a telephone interview to call on the GOP to cut the cord and let him go. What Pat had to say about World War II dishonored all those who had fought in it, he said. Furious, Buchanan called it "a vicious and damnable lie . . . Of course it was a noble cause," to defeat Hitler. But he reiterated his argument that Hitler was not a direct threat to America, so it was wrong to force war with him.[5] Pat only made matters worse when he suggested in an article that the Ivy League universities should try to "look more like America" by reserving 75 percent of their undergraduate places for "non-Jewish whites."[6]

At first look, Reform was the perfect audience for the eccentric controversy Buchanan generated. The 1999 national convention ended when the party's lease expired on the small ballroom at the Hyatt Regency in Dearborn, Michigan.

The exhausted delegates—drained by battles over whether to drop the word "paperless" from the platform or to change "government reform" to "political reform"—were thrown out by security. "The party's not sophisticated yet," said Hoppy Heidelberg, a member of the Oklahoma delegation. Hoppy was thrown off the grand jury investigating the Oklahoma City Bombing for pursuing his own suspects ("Middle Easterners on contract to the CIA"). "But, in time," he predicted, "you will see planks in our platform to get rid of the UN and the Federal Reserve."[7]

However, few in Reform shared Pat's social conservatism. It attracted a different variety of conspiracy theorist. The movement's biggest issue was ending the two-party system. Its demographic included some who were moved by the trade issue, but the vast majority was quasi-libertarian—fiscally conservative, socially tolerant. Perot's personality papered over the cracks in the coalition and kept the focus on third-party politics and jobs. But, since 1996, the party's base and message had expanded. A new generation of Reformers emerged, and their poster boy wasn't Perot or Pat. It was the former pro wrestler Jesse Ventura.[8] And Ventura did not like Pat's new book.

Ventura—aka The Body—played the villain in the ring (his catchphrase was: "Win if you can, lose if you must, but always cheat!"). After serving as mayor of Brooklyn Park, Minnesota, he entered the 1998 Minnesota gubernatorial race on an independent ticket. The state was running a budget surplus and Ventura promised to return the money in a tax refund. He ran as the outsider, with the slogan, "Don't vote for politics as usual." Incredibly, his underfunded, high-camp campaign won. Ventura admitted that he was "basically an entertainer" and that "the bottom line is that my opponents were boring." As governor he threatened to closet unfriendly lawmakers with his flatulent bulldog.[9]

Ventura was a fiscal conservative but a social liberal. In an interview with *Playboy,* he said that, "organized religion is a sham and a crutch." It "tells people to go out and stick their noses in other people's business." Reform chair Russell Verney faxed him a letter demanding he quit the party. He wrote that his comments "about religion, sexual assault, overweight people, drugs, prostitution, women's undergarments, and many other subjects do not represent the values, principles, or ethics upon which this party was built." Ventura's response, as spelled by his spokesman for reporters was, "Pfffff!"[10]

Pat met Ventura once, in September 1999. The meeting was subdued and surreal—the wrestler and the speechwriter sat in silence for long periods, unsure of what to say. Both had a low opinion of each other. Ventura thought Buchanan was a Nazi, and Buchanan thought Ventura was a circus performer who got lucky. Both men felt they had lowered themselves just to meet.[11]

But Pat didn't have to worry about Ventura, said Bay. The Reform nomination process was Byzantine and expensive. Only the brigaders had the money and manpower to win it.[12] A prospective nominee needed to qualify personally for the ballot in the fifty states, by gathering tens of thousands of signatures. Once several nominees had proven their electability, on July 1, 2000, party officials would send ballots to people who signed a petition, who were on the rosters of state Reform Party organizations, or who requested one. The result would be declared at the party convention in August 2000.[13] Ventura didn't have the national organization necessary to compete with Pat, Bay assured her brother. And she was now meeting regularly with Russell Verney and Pat Choate, who assured her that Perot hated Ventura and would not stand in the way of Buchanan's nomination.[14]

But there was a catch. A clause in the nomination process said that the party convention could overturn the primary vote if it didn't approve of the nominee. Perot could use Pat to break Jesse, and then use the convention to dump Pat. The Buchanans were being set up.[15]

The phony war with Ventura gave Buchanan a new lease of life. Journalists noticed how vital he suddenly was. Back on the front page of *The New York Times* and *The Washington Post*, he *meant* something again. Pat spent the mornings of those long few weeks jogging around the perimeter of his CIA neighbor's estate. "It's exhilarating, waking up at 3 in the morning, running, planning things," he said to an interviewer. "You think of what you're going to say, how they'll come at you in sound bites, how much time you'll have to make your proper point. Very exhilarating." His plan for the fight was thus: wrest the

Reform nomination from Ventura, collect the $12.6 million in federal cam-
paign funds, maintain a free-media blitz, and climb to 15 percent to make it to
the debates. That would give him a shot at the presidency. Of course, Ventura
was a problem. "I think he has in mind body-slamming me," Pat said with a
grin of delight. "You're up there on that high diving board my friend," he
added, offering an image of himself, poised, uncertain whether or not to jump.
"It seems a thousand feet down to the water. It's go, or no-go." But Buchanan
was no chicken. "If I come down that ladder, you know what people will say."[16]

On October 25, 1999, Buchanan quit the Republicans for the Reform Party.
A crowd of 350 brigaders turned out, shouting "Go Pat, go! Go Pat, go!," terrifying the press corps. Pat Choate introduced him and, as was his way, Buchanan
didn't just declare his candidacy: He declared war. "Let me say to the money
boys and the Beltway elites who think that, at long last, they have pulled up their
drawbridge and locked us out forever: You don't know this peasant army. We
have not yet begun to fight!" He didn't mention Bush by name, but dismissed
"the hollow men, the malleable men, willing to read from teleprompters
speeches scripted by consultants." What America needed now was a leader
prepared to tell it how it is—to purge the temple of the money lenders.[17]

Pat didn't bother to play to the Reformers' sensibilities. He threw paleocon
ideas at a largely paleocon audience. "They call us isolationists and that's one
of the nicest things they call us," he said, getting a big laugh from the crowd.
"Well, if they mean I intend to isolate America from all the bloody, territorial,
tribal and ethnic wars of the 21st century, I plead guilty!"[18] Once again, battle
was joined. It was, after all, St. Crispin's day—the day that Henry V defeated
superior forces at Agincourt in 1415. "Can America remain forever a light
unto the nations . . . a republic above whose sovereignty stands the sovereignty of God alone?" he asked. "That is our cause. And so it is that in the
name of the Founding Fathers, we go forth to rescue America."[19]

But unbeknownst to Pat Buchanan, Jesse Ventura had a card up his sleeve.
From the top of his tower in Manhattan, property tycoon Donald Trump
called up a newspaper and told a journalist that he had just finished reading
A Republic, Not an Empire. Reform, he decided, needed rescuing from this
madman. "Pat says Hitler had no malicious intent toward the United States,"

Trump spat. "Well, Hitler killed six million Jews and millions of others. Don't you think it was only a question of time before he got to us? He tackled Europe first and we were next. Pat's amazing."[20] And so began the Reform Party's descent into farce.

For many of his Republican friends, Pat's defection to Reform was the end of the road. He had gone too far and they could follow him no further.[21]

But southern traditionalists felt differently. From North Carolina, Boyd Cathey wrote Pat:

> Just the other day I received a note and request from your sister Bay concerning your possible run for the Reform Party nomination. I immediately sent her a check for $50.00, with the promise to send more . . . I have been observing carefully what has been happening in our Grand Old Party—and what has been happening to you. What is occurring clearly reveals what the cabals of poltroons in our two major political parties have done to the parties of Lincoln and Taft and Jackson and Cleveland. Like you, I worked for years in the Republican Party. Although from a Southern Democrat family, when I was old enough to register, I became a Republican, due in no small measure to Goldwater and Jesse Helms. For me, and thousands like me, the "Southern Strategy" was a living reality.

But the strategy, Boyd argued, was based on shared values. And people had entered the GOP since the 1980s who did not share those values.

> During those years when Ronald Reagan helped put the pride back in the term "American," Republicans worked together, but apparently only on the surface. We were facing the "evil empire" abroad and the McGovernite-Mondale liberals at home. But, Pat, that coalition was as fragile as it was brief.

The wrong people were running the GOP, wrote Boyd. There were the big money men—"a managerial class, with no allegiance to anything but its own conservation and enhancement"—and the dreaded neocons. Did Pat remember how they took the chair of the National Endowment for History from Mel Bradford ("that great Texas Confederate")? And now these same people— these closet liberals—were calling the shots and using the label of racist to silence the opposition.

> How strange it is to have ex-Democrat Bill Bennett and son of ex-Democrat leftist Irving Kristol telling YOU that you are not welcome in the party that once boasted of a Robert Taft, William Knowland, and Calvin Coolidge! . . . I believe Chesterton wrote once about "the world being turned upside down." Well, we are there.[22]

Across the South, it was mostly the Sons of Confederate Veterans who collected signatures to make Pat Buchanan the Reform nominee.[23] Tired of the threats to his job, Boyd didn't accept the position of state chair this time round. But the convention for his county was held in his front room, the dozen or so delegates entertained by his handsome spaniel, Mozart.[24]

Across the country, the brigaders moved in on the local Reform Party. A member of the national rules committee griped, "If Pat Buchanan brings enough people, we become the Pat Buchanan Party and there's nothing we can do about it. Their votes will far outweigh those of the indigenous Reformers. They can put all our issues on the back burner." In a last-minute decision, the Reform Party of New Hampshire canceled a state convention because officials feared a takeover by Buchanan brigaders. A tip-off told the state party's spokesman that they intended to pack the convention and elect their own people to the party's offices.[25]

The New Hampshire people had good cause to worry. A couple of days later, newly elected national chair John J. Gargan (replacing Russell Verney) came to a state party meeting in Connecticut. He found the room packed with Buchanan people. Peter Sullivan, sixty, had never been to a Reform meeting before. He kept a red-and-white Buchanan cap in his pocket, until he realized this was friendly turf and proudly put it on his head. The keynote speaker was Pat Choate, who sang Buchanan's praises. John Gargan was disgusted to find that the state party had imposed a $25 entrance fee for the banquet. Some old Reformers arrived and tried to break in without paying and things turned nasty. Gargan stormed out, saying he was going to "go get a hot dog. As a matter of principle, I can't talk to half the group. This party is open to everybody, whether they have a dollar or nothing, or a thousand dollars." He ate with the dissenters and was only tempted back after Buchanan's people opened the hall again. Perot's day was over. A banner said "Ross Was Right," the past tense underlined. His books were on sale for 50 cents and delegates could pose with a cardboard cut-out for $4. There were no takers.[26]

Down in North Carolina, Buchanan's people started to collect signatures. There was some gesture at popular campaigning, when activists targeted universities or stood on the roadside waving signs. But this was a Buchanan campaign, not a Reform one.[27] Boyd's guide to campaigning told activists to target "the pastor and priest . . . of fundamentalist (Pentecostal, Church of God, Free-will Baptist, Baptist) and Catholic churches. Contact other denominations after contacting mentioned churches first. Ask if you can provide specific literature such as nonpartisan voter guides . . . If you can, provide specific literature regarding the abortion issue . . . Point out to Catholics that Pat is a devout Catholic." Happenings to attend included, "small town parades, farm and rural events, bluegrass, gospel, country music festivals." And appropriate organizations included "home schoolers, religious schoolers, conservative groups, Sons and Daughters of the Confederacy, Boy and Girl Scout Leaders, Right to Life groups, pro family groups."[28]

As its name suggested, the Reform Party was primarily about reforming the political system—not banning abortion. Yet Boyd's Confederate troops took it over county by county, electing delegates with pure paleocon views. Jesse Ventura was furious.[29]

To deny Pat the nomination, Ventura threw his weight behind Donald Trump. Few people better represented the glamour and tawdriness of the 1980s than Trump. The son of a real estate developer, he made a fortune out of redeveloping Manhattan and constructing a number of glitzy casinos. He married a beautiful wife—Ivana—and his mix of fabulous wealth and media-friendly vulgarity made him a business star. Some of this was funded though junk bonds that went awry in the late 1980s, but he rebounded with a series of big-scale hotel and residential projects. Short, loudmouthed, and covered in businessman bling, he found a home in professional wrestling. It was at the ringside that Trump met his new best buddy—Jesse Ventura.[30]

Jesse adored Trump. To quote Trump's political consultant, Roger Stone, they shared a "Fuck you attitude." Ventura's ego was flexed through his muscles, Trump's through his money. Either man could have whatever he wanted, or whoever he wanted. Being in their company was like dining with a pair of lions mashed out on steroids. Ventura got it into his head that Trump would make a good candidate; or at least a better one than Pat Buchanan.

According to Stone, Trump held the Reform Party in contempt. "And you could see why. These were folks with an extra chromosome . . . A collection of kooks: gun people, anti-gun people, Nazis, vegetarians, gold standard, anti-gold standard, all freaks."[31] But Trump spotted a good opportunity. In late 1999 the Republican and Democratic races looked sewn up and dull. The media coverage of the Reform nomination suggested that the third-party race was where it was at. If Trump could get in early, say some outrageous stuff, and jump out before any of those freaks thought of actually voting for him, then it could be a fantas-tic publicity stunt. It was like play wrestling—a lot of sound and fury, but no one would really get hurt. No one except Jesse, whose feelings were bruised when he realized his pal was only in it for the free advertising.

On October 24, 1999, a few days after Buchanan, Trump joined Reform. He got an instant guest spot on Leno. In a sharp suit and tie, Trump called Pat "a Hitler lover . . . I guess he's an anti-Semite. He doesn't like the blacks, he doesn't like the gays. It's just incredible that anybody could embrace this guy, and maybe he'll get 4 or 5 percent of the vote and it'll be a really staunch-right wacko vote."[32] Watching at home, Buchanan was furious. His reputation was being challenged by a man with no political experience whatsoever. In fact, Trump's brand of eccentricity probably suited Reform better than Buchanan's—more cosmopolitan and fiscal, less rural and gospel.[33]

Things still looked and felt good from Pat's perspective. More than 500 cheered him at a rally in a Detroit suburb, shortly after he declared. Several hundred came out in depressed Warren, Michigan. Buchanan recalled New Hampshire in 1996 and cried, "This thing's caught fire again!" He defended the Confederate flag before 250 people at a barbecue in the Deep South. Then, best of all, he got a nice reception at a factory line in Gaffney, South Carolina. Before now, his Republican label had turned workers off. Now they shook his hand, all suspicion gone from their eyes. He cared about them enough to quit the party he loved and they respected that. "Free at last!" he laughed, handing out buttons and balloons. "Free at last!"[34]

But *A Republic, Not an Empire* would not go away. Trump read passages aloud on talk shows, his harsh New York vowels making it sound like the audiobook version of *Mein Kampf*.[35] Then he turned up in Miami, to show solidarity for anti-Castro Cubans. Trump got a good reception and took the chance to remind locals of all the nasty things Pat had said about Spanish Americans through the years. A stunning Slovenian supermodel called Melania Knauss hung from his arm. A reporter asked her if she had any plans to redecorate the White House. She smiled and the press pack smiled back. "Let us see where it is going," she replied in a sugarcoated, East-European accent. What is your biggest qualification, the press asked Trump? "It's success," he replied. "Some people have a way of getting things done." He wouldn't even require contributions and he could outspend Bush and Gore with the spare cash in his wallet.[36] "I don't want to toot my own horn," he said later on the *Late Show With David Letterman,* "but everybody says two things about Trump: He's very competent and he's very rich. That's not so bad. If you had to have two traits, I mean you might as well have those two." His speeches read like self-help books for lonely businessmen. "You don't need money to get a beautiful woman," he reassured the readers of *The New York Times.* "All my life, I've had friends who were successful and can't get a date, let alone a date with a beautiful woman."

A trip to California went less well. Arriving in his black-and-gold jet, Trump started at the Holocaust museum, which he advised Buchanan to go visit.[37] Then he met with the state Reform Party in Beverly Hills. Someone asked him if he supported their platform. Trump looked confused. "Well," he said, "nobody knows what the Reform Party platform is." A swell of boos rippled through the crowd. Asked what he thought of a national sales tax, he replied, "How do I feel about sales tax? I try to avoid paying it whenever possible. But the idea is an idea that a lot of people like very much." The audience was silent. Some got the sense that Trump wasn't taking this seriously.[38]

D onald Trump was running to promote himself. In contrast, Pat Buchanan's campaign was driven by ideas. Pat's dream was that the Reform bid would bring together the left and the right in a coalition against the middle. This was to be the highest stage of Sam Francis's Middle American Revolution, the point at which partisanship was replaced by patriotism. There was so much that the fringes of the left and right agreed on: war, trade, the slow decline of American capitalism into a kind of Walmart communism—materialist, greedy, heartless. The very fact that the 1990s were a period of rapid economic growth made those left behind feel more marginalized than ever before. The trade unions and small businessmen that had been at each other's throats for decades suddenly found that they had something in common. Their world was disappearing fast.[39]

Pat made sure he was there when the World Trade Organization convened in Seattle for talks on trade, on November 30, 1999. It was the scene of the largest popular demonstration against a world meeting related to globalization to date. A journalist noted that the crowd of 40,000 was composed of "Steelworkers, animal rights activists, the Sisters of Perpetual Indulgence . . . French makers of Roquefort cheese, anarchists, fans of a Free Tibet, students against sweat-shopped sweatshirts, grandmas, and a fine turn out of local folk too."[40] The anarchists drew up a list of corporations who they charged with raping the Third World—among them Gap, McDonald's, Levi's, Bank of America, Starbucks, Banana Republic, and Planet Hollywood—and planned to smash in their windows and close them down. They blocked the streets and prevented the delegates from entering the convention centers. Around noon, the activists started tipping over dumpsters and setting fire to them. The streets reclaimed, Seattle became an anarchist commune. The police fought back with tear gas and pepper spray and tried to drive the protesters back from the convention center. Six hundred people were arrested. It resembled Chicago in 1968, when

Pat had leaned over his hotel balcony and pointed out to the cops the hippies they had missed. But this time Pat's sympathies were reversed.[41]

The Battle of Seattle was a media coup for Buchanan. He told Fox News that the Middle American Revolution had arrived, that the left and right were now as one against globalization. The press believed him. Pat was interviewed across the day on CNN and received a huge amount of newspaper coverage. Thomas Friedman made the remarkable claim in *The New York Times* that Buchanan had personally "duped" the demonstrators ("a Noah's ark of flat-earth advocates, protectionist trade unions and yuppies looking for their 1960s fix") into thinking that the WTO had power over global finance.[42] Liberals at Seattle were incensed. New Left guru Tom Hayden wrote:

> To the young people who fasted in jail and froze in the streets, the WTO represents all that they fear about the future. They will not find a home in the market globalism of Clinton, who appeared tone-deaf by referring to the protests as "hoopla" while endorsing their goals in the same breath. Still, they are just as unlikely to be part of Pat Buchanan's anti-WTO model and narrow nationalist constituency.

Hayden pointed out that Buchanan spent the day on the phone to CNN in his hotel room.[43]

Left and right had a common enemy, but contrasting motivations. True, some people went to Seattle to defend their jobs. But many were wealthy and middle class. What Pat and some in the media missed was that the antiglobalization movement was internationalist. It cared less about factory jobs in Detroit than it did about working conditions in Mogadishu. It was Pat's cause, but these were not Pat's people. They were not going to vote Reform. "One of the most important lessons of Seattle," wrote one friendly commentator, "was that it had nothing to do with protectionism." Rather, "there are now two visions of globalization on offer, one led by commerce, one by social activism."[44]

Still, Buchanan believed that the hour for a left-right axis had come. Eugene McCarthy, whose liberal presidential campaign had brought down Lyndon

Johnson in 1968, gave an encouraging quote about Pat to *The New York Times*. A couple of Buchanan people invited him to dinner and tried to solicit an official endorsement. "He would have done it," recalled one, "but he was a Minnesota man and was friendly with Ventura . . . Yet it was instructive that someone so associated in the popular mind with liberalism thought Pat was the only man he could vote for that year." Brian Moore, the Socialist Party's 2008 presidential candidate, stumped for him, too.[45]

In the fall of 1999, Buchanan went to New York to win the endorsement of black community activist Lenora Fulani. Fulani had run for president in 1988 on the New Alliance Party ticket, gathering a quarter of a million votes. Her politics mixed Marx and Freud to create a new brand of therapeutic activism. In the early 1990s, realizing the limits of any third-party run without money, she registered with the Reform Party. Fulani believed that the only way to transform America was to break the stranglehold of the two main parties. She was prepared to do anything to shake things up.

Fulani and Buchanan met in a restaurant in New York City. The conversation was polite. The two disagreed on most substantive issues, but they found a common enemy in corporate power. Both had also been accused of anti-Semitism (Fulani was an anti-Zionist). Both were marginalized radicals. Both felt they had been mistreated by the media. Pat brought a big name and money to the table. Fulani promised to use her black activist network to get him on the ballot.[46] At the airport, reporters asked Pat what had happened. "I'm only going to say this just once," he said in a Bill Clinton voice. "I did not have sex with that woman." Pat described a dull but worthy lunch, discussing mainline political and social affairs. "I did not convert to Marxism," he continued. "I was in Beijing in 1972 when Richard Nixon toasted the greatest mass murderer of all time, Mao Tse-tung. If we can do that, why is it wrong for me to have a Caesar salad with Lenora Fulani?"[47]

A couple of weeks later, Leonora Fulani endorsed Pat Buchanan and became a co-chair of his campaign. She admitted that "In traditional political terms, Pat Buchanan stands for all the things that black progressives such as myself revile." But he wasn't all bad. He "is not a racist or a fascist or a bigot. He is not a hater." Referring to the brigades, she added, "We're going to integrate that peasant army of his. We're going to bring black folks and Latino folks and gay folks and liberal folks into that army."[48] The polls put Buchanan at 9 percent and most commentators gave him a shot at getting into the presidential debates. Another poll asked registered voters which candidate "would make the scariest Halloween mask." Buchanan won, Gore came second.[49]

I n the New Year of 2000, Jesse Ventura quit the Reform Party. He appeared outside the governor's residence in St. Paul, wearing a black-and-yellow Rolling Stones baseball jacket. The weather was freezing cold, but Ventura was too angry to notice. He called the national party leadership "hopelessly dysfunctional." They had begun a move to oust his friend, Jack Gargan, as national chair. Perot's pal, Russell Verney, was behind it. Ventura let his anger show by referring to him alternately as Russell Varmint and Russell Vermin. The Body said he couldn't stomach a party that could consider Pat Buchanan as a leader. When he heard that David Duke had joined, he picked up the phone and quit.[50]

Shortly after, Trump bowed out, too. Pat Choate presumed that Trump was a Republican dirty trick, but actually the publicity stunt had just run its course.[51] He couldn't resist a last dig though. "The Reform Party now includes a Klansman, Mr. Duke; a neo-Nazi, Mr. Buchanan; and a communist, Ms. Fulani," he said. "This is not company I wish to keep."[52] Months later, Trump said of the Reform experience:

> I saw the underside of the Reform Party. The fringe element that wanted to repeal the federal income tax, believed that the country was being run by the Trilateral Commission, and suspected that my potential candidacy was a stalking horse for (take your pick) Gov. George W. Bush, Senator John McCain, or Vice President Al Gore. When I held a reception for Reform Party leaders in California, the room was crowded with Elvis look-alikes, resplendent in various campaign buttons and anxious to give me a pamphlet explaining the Swiss-Zionist conspiracy to control America.[53]

Momentum was with Pat. Gargan was gone by the New Year of 2000. He had agreed with Ventura's plan to host the Reform convention in Minnesota.

Gargan calculated that this central location was cheaper than many alternatives, but also that Reform should be exploiting its best asset—Governor Ventura. The Perot and Buchanan people were outraged, seeing it as an attempted coup by Ventura. They called a meeting of the national committee and voted Gargan out 3–1. Pat Choate took his place. The meeting was rowdy and garnered bad press. At one point the cops were called to separate two women fighting over a microphone.[54]

And then . . . there was silence.[55] The struggle against Trump had at least kept Pat in the headlines. But with Jesse and Donald gone, Reform went back to being all about Buchanan. The press was uninterested, the headlines ceased. A journalist discovered Pat in Minnesota and found him cheerful but lonely. The rise in the Republican primaries of Sen. John McCain had stolen his thunder and the primaries obscured his candidacy. "I feel like I'm walking the sidelines at the Super Bowl on crutches and can only yell to the guys on the field about what they're doing," he said. Some of the signature gathering was arduous and costly (50,000 were needed in Texas and Buchanan had to spend $2 million overall).[56] Much of it was small and petty. The West Virginia caucus took place in a bowling alley. It took Buchanan hours to find it and it was nighttime when he finally pulled into a dusty town called Fleetwoods. Someone didn't like the result and there was a fistfight after the voting.[57]

The biggest winner of the Ventura-Buchanan fight was Ross Perot. Pat had done his job; he had wiped out the man who threatened to take the party away from him. Now Perot looked for a stick to club Pat with.[58] At first, he hoped John McCain might help. In the Republican primaries, McCain was soaring among independents and moderates. His willingness to distance himself from the Christian Right and his Vietnam War record set him apart as the Colin Powell of 2000—a maverick figure whose integrity few would dare to question. Bush comfortably won the Iowa primary, showing that he had sewn up the religious right. But in February 2000, McCain took New Hampshire.[59] On the same day, Democratic outsider Bill Bradley was defeated by Vice President Al Gore by just 50–46 percent. Rumors flew that a McCain-Bradley Reform ticket was possible.[60] McCain probably stood a better chance than Buchanan of putting together a left-right coalition. Pat's people were allied by economics but alienated by culture. McCain's were allied by culture and largely indifferent to economics.

McCain reinvented himself as a conservative to win the 2008 Republican primaries. But back in 2000, he was considered hip enough to win the endorsement of liberal Hollywood actor Warren Beatty.[61] The left were so alienated by the corruption and materialism of the Clinton years that they were prepared to back a Republican to herald a fresh start.

Perot realized that McCain's independent spirit was more in touch with the America of 2000 than Buchanan's. He made overtures and tried to get him to commit to enter the Reform process. McCain confirmed that he would run on a joint Reform–Republican ticket if he won the GOP nomination.[62] Team Buchanan was upset. Perot had always been distant and mysterious. But his outreach to McCain was right out in the open. Had Perot been using them all along?

Bush broke McCain in South Carolina. McCain recovered with a victory in Michigan, but the voting in South Carolina reflected the opposition to him from the religious community and party establishment. His notorious temper got the better of him. At a February 28 speech at Virginia Beach he distanced himself from the organized Christian right. "We embrace the fine members of the religious conservative community," he said. "But that does not mean that we will pander to their self-appointed leaders." A few days later he let slip a wisecrack on the Straight Talk Express in which he called Robertson, Reed, et al "the forces of evil."[63] McCain was knocked out of the race on Super Tuesday and Bush was guaranteed the nomination.[64] McCain turned down Perot's advances. He was a party man. It wasn't worth alienating the GOP for the sake of a protest candidacy.

Having lost McCain, Perot had to look elsewhere for someone to rescue him from Buchanan. In the spring of 2000, the North Carolina Reform Party held its state convention to decide who would go to the national. The Buchanan brigades were well prepared. The people on Boyd Cathey's slate from the 8th District were almost all Sons of Confederate Veterans, headed up by a Civil War reenactor called William W. Williams (the "W." stood for William).[65] Williams wrote an incriminating e-mail to his electors that made it into *The Washington Post* that read: "It's our job to get out there in our areas, to raise consciousness, attract and radicalize 'those very people'—OUR people—then organize them into a majority. Many good people will have joined a much more radicalized,

White-friendly Reform Party come November . . . It is going to be a very interesting year with the Jews constantly screaming 'NAZI!' at PB." In an e-mail interview, Williams refused to back down from his remarks. He said he was "interested in the Reform Party becoming the party of the White."[66]

The Buchanan forces entered the North Carolina convention expecting a walkover, but were surprised by what they found. Boyd Cathey called it "just dreadful." The opposition turned out in full force and opposed every Buchanan motion and challenged the credentials of every delegate. Reform stalwarts who didn't like the idea of Pat taking over the party. But there were other, stranger people there, too.[67] "Some were these Buddhist types," recalled Buchanan delegate Tom Smith. "We didn't understand where they had come from. They could be very nice, but they could be very nasty. Not what you'd expect of a bunch of Buddhist monks or whatever."[68]

Having beaten Ventura and Trump, Buchanan would see his political career finally brought down by a flock of flying Buddhists.

TWENTY-SIX

Pat Buchanan vs.
the Flying Buddhists

Pat Buchanan's nemesis was a nuclear scientist called John Samuel Hagelin. A brilliant academic, Hagelin was a fan of Transcendental Meditation and a skilled yogic flyer. Yogic flyers sit cross-legged on the floor, enter a deep trance, and "fly" across the room by bouncing on their knees and feet. Practitioners believe that the flying has a wider effect on the behavior of people in the surrounding area. In 1993, Hagelin conducted a large-scale study whereby 4,000 flyers gathered in Washington, D.C., and bounced around the room twice daily for several weeks. Using data obtained from the District of Columbia Metropolitan Police Department, Hagelin claimed that during the eight weeks of the study the overall level of violent crime (homicides, rapes, and assaults) decreased by 23 percent, with rapes declining by 58 percent. Hagelin used this to argue that federal and state governments should adopt a more holistic approach to crime fighting that included yogic flying. In 1992, Hagelin helped form the Natural Law Party, which argued for flying centers to be established across the country—as well as sustainable farming, a flat tax, and gun control. Hagelin was the party's presidential candidate in 1992 and 1996. In 2000, he decided to enter the Reform Party primaries.

Hagelin realized early that Transcendental Meditation would be a hard sell. So he ran a campaign that demanded a return to the basic principle of the Reform Party—electoral reform.[1] He became a rallying point for all those angry with Buchanan's attempt to turn Reform into a vehicle for the Buchanan brigades. In the spring of 2000, Fulani stepped down as Buchanan's co-chair because he wouldn't stop talking about abortion. "I must and do object," she wrote Pat, "to your efforts to transform the party into a party of and for only social conservatives." Fulani declared for Hagelin instead.[2] Her defection was the first of many.[3] The Texas state party denounced Buchanan when its convention was overrun by evangelical Christians.[4] Colorado and Georgia called Pat a homophobe.[5] California pledged to sit out the election if he was nominated.[6]

Suddenly the nomination looked in doubt. While Pat scooped up signatures, the Hagelin people concentrated on securing delegates to the national convention, where they could overturn the primary vote. Buchanan's friend Tom Piatak found the Ohio event overrun by respectable-looking professors and social workers in suits and ties. He gave a speech on behalf of Pat and called them out as yogic flyers.

"That is a distortion," said the leader of the Hagelin people. "We are ordinary Americans determined to take this party back from the Buchanan brigades." The Hagelin folks carried the convention. Later, when he went to his car, Piatak spotted them sitting under a tree in the yoga position reciting the sacred "ohm."

"These were crazy people," said Piatak. "But they did a good job of looking normal and making us look mad."[7]

Pat decided to relaunch himself and reach out to mainline Reformers. It didn't work.[8] In mid-March, he went to Harvard University and unveiled a giant check for millions of dollars made out to "the major parties," signed "Influence Peddlers." It was a clumsy pitch to the McCainiacs. Campaign reform was, he conceded, "the only real issue" this year. "Both Beltway parties are chemically dependent on soft money," he said. "We get no soft money and we take no PAC money. Neither Beltway party is going to drain this swamp. It's a protected wetland; they breed in it, they spawn in it." He got plenty of laughs, but the audience found it hard to swallow that he had suddenly become a convert to a cause liberals regarded as their own. A critic asked him angrily what he meant by his accusation that Harvard favored giving places to Jews and Asian Americans at the expense of white Christians. "Simply because you're at Harvard does not exempt you from the same kind of rules and regulations that Harvard lovingly imposes upon the rest of America," he shot back. "Pat Buchanan is not a beloved figure in America, but neither is Harvard."[9]

He did come close to engaging the left seriously. Pat spoke movingly of the impact of sanctions upon Iran and Iraq.[10] Conceding "a dramatic departure from what I've argued and believed," Buchanan called sanctions "a sword that slaughters children. Our sanctions are sowing seeds of hatred that will one day flower in acts of terrorism against us."[11] But he couldn't run away from the charge that he was a rabid right winger, an unpopular one at that. In April 2000, Ralph Nader announced that he would run on the Green ticket. He immediately took 5 percent in the polls, a little ahead of Buchanan's 3 percent.[12] Nader sucked up most of Buchanan's left-wing Reform support and reduced his chances of making it into the debates even further. Why should Pat be invited and not Ralph Nader?[13] At its national convention, the UAW discussed endorsing Buchanan.[14] But they backed off because he was too culturally divisive, too Catholic.[15]

A few days before the Reform convention, Buchanan collapsed in pain. He was rushed to the hospital and the doctors removed a gallstone.[16]

On July 29, 2000, the Reform executive met to discuss the Buchanan problem. The heated exchange lasted two hours. Finally, they voted to throw him off the ballot. Under party rules, the 164-member national committee would then vote on whether or not to uphold their decision.[17] "We plan to ignore it," said Bay of Perot's gambit. "It is of no consequence to us, and we plan to stand very, very strongly against the handful of mean-spirited dissidents who have refused to recognize that at every single turn of the process they have been whupped."[18] Bay had done the math and found that Pat had a two-thirds majority among the delegates. He could take the nomination even without winning the primary ballot. But she naively thought that Hagelin's flyers would accept defeat and rally around. That's what Pat had always done, so why wouldn't they?[19]

A week before the convention, the 164-strong Reform national committee met at the Westin Hotel at Long Beach, California, to discuss whether or not to keep Pat on the ballot. They disappeared inside a locked room for several hours. Party members gathered outside, kept at bay by a phalanx of security guards. As the clock ticked on, tempers flared and things turned nasty. The Hagelin people screamed to get in and Buchanan brigaders blocked the doors, chanting "Go Pat, go! Go Pat, go!" Russell Verney argued with a security guard to let him through. "The party is voting and I have every right to be inside!" he pleaded. The doors flew open and a quarter of the national committee broke out. They had lost control of the meeting. Buchanan had won the vote and overturned the executive's decision. The angry mob crossed the road to the Renaissance Hotel and "reconvened the meeting of the one we walked out of." They voted to take Buchanan off the ballot. Meanwhile, the rump national committee voted again, minus the Perot people, to keep him on.[20]

Hagelin said that Buchanan had used his Republican lists to take over the party by stealth. He was changing its message, creating a conservative party in his own image. Buchanan didn't help matters with some fiery performances on TV that week that emphasized his conservative credentials. The GOP had just nominated Bush at its annual convention. The Republicans were at pains to look moderate, giving primetime to McCain, Elizabeth Dole, and Colin Powell. On CBS Buchanan said, "There wasn't a single voice up there for the unborn. There was nobody that got up and spoke about right to life." On ABC he attacked "Affirmative action, quotas, racial preferences . . . They're unjust discrimination against white folks because of the color of their skin or where their ancestors came from." He even went after "Saint" Colin: "And I don't care if General Powell gets up and says they're right. For heaven's sakes, why did not a single Republican get up and say, 'That is wrong?'"[21]

Leaders of the Buchanan and Hagelin factions met the day before the convention to try to thrash out a compromise. They failed. Buchanan offered a fundamentally different philosophy and organizing principle. Any settlement would require surrender of the Reform movement to a maverick Republican. In his press conference, Buchanan declared that he had already won. Before a crowd of one hundred, Bay laid out the game plan: get the money within three weeks, target key states with advertising, reach double figures, go into the debates, and cripple the Bush candidacy. On the other side of town, Hagelin accused Buchanan of "brown-shirt tactics," of physical intimidation. He predicted, more astutely, that whichever side won the battle would go to the federal courts. The $12.6 million wasn't going anywhere just yet.[22]

The 2000 Reform convention was the first and last of its kind—a federally funded event for a third party. With $2.5 million to play around with, the Reform people went wild. They threw an opening night party on a cruise ship. Tom Smith, who had come all the way from North Carolina, was astonished and thrilled by the lashings of champagne and oysters: "They brought in French chefs and there was a ball on the boat. Everyone was drinking, having a great time. They fired fireworks off the bow."[23]

The Buchananites were also surprised to find that the Reform Party attracted a fair amount of the counterculture people they despised. On the streets of Long Beach, hairy youths handed out leaflets about meditation and alien abduction. Of course, Pat had brought along his own contingent of fundamentalists and militiamen. Thomas Edsall in *The Washington Post* reported that "Patrick J. Buchanan's presidential bid has turned the once-centrist Reform Party into a magnet attracting leaders and activists of such extreme right organizations as the National Alliance, the Liberty Lobby, the Council of Conservative Citizens, and the League of the South." Edsall's evidence was thin. The first two organizations had given tacit Internet endorsements, but would withdraw them by the end of the year. They gave no money and offered no activist muscle; nor was any sought. It was true, however, that Francis Bell, chair of the South Carolina Council of Conservative Citizens, won the post of secretary-treasurer of the Aiken County Reform Party chapter. But mostly, Edsall confused heritage people like Tom Smith with white nationalists.[24]

On the first day of the convention, Hagelin gave a news conference calling for a return to the good old Perot days. His people marched to the convention hall, chanting, "Reform, Reform, Reform." Inside, the brigades were gathering. A fight looked likely. Chair Gerald Moan took the microphone and hastily appealed for calm. "I'm asking you to be nonconfrontational," he said. "We are professional and hospitable." The Hagelin group marched into the hall and occupied the front quarter. Moan politely told them that they could not be seated. They began to sing "We Shall Overcome." Then, slowly, they drifted away.[25]

Finally, the much-disputed primary ballot was opened. It was a disappointment. Just under 80,000 people had bothered to participate—only 10 percent of the ballots distributed. Nevertheless, Buchanan won handily, 49,529 to 28,539. At their alternative convention, Hagelin's people threw the ballot out and nominated their own man. Buchanan's convention did the same. After many months of complex democratic process, everything was decided on the whim of two men—Buchanan at the convention and Ross Perot watching from his home in Texas.

"I feel better about things now that we've split off from the Buchananites," said Leroy Mueller, a retired machinery parts distributor from Wisconsin. "But I worry still about the party's future. I was with Ross from the start, from back in 1992, and he never meant for the party to have a right-wing slant. Reform was his thing . . . not abortion and gun control and prayers and the like. Can we ever get it back to the way Ross had it, to the time when we were all excited and ginned up and had our eyes on a new horizon? I just don't know."

"Look," replied Paul Rezel, an orthopedist from Indiana, "reform is fine but I came to the Reform Party because Pat Buchanan was the Reform Party. The Republicans weren't doing it for me, and neither were the Democrats. What Pat says is what I care about."[26]

Buchanan had triumphed. But there was one small problem: He didn't have a vice presidential candidate. Bay claimed that she had an office holder ready to declare, but he pulled out a couple of hours before the announcement had to be made.[27] Team Buchanan gathered in a small room and tried to come up with a name. Someone suggested Ezola Foster, a public school teacher from Los Angeles. Incredibly, Bay said yes.[28]

Ezola Foster was a little-known black conservative. In the 1980s, she registered as a Republican and spoke out against affirmative action, immigration, gay rights, and feminism. This made her unpopular in her school and she often had to receive protection against threats of violence. Foster was arrested in 1987 when she protested the attendance of the gay Log Cabin Republican group at a state GOP convention. In 1992, she testified in defense of the policemen who beat up Rodney King.[29]

Coming after weeks of exhausting fighting, tired and emotional, Team Buchanan's decision to go with Foster was understandable. She had impeccable conservative credentials and was a good speaker. Best of all, she was guaranteed massive press exposure. Pat standing next to a black running mate would put to rest claims that he was a racist and would shake things up. "I thought it would send a good message," said staffer Scott McConnell. "It said that we were nothing to do with race, that Pat was a mainstream conservative."[30] Although the appointment was made because they had nowhere else to go, Bay and her team convinced themselves that it was a brilliant piece of political theater. She ran the idea by her brother and, as always, he did what he was told. Ezola Foster was presented to a bemused press. They put her and Pat on the front page.[31]

The decision to give the second spot to Ezola Foster backfired. Tom Smith knew as soon as he heard it that the party was over.

> In the beginning, everyone seemed to be more energized than they were when that nomination was announced . . . I stopped paying attention from that point on because I was disenchanted . . . I won't say I felt sold out, but Pat was never supposed to be like other politicians. But, with her qualifications being so poor, this looked like tokenism . . . It reminds me of what John McCain did in 2008. Sarah Palin wasn't chosen because she was the most qualified candidate. She was chosen because she was a female . . . I didn't expect Pat Buchanan to act like that.[32]

In fact, Buchanan did a great, historical thing. Foster was the first black lady to run for a major party. But she was an affirmative action appointment, and that didn't sit right on a Buchanan ticket.

Foster was the wrong black woman. On the one hand, she was able to say with conviction, "I was born black, I attended all-Negro schools including college, I grew up in the segregated South during Jim Crow. If anybody knows a racist, I do. Pat Buchanan ain't no racist." On the other hand, her conservatism was such that she sometimes sounded like a shill for the racist right. "Our people were better off under the bondage of slavery than the Marxist 'Great Society' of Johnson," she once said.[33] And if Foster's appointment didn't allay the suspicions of moderates as it was supposed to, it did drive the racist right back to the Republican Party. David Duke's manager told reporters that "After

Buchanan chose a black woman as his veep [Duke] now thinks that Pat is a moron and there is no way that we can support him at this point." With the Democrats running the Jewish Joe Lieberman for vice president, most white supremacists backed Bush.[34] A discussion on the racist *Stormfront* Web site was indicative of the mood. One supporter tried to justify the move as a way of silencing the media: "The media portrayed Pat as a 'racist,' his choice of a black woman, conservative, John Birch Society member, was a slap in the face to those who were criticizing him." But an opponent replied, "I don't care if she was a Nobel prize winning queen of Egypt . . . Buchanan chose a BLACK WOMAN as his VP!"[35] Ethically, Pat was better off without the support of these racist goons. Electorally, however, their disillusionment cut off one of the few remaining pools of support.

In his acceptance speech, Buchanan thanked the Reform Party for giving his supporters, "a home of our own." And then, predictably, he launched into a tirade against "arrogant, unelected judges, ending racial quotas, and preferences." To wild cheers, he attacked the United Nations, imported chopsticks, gay congressman Barney Frank, and the "money changers" whom he said the party had to "drive out of the temples of our civilization."[36] In the middle of the thunder, there was a moment of quiet introspection. He talked about how he had visited his oldest brother, Bill, at the Maryknoll seminary in New York in 1964.

> I asked him why he did it. He told me: "God has been good to our family and we have to give something back." My brother Bill is gone now, but his words haunt me still: God has been good to our family and we have to give something back. That is why we are here: To create something new and good and alive, and give something back to this country that has been so good to all of us.

Then he pounded the air with his fist and asked, "What are we fighting for?" He replied:

> To save our country from being sold down the river into some godless New World Order, and to hand down to our children a nation

as good and as great as the one our parents gave to us—forever independent, forever free. That's what this Gideon's Army is fighting for; and we will fight on and on and on and on—until God himself calls us home."[37]

The polls put Buchanan at 2 percent. Hagelin was at 1 percent. Russell Verney joked, "It's a close one all right. John Hagelin is within one point of Pat Buchanan."[38] Hungover, dazed, and disappointed, the delegates packed their bags and returned to their states.

A nd that was that.
Hagelin decided to challenge Buchanan's right to appear on the ballot as the named Reform nominee. So, for over a month, the campaign became stuck in the courts. Hagelin and Buchanan went to the Federal Election Commission to fight for the $12.6 million.[39] Meanwhile, they had to appeal individually to each state for ballot access as the Reform candidate. The way many states chose between the two was surreal. In Iowa, an aide to the secretary of state put a slip of paper inside each of two black canisters. On one was written "Buchanan-Foster." On the other: "Hagelin-Goldhaber." When the canisters had been placed in a glass bowl on a stand outside his office in the Capitol rotunda, the secretary of state walked up, stirred the bowl around, and lifted one out. That was how Buchanan and Foster became the official Reform ticket in Iowa. Even fate was no guarantee of good fortune. In Montana, the secretary of state picked a name out of a ballot box that contained ten canisters with "Buchanan" written on index cards and ten with "Hagelin." After he had plucked out a "Hagelin," a lawyer for Buchanan presented papers placing a temporary restraining order on the ballot.[40]

Meanwhile, Buchanan's condition grew worse. He had another gallstone removed a few days after the convention, on August 17. As soon as he returned home, he got abdominal pains again and was rushed to hospital. A third stone was taken out on August 23 and he was told to do nothing until early September. When the pains returned yet again, the gallbladder was removed altogether.[41] A *New York Times* reporter visited Buchanan at his home in McLean and found him resigned and cynical. At twelve pounds lighter, his suit hung off his body, his face was gray and downcast. His cat Gipper sat on his lap. "There are a lot of people who don't want us to be alive," he said to the cat. "At least that's a good feeling." The doorbell rang and someone handed him an envelope. "It's the Ross Perot people again," he sighed, throwing the subpoena on the couch. Buchanan was convinced that the money for the endless court cases against him was coming from Texas. Then, perhaps realizing that his pain was all too obvious, Buchanan cried "Vote Lazarus!" and laughed. He cited the case of Frederick the Great, handed a triumph by bizarre political accident after staring defeat in the face. His opponent had died and was succeeded by a fan who immediately signed a peace treaty. But then, the gloom returned. Frederick had armies and a nation at his command. Buchanan had Ezola Foster and 1 percent in the polls. "If we had gotten our money the day after the convention, and I'd have been healthy, we'd be about 5 percent now in the polls. And if we got into the debates, we'd get far more than Ross Perot got in 1996." He scratched Gipper's ears. "Yeah well, of all the words of tongue and pen, the saddest of these is 'might have been.'"[42]

By the time the FEC ruled in his favor and the money finally came through, the Buchanan campaign had disappeared from view. The media wasn't interested in a candidate at 1 percent. Pat tried to relaunch himself with a speech at Bob Jones University. It was a bravura performance, cheered along by a 1,500-strong crowd of fundamentalists. Delivering a stunning sermon, he said:

> God and the Ten Commandments have all been expelled from the public schools. Christmas carols are out, Christmas holidays are out. The latest decision of the Supreme Court said that children in stadiums or young people in high school games are not to speak an inspirational moment for fear they may mention God's name, and offend an atheist in the grandstand.

His fist pumping the air, Buchanan cried:

> We may not succeed, but I believe we need a new fighting conservative traditionalist party in America. I believe, and I hope, that

one day we can take America back. That is why we are building this Gideon's army, and heading for Armageddon, to do battle for the Lord.

Hundreds of students in suits and crew cuts gathered around for autographs. Many said they would vote for him whether he had a chance or not. Bob Jones III was friendly but sad. He called Buchanan "a lonely man, bravely annunciating the truth." Alas, nobody was listening.[43] At a school board luncheon in Florida, he was introduced thus: "Pat says he is a serious candidate. The polls say he's *dead* serious."[44]

The money didn't last long and what the campaign did with it wasn't worth waiting for. In the first half of October, Buchanan spent $10.7 million on advertising. The TV ads were on strong, conservative themes that didn't reflect either Reform's reformism or Buchanan's economic populism. Given that the national race was narrow and that Bush had made a big play for the votes of social conservatives, this was a mistake. One ad promoted organized prayer in schools and supported the Boy Scouts for excluding gay scout leaders. Neither was a big issue in 2000.[45] In a surreal twist, Buchanan's people took a North Carolina Internet company to court for the misuse of the candidate's name. Rendina Solutions of Durham, North Carolina, had created several porn sites and registered domain names that sounded like campaign pages for Buchanan. The principle was that consumers lazily surfing for information on the candidate might wander onto a blue site, get distracted, and spend some money. The head of the company, Mark Rendina, tried to persuade Buchanan to buy the offending sites for $10,000. A federal court's ruling against Rendina established for the first time the offense of registering another person's name on the Internet with the intent to profit.[46]

Buchanan focused his energies on states that were sewn up for the Democrats, to attract votes from conservatives.[47] But running a right-wing message in Democratic areas brought little benefit. And Perot stepped in to make sure that he didn't draw any votes among independents. Perot signed an affidavit supporting Hagelin's claims to be nominee. Then he made a surprise appearance on *Larry King Live* and endorsed Bush. He waxed lyrical about Bush's experience as governor of Texas. Probably still smarting from his defeat over NAFTA, he called Gore "unethical" and accused him of outright corruption as Vice President. Bush was a moral, decent man and "clearly the better of the two." Suddenly, CNN cut to a live news conference of Bush confirming that he had been arrested in Maine in 1976 for drunk driving. The TV screen flashed back to a surprised Perot. Perot swallowed hard and said, "There's something rotten about our press corps." It was, he said, another conspiracy to undermine his own integrity. But it didn't reflect poorly on Bush. "Here's a guy who made a mistake, and it was a dumb mistake, and I'm not trying to rationalize it." King asked for a comment on Pat Buchanan's candidacy. Perot refused to give one.[48]

Buchanan's enthusiasm never dimmed. One reporter was surprised, given his illness and bad polls, to find him more animated than ever. As in 1992 and 1996, he played both politician and pundit—offering a frank assessment of his candidacy. "Look," he said, "as long as we're fighting wars from 15,000 feet and not losing a soldier, when the unemployment rate is 3.9 percent, the Dow is at 11,500 and the Nasdaq is at 5,000, it's not going to be easy for us. But when the chickens come home to roost, this whole coalition will be there for somebody, and then they're going to think, 'What ever happened to that guy back in 2000?' There's no doubt these issues can win. But 2000 might not be the year for them." If only he had gotten into the debates, he'd be "in the teens right now, the upper teens. But the perception is now that it's a very, very close race and people want to bet on it like the Super Bowl because there are only two people in it." He laughed. "We're in the Fiesta Bowl with Nader." He wouldn't give in. "We're going to go all out for the next three weeks," he said enthusiastically, and "then I don't know what I am going to do after that. A lot depends on how well the Reform Party does. But I know one thing: I'm not going back to the Republican Party. The further away from it I get, the better I feel."[49]

On election night, the Buchanan gang met and cracked open a few beers to celebrate defeat. Pat Buchanan was getting less than 1 percent of the vote. He whooped when he reached a high of 2.5 percent in North Dakota.[50] As the night dragged on, the count in Florida looked close. Gore and Bush were running neck and neck while Nader was taking enough votes to lose it for the Democrats.

"Heck, I wouldn't want to be Ralph Nader right now," Pat laughed.[51]

Bush won Florida by a margin of 2,912,790 votes to 2,912,253. And Pat could just as easily be blamed for that as Nader. In Palm Beach County, voters used a "butterfly ballot" whereby they punched holes next to listed names. The ballot was complex and poorly designed, with names placed either side of the vertical line of holes so that it was difficult to work out which hole went with which name. Seen from an angle, it looked like the voter had to punch Pat's hole to vote for Gore. Early reports gave Buchanan about 0.8 percent of the vote in Palm Beach County (a total of 3,407 votes), outperforming his statewide vote share of 0.29 percent. Given that Palm Beach is heavily Democratic (62 percent of the county voted for Gore), it is reasonable to assume that Buchanan won those votes by accident—thus denying Gore the state and the election. This is particularly ironic considering that much of Palm Beach is Jewish and African American. Many Jewish voters in their enthusiasm to vote for the first-ever Jewish vice presidential candidate accidentally voted for Pat Buchanan.

Team Buchanan didn't defend their total in Palm Beach. A spokesman for Bush said, "Palm Beach County is a Pat Buchanan stronghold and that's why Pat Buchanan received 3,407 votes there." But when asked about the statement, Buchanan's Florida coordinator, Jim McConnell, responded: "That's nonsense." He estimated the number of Buchanan activists in the county to be between 300 and 500—nowhere near the 3,407 who voted for him. "Do I believe that these people inadvertently cast their votes for Pat Buchanan? Yes, I do," said McConnell. "We have to believe that based on the vote totals elsewhere."[52]

That was the final word from the Buchanan campaign. Few have ended so ignominiously—denying that its voters even existed.

TWENTY-SEVEN

Pat Takes Tea in the
Twenty-first Century

The Reform campaign ended Pat's hopes of high office. What remained of the Buchanan brigades slunk back to their trailer parks and ivory towers. Bay took over The American Cause and sold her fund-raising services to the highest bidder. Pat returned to his basement study to work on a new Jeremiad. Called *The Death of the West: How Dying Populations and Immigrant Invasions Imperil Our Country and Civilization,* it was an audacious account of an America on the brink of destruction. It was also the closest that Pat had yet come to conflating culture and race. Sam Francis wanted him to call it *The Death of Whitey.*[1]

The Death of the West argued that America had become two countries: old and new. Pat calculated that about 51 percent of Americans were hardworking, God-fearing, and liberty loving; and about 49 percent were cultural revolutionaries looking for a government handout. Decent conservatives were making a superhuman effort to hold on to their country, but the demographics were stacked against them. Year by year, wrote Pat, Latino immigration and dependence on the welfare state put more people in the liberal column. Abortion, contraception, feminism, and homosexuality reduced the number of potential newborns in the conservative column. ("The pill and condom have become the hammer and sickle of the cultural revolution.")[2] The bad Americans were outbreeding the good. Time is short, concluded Buchanan. Unless the conservative movement does something drastic soon, it will lose the old republic for good.[3]

Critical reaction was scathing. The neoconservative Christopher Caldwell was typical for charging Buchanan with racism, for creating an artificial link between racial origin and national character. If the author of *The Death of the West* wanted a Christian republic, then why didn't he stand on the Mexican border and cry, *"Bienvenidos, amigos!"*? After all, most Spanish-speaking immigrants are hardworking Catholics chasing the American dream—an apt description of Pat's own Irish ancestors. Sure, they might speak Spanish at the dinner table and fly the Mexican flag in their backyards. But previous generations of Italians, Germans, and East Europeans kept their language and traditions, too. Part of Pat's favorite movie, *The Godfather*, is in Italian.[4]

Whatever the flaws of his argument, *The Death of the West* sold 200,000 copies and hit the top of *The New York Times* bestseller list. The tone of the book captured the postmillennial mood of the conservative movement. Under George W. Bush, America seemed to be divided into two equally proportioned camps: red state and blue state. They had different economic needs and opposing cultural outlooks. The elections of 2000 and 2004 were close, with fewer people making their minds up at the last minute and a dwindling pool of self-defined independents.[5] The hostile mood that placed enormous stakes on the smallest of policy debates was made worse by the horror of 9/11. For many conservatives, politics became about a clash of civilizations; an end-times battle between good and evil, right and left. They saw themselves in a war against Islamic terrorists abroad and cowardly liberals at home.[6] In words that could have been plagiarized from *The Death of the West*, pundit Bill O'Reilly wrote:

> On one side of the battlefield are the armies of the traditionalists like me, people who believe the United States was well founded and has done enormous good for the world. On the other side are the committed forces of the secular-progressive movement that want to change America dramatically: mold it in the image of Western Europe.

O'Reilly urged readers to "become a cultural warrior," which largely involved watching his TV show and buying his books.[7] The media encouraged partisanship because it made for good viewing. They even helped publicize the absurd idea that conservatives and liberals have different-shaped brains.[8]

Where Pat departed from the post-9/11 conservative movement was his suspicion that the battle was already lost. Buchanan's America—a world of religious mystery, Joe McCarthy, obedient wives, patriotic teamsters, Latin Masses, *Saturday Night at the Movies,* Buck Rogers, apple pie, stink bombs, and Sputniks—was long gone. Even Georgetown was now a plush shopping district, more Ralph Lauren than Roman Catholic. When country-and-western singer Johnny Cash died in 2003, Pat said in an interview, "Johnny Cash is gone and it is fitting, because the America we grew up in is gone, too. We grew up in another country. Johnny Cash wrote and sang our songs."[9] In *The Death of the West,* contradicting his case that America was in balance between the present and the past, Pat wrote that liberals had already "replaced the good country we grew up in with a cultural wasteland and a moral sewer that are not worth living in and not worth fighting for—their country, not ours."[10]

P at Buchanan's culture war thesis was perfectly suited to the politics of the new millennium. But, as a personality, he was out of step with Bush II conservatism. Pat took exception to almost everything the Republican President did. He disapproved of the money the White House threw at education and Medicare, of its flirtation with immigration reform, and its embrace of free trade. Buchanan asked, "What is there about Bush that is conservative? His foreign policy is Wilsonian. His trade policy is pure FDR. His spending is LBJ all the way. His amnesty for illegals is Teddy Kennedy's policy."[11] The Republican base might have been more receptive to Buchanan's criticisms, were it not for one issue that galvanized support for the administration: the War on Terror.

After 9/11, the vast majority of Republicans rallied around the President. Their country had been attacked and their patriotism came to the fore. But Pat Buchanan accused Bush of having "embraced a neo-imperial foreign policy that would have been seen by the Founding Fathers as a breach of faith."[12] September 11, he said, was the result of America's "meddling" in the Middle East. "What took place . . . was an atrocity. What is coming may qualify as tragedy.

For the mass murder of our citizens has filled this country with a terrible re-solve that could lead it to plunge headlong into an all-out war against despised Arab and Islamic regimes that turns into a war of civilizations, with the United States almost alone." To the average Republican, Buchanan's words were bor-derline treachery.[13]

Buchanan made his case through a magazine he helped set up in 2002, called *The American Conservative*. Pat was a co-owner and the first editor was former Reform campaign staffer Scott McConnell. When America in-vaded Iraq on March 20, 2003, Buchanan wrote an editorial denouncing the invasion as a proxy war for Israel, fought by lions and led by neocon donkeys.

> We charge that a cabal of polemicists and public officials seek to ensnare our country in a series of wars that are not in America's interests. We charge them with colluding with Israel to ignite those wars . . . We charge them with deliberately damaging US relations with every state in the Arab world that defies Israel or supports the Palestinian people's right to a homeland of their own. We charge that they have alienated friends and allies all over the Islamic and Western world through their arrogance, hubris, and bellicosity. Not in our lifetimes has America been so isolated from old friends. Far worse, President Bush is being lured into a trap baited for him by these neocons that could cost him his office and cause America to forfeit years of peace won for us by the sacrifices of two genera-tions in the Cold War.[14]

The American Conservative became a soapbox for anti-Bush conservatives. "We got lucky," recalled McConnell. "The Iraq War gave us a prominence that we otherwise wouldn't have had. Our readership really went up." During the magazine's boom years, it published articles by people from across the antiwar spectrum, including the actor Robert Dreyfus, the civil libertarian Glen Green-wald, Paul Gottfried, Robert Novak, and Justin Raimondo.[15] To neocons, Pat Buchanan and *The American Conservative* were anti-Semites and traitors. The liberal company they kept was proof that they and their sanity had long parted company. Responding to Buchanan's anti-invasion editorial, David Frum wrote in *National Review*:

> There is . . . a fringe attached to the conservative world that . . . are thinking about defeat, and wishing for it, and they will take pleasure in it if it should happen. They began by hating the neoconservatives. They came to hate their party and this president. They have finished by hating their country. War is a great clarifier. It forces people to take sides. The paleoconservatives have chosen—and the rest of us must choose too. In a time of danger, they have turned their backs on their country. Now we turn our backs on them.[16]

That's precisely what happened. Pat's two best friends ended their lives this way: marginalized and destroyed by their war against the modern world.

Sam Francis was fired from *The Washington Times* in 1995, after he wrote a column criticizing the Southern Baptist Convention for having apologized for slavery.[17] The *Pittsburgh Tribune-Review* continued to publish him until 2004, when he complained about interracial dating on *Desperate Housewives* and lost that job, too. The underemployed bachelor moved into an apartment on the third floor of Robert E. Lee's childhood home on Cameron Street in Alexandria, Virginia. His rent was paid by a patron, Sylvia Crutchfield, who toured the country raising funds for the continued printing of his column.[18] Pat stayed loyal. He quoted Francis extensively in his books and encouraged him to keep on writing. "Sam was denounced as a racist," Pat said. "But Sam did not hate anyone. He was a victim of hatred, of those who advance by slandering, censoring, and silencing braver men to appease the prevailing power." In 2004, after years of pestering by friends, Francis went on a diet. He lost about twenty pounds and started dating again; he was even thinking about marriage. But one morning in January 2005, he woke up in great pain. He couldn't get an ambulance to come, so he drove himself to the hospital. The doctors told him he was having an aneurysm. They performed several hours of painful surgery and sedated him heavily afterward, in fear that if he moved his heart would give out. After a tiresome week spent lying on his back, Francis ordered that they sit him up in a chair. They did so, and he died.[19]

After being sacked by the *National Review* in 1993, Joe Sobran barely survived off columns he wrote for paleocon journals like *Chronicles*. His marriage ended in divorce and his health declined.[20] In 2001, Pat offered him a column in *The American Conservative*. Sobran was delighted, but, a week before he was due to start writing, Scott McConnell discovered that he had accepted an invitation to speak at a conference of the Holocaust-denying Institute for Historical Review. McConnell rang Sobran and begged him not to do it: "I said that I couldn't employ him if he gave that speech. It would ruin our reputation, rightly so." Sobran seemed angry and upset. He clearly didn't want to lose the column, but he also refused to pull out of the conference. "You don't understand," he told McConnell. "We can't let these people win." Perhaps Sobran had been consumed by far-right conspiracy theories. Perhaps, as McConnell suspected, he needed the money that the IHR was offering. Sobran gave the speech and McConnell—who, as editor, had final say on appointments—dropped his column. Joe Sobran died in 2010, in a nursing home in Virginia.[21]

Some of what Pat and his friends had to say was too strong even for his own magazine. After Pat stood down as an owner in 2007, *The American Conservative* continued to run his column but distanced itself from its more controversial content. In 2008, Pat published his most contentious book yet, *Churchill, Hitler, and "The Unnecessary War": How Britain Lost Its Empire and the West Lost the World*. In it, he argued that Britain should have stayed neutral when Germany declared war on Poland in 1939. British policy during the 1930s, he wrote, was motivated by "Germanophobia," and Hitler's ambitions were limited to colonizing Eastern Europe. If he had been placated, the Führer might have joined an anti-Soviet alliance with the West. Buchanan concluded that, in his conduct of the war, Churchill was as morally reprehensible as Hitler.[22]

Churchill, Hitler, and "The Unnecessary War" received predictably negative reviews from the mainstream media. What was surprising was that *The American Conservative* didn't like it, either. Editor Scott McConnell commissioned a critique by John Lukacs. "There is," wrote Lukacs, "a fatal contradiction in Buchanan's theses: Hitler's regime—including, one may think, its expansion— was evil, but warring against him was unnecessary and wrong. Either thesis may be argued, but not both." By consistently denying the historical uniqueness of Hitler's crimes, Buchanan failed to appreciate why Churchill was revered in classrooms, or why Pat's words distressed so many people who had lost relatives in the death camps and gas chambers of the Third Reich.[23]

Buchanan felt betrayed by *The American Conservative*. He had helped found the magazine and, understandably, expected a warm reception for the book. But many staff members felt that the antiwar conservative movement had grown bigger than Pat Buchanan. A younger generation was coming that was uninterested in arguments about Churchill and Hitler. Discussing the pros and cons of the Second World War threatened to give the movement the tinge of racism, which would put off potential allies. Pat had become a distraction.[24]

So many friends ended their careers poor and maligned. And yet, despite his eccentricity, Buchanan survived and prospered. In 2009, MSNBC put him on contract as a pundit. He was a good foil for the network's liberal hosts, and had impressed producers with his balanced commentary on the 2008 election. Buchanan credited Barack Obama with delivering "the greatest convention speech" he'd ever heard. Pat didn't agree with Obama on much, but after eight years of listening to George W. Bush's malapropisms he probably appreciated the marked improvement in presidential rhetoric.

Pat's career might have also been saved by his charm. He came from an era when Republicans and Democrats disagreed in public but were civil in private. Joe Scarborough recalled that all of his liberal interns would cringe when they first heard that they would be meeting Pat Buchanan: "They'd really squirm and say, 'Isn't he an awful person? He's so right wing.' But after a couple of days with him, they'd all want to adopt him as their father . . . He's very funny and disarming and great with young people."[25] Rachel Maddow, who had been drawn to politics by Pat's culture war speech, had several on-air arguments with "him." But, behind the scenes, she took to calling him "Uncle Pat." "I like debating things with him," she admitted. "He's funny and quick and intellectually coherent, even when his views are totally toxic."[26]

And program makers couldn't ignore Pat Buchanan's remarkable CV. No producer would blacklist a man who worked for Nixon, survived Watergate, accompanied Reagan to Reykjavik, forced George H. W. Bush to the right, and won New Hampshire.[27] Chris Matthews observed, "I wouldn't compare Pat

Buchanan with Glenn Beck and all those guys we have now, because Pat actually had brains. He went right back to Nixon, was there on the trip to China, and he had gravitas . . . With Pat, you're arguing with a brilliant guy, not just a loudmouth celebrity."[28]

Buchanan's incredible career gave him contemporary relevance.[29] The press rediscovered that in 2008, when Republican presidential nominee John McCain selected Sarah Palin to be his running mate. On MSNBC, Pat called her "probably the most dynamic young conservative in the country" and "beloved by the base." He said that he was certain she had thrown a fund-raiser for him in 1996 or 1999. The discovery that the Palins might have been Buchanan brigaders became a major news story. Whether they were or not remains the stuff of gossip and rumor. All that can be substantiated is that when Pat visited Alaska in 1999, Wasilla mayor Sarah Palin greeted him wearing a "Vote Buchanan" button. Palin insisted that she only put it on to be polite.[30]

Sarah Palin was a Buchanan brigader in style and spirit. She entered Republican politics when Buchananmania was at its height, as Pat was expanding the party's appeal to poor and middle-class conservatives. Sean Scallon, writing in The American Conservative, noticed parallels between their careers:

> Her first race for public office came the same year as Buchanan's: 1992. From the Wasilla City Council, she rose to become mayor in 1996, the year of his second campaign [and victory in the Alaskan caucus]. Like many of Buchanan's culturally conservative voters in the early and mid-1990s, she become politically active thanks to groups like the Christian Coalition and used her church at that time, the Wasilla Assembly of God, as her base. Like Buchanan, she styled herself as a reformer and outsider. Even today, he recognizes her, both literally and figuratively, as his kind of Republican, writing in a recent column: "She is a traditionalist whose values are those of family, faith, community and country, not some utopian ideology."

Scallon argued that Palin and Buchanan's constituencies were identical. She "describes [her] constituency as 'hockey moms' and 'snowmobiling dads.' Through the years, they've been called 'Jacksonians,' 'Scots-Irish,' 'Middle

American Radicals,' 'blue collar,' and 'lunchbucket' voters. In the 1990s, many also called themselves Buchananites."[31] After the 2008 election they became known as the Tea Party.

There were, however, big differences between the Buchanan brigades and the Tea Party revolt. The Tea Party was founded in reaction to profligate spending, not free trade. Its foreign policy is comparatively neoconservative and pro-Israel.[32] But, culturally and demographically, the Tea Party and the brigades are cut from the same cloth. "These are basically the same people, motivated by the same issues," opined Connie Mackey, who went to work for the socially conservative Family Research Council after staffing for Pat in 1996. "All the Tea Party favorites are pro-life and anti-gay marriage . . . The media tends to overlook the culturally conservative element because the recent focus has been on spending issues . . . But Tea Party people would agree with Pat on a lot."[33]

"Unsurprisingly, many of Buchanan's former activists claim responsibility for the Tea Party. Terry Jeffrey: "We raised the kinds of issues that the Tea Party are now talking about."[34] Greg Mueller: "Sarah Palin might not actually be a brigrader, but she looks like one . . . An ordinary hockey-mom, anti-Washington, anti-big government."[35] Jerry Woodruff (Pat's press spokesman in 1992): "The issues that Pat raised and the people who were drawn to him back in 1992 and the Tea Party revolt today are identical. And the Tea Party thing isn't just about balanced budgets and taxes . . . It's about god and guns and the death of our culture."[36] Pat Buchanan agreed. The contemporary political battle, he wrote in 2010, "is cultural, political and tribal." He saw the Tea Party revolt as an act of secession, a Middle American war of independence from the brave new republic that Democrat and Republican elites were determined to build.[37] "However, he was cynical about its chances of success. In his 2011 book, *Suicide of a Superpower: Will America Survive to 2025?*, Pat argued that the Tea Party's goal was to restore the USA he had grown up in. But, he asked, "Can we restore America? Or has the America we grew up in already been transformed into another country?" He concluded, with regret, that it had. "Though we appear to the world the same country, we are on a course far off from the one our fathers set."[38]

The Tea Party and the Buchanan brigades were both a part of a postwar tradition of conservative revolt against mainstream politics. Their forebears were the New Right of the 1970s, the Goldwater Republicans of the 1960s, and the anticommunists of the 1950s. But, by defining the culture war so well in the 1990s, Pat may be given unique credit for shaping the worldview from which the Tea Party emerged: us vs. them, small vs. big, Christian vs. atheist, straight vs. gay, hardworking vs. work shy, conservative vs. liberal. Yes, these conflicts had been around for a very long time before Pat Buchanan bundled them together and called them a "religious war" at the 1992 Houston convention. But, for post–Cold War conservatives, Pat Buchanan set the tone of the debate. Sarah Palin owed her nomination in 2008 to Buchanan in the sense that he helped foster a conservative identity that was folksy and working class. To the permanent annoyance of liberals, the cultural politics he spawned continues to attract people to the Republican Party whose income would normally incline them toward voting Democrat.[39]

Today, Pat Buchanan is a comfortable man. He has a beautiful home, a small real estate fortune, a generous contract with MSNBC, and millions in savings and investments. He has a fan base that—judging by his book sales and newsletter subscriptions—reaches into the hundreds of thousands. Right-wing outrage is a profitable business. All, but one, of his books have been bestsellers. His publisher told me that Buchanan once complained to him of writer's block. Pat said, "I can't think of what book to do next. The only issue that I really care about right now is immigration, and I wrote about that in my last book."

"Well, Pat," replied the publisher, "in this country you can never, ever go wrong with xenophobia." Pat chuckled appreciatively. And so, he wrote *State of Emergency: The Third World Invasion and Conquest of America,* and the money kept rolling in.[40]

Buchanan's hair is graying and he wears thick glasses. He has the academic air of a man who might be able to recite the entire history of the War of 1812, but not recall where he parked the car. His friends love him and believe in him. When I interviewed Howard Phillips for this book, he told me that he had begged Pat to run for president in 2008. A year later, I met Phillips again at a funeral. He had forgotten who I was, so I said that I was writing a biography of Pat Buchanan. "Pat's fantastic!" said Phillips. "Is he going to run in 2012?"[41]

Pat Buchanan failed to win the culture war, but he can take some satisfaction in the fact that he helped define it for millions of people on both sides of the conflict. When in New York one day conducting interviews, I went into a shop to put credit on my cell phone. The guy behind the counter asked me why I was in town and I told him I was writing a biography of Pat Buchanan.

"Urgh! Buchanan's an asshole!" he said. "He's such a fascist, he's such a Nazi. Every time I see him on TV, I just want to put my foot through it. Goddammit, he's such a right-wing jerk." The salesman handed me my receipt. "And you want to know what the worst thing about Pat Buchanan is?" he asked.

"Sure," I replied.

"My father voted for him."

ACKNOWLEDGMENTS

This book was made possible by the generous funding of the Leverhulme Foundation and Royal Holloway College, University of London. The Leverhulme Early Career Fellowship was a wonderful honor and I am forever grateful for the work that it helped fund. I also benefited from a Robert J. Dole Institute grant. The Institute's staff was welcoming and kind, and helped me to survive a harsh Kansas winter.

Among the academic colleagues who criticized, praised, and damned the text, I should particularly like to thank Alex Goodall, Daniel Joyce, and Rupert Russell. For their advice, I'd also like to recognize Tony Badger, Don Critchlow, Richard Follett, Iwan Morgan, Andrew Preston, Dominic Sandbrook, and John Thompson. The eminent archivist Carl Ashley has proven a true friend on all my stays in Washington, D.C. Between us we have drunk enough beer to drown an ox. My mother is magnificent and I owe everything I have to her.

The book made it onto the shelves thanks to the work of my agent Lynn Chu and the courage of my publisher, Thomas Dunne. Both took a risk on a bizarre Englishman in a bow tie and blazer. Good for them.

The Crusader belongs to the people I interviewed. Without their trust, it wouldn't have been possible. The Buchanans were kind hosts and I enjoyed my fiery debates with Pat. I hope he feels I have been fair. I may, someday, write a book about the writing of this book. One of my finest memories was my brief stay at the Hines family home in South Carolina. We ate grits on the veranda while the mastiffs wrestled in the street. Less than a month later, Mrs. Hines passed away. She was a gracious lady and will be missed by many.

This book began and ended with Boyd Cathey. I didn't know where to start my research, so I googled "Buchanan right-wing activists crazy" and found Boyd's phone number. Within an hour, he had promised to introduce me to at least half the people I finally interviewed. Boyd and I disagree on many things, except that all dogs go to heaven. But, for all his charity, I am forever in his debt.

NOTES

INTRODUCTION

1. Author interview with Pat Buchanan, subject's home, Virginia, on May 1, 2010.
2. "Bush Rises in Poll, Even Before Speech," *USA Today,* August 21, 1992, 3A.
3. "Buchanan Heaps Scorn on Democrats," *Washington Post,* August 17, 1992, A18.
4. Barbara Bush, *Barbara Bush: A Memoir* (New York: Scribner, 2003), 480.
5. "Buchanan Heaps Scorn on Democrats."
6. "Ask Why Koreatown Voted for Buchanan," *Washington Times,* June 12, 1992, F2.
7. Author interview with Diana Banister, phone, September 3, 2010.
8. http://www.huffingtonpost.com/2008/10/06/rachel-maddow-pat-buchana_n_132145 .html, last accessed November 15, 2010.
9. Bill Clinton, *My Life* (New York: Random House, 2004), 396, 426–27.
10. "Republicans in Houston," *New York Times,* August 19, 1992, 13.
11. "Moderates Feeling Shut Out," *USA Today,* August 20, 1992, 4A.
12. "Conservative vs. Conservative," *Washington Post,* August 21, 1992, A27.
13. "Red Meat and Astro-Turf: Decoding the Convention," *Washington Post,* August 23, 1992, C1.
14. "Religion Shares Convention Stage," *USA Today,* August 18, 1992, 4A.
15. "Merchants of Hate," *New York Times,* August 21, 1992, A25.
16. Mark J. Rozell, *The Press and the Bush Presidency* (Westport, CT: Greenwood, 1996), 126.
17. "Bush Rises in Poll, Even Before Speech," *USA Today,* August 21, 1992, 3A.
18. Author interview with Richard Viguerie, phone, March 18, 2010.
19. See page 197.
20. "Buchanan Takes Conservative Message to Fairbanks," Associated Press, July 17, 1999.
21. Author interview with Boyd Cathey, subject's home, North Carolina, May 12, 2010.

ONE: THE GEORGETOWN GANG

1. Patrick Buchanan, *Right from the Beginning* (Washington, D.C.: Regnery Gateway, 1990), 14–15.
2. Ibid., 24.
3. "Sisters in Arms," *Time,* March 4, 1996, 31.
4. "Buchanan Tries to Soften a Boyhood Bully Image," *New York Times,* February 9, 1992, 26.
5. "The Making of Buchanan," *Time,* February 26, 1996, 32.
6. "Campaign Briefing," *New York Times,* August 30, 2000, A21.
7. Buchanan, *Right from the Beginning,* 49–50.
8. Ibid., 59.
9. "The Making of Buchanan."
10. Buchanan, *Right from the Beginning,* 74–75.
11. "Pat's School Days with the Pope's Marines," *Time,* February 26, 1996, 35.
12. "Remembrance of Things Pat," *Washington Post,* February 19, 1996, B1.
13. James M. O'Toole, *The Faithful: A History of Catholics in America* (Cambridge, MA: Harvard University Press, 2008), 254–55.
14. Michael W. Cuneo, *The Smoke of Satan: Conservative and Traditionalist Dissent in Contemporary Catholicism* (Baltimore, MD: John Hopkins University Press, 1999), 135.
15. Buchanan, *Right from the Beginning,* 72.
16. "Buchanan's Alternative: Neither Kindler nor Gentler," *New York Times,* January 15, 1992, A1.
17. Sarah DeCapua and Edmund Lindop, *America in the 1950s* (Minneapolis, MN: Twenty-First Century Books, 2010), 45–50.
18. Buchanan, *Right from the Beginning,* 131.
19. "Bully in the Pulpit," *New York Times,* September 7, 1995, A27.
20. "Buchanan Tries to Soften a Boyhood Bully Image."
21. "Pat's School Days with the Pope's Marines."
22. Buchanan, *Right from the Beginning,* 178.
23. Ibid., 186.
24. Author interview with Peter Fenn, subject's office, D.C., May 12, 2010.
25. Buchanan, *Right from the Beginning,* 131.
26. "Remembrance of Things Pat."
27. "Daddy's Boy," *New Republic,* January 22, 1996, 15.
28. Buchanan, *Right from the Beginning,* 131.
29. "Daddy's Boy."
30. Richard G. Kurial and David B. Woolner, *FDR, the Vatican, and the Roman Catholic Church in America, 1933–1945* (New York: Palgrave MacMillan, 2003), 129–30.
31. Ellen Schrecker, *Many Are the Crimes: McCarthyism in America* (New York: Little Brown, 1998), 241.
32. Buchanan, *Right from the Beginning,* 87.
33. Schrecker, *Many Are the Crimes,* 240–41.
34. Ibid., 264.

35. Buchanan, *Right from the Beginning*, 80–122.

36. Author interview with Bay Buchanan, restaurant, Virginia, May 3, 2010.

37. Buchanan, *Right from the Beginning*, 145.

38. Author interview with Bay Buchanan, restaurant, Virginia, May 3, 2010.

39. Author interview with Paul Gottfried, restaurant, D.C., February 24, 2010.

40. Robert Griffith, *The Politics of Fear: Joseph R. McCarthy and the Senate* (Amherst: University of Massachusetts Press, 1987), 211.

41. "Patrick J. Buchanan: History Conscious Fighter Focuses on Trade," *Washington Post,* January 26, 1996, A1.

42. Buchanan, *Right from the Beginning*, 162–63.

TWO: LICENSE TO KILL IN ST. LOUIS

1. "The Quayle Quagmire," *Time,* August 29, 1988, 16.

2. Buchanan, *Right from the Beginning*, 213.

3. "The Ugliest Republican," *Penthouse,* April 1987, 12.

4. Buchanan, *Right from the Beginning*, 216.

5. Ibid., 218.

6. Ibid., 226.

7. Ibid., 229.

8. Ibid., 236.

9. "The Ugliest Republican," 8.

10. "A Classmate Remembers," *New York Times,* June 23, 1993, 31.

11. "The Ugliest Republican," 8.

12. Buchanan, *Right from the Beginning*, 243–44.

13. "Daddy's Boy."

14. Buchanan, *Right from the Beginning*, 297–98.

15. "The Pen That Just Grew," *Nation,* November 16, 1964, 355.

16. Buchanan, *Right from the Beginning*, 300.

17. "Daddy's Boy."

18. For conservative frustration with the GOP, see Donald T. Critchlow, *The Conservative Ascendancy: How the GOP Right Made Political History* (Cambridge, MA: University of Harvard Press, 2007), 43.

19. For Goldwater and popular conservative opinion, see Lisa McGirr, *Suburban Warriors: The Origins of the New American Right* (Princeton, NJ: Princeton University Press, 2001), 147–86.

20. "The Globe's Recommendations," *St. Louis Globe-Democrat,* November 2, 1964, 18A.

21. Buchanan, *Right from the Beginning*, 245.

22. Gary Donaldson, *Liberalism's Last Hurrah: The Presidential Campaign of 1964* (New York: M. E. Sharpe, 2003), 103–27.

23. A point conceded by most conservatives, including Buchanan and Buckley: "Uproar over Candidate's Famous Words Hints Caution Is in Order," *Los Angeles Times,* July 23, 1964, 2.

24. For Goldwater and race, see Rick Perlstein, *Before the Storm: Barry Goldwater and the American Consensus* (New York: Hill and Wang, 2001), 460–62.

25. "Captive Voters," *St. Louis Globe-Democrat*, November 2, 1964, 16A.

26. Donaldson, *Liberalism's Last Hurrah*, 293–308.

27. "Power Preying," *Mother Jones*, November–December 1995, 38.

28. Chester Gillis, *Roman Catholicism in America* (New York: Columbia University Press, 1999), 95.

29. For an excellent summary of the cultural politics of Vatican II, including Buchanan's response, see Mary Jo Weaver, *What's Left?: Liberal American Catholics* (Bloomington: University of Indiana Press, 1999), 2.

30. Cuneo, *The Smoke of Satan*, 81–120.

31. "Those Beleaguered Maryknollers," *Time*, July 6, 1981, 24.

32. Author interview with Tom Fleming, phone, August 9, 2010.

33. Author interview with Pat Buchanan, subject's home, Virginia, February 26, 2010.

34. Iwan Morgan, *Nixon* (New York: Oxford University Press, 2002), 63.

35. Author interview with Pat Buchanan, subject's home, Virginia, February 26, 2010.

36. Buchanan, *Right from the Beginning*, 319–21.

37. Rick Perlstein, *Nixonland: The Rise of a President and the Fracturing of America* (New York: Scribner, 2008), 18.

38. Author interview with Pat Buchanan, subject's home, Virginia, May 1, 2010.

39. "The Men Behind Nixon's Speeches," *New York Times*, January 19, 1969, SM21.

THREE: A NEW OLD MAN

1. Author interview with Shelley Buchanan, MSNBC, D.C., May 1, 2010.

2. "Sisters in Arms," *Time*, March 4, 1996, 31.

3. Author interview with Shelley Buchanan, MSNBC, D.C., May 1, 2010.

4. Stephen Ambrose, *Nixon: The Triumph of a Politician, 1962–1972* (New York: Simon & Schuster, 1990), 67.

5. "The Great Right Hope," *New York*, June 10, 1985, 48.

6. Author interview with Pat Buchanan, subject's home, Virginia, February 26, 2010.

7. Herbert S. Parmet, *Richard Nixon and His America* (Boston: Little Brown, 1990), ix, 528.

8. Author interview with Pat Buchanan, subject's home, Virginia, February 26, 2010.

9. Mary Edsall and Thomas Edsall, *Chain Reaction: The Impact of Race, Rights, and Taxes on American Politics* (New York: Norton, 1991), 263.

10. Robert Dallek, *Lyndon B. Johnson: Portrait of a President* (New York: Oxford, 2004), 280.

11. Critchlow, *The Conservative Ascendancy*, 86.

12. Jonathan M. Schoenwald, *A Time for Choosing: The Rise of Modern American Conservatism* (New York: Oxford University Press, 2001), 253.

13. Author interview with Pat Buchanan, subject's home, Virginia, May 1, 2010.

14. Peter Braestrup, *How the American Press and Television Reported and Interpreted the Crisis of Tet 1968 in Vietnam and Washington* (New York: Presidio, 1977), 509.

15. Gary Wills, *Nixon Agonistes: The Crisis of the Self-Made Man* (New York: Mariner, 2002), 89.

16. "Republicans: Nixon's Dream," *Time,* February 9, 1968, 12.

17. Author interview with Pat Buchanan, subject's home, Virginia, February 26, 2010.

18. "Report on the Phenomenon Named McCarthy," *New York Times,* August 26, 1968, SM24.

19. Norman Mailer, *Miami and the Siege of Chicago: An Informal History of the American Political Conventions of 1968* (London: Weidenfeld & Nicolson, 1968), 83.

20. "McCarthy Rides on Student Power," *New York Times,* March 10, 1968, E1.

21. "Romney Is Gaining in New Hampshire," *New York Times,* January 28, 1968, 36.

22. Author interview with Pat Buchanan, subject's home, Virginia, February 26, 2010.

23. Hunter S. Thompson, *The Great Shark Hunt: Strange Tales from a Strange Time* (London: Pan Macmillan, 1979), 248–49.

24. "Effects of Primary; Rockefeller Gets Push Toward Oregon," *New York Times,* March 13, 1968, 1.

25. "Kennedy to Make 3 Primary Races," *New York Times,* March 17, 1968, 1.

26. Author interview with Pat Buchanan, subject's home, Virginia, February 26, 2010.

27. "Nixon's Men Are Smart but No Swingers," *New York Times,* September 29, 1969, SM28.

28. Author interview with Pat Buchanan, subject's home, Virginia, February 26, 2010.

29. "Kennedy Shot and Gravely Wounded After Winning California Primary," *New York Times,* June 5, 1968, 1.

30. Author interview with Pat Buchanan, subject's home, Virginia, February 26, 2010.

31. "The Political Picture Is All Too Clear," *New York Times,* August 18, 1968, D17.

32. Craig Shirley, *Reagan's Revolution: The Untold Story of the Campaign That Started It All* (New York: Thomas Nelson Inc., 2005), 12–13.

33. "Pledges End of War, Toughness on Crime," *New York Times,* August 9, 1968, 1.

34. For Buchanan's take on the Agnew appointment see Jules Witcover, *Very Strange Bedfellows: The Short and Unhappy Marriage of Richard Nixon and Spiro Agnew* (New York: Public Affairs, 2007), 14.

35. David Farber, *Chicago '68* (Chicago: University of Chicago Press, 1994), 17.

36. "Chicago Examined: Anatomy of a Police Riot," *Time,* December 6, 1968.

37. Author interview with Pat Buchanan, subject's home, Virginia, February 26, 2010.

38. Dan T. Carter, *The Politics of Rage: George Wallace, the Origins of the New Conservatism, and the Transformation of American Politics* (New York: Simon & Schuster, 2000), 133–55.

39. Dan T. Carter, *From George Wallace to Newt Gingrich: Race in the Conservative Counter Revolution, 1963–1994* (Baton Rouge: Louisiana State University Press, 1996), 16–17.

40. Carter, *The Politics of Rage,* 349–50.

41. Richard Scammon and Ben Wattenberg, *The Real Majority* (New York: Coward-McCann, 1970), 170.

42. Perlstein, *Nixonland,* 328.

43. A. J. Langguth, *Our Vietnam: The War, 1954–1975* (New York: Simon & Schuster, 2000), 521.

44. Author interview with Pat Buchanan, subject's home, Virginia, February 26, 2010.

45. Perlstein, *Nixonland,* 236.

46. Author interview with Pat Buchanan, subject's home, Virginia, February 26, 2010.

47. "Humphrey Drums on Trust Theme," *New York Times,* November 1, 1968, 51.

48. Author interview with Pat Buchanan, subject's home, Virginia, February 26, 2010.

FOUR: SPEAKING UP FOR THE SILENT MAJORITY

1. "Nixon's Men Are Smart but No Swingers."

2. "The Dirtiest Trick," *New York Times,* September 27, 1973, 39.

3. "The Men Behind Nixon's Speeches," *New York Times,* January 19, 1969, SM21.

4. H. R. Haldeman, *The Haldeman Diaries: Inside the Nixon White House* (New York: Berkley Book Pub. Group, 1996), 20.

5. Ibid., 22.

6. Memo, Buchanan to Haldeman, January 14, 1971, *Documents and News Summaries Annotated by the President, Papers of Richard M. Nixon,* Roosevelt Study Center, Abdij 8, 4331 BK Middelburg, The Netherlands, File 6A-116-04; "Nixon, Reagan Compared," *Washington Post,* June 3, 1985, A3.

7. Author interview with Pat Buchanan, subject's home, Virginia, February 26, 2010.

8. Hal Bochin, *Richard Nixon: Rhetorical Strategist* (New York: Greenwood Publishing Co., 1990), 89–90.

9. "Nixon's Presidency Is a Very Private Affair," *New York Times,* November 2, 1969, SM28.

10. John Anthony Maltese, *Spin Control: The White House Office of Communications and the Management of Presidential News* (Chapel Hill: University of North Carolina Press, 1994), 48–49.

11. "Nixon's Presidency Is a Very Private Affair"; Ambrose, *Nixon,* 248–49, 409.

12. Author interview with David Keene, subject's hotel room, D.C., February 18, 2010.

13. Ambrose, *Nixon,* 369.

14. Author interview with Patrick Buchanan, subject's home, Virginia, February 26, 2010.

15. "Richard Nixon's Collapsing Presidency," *Time,* May 20, 1974, 15.

16. Author interview with Patrick Buchanan, subject's home, Virginia, February 26, 2010.

17. Memo, Buchanan to Nixon, January 31, 1972, *Papers of Patrick J. Buchanan,* Nixon Library, 18001 Yorba Linda Boulevard, Yorba Linda, California 92886-3949, Box 2.

18. Author interview with Pat Buchanan, subject's home, Virginia, February 26, 2010.

19. Memo, Buchanan to Nixon, February 25, 1970, *Annotated Documents, Nixon Papers,* Roosevelt Study Center, File 6A-73-05.

20. Notes on meeting with Nixon, December 1, 1972, *H. R. Haldeman Notes of White House Meetings, 1969–1973, Nixon Papers,* Roosevelt Study Center, File 5-78-40.

21. Matthew D. Lassiter, "Suburban Strategies: The Volatile Center in Postwar American

Politics," in Meg Jacobs, William J. Novak, and Julian Zelizer eds., *The Democratic Experiment: New Directions in American Political History* (Princeton, NJ: Princeton University Press, 2003), 325–49.

22. Notes on meeting with Nixon, January 3, 1969, *Haldeman Minutes, Nixon Papers,* Roosevelt Study Center, File 5-11-77; notes on meeting with Nixon, June 12, 1970, *Haldeman Minutes, Nixon Papers,* Roosevelt Study Center, File 5-80-74.

23. James Landers, *The Weekly War: Newsmagazines and Vietnam* (Columbia: University of Missouri Press, 2004), 220–21.

24. Author interview with Pat Buchanan, subject's home, Virginia, February 26, 2010.

25. "The Breaking of the President," *Washington Post,* October 7, 1969, 21.

26. Author interview with Pat Buchanan, subject's home, Virginia, February 26, 2010.

27. Andrew L. Johns, *Vietnam's Second Front: Domestic Politics, Virginia, the Republican Party, and the War* (Lexington: University Press of Kentucky, 2010), 272.

28. Mara Einstein, *Media Diversity: Economics, Ownership, and the FCC* (New York: Routledge, 2004), 65.

29. Maltese, *Spin Control,* 54.

30. Pat Buchanan, *Conservative Votes, Liberal Victories: Why the Right Has Failed* (New York: Quadrangle, 1975), 89.

31. Author interview with Pat Buchanan, subject's home, Virginia, February 26, 2010.

32. Haldeman, *The Haldeman Diaries,* 106.

33. Spiro T. Agnew, *Go Quietly . . . Or Else* (New York: William Morrow, 1980), 28–29.

34. Author interview with Pat Buchanan, subject's home, Virginia, February 26, 2010.

35. Maltese, *Spin Control,* 56.

36. "The Politics of Polarization," *Time,* November 21, 1969, 16.

37. "The Weekly Agnew Special," *Time,* November 28, 1969, 16.

38. William Safire, *Before the Fall: An Inside View of the Pre-Watergate White House* (New Brunswick, NJ: Transaction Publishers, 2005), 323.

39. "Spiro Agnew," *The Economist,* September 28, 1996, 52.

40. "Four Students Killed by State Troops," *New York Times,* May 5, 1970, 1.

41. "War Foes Here Attacked by Construction Workers," *New York Times,* May 9, 1970, 1.

42. "Nixon, in Pre-Dawn Tour, Talks to Protestors," *New York Times,* May 10, 1970, 1.

43. Dan Berger, *Outlaws of America: The Weather Underground and the Politics of Solidarity* (New York: AK Press, 2006), 204–37.

44. "Gallup Poll Finds 57 Percent of Americans Support President on Cambodia Policy," *New York Times,* May 10, 1970, 173.

45. Jonathan Rider, *Canarsie: The Jews and Italian Americans of Brooklyn Against Liberalism* (Cambridge, MA: Harvard University Press, 1985), 157.

46. Landers, *The Weekly War,* 208.

47. Author interview with Buchanan, subject's home, Virginia, February 26, 2010.

48. Memo, Buchanan to Nixon, September 2, 1969, *Annotated Documents, Nixon Papers,* Roosevelt Study Center, File 6A-32-05.

49. Alice O'Connor, "Financing the Counterrevolution," in Bruce Schulman and Julian Zelizer eds., *Rightward Bound: Making America Conservative in the 1970s* (Cambridge, MA: Harvard University Press, 2008), 148–70.

50. Memo, Buchanan to Nixon, March 9, 1973, *Annotated Documents, Nixon Papers*, Roosevelt Study Center, File 6A-275-10.

51. Memo, Buchanan to Nixon, February 25, 1970, *Annotated Documents, Nixon Papers*, Roosevelt Study Center, File 6A-73-05.

52. Notes on meeting with Nixon, July 10, 1970, *Haldeman Minutes, Nixon Papers*, Roosevelt Study Center, File 5-27-49.

53. "The Middle American Who Edits Ideas for Nixon," *New York Times*, April 12, 1970, SM117.

54. "Pattern Unclear: Vote Is Kaleidoscopic, but President Fails in Primary Goals," *New York Times*, November 5, 1970, 1.

55. Memo, Buchanan to Nixon, January 13, 1973, *Buchanan Papers*, Nixon Library, Box 7.

56. Kevin P. Phillips, *Post-Conservative America: People, Politics, and Ideology in a Time of Crisis* (New York: Random House, 1983), 56.

57. Safire, *Before the Fall*, 220.

58. Memo, Buchanan to staff secretary, January 11, 1971, *Buchanan Papers*, Nixon Library, Box 1.

59. Memo, Buchanan to Haldeman, January 14, 1971, *Annotated Documents, Nixon Papers*, Roosevelt Study Center, File 6A-116-04.

60. Memo, Buchanan to Nixon, January 6, 1971, *Annotated Documents, Nixon Papers*, Roosevelt Study Center, File 6A-114-16.

61. Haldeman, *The Haldeman Diaries*, 234.

62. Safire, *Before the Fall*, 547.

63. Haldeman, *The Haldeman Diaries*, 282.

64. Ibid., 397.

65. Ibid., 192.

66. Eric J. Ladley, *Nixon's China Trip* (Lincoln, NE: Writers Club Press, 2002), 75.

67. "Shelly Scarney and Nixon Aide Plan to Marry," *New York Times*, February 21, 1971, 70.

68. "Patrick J. Buchanan Weds Shelley Scarney," *New York Times*, May 9, 1971, 68.

FIVE: MAO AND MCGOVERN

1. Patrick Buchanan, *Where the Right Went Wrong: How Neoconservatives Subverted the Reagan Revolution and Hijacked the Bush Presidency* (New York: Thomas Dunne, 2004), 92.

2. Michael Kazin, *Populist Persuasion: An American History* (New York: Cornell University Press, 1998), 183.

3. Minutes of meeting, July 16, 1972, *Haldeman Minutes, Nixon Papers*, Roosevelt Study Center, File 5-54-30.

4. Michael P. Riccards, *The Presidency and the Middle Kingdom: China, the United States, and Executive Leadership* (Lanham, MD: Lexington Books, 2000), 181–82.

5. Notes on meeting with Nixon, July 16, 1971, *Haldeman Minutes, Nixon Papers*, Roosevelt Study Center, File 5-54-30.

6. Memo, Kissinger to Nixon, June 26, 1969, *Nixon Presidential Materials, NSC Files, National Archives (Papers of the National Security Council)*, 700 Pennsylvania Avenue Northwest, Washington, D.C. 20408-0002, Box 392.

7. Author interview with Pat Buchanan, subject's home, Virginia, February 26, 2010.

8. "Official Party Names for Nixon China Trip," *New York Times*, February 13, 1972, 3.

9. Ladley, *Nixon's China Trip*, 210.

10. Deborah Strober and Gerald Strober, *The Nixon Presidency: An Oral History of the Era* (New York: HarperCollins, 2003), 135.

11. Author interview with Pat Buchanan, subject's home, Virginia, February 26, 2010.

12. Haldeman, *The Haldeman Diaries*, 423.

13. Author interview with Pat Buchanan, subject's home, Virginia, February 26, 2010.

14. Margaret Macmillan, *Nixon and Mao: The Week That Changed the World* (New York: Random House, 2007), 300–20.

15. Henry Kissinger, *The White House* Years (London: Weidenfeld & Nicolson, 1979), 1093.

16. Author interview with Pat Buchanan, subject's home, Virginia, February 26, 2010.

17. Notes on meeting with Nixon, March 6, 1972, *Haldeman Minutes, Nixon Papers*, Roosevelt Study Center, File 5-71-48.

18. Haldeman, *The Haldeman Diaries*, 426.

19. This was the opinion of Bill Safire, and is shared by the author. "The Last Days in the Bunker," *New York Times*, August 18, 1974, 202.

20. Michael A. Genovese, *The Watergate Crisis* (Westport, CT: Greenwood Press, 1999), 20.

21. Memo, Buchanan to Colson, January 12, 1972, *Buchanan Papers*, Nixon Library, Box 2.

22. Memo, Buchanan to Nixon, undated, *Haldeman Minutes, Nixon Papers*, Roosevelt Study Center, File 5-69-87.

23. Bruce Miroff, *The Liberals' Moment: The McGovern Insurgency and the Identity Crisis of the Democratic Party* (Lawrence: University of Kansas Press, 2007), 52–53.

24. "Text of 2 Memos from Strachan to Haldeman on the 1972 Election Campaign," *New York Times*, July 19, 1972, 17.

25. "Buchanan Sought to Block Muskie," *New York Times*, September 27, 1973, 1.

26. "McGovern Gains 54 of Delegates in Wisconsin Race," *New York Times*, April 6, 1972, 1.

27. Memo, Buchanan to Nixon, July 5, 1972, *Buchanan Papers*, Nixon Library, Box 1.

28. Carter, *The Politics of Rage*, 439–43.

29. "Wallace off the Critical List," *New York Times*, May 17, 1972, 1.

30. Memo, Buchanan to Haldeman, January 11, 1972, *Buchanan Papers*, Nixon Library, Box 2.

31. Miroff, *The Liberals' Moment*, 84–89.

32. "Buchanan Outlined Plan to Harass Democrats in '72, Memo Shows," *Washington Post*, March 4, 1996, A7.

33. "McGovern, Eagleton, Statements and News Parley," *New York Times*, August 1, 1972, 25.

34. Memo, Buchanan to Nixon, September 6, 1972, *Buchanan Papers,* Nixon Library, Box 2.

35. "Nixon Explains His Taped Cryptic Remark About Helms," *New York Times,* March 12, 1976, 15.

36. For Nixon's rising popularity see Robert Mason, *Richard Nixon and the Quest for a New Majority* (Chapel Hill: University of North Carolina Press, 2004), 140. For Nixonian economics, see Edward R. Tufte, *Political Control of the Economy: Booms, Busts, Dollars, and Votes* (Lawrence: University Press of Kansas, 1998), 52.

37. Haldeman, *The Haldeman Diaries,* 573.

38. For discussion of Nixon as a liberal, see David Greenberg, *Nixon's Shadow: The History of an Image* (New York: Norton, 2003), 319–37.

39. "The Ship of Integration Is Going Down," *Harper's,* June 1972, 66.

40. Kevin L. Yuill, *Richard Nixon and the Rise of Affirmative Action: The Pursuit of Racial Equity in an Era of Limits* (Lanham, MD: Rowman & Littlefield, 2006), 225–27.

41. Memo, Buchanan to Nixon, April 11, 1969, *Annotated Documents, Nixon Papers,* Roosevelt Study Center, File 6A-12-43 B.

42. "Nixon Aides Explain Aims of Letter on Abortion Law," *New York Times,* May 11, 1972, 1.

43. Memo, Buchanan to Nixon, June 10, 1972, *Buchanan Papers,* Nixon Library, Box 7.

44. "The Legend of Saint George McGovern," *New York Times,* November 24, 1972, 37.

45. Memo, Buchanan to Nixon, September 7, 1972, *Buchanan Papers,* Nixon Library, Box 2.

SIX: WATERGATE

1. "A Vote for More of the Same . . . Nixon's Victory," *New York Times,* November 12, 1972, E1.

2. Patrick Buchanan, *The New Majority: President Nixon at Mid-Passage* (The Girard Company, 1973), 55–68.

3. Memo, Frank Gannon to Ehrlichman, March 30, 1973, *Annotated Documents, Nixon Papers,* Roosevelt Study Center, File 6A-281-22.

4. Memo, Buchanan to Haldeman, December 21, 1972, *Buchanan Papers,* Nixon Library, Box 7.

5. Briefing notes, 1973, "Budget Cutting vs. Compassion," *William J. Baroody Jr. Papers,* Gerald R. Ford Library, 1000 Beal Avenue, Ann Arbor, Michigan 48109, Box 39.

6. Memo, Buchanan to Nixon, November 10, 1972, *Buchanan Papers,* Nixon Library, Box 7.

7. Bruce J. Schulman, *The Seventies: The Great Shift in American Culture, Society, and Politics* (Cambridge, MA: Da Capo Press, 2002), 41.

8. Memo, Buchanan to Nixon, November 10, 1972, *Buchanan Papers,* Nixon Library, Box 7.

9. Minutes of meeting that took place on November 15. Memo, Buchanan to Nixon, November 30, 1972, *Buchanan Papers,* Nixon Library, Box 7.

10. Ambrose, *Nixon,* 639.

11. For an excellent narrative, see Keith Olsen, *Watergate: The Presidential Scandal That Shook America* (Lawrence: University Press of Kansas, 2003), 89–122.

12. Author interview with Pat Buchanan, subject's home, Virginia, February 26, 2010.

13. "A White House Response," *New York Times,* June 11, 1973, 35.

14. Genovese, *The Watergate Crisis,* 37.

15. Memo, Buchanan to Nixon, May 16, 1973, *Annotated Documents, Nixon Papers,* Roosevelt Study Center, File 6A-286-50.

16. Haldeman, *The Haldeman Diaries,* 652.

17. "Haldeman's Role Viewed as Reduced by Watergate," *New York Times,* April 26, 1973, 89.

18. "End of an Era in Nixon Presidency," *New York Times,* May 1, 1973, 1.

19. Memo, Buchanan to Nixon, May 16, 1973, *Annotated Documents, Nixon Papers,* Roosevelt Study Center, File 6A-286-50.

20. "4 On Writing Staff Promoted by Nixon," *New York Times,* February 12, 1973, 19.

21. Mason, *Richard Nixon and the Quest for a New Majority,* 205.

22. Bob Woodward, *The Choice* (New York: Simon & Schuster, 1996), 147.

23. "Mr. Nixon as the Target," *New York Times,* August 2, 1973, 35.

24. Memo, Buchanan to Nixon, May 3, 1973, *Annotated Documents, Nixon Papers,* Roosevelt Study Center, File 7-35-0087.

25. "Senate Panel to Hear Buchanan, a Nixon Writer," *New York Times,* September 19, 1973, 97.

26. "Buchanan Sought to Block Muskie."

27. "Senate Hears a Chastened Spook and a Lively Ghost," *New York Times,* September 30, 1973, 196.

28. "Watergate Panel to Speed Inquiry," *New York Times,* September 28, 1973, 16.

29. "The Dam Cracks," *New York Times,* October 11, 1973, 45.

30. "Nixon and 4 Advisers in Florida for Weekend," *New York Times,* October 5, 1973, 12.

31. Author interview with Pat Buchanan, subject's home, Virginia, February 26, 2010.

32. "Nixon Reportedly Asserts Cox Reneged on Tapes Compromise," *New York Times,* November 17, 1973, 1.

33. Martin J. Medhurst and Kurt Ritter, *Presidential Speechwriting: From the New Deal to the Reagan Revolution and Beyond* (College Station: Texas A&M University Press, 2003), 149.

34. "Edited Transcripts of Conversations Tapes in the White House," *New York Times,* May 1, 1974, 1.

35. "2 Democrats and Aide to Nixon Urge President Not to Resign," *New York Times,* May 15, 1974, 32.

36. "Mr. Nixon and the Press," *New York Times,* November 1, 1973, 43.

37. "President's Latest Counterattack," *New York Times,* April 9, 1974, 20.

38. Author interview with Pat Buchanan, subject's home, Virginia, February 26, 2010.

39. "Nixon in Moscow, Met by Brezhnev," *New York Times,* July 28, 1974, 69.

40. "US Newsmen Become Tourist Attraction at Yalta," *New York Times,* July 1, 1974, 12.

41. "The Final Days," *Newsweek,* April 5, 1975, 37.

42. "Fear and Loathing in the Bunker," *New York Times,* January 1, 1974, 19.

SEVEN: IN THE CROSSFIRE

1. Letter, Ford to Buchanan, October 11, 1974, *White House Central Files, Name Files: Buchanan,* Ford Library.

2. Author interview with Pat Buchanan, subject's home, Virginia, February 26, 2010.

3. "The Moralists and the Business Apologists Operate in Different Worlds and the Public Is Caught Between Them," *Washington Post,* April 28, 1977, Md. 2.

4. "New Discrimination of Racial Quotas," *St. Louis Globe-Democrat,* September 17, 1977, 15.

5. "The Catholics, the Bishops and Abortion," *St. Louis Globe-Democrat,* September 30, 1976, 15.

6. Phillips, *Post-Conservative America,* 47.

7. Deborah Strober and Gerald Strober, *The Reagan Presidency: An Oral History of the Era* (New York: Houghton and Mifflin, 2003), 23.

8. Schulman, *The Seventies,* 196–99.

9. "America on the Road to the Right," *Washington Post,* July 20, 1980, 5.

10. Paul Gottfried and Thomas Fleming, *The Conservative Movement* (Boston: Twayne, 1988), 92–95.

11. Paul Weyrich, "Blue Collar or Blue Blood? The New Right Compared with the Old Right," in Robert W. Whitaker ed., *The New Right Papers* (New York: St. Martin's Press, 1982), 52–53.

12. Sam Francis, "Message from MARs: The Social Politics of the New Right," in Whitaker, *The New Right Papers,* 74–75.

13. Chilton Williamson Jr., "Country and Western Marxism," *National Review,* June 9, 1978, 25.

14. Author interview with Richard Viguerie, phone, March 18, 2010.

15. Buchanan, *Conservative Votes, Liberal Victories,* 168–69.

16. Article, "The Battle of New York," October 16, 1975, reprinted in *White House Central Files, Name Files: Buchanan,* Ford Library.

17. Schulman, *The Seventies,* 51.

18. Memo, Ron Nessen to Ford, December 31, 1975, *White House Central Files, Name Files: Buchanan,* Ford Library.

19. "Ford's Nearsighted Visions," *Chicago Tribune,* January 6, 1976, 7.

20. Press release, "Should Reagan Junk the 11th Commandment?," February 10, 1976, *White House Central Files, Name Files: Buchanan,* Ford Library.

21. Interview with Pat Buchanan by James Reichley, September 13, 1977, *Reichley Papers,* Ford Library, Box 1.

22. "Ford and Reagan Backers Skirmish in Kansas City," *New York Times,* August 10, 1976, 1.

23. Author interview with Richard Viguerie, phone, March 18, 2010.

24. Author interview with Pat Buchanan, subject's home, Virginia, February 26, 2010.

25. "Wallace, One of a Kind in a Full House," *Daily News,* February 26, 1976, 50.

26. Edward D. Berkowitz, *Something Happened: A Political and Cultural Overview of the Seventies* (New York: Columbia University Press, 2006), 123–28.

27. "US Reports Soviet Flying Many Troops to Afghan Conflict; World Condemnation Asked," *New York Times,* December 26, 1979, A1.

28. Karlyn H. Bowman and Everett Carll Ladd, *What's Wrong: A Survey of American Satisfaction and Complaint* (Washington, D.C.: AEI Press, 1998), 43.

29. Carter, *From George Wallace to Newt Gingrich,* 57.

30. Schulman, *The Seventies,* 202–03.

31. "Urges Defeat of Gay Front," *St. Louis Globe-Democrat,* June 7, 1977, 15.

32. "Vision Lacking in '37 Also Missing Today," *St. Louis Globe-Democrat,* August 25, 1977, 25.

33. "One, Two, Three . . . ," *Washington Post,* June 8, 1977, B1.

34. "AM Radio's Afternoon Specialists," *Washington Post,* December 27, 1979, C3.

35. "The Calls of the Wild," *Washington Post,* November 14, 1979, B1.

36. "Braden Storms Off Own Show," *Washington Post,* January 28, 1983, D4.

37. "PBS' 'Inside' Scoop," *Washington Post,* May 7, 1980, F3.

38. "Mild Weather Causes Heating, Cooling Woes," *Washington Post,* March 11, 1981, B15.

39. "Shriek! Chic! It's Morton Downey!; Talk's Mr. Nasty, Coming on Strong with the Art of Abuse," *Washington Post,* July 6, 1988, C1.

40. "Ringside with Braden and Buchanan," *Washington Post,* July 2, 1981, C1.

EIGHT: REAGAN IN THE WHITE HOUSE

1. "The Republicans in Detroit," *Washington Post,* July 16, 1980, A14.

2. Author interview with Bay Buchanan, restaurant, Virginia, May 3, 2010.

3. Buchanan, *Right from the Beginning,* 76–77.

4. Author interview with Bay Buchanan, restaurant, Virginia, May 3, 2010.

5. "Reagan: Iowa Loss Allowed Him to Campaign His Way," *Washington Post,* June 1, 1980, A2.

6. "GOP Chairman Says It's Time for Debate on US Hostages," *Washington Post,* January 26, 1980, A3.

7. "Buchanan's Sister Shepherds Insurgent's Race," *New York Times,* September 26, 1999, 35.

8. Buchanan, *Right from the Beginning,* 77.

9. Robert Dallek, *Ronald Reagan: The Politics of Symbolism* (Cambridge, MA: Harvard University Press, 1999), xiv.

10. Charles W. Dunn, *The Enduring Reagan* (Lawrence: University Press of Kentucky, 2009), 83.

11. Andrew Busch, *Ronald Reagan and the Politics of Freedom* (New York: Rowman & Littlefield, 2001), 107.

12. "The Rise, Fall and Future of Détente," *Foreign Affairs,* 62:2 1983–1984, 355–77.

13. This view was shared across the breadth of the conservative movement, uniting both New Right and neoconservative critics: Jonathan Clarke and Stefan A. Halper, *America Alone: The Neo-Conservatives and the Global Order* (New York: Cambridge University Press, 2004), 164.

14. Author interview with Paul Erickson, subject's hotel room, D.C., February 21, 2010.

15. "National Defense Highest Priority," *St. Louis Globe-Democrat*, January 11, 1983, 27.

16. Article, *St. Louis Globe-Democrat*, June 20, 1981, reprinted in *Buchanan File, Dole Campaign Files*, Robert J. Dole Institute, Box 1.

17. "Is Reagan Ready for Road Show?," *Washington Times*, undated, reprinted in *Buchanan File, Dole Campaign Files*, Robert J. Dole Institute, Box 1.

18. Article, *St. Louis Globe-Democrat*, March 21, 1984, reprinted in *Buchanan File, Dole Campaign Files*, Robert J. Dole Institute, Box 1.

19. "Out of Step with Reagan," *Washington Post*, February 11, 1985, A2.

20. "Reagan Bid Reopens Rift with Right," *New York Times*, February 19, 1983, 9.

21. "Media Boxer in Reagan Corner," *Washington Post*, February 6, 1985, A2.

22. Article, *St. Louis Globe-Democrat*, March 21, 1984, reprinted in *Buchanan File, Dole Campaign Files*, Robert J. Dole Institute, Box 1.

23. Richard A. Viguerie, *The Establishment vs. The People: Is a New Populist Revolt on the Way?* (Chicago: Regnery Gateway, 1984), 74.

24. Whitaker ed., *The New Right Papers*, xi.

25. Sam Francis, *Beautiful Losers: Essays on the Failure of American Conservatism* (Columbia: University of Missouri Press, 1993), 14.

26. "Group Criticizes Buchanan over Views on Nazi-Hunting New York," *Washington Post*, April 10, 1985, A5.

27. Letter, Linas Kojelis to Buchanan, June 13, 1985, FG017, *White House Office of Records Management (WHORM) Subject File*, Ronald Reagan Presidential Library Papers, 40 Presidential Drive, Simi Valley, California 93065.

28. "Lobbying the Office That Hunts Nazi Suspects," *New York Times*, March 3, 1987, A20.

29. "Acquit Demjanjuk: The Case Is Weak," *New York Times*, March 31, 1987, A35.

30. "A Nazi Past and the Present," *New York Times*, March 29, 1987, LI1.

31. "The Buchanan Aggravation," *New York Times*, February 19, 1987, A28.

32. "Appeal Fails; Nazi Suspect Deported," *New York Times*, April 21, 1987, A20.

33. Memo, Buchanan to Ed Meese, February 9, 1987, IM 471443, *WHORM Subject File*, Ronald Reagan Presidential Library Papers.

34. Letter, Anu Linnas to Buchanan, June 12, 1986, *WHORM Alphabetical, Abu Linnas*, Ronald Reagan Presidential Library Papers.

35. Letter, Abu Linnas to Buchanan, May 3, 1986, *WHORM Alphabetical, Anu Linnas*, Ronald Reagan Presidential Library Papers.

36. Letter, Linas Kojelis to Buchanan, September 11, 1985, PR 013, *WHORM Subject File*, Ronald Reagan Presidential Library Papers.

37. "Three Senior White House Aides Expected to Be Named Today," *Washington Post*, February 5, 1985, A7.

38. "Reagan Wins by a Landslide, Sweeping at Least 48 States," *New York Times*, November 7, 1984, 1.

39. "His Next Challenge: Keeping the Economy Strong," *New York Times*, November 11, 1984, Financial Section, 1.

40. "The Conservatives' Choices," *Washington Post,* December 10, 1984, C3.

41. "Three Senior White House Aides Expected to Be Named Today."

NINE: HELPING REAGAN BE REAGAN

1. "Buchanan's Assessors," *Washington Post,* February 13, 1985, A22.

2. Donald T. Regan, *For the Record: From Wall Street to Washington* (New York: Harcourt Brace Jovanovich, 1988), 132.

3. "White House Names Chavez Director of Public Liaison," *Washington Post,* April 10, 1985, A1.

4. Memo, Regan to Buchanan, July 23, 1985, FG001, *WHORM Subject File,* Ronald Reagan Presidential Library Papers, Box 49.

5. "There Will be Few Tears Shed by Moderate Republicans," *Washington Post,* September 23, 1985, C3.

6. "Personalities," *Washington Post,* November 2, 1985, H3.

7. Memo, Mona Charen to Pat Buchanan, July 3, 1985, FG601, *WHORM Subject File,* Ronald Reagan Presidential Library Papers, Box 51.

8. Gil Troy, *Morning in America: How Ronald Reagan Invented the 1980s* (Princeton, NJ: Princeton University Press, 2005), 121.

9. http://old.swivel.com/data_sets/show/1017281, last accessed November 2, 2010; for an assessment of Reagan's economic success, see Haynes Johnson, *Sleepwalking Through History: America in the Reagan Years* (New York: HarperCollins, 2003), 411–18.

10. "Playing It by Zaire," *Washington Post,* October 22, 1985, B3.

11. "Buchanan's White House Rise," *Washington Post,* April 15, 1985, B3.

12. "No More Mr. Nice Guy," *Washington Post,* March 17, 1985, E1.

13. "The Fallout from Reagan's Joke," *Washington Post,* March 26, 1985, C2.

14. Memo, Buchanan to Regan, March 31, 1985, FG001, *WHORM Subject File,* Ronald Reagan Library Presidential Papers, Box 51.

15. "Post-Election Folly," *Washington Post,* February 26, 1985, A2.

16. "Gorbachev Endorses Idea of Summit Meeting," *Washington Post,* April 2, 1985, A1.

17. "Reagan Reportedly to Offer New Plan on Nicaragua Peace," *Washington Post,* April 4, 1985, A1.

18. "Escrow Account Plan Prevailed After Talks with Hill Leaders," *Washington Post,* April 5, 1985, A22.

19. "McFarlance's Hidden Hand Helps Shape Foreign Policy," *Washington Post,* February 15, 1985, A1.

20. "Buchanan Urges Speech on Nicaragua," *Washington Post,* April 18, 1985, A1.

21. "Reagan Orders Review of Policy on Nicaragua," *Washington Post,* April 27, 1985, A1.

22. Jane Mayer and Doyle McManus, *Landslide: The Unmaking of the President 1984–1988* (New York: Houghton Mifflin, 1988), 137–39.

23. "Speaker Says House May Aid Contras," *Washington Post,* May 7, 1985, A1.

24. Mayer and McManus, *Landslide,* 109–12.

25. "Foggy Bottom Agit Prop," *Harper's,* December 1988, 22.

26. Memo, Noonan to Pat, March 19, 1985, CO114, *WHORM Subject File,* Ronald Reagan Presidential Library Papers, Box 4.

27. "North Role Cited in Bid to Unseat Contra Aid Foes," *New York Times,* December 15, 1986, A1.

28. Lisa Klobuchar, *The Iran-Contra Affair: Political Scandal Uncovered* (Minneapolis: Compass Point Books, 2008), 16–23.

29. "Contradiction," *Mother Jones,* July–August 1989, 26.

30. For a good summary of the internal politics of presentation and Buchanan's speedy fall from grace, see Lou Cannon, *President Reagan: The Role of a Lifetime* (New York: Simon & Schuster, 1991), 569–89.

31. "Nixon, Reagan Compared," *Washington Post,* June 3, 1985, A3.

32. Author interview with Pat Buchanan, subject's home, Virginia, February 26, 2010.

33. "Regan Expects 'Essence' of Tax Plan to Survive," *Washington Post,* June 15, 1985, A4.

34. "Nixon, Reagan Compared."

35. Richard Jay Jensen, *Reagan at Bergen-Belsen and Bitburg* (College Station: Texas A&M University Press, 2007), 122–32.

36. Letter, Joseph B. Glaser to Reagan, March 19, 1985, TR123-01, *WHORM Subject File,* Reagan Library.

37. Memo, Buchanan to Regan, April 14, 1985, TR123-01, *WHORM Subject File,* Reagan Library.

38. Letter, Pete Wilson to Reagan, April 18, 1985, TR123-01, *WHORM Subject File,* Reagan Library.

39. "2 Congressmen Warned White House About Trip," *Washington Post,* May 1, 1985, A13.

40. Memo, Marshall Breger to Buchanan, April 22, 1985, 31248655, *WHORM Subject File,* Reagan Library.

41. Letter, Anne Higgins to Buchanan, April 17, 1985, 310942, *WHORM Subject File,* Reagan Library.

42. Press release from Elizabeth Holtzman, October 18, 1985, FG006-01, *WHORM Subject File,* Reagan Library.

43. "Buchanan's Jottings Cited 'Pressure' of Jews," *Washington Post,* May 3, 1985, A13.

44. "Buchanan Says Story on His Note-Taking Is Silly," *Washington Post,* May 4, 1985, A5.

45. "Honoring Wiesel, Reagan Confronts the Holocaust," *Washington Post,* April 20, 1985, A1.

46. Memo, Buchanan to Michael K. Deaver, April 24, 1989, TA313089, *WHORM Subject File,* Reagan Library.

47. Letter Linas Kojelis to Buchanan, June 13, 1985, FG017, *WHORM Subject File,* Reagan Library.

48. Letter, Robert Torricelli to Reagan, April 2, 1985, ALL30094, *WHORM Subject File,* Reagan Library.

49. Memo, Buchanan to Reagan, September 17, 1986, C0074, *WHORM Subject File,* Reagan Library.

50. Memo, Buchanan to Regan, September 17, 1986, C0074, *WHORM Subject File,* Reagan Library.
51. Memo, Buchanan to Meese, February 9, 1987, IM471443, *WHORM Subject File,* Reagan Library.
52. "Meese Gives Nazi Suspect Time to Find a Country," *New York Times,* March 6, 1987, A32.
53. "Nazi Guard Demjanjuk Wheeled into Munich Trial," Reuters Dispatch, November 30, 2009.
54. "The Buchanan Aggravation," *New York Times,* February 19, 1987, A28.
55. Letter, Buchanan to Olgert to R. Pavlovskis, December 19, 1985, HU013-50, *WHORM Subject File,* Reagan Library.
56. "Grab a Post-Election Scorecard," *New York Times,* November 4, 1986, A28.
57. "Appeal Fails; Nazi Suspect Deported," *New York Times,* April 21, 1987, 21.
58. "The Buchanan Aggravation," *New York Times,* February 19, 1987, A28.
59. Letter, Oscar Stadtler to Regan, July 25, 1985, FG006-01, *WHORM Subject File,* Reagan Library.
60. "Regan: After Four Months, Chief of Staff Is New Strongman in White House," *Washington Post,* June 3, 1985, A1.
61. "Chief of Staff More Firmly in Charge," *Washington Post,* July 18, 1985, A1.
62. "Let the Games Begin!," *New Republic,* January 29, 1996, 25.
63. "The Great Right Hope," *New York,* June 10, 1985, 48; "Dinner Guests," *Jet,* October 8, 1984, 6.
64. "Ex-Speechwriter for First Lady: Men and Mice," *Washington Post,* September 1, 1985, A13.
65. "Deaver's Departure Will Create a Void," *Washington Post,* April 15, 1985, A4.
66. "Reagan, His Aides Split, Still Backs Attack on Deficit," *New York Times,* October 30, 1985, A1.
67. "McFarlane Reported Set to Quit as the National Security Advisor," *New York Times,* December 3, 1985, A24.
68. "State of Union Prompts Debate in White House," *New York Times,* January 28, 1986, A1.
69. "Reagan Lauds 'Heroes,'" *New York Times,* January 29, 1986, A1.
70. Author interview with Pat Buchanan, subject's home, Virginia, February 26, 2010.
71. "Reagan Lauds 'Heroes.'"

TEN: IRAN-CONTRA

1. Author interview with Pat Buchanan, subject's home, Virginia, February 26, 2010.
2. "Patrick Buchanan: From Street Corner to White House He's the Roaring Lion of the Far Right, but Privately He's a Pussycat," *People,* August 29, 1988, 67.
3. "Gay Times and Diseases," *American Spectator,* August 1984, 5.
4. Troy, *Morning in America,* 202.
5. Memo, Buchanan to Regan, October 14, 1985, *Patrick Buchanan Files,* Reagan Library, Box SP601.

6. Memo, Tom Gibson to Buchanan, undated, 1985, *Patrick Buchanan Files,* Reagan Library, Box HE001.

7. Joe Sobran, "Virtue Is Practical and Desirable," *Conservative Chronicle,* November 27, 1991, 1.

8. Memo, Tom Gibson to Buchanan, October 16, 1985, *Patrick Buchanan Files,* Reagan Library, Box HE001.

9. "Counter Culture; Enemies, a Love Story," *New York Times,* April 16, 2000, 6–28.

10. "2 House Units Bar Contra Aid Plan and One Backs It," *New York Times,* March 7, 1986, A1.

11. "President Turns to the Senate in Fight for Bill," *New York Times,* March 21, 1986, A1.

12. "Reagan Angered, Denies His Policy Aims at Latin War," *New York Times,* March 23, 1986, 1.

13. "Reagan's Speechwriter Says He Was Dismissed in Dispute," *New York Times,* June 10, 1986, A20.

14. "Hot and Angry Words from the Wordsmiths," *New York Times,* June 12, 1986, B6.

15. Author interview with Pat Buchanan, subject's home, Virginia, February 26, 2010.

16. John O'Sullivan, *The President, the Pope, and the Prime Minister: Three Who Changed the World* (Washington, D.C.: Regnery, 2006), 271.

17. "US Acts to Enhance Image After Talks," *New York Times,* October 15, 1986, A13.

18. "Reagan Triumphs from Failure in Iceland," *New York Times,* October 17, 1986, A22.

19. "Reagan's Revolution Ended?," *New York Times,* November 9, 1986, 4–23.

20. Mayer and McManus, *Landslide,* 427.

21. Ibid., 434.

22. Presidential televised address, November 13, 1986, Reagan Library, Box 307.

23. Mayer and McManus, *Landslide,* 443.

24. Ann Wroe, *Lives, Lies and the Iran-Contra Affair* (New York: I.B. Taurus, 1991), 244–45.

25. "Reagan Describes Domestic Moves to Press 'Business of Governing,'" *New York Times,* December 13, 1986, 1.

26. "White House Vigilante," *New Republic,* January 26, 1987, 17.

27. "Reagan Refuses to Intercede," *New York Times,* December 9, 1986, A1.

28. "Saudi Arms Trader Describes Role in Iran Weapons Deal," *New York Times,* December 11, 1986, A21.

29. "3,000 Rally for Reagan," *New York Times,* December 9, 1986, B16.

30. "Buchanan Pursues Attacks on Critics of the President," *New York Times,* December 10, 1986, A20.

31. "The President's Allies Are Rallying Round," *New York Times,* December 19, 1986, A36.

32. "When TV Zooms In on a White House Crisis," *New York Times,* December 21, 1986, H27.

33. Author interview with Bay Buchanan, restaurant, Virginia, May 3, 2010.

34. "Buchanan: Not Just Another Wordsmith," *Chicago Tribune,* January 29, 1987, 25.

35. Author interview with Richard Viguerie, phone, March 18, 2010.

36. "To Be or Not to Be a Protest Candidate," *New York Times,* January 19, 1987, A21.

37. Author interview with Howard Phillips, phone, March 9, 2010.

38. Author interview with Phyllis Schlafly, subject's hotel room, D.C., February 19, 2010.

39. Author interview with Carter Wrenn, subject's office, North Carolina, May 5, 2010.

40. Author interview with Boyd Cathey, subject's home, North Carolina, May 5, 2010.

41. Letter, Cathey to Buchanan, January 16, 1987, *Boyd Cathey Private Papers,* Box 1.

42. Letter, Thomas Kennelly to Buchanan, undated, *Boyd Cathey Private Papers,* Box 1.

43. Letter, Cathey to Howard Phillips, December 10, 1986, *Boyd Cathey Private Papers,* Box 1.

44. Author interview with Bay Buchanan, restaurant, Virginia, May 3, 2010.

45. Buchanan, *Right from the Beginning,* 3–4.

46. Author interview with Howard Phillips, phone, March 5, 2010.

47. Hunter S. Thompson with Kevin Simonson and Beef Torrey, *Conversations with Hunter S. Thompson* (Jackson: University Press of Mississippi, 2008), 78.

48. Author interview with Pat Buchanan, subject's home, Virginia, February 26, 2010.

49. Author interview with Richard Viguerie, phone, March 18, 2010.

50. Buchanan, *Right from the Beginning,* 9.

51. "White House Facing Crisis of Confidence," *New York Times,* February 8, 1987, 36.

52. "New Political Winds May Affect Response to President's Message," *New York Times,* January 27, 1987, A13.

53. "Buchanan, a Tough Conservative, Is Leaving Post at White House," *New York Times,* February 4, 1987, A19.

54. Buchanan, *Right from the Beginning,* 10–11.

ELEVEN: NEW WORLD ORDER

1. Buchanan, *Right from the Beginning,* 123.

2. "Losing the War for America's Culture," *Washington Times,* May 22, 1989, D1.

3. Author interview with Pat Buchanan, subject's home, Virginia, February 26, 2010.

4. Troy, *Morning in America,* 298; "Abortion's Dividing Line," *Newsweek,* October 23, 1989, 31.

5. "Can Bush as Bush Steal the Show?," *New York Times,* August 21, 1988, A21.

6. David Mark, *Going Dirty: The Art of Negative Campaigning* (Lanham, MD: Rowman & Littlefield, 2009), 201.

7. "The End of History," *National Interest,* Summer 1989.

8. "Peace Terms for the Cold War," *Washington Times,* February 22, 1989, F1.

9. Joseph Scotchie, *Revolt from the Heartland: The Struggle for an Authentic Conservatism* (New Brunswick, NJ: Transaction Publishers, 2002), 79.

10. "Into Panama . . . for All the Right Reasons?," *Washington Times,* December 25, 1989, D3.

11. "Three Little Words," *New York Times,* February 11, 1996, E15; for a detailed account of the conflict between neocons and paleocons, see Mark Gerson, *The Neoconservative Vision: From the Cold War to the Culture Wars* (Lanham, MD: Madison Books, 1996),

309–20; Patrick Allitt, *The Conservatives: Ideas and Personalities Throughout American History* (New Haven, CT: Yale University Press, 2009), 261–62.

12. Clarke and Halper, *America Alone*, 112–56.

13. Patrick Buchanan, *A Republic, Not an Empire: Reclaiming America's Destiny* (New York: Regnery, 1999), 324.

14. "America First—and Second, and Third," *National Interest*, Spring 1990, 77.

15. Letter, Buchanan to Ryn, July 9, 2003, *Claes Ryn Private Papers*.

16. Bill Kauffman, *Ain't My America: The Long, Noble History of Antiwar Conservatism and Middle-American Anti-Imperialism* (New York: Metropolitan, 2008), 181.

17. Buchanan, *A Republic, Not an Empire*, 364–65.

18. "The Democracy Boosters," *National Review*, March 24, 1989, 30.

19. Buchanan, *Where the Right Went Wrong*, 12–13.

20. Author interview with Paul Erickson, subject's hotel room, D.C., February 21, 2010.

21. "Bush Trying a New Topic," *New York Times*, October 31, 1990, A2.

22. "Accord to Reduce Spending and Raise Taxes Is Reached," *New York Times*, October 1, 1990, 1.

23. Copy of speech, October 13, 1990, *Chuck Douglas Private Papers*.

24. Author interview with Chuck Douglas, phone, February 12, 2010.

25. "With Budget Wars Ended, Frantic Campaign Begins," *New York Times*, November 2, 1990, 1.

26. Author interview with Signe McQuaid, phone, February 11, 2010.

27. Henry N. Pontell, Stephen M. Rosoff, and Robert Tillman, *Profit Without Honor: White-Collar Crime and the Looting of America* (New York: Prentice Hall, 2003), 55.

28. "Irate Voters Approach Ballot Box with Sharpened Axes," *New York Times*, November 4, 1990, A15.

29. "The Man Behind the Mask," *Advocate*, May 2, 1995, 29.

30. "Duke: Anatomy of an Upset," *Times-Picayune*, March 5, 1989, 1.

31. Lawrence N. Powell, "Slouching Toward Baton Rouge: The 1989 Legislative Election of David Duke," in Douglas D. Rose ed., *The Emergence of David Duke and the Politics of Race* (Chapel Hill: North Carolina University Press, 1992), 23.

32. "New Republicanism vs. The Old Klansman," *Washington Times*, February 27, 1989, D1.

33. Martin Durham, *The Christian Right, the Far Right and the Boundaries of American Conservatism* (New York: Manchester University Press, 2001), 152.

34. "Respectable Racism?," *Washington Times*, November 6, 1990, G2.

35. Tyler Bridges, *The Rise of David Duke* (Jackson: University Press of Mississippi, 1994), 265.

36. "Louisiana Talley Is Seen as a Sign of Voter Unrest," *New York Times*, October 8, 1990, 22.

37. "Bush and Buchanan Trade Punches in the South," *Atlanta Journal-Constitution*, February 22, 1992, A1.

38. "Bring on the Primary," *Manchester Union-Leader*, January 16, 1991, 1.

39. Clarke and Halper, *America Alone*, 180.

40. "Mideast Tensions," *New York Times,* November 9, 1990, 1. The italics are mine.

41. "Disbelievers in Pax Americana," *San Jose Mercury News,* November 16, 1990, 10.

42. Ryan J. Barilleaux and Mark J. Rozell, *Power and Prudence: The Presidency of George H. W. Bush* (College Station: Texas A&M University Press, 2004), 32.

43. "Bush's Worst Political Nightmare: Banks and Oil Fields Shut on Same Day," *Los Angeles Times,* January 13, 1991, M-4.

44. "Pat Buchanan's Small World," *New York Times,* January 13, 1992, A12.

45. "A. M. Rosenthal's Outrage Reeks of Fakery," *St. Louis Post-Dispatch,* September 21, 1990, 3C.

46. "The Heresies of Pat Buchanan," *New Republic,* October 22, 1990, 27.

47. Buchanan, *Right from the Beginning,* 377.

48. "The Pat and Abe Show," *Nation,* November 5, 1990, 517.

49. "Enter the Peace Party," *Commentary,* January 1991, 21.

50. "Buchananism or Barbarism," August 12, 2000, *Boyd Cathey Private Papers.*

TWELVE: PAT BECOMES A PALEOCON, RUNS FOR PRESIDENT

1. "Buchanan Speech Sounds Strong Conservative Theme: Tells State Republican Committee That Foreign Policy Debate Is Needed, but Not Until After War Ends," *Manchester Union-Leader,* January 17, 1991, 9.

2. Memo, Utley to Larry Moffit, undated, 1990, *Jon Utley Private Papers.*

3. "Not the World's Policeman," *Nation,* October 29, 1990, 18.

4. "Conservative War Opponents Facing Dilemma," *National Catholic Reporter,* January 25, 1991, 12.

5. "Cry of Anti-Semitism Seeps into Gulf Debate," *Washington Times,* September 17, 1990, A1.

6. Author interview with Jon Utley, restaurant, D.C., July 6, 2010.

7. Buchanan interview on *Larry King Live,* February 19, 1992, reprinted in *Dole Campaign Collection,* Robert J. Dole Institute, Box 32.

8. Author interview with Jon Utley, restaurant, D.C., July 6, 2010.

9. Chip Berlet, "The New Political Right in the United States: Reaction, Rollback and Resentment," in Michael J. Thompson ed., *Confronting the New Conservatism: The Rise of the Right in America* (New York: New York University Press, 2007).

10. Joseph Scotchie, *The Paleoconservatives: New Voices of the Old Right* (New Brunswick, NJ: Transaction Publishers, 1999), 12–15; Scotchie, *Revolt from the Heartland,* 1–14. See also Paul Edward Gottfried, *Conservatism in America: Making Sense of the American Right* (New York: Palgrave Macmillan, 2007), 128–32.

11. "Crackup of the Conservatives," *Washington Times,* May 1, 1991, G2.

12. Paul Gottfried, "A Conservative War?," in D. L. O'Huallachain and J. Forrest Sharpe eds., *Neo-Conned!: Just War Principles: A Condemnation of War in Iraq* (Norfolk, VA: IHS Press, 2007).

13. Justin Raimondo, *Reclaiming the American Right: The Lost Legacy of the Conservative Movement* (Wilmington, DE: ISI Books, 2008), 274.

14. Author interview with Fran Griffin, restaurant, Virginia, February 27, 2010.

15. http://www.sobran.com/bio.shtml, last accessed November 12, 2010.

16. Author interview with Joe Sobran, restaurant, Virginia, February 27, 2010.

17. http://www.sobran.com/columns/2002/020124.shtml, last accessed November 2, 2010.

18. Linda Bridges and John R. Coyne Jr., *Strictly Right: William F. Buckley Jr. and the American Conservative Movement* (Hoboken, NJ: Wiley and Sons, 2007), 158.

19. http://www.yaliberty.org/, last accessed November 2, 2010.

20. Joe Sobran, *Hustler: The Clinton Legacy* (Vienna, VA: Griffin Communications, 2000), xi.

21. Author interview with Joe Sobran, restaurant, Virginia, February 27, 2010.

22. Author interview with Pat Buchanan, subject's home, Virginia, February 26, 2010.

23. "Why National Review Is Wrong," *National Review,* October 15, 1990, 64.

24. "Cheney Had It Right First Time," *Congressional Record,* September 30, 2004, 20044.

25. H. Bruce Franklin, *Vietnam and Other American Fantasies* (Boston: University of Massachusetts Press, 2000), 27.

26. "The New World Order," *New York Times,* April 5, 1991, A25.

27. "Utley Ousted," *Washington Times,* March 26, 1991, A6.

28. Author interview with Jon Utley, restaurant, D.C., July 6, 2010.

29. "In Search of Anti-Semitism," *National Review,* December 30, 1991, 56.

30. "War of Words Raging at National Review," *Washington Times,* October 7, 1993, 5.

31. "Buchanan and Anti-Semitism," *Wall Street Journal,* October 25, 1999, A52.

32. "It's Respectable Buchanan Who Tars the Republicans," *Los Angeles Times,* January 1, 1992, B-7.

33. "Buchanan an Anti-Semite? It's a Smear," *Los Angeles Times,* January 6, 1992, B-5.

34. "Forgive Them Not," *New York Times,* September 13, 1990, A33.

35. "Behind Duke's Success, Campaign Without End," *New York Times,* October 27, 1991, 22.

36. "Ex-Klan Chief Has Even Odds in Governor's Race," *New York Times,* October 19, 1991, 1.

37. "Duke's Loss Brings Joy Even as It Fans Anger," *New York Times,* November 18, 1991, B7.

38. "Fearing Duke, Voters in Louisiana Hand Democrat Fourth Term," *New York Times,* November 18, 1991, A1.

39. Author interview with Bay Buchanan, restaurant, Virginia, May 3, 2010.

40. Author interview with Paul Erickson, subject's hotel room, D.C., February 21, 2010.

41. Author interview with Tony Fabrizio, phone, March 9, 2010.

42. Author interview with Paul Erickson, subject's hotel room, D.C., February 21, 2010.

43. Author interview with Brent Bozell Jr., Mt. Vernon House, Washington, D.C., February 17, 2010.

THIRTEEN: THE REPUBLICAN HO CHI MINH

1. Author interview with Chuck Douglas, phone, February 12, 2010.

2. "Candidates Playing to Mood of Protectionism," *New York Times,* January 26, 1992, 20.

3. "Economy Has New Hampshire Votes Looking to the Democrats," *Los Angeles Times,* January 17, 1992, A-1.

4. "Souhegan Job Applicants Submit Resumes, Videos, Cheese," *Manchester Union-Leader,* 17 January 1992, 5.

5. "Residents of Fr. Burns High-Rise Defy Ban on Religious Items," *Manchester Union-Leader,* January 17, 1992, 1.

6. "Gingerbread Float Subject of Lawsuit," *Manchester Union-Leader,* January 17, 1992, 5.

7. Memo, Paul Erickson to Scott MacKenzie and Bay Buchanan, January 2, 1999, *Chuck Douglas Private Papers.*

8. Author interview with Signe McQuaid, phone, February 12, 2010.

9. Author interview with Paul Nagy, email, November 11, 2009.

10. "Plans Being Made for Buchanan Visit," *Foster's Daily Democrat,* November 30, 1991, 4.

11. "Buchanan Won't Compromise on Matters of Principle," *Concord Monitor,* January 7, 1992, 3.

12. Author interview with Pat Buchanan, subject's home, Virginia, February 26, 2010.

13. "Pat for Pres," *Manchester Union-Leader,* November 15, 1992, 16.

14. Author interview with anonymous.

15. "An Editorial," *Manchester Union-Leader,* January 22, 1992, 1.

16. "In Manchester, the Charge Is Mellow Journalism," *New York Times,* January 30, 1992, A14.

17. Author interview with Paul Erickson, subject's hotel room, D.C., February 21, 2010.

18. Memo, Paul Erickson to Scott MacKenzie and Bay Buchanan, January 2, 1999, *Chuck Douglas Private Papers.*

19. Author interview with Paul Erickson, subject's hotel room, D.C., February 21, 2010.

20. Author interview with Peter Robbio, restaurant, Virginia, February 21, 2010.

21. Author interview with Paul Erickson, subject's hotel room, D.C., February 21, 2010.

22. "Buchanan, Urging New Nationalism, Joins '92 Race," *New York Times,* December 11, 1991, A1.

23. C-SPAN video of Buchanan announcement speech, December 10, 1991, *Boyd Cathey Private Papers.*

24. "Bush Challenger Buchanan: We Will Put America First," *Manchester Union-Leader,* December 11, 1992, 4.

25. Memo to file, "Patrick J. Buchanan's Announcement for the Republican Nomination for President," December 10, 1991, *Chuck Douglas Private Papers.*

26. Author interview with E. J. Dionne, restaurant, D.C., February 22, 2010.

27. Author interview with Greg Mueller, restaurant, D.C., February 21, 2010.

28. "Watch What He Does," undated, New Hampshire Political Library, Park Street, Concord, New Hampshire 03301, Box 1.

29. Author interview with Brent Bozell Jr., Mt. Vernon House, Washington D.C., February 17, 2010.

30. Patrick Buchanan, *The Great Betrayal: How American Sovereignty and Social Justice Are Being Sacrificed to the Gods of the Global Economy* (New York: Little Brown, 1998), 17–18.

31. "Panel Votes Down Toshiba Sanctions," *Washington Times,* February 10, 1988, C1.

32. Author interview with Richard Viguerie, phone, March 18, 2010.

33. Author interview with Brent Bozell Jr., Mt. Vernon House, Washington, D.C., February 17, 2010.

34. "Ever the Competitor, Bush Goes Gunning for Support," *Los Angeles Times,* December 28, 1991, A-18.

35. Author interview with Richard Hines, restaurant, Virginia, February 18, 2010.

36. "Something Happened," *New York,* March 2, 1992, 24.

37. Author interview with Charles Black, subject's office, D.C., May 9, 2010.

38. "Bush's Trip Carries Heavy Political Load," *Los Angeles Times,* January 1, 1992, A4.

39. "Bush to Resume Summit After Collapse with Flu Halts Work," *Los Angeles Times,* January 9, 1992, A1.

40. "We Have Become a Bunch of Beggars," *Manchester Union-Leader,* January 13, 1992, 1Y.

41. "Bush Bringing Home Little from Tokyo Quest for Jobs," *Los Angeles Times,* January 10, 1992, A1.

42. Author interview with Terry Jeffrey, restaurant, D.C., February 21, 2010.

43. Author interview with Greg Mueller, restaurant, D.C., February 21, 2010.

44. Author interview with Terry Jeffrey, restaurant, D.C., February 21, 2010.

45. "Tempo," *Chicago Tribune,* March 15, 1992, 5.

46. "Buchanan Knows the Tricks of the Trade," *New York Times,* March 10, 1992, A22.

47. Author interview with Terry Jeffrey, restaurant, D.C., 21 February, 2010.

48. Author interview with Greg Mueller, restaurant, D.C., 21 February, 2010.

49. "Homelessness Rises, but Not as Issue," *New York Times,* December 25, 1991, 9.

50. Author interview with Pat Buchanan, subject's home, Virginia, May 1, 2010.

51. Author interview with Greg Mueller, restaurant, D.C., 21 February, 2010.

52. Author interview with Peter Robbio, restaurant, D.C., 21 February, 2010.

53. Erickson's emphasis. Author interview with Paul Erickson, subject's hotel room, February 21, 2010.

54. Author interview with Pat Buchanan, subject's home, Virginia, May 1, 2010.

55. Author interview with E. J. Dionne, restaurant, D.C., 22 February, 2010.

56. Press release, "Read Our Lips: No Second Term," January 1992, *Boyd Cathey Private Papers,* Box 3.

57. "Buchanan: Extension Was Needed," *Manchester Union-Leader,* January 11, 1992, 6.

58. "Pat Buchanan's Politics of Pain," *New York Times,* February 16, 1992, E14.

59. Author interview with Paul Erickson, subject's hotel room, D.C., February 21, 2010.

60. "Bush Supporters Try to Figure Out How Their Candidate Went Wrong," *New York Times,* February 20, 1992, A20.

61. "Poll: Buchanan Gains on Bush; Clinton and Tsongas Lead Dems," *Manchester Union-Leader,* January 13, 1992, 1.

62. "Political Perennial Pat Paulsen Is Still Running for President, Getting Laughs," *Los Angeles Times,* January 19, 1992, B-1.

63. "Quayle's New Hampshire Theme: A Vote for Bush Is a Message to Congress," *New York Times,* February 2, 1992, 24.

64. "Uncommon Effort Aids Quayle," *New York Times,* January 10, 1992, A15.
65. Author interview with Pat Buchanan, subject's home, Virginia, May 1, 2010.
66. Author interview with Greg Mueller, restaurant, D.C., 21 February, 2010.
67. Letter, Buchanan to Cathey, January 8, 1992, *Boyd Cathey Private Papers,* Box 3.
68. Author interview with Kara Hopkins, subject's office, D.C., 23 February, 2010.
69. Author interview with Paul Erickson, subject's hotel room, D.C., 21 February, 2010.
70. "The Photo Op: Making Icons or Playing Politics?," *New York Times,* February 9, 1992, H1.
71. Letter, Buchanan to Rev. Gary Minery, February 5, 1992, *Chuck Douglas Private Papers.*
72. Memo, Bruce Hawkins to state directors, January 16, 1992, *Boyd Cathey Private Papers,* Box 3.
73. "Clinton and Bush Lead in Donations," *New York Times,* February 1, 1992, 8.
74. "The Checks Are in the Mail, and Made Out to Buchanan," *New York Times,* February 24, 1992, A16.
75. "Buchanan Says Party Needs Little Rebellion," *New York Times,* February 10, 1992, A15; "Buchanan Steals Show from Bush," *Manchester Union-Leader,* February 10, 1992, 4.
76. "Pat Buchanan and the Intellectuals," *National Review,* February 17, 1992, 41.
77. "Bush in NH Goes on Attack for a 2nd Term," *Los Angeles Times,* January 16, 1992, A1.
78. "Immersing Himself in Nitty-Gritty, Bush Barnstorms New Hampshire," *New York Times,* January 16, 1992, A1.
79. Letter, Paul Overgaard to Teeter, February 6, 1992, *Robert M. Teeter Papers,* Ford Library, Box 140.
80. Author interview with Charlie Black, subject's office, D.C., May 9, 2010.
81. "Bush Promises Economic Relief and Promises Modest Steps in State of the Union Talk," *New York Times,* January 29, 1992, 1.
82. Letter, Elsie H. Hillman to Teeter, February 19, 1992, *Robert M. Teeter Papers,* Ford Library, Box 140.
83. "Poll: Bush Lead Is Large in NH: 30 Percent Undecided," *Manchester Union-Leader,* February 3, 1992, 5.
84. Press release, "Chuck Douglas on Pinocchio Politics," February 13, 1992, *Chuck Douglas Private Papers.*
85. "Bush Slipping in New Hampshire, Hopes for Rally and Home Run," *New York Times,* February 15, 1992, 1.
86. "Barbara Bush in Key Role, Far More Than Everybody's Grandmother," *Los Angeles Times,* February 16, 1992, A30.
87. "Toward a New Hampshire Decision—Republicans: Bush, Buchanan Battle for Votes of Disgruntled and Undecided," *Los Angeles Times,* February 16, 1992, A1.
88. "Voters Grapple for Choices They Can Live With," *Los Angeles Times,* February 16, 1992, A17.
89. "Candidates Take Their Last Shots in New Hampshire," *New York Times,* February 18, 1992, A1.

90. "Primaries: A Cocktail Consensus—Election Returns Alone Won't Measure Success," *Los Angeles Times,* February 16, 1992, A-1.

91. "Bush and Buchanan, Scrappy to the End, Go for Knockout," *Los Angeles Times,* February 18, 1992, A-1.

FOURTEEN: LEATHER DADDIES AND FREE TRADE

1. "Poll of Republicans Was off the Mark," *New York Times,* February 20, 1992, A21.

2. Author interview with Paul Erickson, subject's hotel room, D.C., February 21, 2010.

3. "Poll of Republicans Was off the Mark."

4. "Stunned by Voting, Bush Plans to Travel to Boost Campaign," *New York Times,* February 19, 1992, A1.

5. Author interview with Richard Viguerie, phone, March 18, 2010.

6. "Buchanan Knows the Tricks of the Trade," *New York Times,* March 10, 1992, A22.

7. "Buchanan at 40 Percent," *New York Times,* February 20, 1992, A1.

8. "Lessons from New Hampshire," *New York Times,* February 20, 1992, A24.

9. "Buchanan Shock," *New York Times,* February 20, 1992, A20.

10. "Bush Allies Told Not to Attack Buchanan in Georgia, the Next Battleground," *New York Times,* February 21, 1992, A14.

11. Author interview with Charlie Black, subject's hotel room, D.C., May 9, 2010.

12. "Old Guard May Usher in New Age of Politics," *Atlanta Journal-Constitution,* February 28, 1992, B1.

13. "Bush and Buchanan Trade Punches in the South."

14. "Bush Sounds Patriotic Theme in Maryland," *New York Times,* February 25, 1992, A16.

15. "Bush Considering a Shift in Tactics to Fight Buchanan," *New York Times,* February 20, 1992, A1.

16. "Bush and Buchanan Trade Punches in the South."

17. "Head of Endowment for the Arts Is Forced from His Post by Bush," *New York Times,* February 22, 1992, 1; "The Political Interest," *Time,* March 9, 1992; Doug Bandow, *The Politics of Envy: Statism as Theology* (New Brunswick, NJ: Transaction Books, 1994), 331–34.

18. "Bush Pushes Plan to Revive Economy," *New York Times,* February 23, 1992, 21.

19. "Buchanan Vows to Stay in Race, Despite Vote," *New York Times,* March 8, 1992, 25.

20. "Republican Duel: A Party Wounded," *New York Times,* February 29, 1992, 1.

21. "GOP Air War Reflects Competitiveness of Georgia Contest," *New York Times,* February 28, 1992, A16.

22. "Hopefuls Turn South, Taking the Low Road," *New York Times,* March 3, 1992, A19.

23. Author interview with Bay Buchanan, restaurant, Virginia, May 3, 2010.

24. Letter to supporters, undated, *Boyd Cathey Private Papers.* Box 3.

25. Matthew Lassiter, *The Silent Majority: Suburban Politics in the Sunbelt South* (Princeton, NJ: Princeton University Press, 2005), 276–300.

26. "In Georgia, Buchanan Plays Up His Role as a Republican Outsider," *New York Times,* February 25, 1992, A16.

27. "For Southerners, Issues Go Beyond the Economy," *New York Times*, February 28, 1992, A17.

28. "Challenger Lambasts Rights Act," *Atlanta Constitution*, March 1, 1992, B1.

29. "Buchanan Invokes Confederate Forebears in Bid for South's Votes," *Atlanta Journal-Constitution*, February 26, 1992, A5.

30. "Pat Buchanan Visit to CS Cemetery, Okolona, Mississippi," *Confederate Veteran*, March–April 1992, 31.

31. "Hopefuls Turn South, Taking the Low Road."

32. "White House Hopes to Trip Buchanan on His Paper Trail," *New York Times*, March 1, 1992, 1.

33. "Buchanan's Peppery Prose," *New York Times*, March 1, 1992, 20.

34. "An Acid Tongued Buchanan Lashes Out: Ambiguity Is the Last Unpardonable Sin," *New York Times*, February 29, 1992, 8.

35. "Campaigning in the Big Country," *Atlanta Journal-Constitution*, March 2, 1992, A4.

36. "Kerrey Is South Dakota Victor: Keeps Presidential Hopes Alive," *New York Times*, February 26, 1992, A1.

37. "Louisiana GOP Leader Backs Buchanan," *New York Times*, February 27, 1992, A22.

38. "Now Read His Lips; Bush Says He Erred," *New York Times*, March 4, 1992, A1.

39. "Buchanan Has Bush Allies Anxious in Georgia," *New York Times*, March 2, 1992, A12.

40. "White House Says Buchanan Is Likely to Remain in Race," *New York Times*, February 29, 1992, 1.

41. "President Focuses upon Family Values," *New York Times*, March 10, 1992, A21.

42. "Bush Cheered in Savannah," *Atlanta Journal-Constitution*, March 2, 1992, A5.

43. "Bush Takes Dinner Break in Buckhead," *Atlanta Journal-Constitution*, March 2, 1992, A4.

44. "Buchanan's Georgia Visits Are Paying Off," *Atlanta Journal-Constitution*, March 3, 1992, A4.

45. "Rallies Around the Candidates," *Atlanta Constitution*, March 4, 1992, A9.

46. "Around the Perimeter, Voters Love Bush, Like Clinton," *Atlanta Constitution*, March 4, 1992, A1.

47. "A Worry For Bush: Independent Voters," *New York Times*, March 5, 1992, A1.

48. "Georgia's GOP Vote 'Awesome,'" *Atlanta Constitution*, March 4, 1992, A11.

49. "Clinton Wins Georgia Primary and Tsongas Takes Maryland," *New York Times*, March 4, 1992, A1.

50. Leonard Zeskind, *Blood and Politics: The History of the White Nationalist Movement from the Margins to the Mainstream* (New York: Farrar, Straus and Giroux, 2009), 277–80.

51. Martin Durham, *The Christian Right: The Far Right and the Boundaries of American Conservatism* (Manchester, UK: Manchester University Press, 2000), 163–64.

52. "Duke's Followers Lean to Buchanan," *New York Times*, March 8, 1992, 26.

53. "Duke Plays to Empty Houses as Spotlight Trails Buchanan," *New York Times*, March 6, 1992, A1.

54. "Bush and Clinton Score Big Victories," *New York Times*, March 8, 1992, 26.

55. Author interview with Pat Buchanan, subject's home, Virginia, May 1, 2010.
56. Author interview with Jerry Woodruff, restaurant, North Carolina, March 2, 2010.
57. "The Die-Hard Delegate, Standing by His Man," *Washington Post*, August 16, 1992, D1.
58. "Bush Gets Two Cheers from Religious Right," *New York Times*, March 10, 1992, A21.
59. "Campaigners Rush to Super Tuesday with a Testy Edge," *New York Times*, March 10, 1992, A1.
60. "Schwarzkopf Offers Praise, Not Endorsement," *New York Times*, March 5, 1992, A24.
61. "President Goes South, Tooting His Own Horn," *New York Times*, March 6, 1992, A20.
62. "Bush Goes Back to His Favorite Role," *New York Times*, March 8, 1992, 26.
63. "Tsongas Set Back," *New York Times*, March 11, 1992, A1.

FIFTEEN: THE MESSAGE FROM MARS

1. "Buchanan: The Most Interesting Candidate," *Washington Post*, August 27, 1999, A29.
2. Tim Hames and Nicol C. Rae, *Governing America: History, Culture, Institutions, Organization, Policy* (Manchester, UK: Manchester University Press, 1996), 203; "Threshold of New Political Identities?," *Washington Times*, December 3, 1991, F1.
3. "Perot, the 'Simple' Billionaire, Says Voters Can Force His Presidential Bid," *New York Times*, March 29, 1992, A21.
4. Ronald B. Rapoport and Walter J. Stone, *Three's a Crowd: The Dynamic of Third Parties, Ross Perot, and Republican Resurgence* (Detroit: University of Michigan Press, 2008), 54.
5. "He's Ready, but Is America Ready for President Perot?," *Time*, June 24, 1992, 12.
6. Kenneth D. Nordin, "The Television Candidate: H. Ross Perot's 1992 and 1996 Presidential Races," in Ted G. Jelen ed., *Ross for Boss: The Perot Phenomenon and Beyond* (New York: SUNY Press, 2001), 15–34.
7. Jack Germond and Jules Witcover, *Mad as Hell: Revolt at the Ballot Box, 1992* (New York: Warner Books, 1993), 224.
8. "Perot the Non-Candidate Overtakes Bush in Poll," *The Times of London*, May 18, 1992, 8.
9. "This Season's Political Mavericks See Perot's Rise as Validation," *Washington Post*, May 31, 1992, A16.
10. Sam Francis, *Revolution from the Middle* (Raleigh, NC: Middle American Press, 1997), 141.
11. Author interview with John Judis, phone, February 12, 2010.
12. Paul Gottfried, *Encounters: My Life with Nixon, Marcuse, and Other Friends and Teachers* (Wilmington, DE: ISI Books, 2009), 150–51.
13. Francis, *Beautiful Losers*, 62.
14. "From Household to Nation," *Chronicles*, March 1996, 12.
15. B. Bruce Briggs, *The New Class?* (New Brunswick, NJ: Transaction, 1979), 144.
16. Buchanan, *The Death of the West*, 215.
17. Martin Durham, *White Rage: The Extreme Right and American Politics* (New York: Taylor and Routledge, 2007), 126.

18. "Wooing the Middle Class: Beyond Bush Bashing," *Washington Times,* August 2, 1991, F1.

19. For a discussion of the similarity between the two, see Zeskind, *Blood and Politics,* 293.

20. Author interview with Jon Utley, restaurant, D.C., July 6, 2010.

21. Gerald J. Russello, *The Postmodern Imagination of Russell Kirk* (Columbia: University of Missouri Press, 2007), 28–66.

22. Author interview with Annette Kirk, phone, February 13, 2010.

23. Author interview with Harry Veryser, restaurant, Detroit, February 11, 2010.

24. "Midwest Showdown," *Los Angeles Times,* March 12, 1992, A-5.

25. "Buchanan Raises Specter of Intolerance, Critics Say," *Los Angeles Times,* March 17, 1992, A-1.

26. Author interview with Harry Veryser, restaurant, Detroit, February 11, 2010.

27. Author interview with Tom Fleming, phone, August 16, 2010.

28. "Bush, Buchanan Both Promise Aid for Automobile Industry," *Los Angeles Times,* March 14, 1992, A-22.

29. Author interview with Harry Veryser, restaurant, Detroit, February 11, 2010.

30. "Buchanan's Wife Stays in Step with a Smile, but Seldom a Word," *New York Times,* March 15, 1992, A21.

31. Author interview with Connie Mackey, phone, October 19, 2010.

32. Author interview with Bay Buchanan, restaurant, Virginia, May 3, 2010.

33. "Ads Shift to Impact of Foreign Built Cars," *Los Angeles Times,* March 13, 1992, A-20.

34. "Word Warrior Packs a Punch—Buchanan Rushes Opponents with Stinging Rhetoric," *Chicago Tribune,* March 16, 1992, 1.

35. Author interview with Harry Veryser, restaurant, Detroit, February 11, 2010.

36. "Bush Goes Low-Key as Buchanan Falters," *Los Angeles Times,* March 17, 1992, A-14.

37. "New Hampshire, Seriously," *New York Times,* February 16, 1992, E15.

38. Author interview with Paul Erickson, subject's hotel room, D.C., February 21, 2010.

39. "Brown Is Betting on Michigan to Give His Campaign Credibility," *New York Times,* March 17, 1992, A24.

40. "In High Tech Politics, Location Is Not Everything," *Chicago Tribune,* March 12, 1992, 25.

41. "For the Republicans: President Bush," *Chicago Tribune,* March 13, 1992, 18.

42. "Buchanan Gets Needed Boost in Chicago," *Los Angeles Times,* March 15, A32.

43. "Buchanan Strikes Ethnic Chord," *Chicago Tribune,* March 15, 1992, 15.

44. "A Blow to Tsongas," *New York Times,* March 18, 1992, A1.

45. "Brown's Supporters: A Diverse Group," *New York Times,* March 18, 1992, A18.

46. "Buchanan Pledges to Go On, but at a Quieter Pace," *New York Times,* March 19, 1992, A19.

47. Author interview with Roger Stone, phone, February 12, 2010.

48. Monica Crowley, *Nixon in Winter: The Final Revelations, Volume 1998, Part 2* (London: I.B. Tauris, 1998), 287.

49. Letter, Nixon to Ryn, May 3, 1991, *Claes Ryn Private Papers.*

50. Author interview with Pat Buchanan, subject's home, Virginia, February 26, 2010.

51. "Nixon's Advice for Buchanan," *New York Times,* March 22, 1992, A21.

52. Author interview with Bay Buchanan and two anonymous sources, restaurant, Virginia, May 3, 2010.

53. "For the Republicans: President Bush."

54. "Buchanan Looks for Sustenance in the Heart of Helms Country," *News & Observer,* March 20, 1992, 3.

55. Press release, December 12, 1991, *Boyd Cathey Private Papers,* Box 3.

56. "Helms Pays Buchanan Surprise Call," *News & Observer,* December 19, 1991, B1.

57. Press Release, "Funderbunk Joins North Carolina Buchanan Campaign," undated, *Boyd Cathey Private Papers,* Box 3.

58. Memo, Cathey to supporters, undated, *Boyd Cathey Private Papers,* Box 3.

59. Letter, Cathey to Buchanan, November 19, 1991, *Boyd Cathey Private Papers,* Box 4.

60. Letter, Bruce E. Hawkins to Cathey, January 15, 1992, *Boyd Cathey Private Papers,* Box 3.

61. "The Excess of Anti-Anti-Semitism," *Southern Partisan,* Fourth Quarter 1991, 10.

62. "White-Shoed Supremacy," *Nation,* June 10, 1996, 21.

63. Author interview with Boyd Cathey, subject's home, North Carolina, August 16, 2010.

64. Zeskind, *Blood and Politics,* 282–83.

65. Letter, Cathey to Buchanan, November 19, 1991, *Boyd Cathey Private Papers,* Box 4.

66. Memo, Cathey to Buchanan, January 10, 1992, *Boyd Cathey Private Papers,* Box 4.

67. Ibid.

68. Press release, "Helms Field Man Heads NC Political Effort," March 16, 1992, *Boyd Cathey Private Papers,* Box 3.

69. "Buchanan Looks for Sustenance in the Heart of Helms Country."

70. Memo, Cathey to Terry Jeffrey, March 25, 1992, *Boyd Cathey Private Papers,* Box 4.

71. Author interview with Boyd Cathey, subject's home, North Carolina, August 16, 2010.

72. Brochure, "Culture Wars," 1992, *Boyd Cathey Private Papers,* Box 3.

73. "Buchanan Eyes Leadership on Conservative Cause," *Washington Times,* March 19, 1992, A5.

74. Video recording, undated, *Boyd Cathey Private Papers.*

75. "Buchanan Staff Plays Down Helms' Role in Bush Campaign," *News & Record,* April 22, 1992, 4.

76. "Clinton and Bush Win Easily," *New York Times,* May 6, 1992, A1.

77. "Connecticut Presidential Exit Poll," *Washington Post,* March 26, 1992, A24.

78. "Clinton Leads NY; Tsongas, Brown Vie for Second," *Washington Post,* April 8, 1992, A1.

79. "Clinton Foes Push Electability Issue," *New York Times,* March 17, 1992, A1.

80. "Losing, Buchanan Says He's Winning," *New York Times,* May 31, 1992, 22.

SIXTEEN: THE CULTURE WAR

1. "Riots in Los Angeles: The Overview," *New York Times,* May 5, 1992, A1.

2. "Politicians Warily Gauge the Effects of Los Angeles's Rioting at the Polls," *New York Times,* May 17, 1992, A15.

3. Hugh Davis Graham, *Collision Course: The Strange Convergence of Affirmative Action and Immigration Policy in America* (New York: Oxford University Press, 2003), 159.

4. Maxine Waters, "Testimony Before the Senate Banking Committee," in Don Hazen ed., *Inside the L.A. Riots: What Really Happened—and Why It Will Happen Again* (Houston, TX: Institute for Alternative Journalism, 1992), 26–27.

5. "Quayle Says Riots Sprang from Lack of Family Values," *New York Times,* May 20, 1992, 1.

6. "After the Riots: Excerpts from Speech by Bush in Los Angeles," *New York Times,* May 9, 1992, A21.

7. "Dan Quayle vs. Murphy Brown," *Time,* June 1, 1992, 12.

8. Robert Gooding-Williams, *Reading Rodney King/Reading Urban Uprising* (New York: Routledge, 1993), 98.

9. "Clinton: Parties Fail to Attack Race Divisions," *Los Angeles Times,* May 3, 1992, 1.

10. "The Right Message," *New York Times,* March 17, 1992, A15.

11. "Sister Souljah's Call to Arms," *Washington Post,* May, 13, 1992, B1.

12. "Black and White," *New York Times,* June 18, 1992, A15.

13. "Buchanan Quits Race, but Won't Bow to Bush," *Washington Times,* June 3, 1992, A4.

14. "A Good Day for Perot and a New Politics," *New York Times,* June 3, 1992, A1.

15. "Disaffected White Male Viewed as Most Likely Backer of Perot," *Washington Post,* June 3, 1992, A15.

16. "A Feast of Fear and Hate," *Newsweek,* August 31, 1992, 32.

17. "Buchanan's Heart Valve Replaced," *Chicago Tribune,* June 6, 1992, 4.

18. Author interview with Bay Buchanan, restaurant, Virginia, May 3, 2010.

19. "Democratic Convention Speeches," *New York Times,* July 16, 1992, A14.

20. "Behind Gore's Choice," *New York Times,* July 10, 1992, 1.

21. "Perot Quits Race," *New York Times,* July 17, 1992, 1.

22. "Bush's Warm-Up Jabs Cheer His Action Starved Backers," *Washington Times,* August 2, 1992, A1.

23. Author interview with Bay Buchanan, restaurant, Virginia, May 3, 2010.

24. Author interview with Terry Jeffrey, restaurant, D.C., February 21, 2010.

25. Author interview with Greg Mueller, restaurant, D.C., February 21, 2010.

26. "Family Values," *New York Times,* September 21, 1992, A21.

27. Author interview with Charlie Black, subject's office, D.C., May 9, 2010.

28. "Inside Politics," *Washington Times,* August 16, 1992, A4.

29. "Buchanan Brigade Gets a Brief Look at Its Hero," *Washington Times,* August 17, 1992, D1.

30. "Inside the Beltway," *Washington Times,* August 4, 1992, A6.

31. "Bush Rises in Poll, Even Before Speech," *USA Today,* August 21, 1992, 3A.

32. George Grant, *Buchanan: Caught in the Crossfire* (Nashville, TN: Thomas Nelson, 1996), 62.

33. "Buchanan Touched by Warm Reception," *Washington Times,* August 21, 1992, A4.

34. "Big Tent Fills Up on Right," *Washington Times,* August 19, 1992, A1.

35. "Marilyn Quayle Says the 1960s Had a Flip Side," *New York Times,* August 20, 1992, A20.

36. "Taking No Prisoners in a Culture War," *New York Times,* August 21, 1992, A11.

37. "Some Republicans See Party's Divisions Growing on Trade, Abortion, Immigration," *Christian Science Monitor,* August 21, 1992, 1.

38. "Conservative vs. Conservative," *Washington Post,* August 21, 1992, A27.

39. "Ex-President Is of Two Minds About Bush's Loss," *New York Times,* November 5, 1992, B4.

40. "Resurgence of the Right," *Washington Post,* August 18, 1992, A2.

41. "George Bush, Prisoner of the Crazies," *New York Times,* August 16, 1992, 17.

42. "Bush's Gains from Convention Nearly Evaporate in Latest Poll," *New York Times,* August 26, 1992, A19.

43. "Clinton Says Foes Sow Intolerance," *New York Times,* September 12, 1992, 1.

44. "Republicans Talk, but Split Remains," *New York Times,* May 11, 1993, A19.

45. Author interview with Pat Buchanan, subject's home, Virginia, February 26, 2010.

46. Author interview with Greg Mueller, restaurant, D.C., February 21, 2010.

47. Author interview with Jerry Woodruff, restaurant, North Carolina, March 2, 2010.

SEVENTEEN: HUNTING THE CLINTONS

1. "Remembrance of Things Pat," *Washington Post,* February 19, 1996, B1.

2. Author interview with Connie Mackey, phone, October 19, 2010.

3. Author interview with anonymous.

4. Author interview with Greg Mueller, restaurant, D.C., February 21, 2010.

5. Good works on Clinton's first two years in office include: E. J. Dionne, *They Only Look Dead: Why Progressives Will Dominate the Next Political Era* (New York: Simon & Schuster, 1995); Elizabeth Drew, *On the Edge: The Clinton Presidency* (New York: Simon & Schuster, 1995).

6. "Nixon on 1996," *New York Times,* May 12, 1994, A25.

7. "Buchanan to Sue over Retroactive Tax Boost," *Washington Times,* August 12, 1993, A4.

8. Steve Gillon, *The Pact: Bill Clinton, Newt Gingrich, and the Rivalry That Defined a Generation* (New York: Oxford University Press, 2008), 114.

9. Edward D. Berkowitz, *To Improve Human Health: A History of the Institute of Medicine* (Washington, D.C.: New Academies Press, 1998), 266.

10. R. Emmett Tyrell, *Boy Clinton: The Political Biography* (Washington, D.C.: Regnery, 1996), 93.

11. "The Faltering of Clintonism," *Washington Times,* May 12, 1993, G1.

12. "Lowered Ears . . . and Approval Ratings," *Washington Times,* May 26, 1993, G1.

13. "When Will the Looting Cease?," *Washington Times,* June 21, 1993, E1.

14. "Mall Proposal Pits Residents Against Builder," *New York Times,* July 23, 1995.

15. Author interview with Pat Choate, phone, August 27, 2010.

16. Christopher J. Bailey, "Clintonomics," in Paul S. Herrnson and Dily M. Hill eds., *The Clinton Presidency: The First Term, 1992-1996* (London: Macmillan Press, 1999).

17. "The Downsizing of America," *New York Times,* March 5, 1995.

18. "New Appeals to Pocketbook Patriots," *New York Times,* January 23, 1993, 37.

19. John C. Hulsman, *A Paradigm for the New World Order: A Schools-of-Thought Analysis of American Foreign Policy in the Post-Cold War Era* (London: Macmillan, 1997), 108-09.

20. "Splintered on Trade," *New York Times,* September 15, 1993, B12.

21. "Democratic Whip in House to Fight Free-Trade Pact," *New York Times,* August 28, 1993, 1.

22. "Splintered on Trade," *New York Times,* September 15, 1993, B12.

23. "Gore, Perot Tangle in Heated NAFTA Debate," *Los Angeles Times,* November 10, 1993, 1.

24. John R. MacArthur, *The Selling of "Free Trade": NAFTA, Washington, and the Subversion of American Democracy* (Los Angeles: University of California Press, 2000), 233.

25. "Why Are Republicans Rescuing Bill Clinton," *Washington Times,* September 11, 1993, 24.

26. "Revolt Brewing Among Middle Americans," *Washington Times,* August 30, 1993, G1.

27. "Buchanan Joins the Foes of Trade Pact," *New York Times,* August 27, 1993, D2.

28. "The Asking Price of NAFTA Is Our Sovereignty," *Washington Times,* undated, reprinted in *Dole Campaign Papers,* Robert J. Dole Institute, Box 38.

29. "The Free Trade Accord," *New York Times,* November 18, 1993, A20.

30. Steven E. Schier, *The Postmodern Presidency: Bill Clinton's Legacy in U.S. Politics* (Pittsburgh: University of Pittsburgh Press, 2000), 49.

31. "America First Movement Is Gaining Converts," *Washington Times,* November 20, 1993, 24.

32. "The Shape of Things to Come," *Washington Times,* August 10, 1993, reprinted in *Dole Campaign Papers,* Robert J. Dole Institute, Box 38.

33. "Trade Vote Effect May Ebb Over Time," *New York Times,* November 21, 1993, 23.

34. "The GOP Looks Homeward on Trade," *New York Times,* October 16, 1994, E3.

35. "Buchanan Launches Foundation, Sets Culture Debate," *Washington Times,* March 20, 1993, A4.

36. Letter, Terry Jeffrey to Cathey, April 12, 1993, *Boyd Cathey Private Papers.*

37. Letter, Terry Jeffrey to Cathey, undated, *Boyd Cathey Private Papers.*

38. Gottfried, *Encounters,* 131.

39. "Buchanan Broadens Base, Cultivates GOP Moderates," *Washington Times,* November 12, 1993, A4.

40. "Buchanan, Allies Promote New Vision of Conservatism," *Washington Times,* November 15, 1993, A1.

41. http://buchanan.org/blog/pjb-the-great-betrayal-cspan-interview-317, last accessed December 7, 2010.

42. "Richard Nixon's Long Journey Ends," *Washington Post,* April 28, 1994, 1.

43. "Dole, Campaigning from Afar, Wins an Early Republican Straw Poll in Iowa," *New York Times,* June 26, 1994, 12.

44. "Republicans Form Group to Regain Centrist Votes," *New York Times,* December 16, 1992, A24.

45. "Oregon GOP Faces Schism over Agenda of Christian Right," *New York Times,* November 14, 1992, 6.

46. "Conservatives Struggle for Something to Say," *New York Times,* August 1, 1993, E4.

47. "Departing Chairman Scolds Republicans over Zealotry," *New York Times,* January 30, 1993, 1.

48. "Buchanan Launches Foundation, Sets Culture Debate."

49. "How Houston's Angry Din Still Haunts Republicans," *New York Times,* March 27, 1994, 126.

50. "Gingrich, Buchanan Clash on Role of Government in Economy," *North Carolina Democrat,* July 15, 1995, 1.

51. "Gingrich's Life: The Complications and Ideals," *New York Times,* November 24, 1994, A1.

52. "A Suburban Eden Where the Right Rules," *New York Times,* August 1, 1994, B6.

53. Gillon, *The Pact,* 121.

54. Matthew Continetti, *The K Street Gang: The Rise and Fall of the Republican Machine* (New York: Doubleday, 2006), 1–21.

55. Chris R. Edwards and John Curtis Samples, *The Republican Revolution 10 Years Later: Smaller Government or Business as Usual?* (Washington, D.C.: Cato Institute, 2004), 17–22.

56. Interview with Terry Jeffrey, restaurant, D.C., February 23, 2010.

57. http://www.mediaite.com/tv/pat-buchanan-slams-94-contract-with-america-as-over rated-silly/, last accessed December 7, 2010.

58. Joseph A. Aistrup, *The Southern Strategy Revisited: Republican Top-down Advancement in the South* (Lawrence: University Press of Kansas, 1996), 57.

59. "Clinton's Grip on the '96 Ticket Isn't So Sure," *New York Times,* November 21, 1994, A1.

60. "Second Dawn of Conservatism May Be at Hand," *Washington Times,* November 2, 1994, 24.

61. "Nation Shows Its Dissatisfaction with Clinton," *Washington Times,* undated, reprinted in *Dole Campaign Papers,* Robert J. Dole Institute, Box 38.

62. David B. Kopel, *Guns: Who Should Have Them?* (New York: Prometheus, 1995), 61.

63. Author interview with Grover Norquist, subject's office, May 12, 2010.

64. Gregg Lee Carter, *Guns in American Society* (Santa Barbara, CA: ABC-CIO, 2002), 157.

65. David S. New, *Holy War: The Rise of Militant Christian, Jewish, and Islamic Fundamentalism* (Jefferson, NC: McFarland, 2001), 105.

66. Author interview with Joe Scarborough, phone, August 13, 2010.

67. "Advertising," *New York Times,* November 30, 1994, D18.

68. "US Workers Will Lose If GATT Is Approved," *Conservative Chronicle,* undated, reprinted in *Dole Campaign Papers,* Robert J. Dole Institute, Box 38.

69. Author interview with Joe Scarborough, phone, August 13, 2010.

70. "GATT Is an End Run Around Sovereignty," *Washington Times,* November 21, 1994, 27.

71. "Escape Clause for Congress Is a Key," *New York Times,* November 21, 1994, A1.

72. "A New Quest by Buchanan for President," *New York Times,* March 21, 1995, A16.

EIGHTEEN: WEIGHING UP THE OPPOSITION

1. "Now Officially, Dole Is Making a Run for '96," *New York Times,* April 11, 1995, A1.
2. "The Making of Bob Dole," *Boston Globe Magazine,* July 18, 1995, 1.
3. "Dole Builds Loyal, If Uninspired, Support," *New York Times,* October 16, 1995, B5.
4. Author interview with Paul Erickson, subject's hotel room, D.C., February 21, 2010.
5. "Dole: Opposed Only by Voters," *Manchester Union-Leader,* December 24, 1995, 7.
6. "Buchanan Dares Dole on Depth of Conservatism," *Manchester Union-Leader,* November 10, 1995, A6.
7. Author interview with Larry Pratt, restaurant, D.C., February 25, 2010.
8. "A Potent Trinity: God, Country, and Me," *Nation,* June 26, 1996, 13.
9. Oral archive interview with Sheila Burke, *Dole Campaign Papers,* Robert J. Dole Institute, Box 5.
10. Author interview with Bill Lacy, subject's office, Kansas, February 2, 2010.
11. Memo, Dennis Shea to Dole, May 23, 1996, *Dole Campaign Papers,* Robert J. Dole Institute, Box 122.
12. "Challenge for Dole's Team Is to Serve a Man Who Keeps His Own Counsel," *New York Times,* March 17, 1996, A21.
13. "Stolid on the Stump, Dole Wages a Battle to Inspire Voters," *Washington Post,* February 19, 1996, A6.
14. Author interview with Carter Wrenn, subject's office, North Carolina, May 5, 2010.
15. "New Hampshire: And the Race Has Started," *Arizona Republic,* March 1, 1995, B5.
16. "When Good Republicans Make Bad Moves," *New York Times,* April 23, 1995, E2.
17. "Gramm's Campaign Serious?," *Dallas Morning News,* February 5, 1995, 2J.
18. "He's Nice, and He Wants the Job," *New York Post,* March 4, 1995, 10.
19. "Alexander Challenges Manchester Union Leader," *Manchester Union-Leader,* March 1, 1995, A6.
20. "A Candidate Plans Some Spontaneity," *New York Times,* February 21, 1995, A16.
21. "Joining Race, Specter Attacks the Right," *New York Times,* March 31, 1996, A1.
22. "Ready to Join Presidential Race, Specter Is Looking for His Niche," *New York Times,* March 30, 1996, A1.
23. "Morry Taylor, Tire Magnate, Stops His Campaign," *New York Times,* March 9, 1996.
24. "Illinoisian Gives Up Quixotic Campaign," *St. Louis Post-Dispatch,* March 9, 1996, 1A.
25. "A Little Known Candidate with a Big Issue," *New York Times,* August 9, 1996, A16.
26. "Black Conservative Enters Race for GOP Nomination," *New York Times,* March 27, 1995, A16.
27. "Dornan Files for NH Run," *Manchester Union-Leader,* December 13, 1995, A6.
28. "Appearing Nightly: Robert Dornan, Master of the Put Down," *New York Times,* June 27, 1995, A14.
29. "Dornan, House Firebrand, Joins the '96 Race," *New York Times,* April 14, 1995, A11.
30. "No More Mr. Nice Guys," *New York Times,* July 6, 1995, A21.
31. Author interview with Bay Buchanan, restaurant, Virginia, May 3, 2010.
32. "Buchanan Taps a Populist Vein," *New York Times,* September 12, 1995, A21.

33. "Deadbeat Pat?," *Nation,* June 26, 1995, 25.

34. Author interview with Connie Mackey, phone, October 19, 2010.

35. Author interview with Bay Buchanan, restaurant, Virginia, May 3, 2010.

36. "In Iowa, Buchanan Tries to Convince Conservatives That He's Their Man," *New York Times,* December 3, 1995, 34.

37. "Seismic Shift in the Parties Reflects View on Business," *New York Times,* September 24, 1995, E1.

38. Continetti, *The K Street Gang,* 148–50.

39. "Look Who Wants to Tinker with Market Forces," *BusinessWeek,* October 2, 1995, 26.

40. "Buchanan's Tough Tariff Talk Rattles GOP," *New York Times,* October 8, 1995, 1.

41. "The Meaning of Timothy McVeigh," *Vanity Fair,* September 2001, 38.

42. "Speaking Up for Guns, Lots of Them, for Nearly Everyone," *New York Times,* April 26, 1999, A21.

43. "Armed and Dangerous (The NRA, Militias and White Supremacists Are Fostering a Network of Right Wing Warriors)," *Rolling Stone,* November 2, 1995, 55.

44. Author interview with Larry Pratt, restaurant, D.C., February 25, 2010.

45. David Henry Bennett, *A Party of Fear: From Nativist Movements to the New Right in American History* (Chapel Hill: University of North Carolina Press, 1988), 450–51.

46. "A Plausible Hothead," *Newsweek,* May 29, 1995, 45.

47. "Christian Coalition Is United on Morality, but Not Politics," *New York Times,* September 8, 1995, D18.

48. "Life in Iowa May Not Have Changed, but the Political Turf Is Another Story," *New York Times,* October 28, 1995, 6.

49. "Buchanan Challenges Gramm to Debate," *New York Times,* July 15, 1995, 9.

50. Author interview with Scott Reed, subject's office, D.C., February 23, 2010.

51. "Politicians of Every Stripe Troop to a Perot Convention in Dallas," *New York Times,* August 12, 1995, 1.

52. "Poll Shows Disenchantment with Politicians and Politics," *New York Times,* August 12, 1995, 1.

53. "In Iowa, Buchanan Tries to Convince Conservatives That He's Their Man."

54. "Surprising Straw Poll Gives Dole a Glimpse of the Battles Ahead," *New York Times,* August 21, 1995, A1.

55. Woodward, *The Choice,* 243–44.

56. Author interview with Bay Buchanan, restaurant, Virginia, May 3, 2010.

57. Author interview with Shelley Buchanan, MSNBC, D.C., May 1, 2010.

58. Author interview with Bay Buchanan, restaurant, Virginia, May 3, 2010.

59. Author interview with Connie Mackey, phone, October 19, 2010.

60. "Surprising Straw Poll Gives Dole a Glimpse of the Battles Ahead."

61. Author interview with Bay Buchanan, restaurant, Virginia, May 3, 2010.

NINETEEN: COMING FROM BEHIND

1. "Primaries Ending Before They Begin," *New York Times,* October 15, 1995, E4.
2. "New Hampshire Poll Finds Powell with an Edge," *New York Times,* October 19, 1995, B13.
3. "A Bigger Tent for the GOP," *New York Times,* October 30, 1995, A1.
4. "Politicians Find a Window into the Heart of the Christian Right," *New York Times,* November 1, 1995, A14.
5. "Buchanan Says Powell Would Split GOP," *New York Times,* October 30, 1995, A12.
6. "A Decision Relieving Some, but Disappointing Others," *New York Times,* November 9, 1995, B12.
7. "Abortion Foes Flex Their Political Muscle," *New York Times,* November 12, 1995, 24.
8. Article in the *Washington Post,* undated, reprinted in *Dole Campaign Papers,* Robert J. Dole Institute, Box 15.
9. "With the Field Now Scrambled, Iowans Prepare to Vote," *New York Times,* February 11, 1996, 26.
10. "A Stroll down Steve Forbes' Paper Trail," *New York Times,* January 30, 1996, D7.
11. "In Political Quest, Forbes Runs in Shadow of Father," *New York Times,* February 11, 1996, D7.
12. "Forbes, King of the Island," *Washington Post,* January 14, 1996, C2.
13. "Under a Rock," *New Republic,* January 29, 1996, 22.
14. "Forbes Is Trying to Buy the Republican Primary," *Portsmouth Herald,* January 26, 1996, A4.
15. "Long, Costly Prelude Does Little to Alter Plot of Presidential Race," *New York Times,* January 3, 1996, A1.
16. "Going by Foot and Searching for Respect," *New York Times,* January 5, 1995, B1.
17. "After Tough Tuesday, Gramm's on the Spot," *Washington Post,* February 8, 1996, A14.
18. "Flat Tax, Once Obscure Idea, Is Set to Enter Campaign Debate," *New York Times,* January 9, 1996, 7.
19. "A Flawed Flat Tax and the Way Out," *New York Times,* January 17, 1996, A19.
20. "Who'll Cross the Delaware?," *Manchester Union-Leader,* November 30, 1995, A6.
21. "Mr. Momentum? Steve Forbes Hasn't Got Much Spark, but His Campaign May Be Catching Fire," *Washington Post,* January 6, 1996, C1.
22. "Buchanan and Forbes: Odd Couple of GOP Field," *Washington Post,* January 9, 1996, A1.
23. Memo, Anette Guarisco to Dole, February 6, 1996, *Dole Campaign Papers,* Robert J. Dole Institute, Box 122.
24. New Hampshire Briefing, February 9, 1996, *Dole Campaign Papers,* Robert J. Dole Institute, Box 122.
25. Andrew Busch and James W. Ceaser, *Losing to Win: The 1996 Elections and American Politics* (Lanham, MD: Rowman & Littlefield, 1997), 80.
26. Rich Lowry, *Legacy: Paying the Price for the Clinton Years* (Washington, D.C.: Regnery, 2003), 355.
27. Gillon, *The Pact,* 159.

28. Lee Edwards, *The Conservative Revolution: The Movement That Remade America* (New York: Free Press, 1999), 305.

29. "For Twice Victorious Dole, the Main Thing Isn't Winning, but Not Losing," *New York Times*, November 21, 1996, A16.

30. Author interview with Scott Reed, subject's office, D.C., February 23, 2010.

31. Memo, John Schall and Sheila Burke to Dole, January 16, 1996, *Dole Campaign Papers*, Robert J. Dole Institute, Box 122.

32. "Republican Newcomer Gets His Rivals' Attention," *New York Times*, January 13, 1996, 1.

33. "GOP Candidates Spar in Long Distance Debate," *New York Times*, November 18, 1995, 6.

34. Author interview with Connie Mackey, phone, October 19, 2010.

35. "Gramm, After a Torrid Start, Slips and Slides in 1996 Race," *New York Times*, June 20, 1995, A1.

36. "Buchanan for President," *New York Times*, December 24, 1995, E9.

37. "Buchanan in Unfamiliar Role, Is Under Fire as a Left-Winger," *New York Times*, December 31, 1995, 1.

38. "Candidate Visits Louisiana Again," *Advocate*, December 19, 1995, 9A.

39. "Buchanan Attacks Gambling, Rivals on Stopover in BR," *Advocate*, January 4, 1996, 2B.

40. "Former Consultant to Aid Buchanan," *Advocate*, December 30, 1996, 13A.

41. "Foster to Back Buchanan; but Vote Isn't an Endorsement," *Advocate*, February 3, 1996, A3.

42. Author interview with Scott Reed, subject's office, D.C., February 23, 2010.

43. "Texas Senator Gets Nod in Louisiana Republican Straw Poll," *New York Times*, January 8, 1995, 15.

44. Author interview with Terry Jeffrey, restaurant, D.C., February 21, 2010; author interview with Pat Buchanan, subject's home, Virginia, March 13, 2010.

45. "The GOP's Fat Tuesday—Hopefuls Phil Gramm and Pat Buchanan Hustle to the Hustings," *Washington Post*, February 1, 1996, C1.

46. "3 Republicans Seek a Boost in Louisiana," *New York Times*, January 28, 1996, 16.

47. "The GOP's Fat Tuesday—Hopefuls Phil Gramm and Pat Buchanan Hustle to the Hustings."

48. Author interview with Diana Banister, phone, September 3, 2010.

49. Author interview with Bay Buchanan, restaurant, Virginia, May 3, 2010.

50. Author interview with Connie Mackey, phone, October 19, 2010.

51. "Buchanan and Forbes Beat Dole in an Alaska Poll," *New York Times*, January 31, 1996, A13.

52. Author interview with Ralph Reed, phone, September 14, 2010.

53. "Presidential Hopeful Swings Through State," *Anchorage Daily News*, November 5, 1995, B1.

54. "Presidential Hopeful Buchanan Stumps in Alaska," *Anchorage Daily News*, November 3, 1995, B3.

55. "Aiming at History: Gun Show Draws Fans of the Past as Well as Hunters," *Anchorage Daily News*, November 6, 1995, F1.

56. Author interview with Bay Buchanan, restaurant, Virginia, May 3, 2010.

57. "Buchanan and Keyes Press Social Issues," *New York Times,* February 3, 1996, 8.

58. "Voters Flood GOP Caucuses," *Anchorage Daily News,* January 28, 1996, B1.

59. "Bush Wins in Alaska Straw Poll," *Anchorage Daily News,* January 25, 2000, B1.

60. "Buchanan Wins GOP Poll," *Anchorage Daily News,* January 30, 1996, A1.

61. "Buchanan, Forbes Top Dole in Alaska GOP Straw Poll," *Washington Post,* January 31, 1996, A4.

62. "Energized Buchanan Takes Aim at Forbes," *Manchester Union-Leader,* February 1, 1996, A16.

63. "Poll Has More Than One Winner," *Anchorage Daily News,* January 21, 1996, B1.

64. "Buchanan Stumps LA on Eve of Caucuses," *Times-Picayune,* February 6, 1996, A3.

65. "Buchanan, Gramm Target Gun Control," *Washington Post,* January 15, 1996, A14.

66. "LA Caucus: Buchanan Wins," *Advocate,* February 7, 1996, 1A.

67. "Louisiana Cajun Casts First 1996 Presidential Vote," *Advocate,* February 7, 1996, 7A.

68. "After the First Votes, Ecstasy and Agony," *New York Times,* February 8, 1996, A1.

69. "Buchanan Overwhelms Gramm to Take Caucus," *Times-Picayune,* February 7, 1996, A1.

70. "Buchanan Caucus Win Is Closer Than It Looked," *Times-Picayune,* February 8, 1996, A1.

71. "In Their Own Words," *New York Times,* February 8, 1996, B12.

TWENTY: WINNING WITHOUT WINNING

1. "Iowans Trudge Through Mud to Reach Decisions," *Los Angeles Times,* February 12, 1996, A1.

2. Memo, Frank J. Donatelli to Dole, February 9, 1996, *Dole Campaign Papers,* Robert J. Dole Institute, Box 122.

3. "In Sharp Words, Gingrich Notes Forbes Flat Tax," *Washington Post,* February 9, 1996, A6.

4. "Rivals Pile on Forbes, Dole at Iowa Debate," *Washington Times,* January 14, 1996, A7.

5. "Forbes: Newcomer in Perot's Clothing," *New York Times,* January 15, 1996, A12.

6. "Top Target in Iowa Debate: Forbes, the No. 2 Candidate," *New York Times,* January 14, 1996, 1.

7. "Dole in Iowa, Makes Pitch for Backing of Anti-Abortion Voters," *New York Times,* February 4, 1996, 23.

8. "A Pledge Against Gays," *Washington Post,* February 13, 1996, A19.

9. "Fight for Religious Right's Votes Turns Bitter," *New York Times,* February 10, 1996, 1.

10. New Hampshire briefing, February 9, 1996, *Dole Campaign Papers,* Robert J. Dole Institute, Box 122.

11. "Dropping in Polls, Forbes Lashes Out," *Washington Post,* February 10, 1996, A1.

12. "Returning to Iowa, Dole Stresses Moral Values," *New York Times,* February 10, 1996, B10.

13. "Bashing to Victory," *New York Times,* February 14, 1996, A21.

14. "Dole Holds onto Lead as Iowans Head to Polls," *Los Angeles Times,* February 12, 1996, A1.

15. "Buchanan Tries to Trim GOP Field," *New York Times,* February 11, 1996, 29.

16. "Fueled By Success, Buchanan Revels in Rapid-Fire Oratory," *New York Times,* February 15, 1996, A1.

17. "With Fervor of a Prophet, Gramm Keeps Fighting," *New York Times,* February 11, 1996, 27.

18. Memo, Hilton to Scott Reed, February 1, 1996, *Dole Campaign Papers,* Robert J. Dole Institute, Box 48.

19. "In No Frills Message, Modesty Vies with Pride in Service," *New York Times,* February 12, 1996, A1.

20. "For Alexander, Upbeat Campaign Brings Modest Gains in Iowa," *New York Times,* February 11, 1996, 1.

21. "New Hampshire Voters Buried by Avalanche of Negative Advertisements," *Washington Post,* February 10, 1996, A11.

22. "Alexander's Advisers See Gains at Expense of Gramm and Forbes," *Washington Post,* February 9, 1996, A4.

23. "Candidates Look for Last-Minute Dazzle in Iowa," *New York Times,* February 12, 1996, A1.

24. "For Buchanan, the Voice Is His Weapon of Choice," *New York Times,* February 16, 1996, A27.

25. "Let the Games Begin!," *New Republic,* January 29, 1996, 21.

26. "Ads for Forbes Played Role in Outcome but Not the One He Intended," *New York Times,* February 14, 1996, B8.

27. "Buchanan Gets Strong Second in Surprise," *New York Times,* February 13, 1996, A1.

28. Woodward, *The Choice,* 379.

29. "Hard on the Heels of Dole, Buchanan Celebrates 2nd Place," *Washington Post,* February 13, 1996, A9.

30. "Dole Edges Buchanan in Iowa GOP Vote," *Washington Post,* February 13, 1996, A1.

31. Author interview with Terry Jeffrey, restaurant, D.C., February 21, 2010; this story was investigated and confirmed by James J. Condit, based on comparing results released by the media-favored Voter News Survey and those recorded in the *Des Moines Register.* After the caucus, Sen. Charles Grassley officially complained to the VNS: James J. Condit, Jr., "A House Without Doors: Vote Fraud in America," *Chronicles,* November 1996, 14.

32. Author interview with Connie Mackey, phone, October 19, 2010.

33. "Poor Showings in 2 Contests Lead Gramm to Withdraw," *New York Times,* February 14, 1996, A1.

34. "A Strong Second Place Gives Heart to Buchanan," *New York Times,* February 13, 1996, A19.

TWENTY-ONE: THE PEASANTS' REVOLT

1. "Buchanan Hits Back—Gramm Endorses Dole—Establishment Panicking, Commentator Says," *Washington Post,* February 19, 1996, A1.

2. "Eating Presidential Dust on the Campaign Trail," *Washington Post,* February 19, 1996, B1.

3. "Dole Takes a Page Out of Buchanan's Populist Pitch," *Washington Post*, February 18, 1996, A20.

4. "Dole Opens Drive in New Hampshire with New Theme," *New York Times*, February 14, 1996, A1.

5. "Bugle Call for Dole: Reveille, or Taps?," *New York Times*, February 14, 1996, B8.

6. "Cap over the Wall," *New York Times*, February 15, 1996, A27.

7. "The Pat Solution," *Time*, November 6, 1995, 26.

8. "New England Finds GOP Trying Out New Tactics," *New York Times*, February 15, 1996, B15.

9. "Fueled by Success, Buchanan Revels in Rapid-Fire Oratory."

10. "Dole Stepping Carefully in New Hampshire Race," *New York Times*, February 15, 1996, B15.

11. "Panic in the Party Ranks," *Washington Post*, February 19, 1996, A25.

12. ". . . And the Cant on Character," *Washington Post*, February 20, 1996, A11.

13. "Alexander, the Contender, Says He Avoids the Negative," *New York Times*, February 16, 1996, A27.

14. "Alexander Builds His Hopes on Some Radical Departures," *New York Times*, February 18, 1996, 1.

15. "Alexander: From Asterisk to Exclamation Point," *Washington Post*, February 18, 1996, A20.

16. "Ignored and Indignant—Moderates Feel Slighted in New Hampshire," *Washington Post*, February 19, 1996, A1.

17. "Never Mind His Politics: Is the Man Telegenic?," *New York Times*, February 20, 1996, C18.

18. "Struggle in the Snow," *New York Times*, February 20, 1996, A18.

19. "Three Little Words," *New York Times*, February 11, 1996, E15.

20. "Your Wish Is My Campaign," *St. Louis Post-Dispatch*, February 25, 1996, 1B.

21. "Conservatism Gets Soiled," *Newsweek*, March 4, 1996, 74.

22. "Sen. Smith Dismisses Criticism of Buchanan," *Manchester Union-Leader*, February 19, 1996, 1.

23. "Buchanan Co-Leader Quits Under Fire," *New York Times*, February 16, 1996, A27.

24. "And Now, the Hate Show," *New York Times*, November 16, 1993, A27.

25. Author interview with Larry Pratt, restaurant, D.C., February 25, 2010.

26. "The Pratt Fall," *New York Times*, February 17, 1996, 23.

27. "Arizona Hails Dual Message of Buchanan," *Washington Post*, February 24, 1996, A10.

28. "7,000 Rally Against Governor in Baton Rouge," *Washington Post*, February 25, 1996, A3.

29. "Buchanan, Beset by Many Critics, Still Unbowed," *New York Times*, February 17, 1996, 1.

30. Author interview with Yehuda Levin, restaurant, New York, April 26, 2010.

31. "New Hampshire Will Be Close, Polls Say: Gramm Endorses Dole," *New York Times*, February 19, 1996, A1.

32. Author interview with Larry Pratt, restaurant, D.C., February 25, 2010.

33. Author interview with Pat Buchanan, subject's home, Virginia, February 26, 2010.

34. Author interview with Greg Mueller, restaurant, D.C., February 21, 2010.

35. Author interview with Bay Buchanan, restaurant, Virginia, May 3, 2010.

36. "GOP Rivals Clash over Attack Ads," *New York Times,* February 16, 1996, A1.

37. "The Manchester Burlesque," *Washington Post,* February 18, 1996, C1.

38. "Buchanan, Beset by Many Critics, Still Unbowed."

39. "Mr. Buchanan Stumbles," *New York Times,* February 16, 1996, 22.

40. "Buchanan Plugs into Voters' Anxieties," *Washington Post,* February 18, 1996, A21.

41. "Down to the Wire, a Clutch of Candidates and Choices," *New York Times,* February 21, 1996, A1.

42. Author interview with Bay Buchanan, restaurant, Virginia, May 3, 2010.

43. "Stakes Are High as NH Voters Go to the Polls," *Los Angeles Times,* February 20, 1996, A1.

44. "Direct from New Hampshire, Thanks to Web," *New York Times,* February 20, 1996, A14.

45. "Inside the Race," *Time,* February 26, 1996, 21.

46. "Campaign '96—Enough Already, Weary NH Voters Say of the Electioneering," *Los Angeles Times,* February 20, 1996, A12.

47. Author interview with Bay Buchanan, restaurant, Virginia, May 3, 2010.

48. Woodward, *The Choice,* 385.

49. "May the Batter Man Win," *Washington Post,* February 20, 1996, D1.

50. "New Hampshire: Backdrop for Outlandish Political Drama," *Washington Post,* February 19, 1996, A7.

51. "Long Shots Hope to Hit the Jackpot," *Washington Post,* February 20, 1996, A5.

52. "May the Batter Man Win."

53. "Candidates Clash over Trade Issues Heading into Vote," *New York Times,* February 20, 1996, A1.

54. "Stakes Are High as NH Voters Go to the Polls," *New York Times,* February 20, 1996, A1.

55. Author interview with Signe McQuaid, phone, February 12, 2010.

56. "Mob Scene," *Time,* March 4, 1996, 32.

57. "Alexander—When Third Place Is a Tremendous Win," *Washington Post,* February 21, 1996, A12.

58. Woodward, *The Choice,* 386–87.

59. "The Night Was Anything but Bittersweet for Supporters," *Manchester Union-Leader,* February 21, 1996, A1.

60. "We Are Taking Back Our Party, Victor Says," *Washington Post,* February 21, 1992, A1.

61. "Exit Poll—Angry White Working Class Voter Came to the Fore," *Washington Post,* February 21, 1996, A14.

TWENTY-TWO: LOSING

1. "Buchanan Steps Up Campaign as Dole Remains Confident," *Los Angeles Times,* February 22, 1996, A1.

2. "Buchanan Supporter Disarmed in SD," *Washington Post,* February 25, 1996, A10.

3. "In Farm State, Buchanan Finds No Help in History," *New York Times*, February 27, 1996, A18.

4. "Stop Attacking Buchanan," *Times and Democrat*, February 27, 1996, 15.

5. "Buchanan Pushes His Arizona Bid," *Post and Courier*, February 26, 1996, A5.

6. "Social Issues Give Buchanan Boost, a New Poll Finds," *New York Times*, February 27, 1996, A1.

7. "Appealing to Gun Owners and Perot Camp," *New York Times*, February 26, 1996, B6.

8. "The Populist Blowup," *Time*, February 26, 1996, 28.

9. "Buchanan's Brash Rhetoric Ruffles Convention," *Washington Post*, February 22, 1996, A1.

10. "Pundit's Success in Primaries Stirs Concern and Opposition," *Washington Post*, February 24, 1996, A10.

11. "Your Wish Is My Campaign," *St. Louis Post-Dispatch*, February 25, 1996, 1B.

12. "Buchanan's Supporters Bristle with Ire for News Media," *Washington Post*, February 26, 1996, A7.

13. "Patrick Buchanan . . . Liberal?," *Washington Post*, February 23, 1996, B1.

14. "The Castle Storms Back," *Washington Post*, February 23, 1996, C1.

15. "Mayor and Local GOP Seek to Stop Buchanan," *New York Times*, February 27, 1996, A19.

16. "After Luring Disaffected, GOP Elite Is Uneasy," *Washington Post*, February 22, 1996, A12.

17. "Republicans Assess Buchanan's Impact," *Washington Post*, February 22, 1996, A1.

18. "Dole Names His Reason for Running—Nomination of Buchanan Might Cost Republicans Control of Congress, Senator Warns," *Washington Post*, February 23, 1996, A12.

19. "Dole Shifts Attack, Drops Extremist Tag," *Washington Post*, February 23, 1996, A1.

20. "Delaware Voters Took Tax Concerns into Primary Booth," *Post and Courier*, February 25, 1996, A10.

21. "Why Delaware Voters Support Him? Because He Was There," *New York Times*, February 26, 1996, B7.

22. Author interview with Scott Reed, subject's office, D.C., February 23, 2010.

23. "In Visit to Arizona, Senator Emphasizes Goldwater Roots," *New York Times*, February 26, 1996, B7.

24. "Candidates Futures Rely on Good Outing," *Arizona Republic*, February 25, 1996, A1.

25. "GOP Rivals into Arizona for Western Showdown," *Los Angeles Times*, February 22, 1996, A10.

26. "Arizona Sits atop Republican Divide," *Washington Post*, February 25, 1996, A10.

27. "At Rallies for Buchanan, Fervent Supporters Are Part of the Show, Too," *New York Times*, February 26, 1996, B6.

28. "Militias See Buchanan as Their Kind of Candidate," *Los Angeles Times*, February 22, 1996, A1.

29. "Rivals Hit Buchanan on Trade at Debate," *Washington Post*, February 23, 1996, A12.

30. Author interview with Greg Mueller, restaurant, D.C., February 21, 2010.

31. Condit, "A House Without Doors."

32. Author interview with Bay Buchanan, subject's home, Virginia, February 26, 2010. I

have found no evidence to support this alleged case of malpractice, but certainly bottle-necks occurred and perhaps 10 percent of all voters were turned away due to an insufficient number of polling booths. Turnout was three times what the Arizona GOP and Bay probably confused ineptitude for fraud. "Bottlenecks Greet Voters at Some Valley Poll Sites," *Arizona Republic,* February 28 1996, A15.

33. Woodward, *The Choice,* 398.

34. "Arizona Voting Puts Forbes Back in Race," *New York Times,* February 29, 1996, A1.

35. "Buchanan Attacking All Fronts," *New York Times,* February 29, 1996, B8.

36. "From Household to Nation," *Chronicles,* March 1996, 12.

37. Author interview with Pat Buchanan, subject's home, Virginia, May 1, 2010.

38. "Dole, Alexander Fight for Middle," *State,* February 27, 1996, A1.

39. "GOP Comes A-Courtin': Vote Split Will Test Coalition," *Post and Courier,* March 1, 1996, A1.

40. "Buchanan Campaign Forges Conservative Coalition in State," *Greenville News,* February 27, 1996, 3.

41. "Textiles May Be Key to Republican Primary," *Herald-Journal,* February 28, 1996, 6.

42. "Free Trade or Tariffs? South Carolina Tests 2 Republican Visions," *Wall Street Journal,* February 28, 1996, A6.

43. "BMW Expansion Plans to Be Unveiled Tuesday," *Herald-Journal,* February 25, 1996, 1A.

44. "South Carolina Is a Crossroads for the GOP," *New York Times,* February 29, 1996, A21.

45. "For Dole, It Again Comes Down to SC," *Post and Courier,* February 26, 1996, A1.

46. Memo, John Schall to Dole, February 27, 1996, *Dole Campaign Papers,* Robert J. Dole Institute, Box 42.

47. South Carolina briefing, February 29, 1996, *Dole Campaign Papers,* Robert J. Dole Institute, Box 122.

48. "South Carolina Is a Crossroads for the GOP."

49. Memo, Rolf Lundberg to Dole, February 26, 1996, *Dole Campaign Papers,* Robert J. Dole Institute, Box 122.

50. "State Politicians Push Hard for Dole," *State,* February 28, 1996, 12.

51. "SC Most Generous in Donations to Dole," *Post and Courier,* February 27, 1996, 5.

52. "GOP Must Make a Choice, and Dole Has Most to Offer," *State,* February 28, 1996, 9.

53. "Countdown 250," *Post and Courier,* February 29, 1996, A11.

54. "Buchanan Attacking All Fronts."

55. "Candidates Dash for State Votes," *New York Times,* March 1, 1996, A1.

56. "As Rivals Take the Stage, Sniping Abounds," *New York Times,* March 1, 1996, A1.

57. "For Buchanan, It's a Costume Change Every Day," *New York Times,* March 2, 1996, A21.

58. "Candidates Dash for State Votes."

59. "Dole Easily Beats Buchanan to Win in South Carolina," *New York Times,* March 3, 1996, A1.

60. "In Their Own Words," *New York Times,* March 2, 1996, A21.

TWENTY-THREE: TRIUMPH OF THE BIG TENT

1. "Buchanan Is Slugging Away, Seeking a Georgia Comeback," *New York Times*, March 5, 1996, A21.
2. "Dole Basks in Wins," *St. Louis Post-Dispatch*, March 4, 1996, 1A.
3. "Dole, Sweeping 8 Primaries, Calls for Party to Unite," *New York Times*, March 6, 1996, A1.
4. Woodward, *The Choice*, 371–74.
5. "Dole Is Victor in New York, Continuing Primary Surge," *New York Times*, March 8, 1996, A1.
6. "Political Circuit," *St. Louis Post-Dispatch*, March 3, 1996, 4D.
7. "Phyllis Schlafly Blasts Anti-Buchanan 'Smears,'" *St. Louis Post-Dispatch*, February 28, 1996, 7A.
8. "Standing Pat: Buchanan Supporters Take Control of Caucus," *St. Louis Post-Dispatch*, March 10, 1996, 8A.
9. "Buchanan Scores Upset in Missouri's Caucuses; He Leads Dole With 35 Percent," *St. Louis Post-Dispatch*, March 10, 1996, 1A.
10. "Buchanan Courts Old Friends with a Warning," *New York Times*, March 9, 1996, A21.
11. "Dole Captures All Seven States in Biggest Day of Primaries," *New York Times*, March 13, 1996, A1.
12. Author interview with Signe McQuaid, phone, February 12, 2010.
13. Letter, Buchanan to supporters, April 1996, *Boyd Cathey Private Papers*, Box 4.
14. Woodward, *The Choice*, 405.
15. "Buchanan Won't Pledge to Back Dole," *New York Times*, March 5, 1996, A21.
16. Woodward, *The Choice*, 404.
17. Author interview with Bay Buchanan, restaurant, Virginia, May 3, 2010.
18. "Buchanan's Sister Shepherds Insurgent Race," *New York Times*, September 26, 1999, 35.
19. "Elbowed Aside in '92: Moderates Expect to Feel Welcome at This GOP Convention," *New York Times*, August 5, 1996, A12.
20. "Abortion Plank Forces GOP to Tread Carefully," *USA Today*, August 5, 1996, 4A.
21. Author interview with Phyllis Schafly, subject's hotel room, D.C., February 14, 2010.
22. Author interview with Diana Banister, phone, September 3, 2010.
23. "Dole Camp Retreats on Abortion: Conservatives Attack 'Personal Conscience' GOP Platform Language," *Washington Post*, August 6, 1996, A01.
24. Author interview with Scott Reed, subject's office, D.C., February 23, 2010.
25. Author interview with Ralph Reed, phone, September 14, 2010.
26. "GOP Moderates Threaten Floor Fight on Abortion," *Washington Post*, August 7, 1996, A01.
27. "GOP Moderates Accept an Accord on Abortion Issue," *New York Times*, August 8, 1996, A1.
28. "GOP Leaders Dismiss Buchanan's Assertion That He Steers Party," *Washington Post*, August 13, 1996.
29. "Republicans Head for San Diego," *New York Times*, August 11, 1996, A1.

30. Author interview with Connie Mackey, phone, October 19, 2010.

31. "Where Competing Views of America Collide in Anger," *Philadelphia Inquirer,* August 16, 1996, A22.

32. "Buchanan Endorses Dole as Clinton's Lead Drops," *Irish Times,* August 13, 1996, 1.

33. Author interview with Connie Mackey, phone, October 19, 2010.

34. "Bill and Bob's Gender Bender Adventures in Oprah-Land," *Guardian,* August 20, 1996, 13.

35. "An Ordinary Boy's Extraordinary Rage," *Washington Post,* July 2, 1995, 1.

36. Author interview with Pat Buchanan, subject's home, Virginia, May 1, 2010.

37. "Voter Interviews Suggest Clinton Was Persuasive on Path of US," *New York Times,* November 6, 1996, 1.

TWENTY-FOUR: THREATENING THIRD PARTY

1. "La Cage aux Folles, but in South Beach," *New York Times,* March 8, 1996, B1.

2. Elaine May, *The Birdcage: The Shooting Script* (New York: Newmarket Press, 1999).

3. "Middle March," *New York,* June 24, 1996, 46.

4. Marc Oxby, *The 1990s* (New York: Greenwood, 2003), 58.

5. "Defender of God, South, and Unborn," *New York Times,* January 13, 1998, A15.

6. "Christian Coalition Shrinks as Debt Grows," *Washington Post,* April 10, 2006, 64.

7. "Dependable Partisans Celebrate 15 Years of Sparring," *New York Times,* June 23, 1997, B3.

8. "The Guttering Out of the GOP Revolution," *Washington Times,* July 22, 1997, A17.

9. Buchanan, *The Great Betrayal,* 6–7.

10. Ibid., 286–87.

11. "A Conservative No More," *National Review,* October 11, 1999, 34.

12. "President Issues Last Minute Plea on Trade Measure," *New York Times,* November 7, 1997, A1.

13. "New World Order Conservative Club," *Washington Times,* September 22, 1997, A17.

14. "Clinton Accused of Urging Aide to Lie," *Washington Post,* January 21, 1998, A1.

15. "First Lady Launches Counterattack," *Washington Post,* January 28, 1998, A1.

16. Gillon, *The Pact,* 223–38.

17. Sobran, *Hustler,* 129–30.

18. "American Voters See Two Very Different Bill Clintons," *Washington Post,* August 23, 1998, A1.

19. "How He Gets Away with It," *Washington Times,* December 29, 1998, A17.

20. Thomas Edsall, *Building Red America: The New Conservative Coalition and the Drive for Permanent Power* (New York: Basic Books, 2007), 192.

21. "Why We Can't Quit the Culture War," *Washington Times,* February 19, 1999, A17.

22. Author interview with Bay Buchanan, restaurant, Virginia, May 3, 2010.

23. David Frum, *The Right Man* (London: Weidenfeld & Nicholson, 203), 17–18.

24. "GOP Aspirants Warned Not to Attack Rivals for Nomination," *New York Times,* February 24, 1999, A7.

25. "Forbes to Try His Fortunes Again," *Washington Post,* March 16, 1999, A1.

26. Author interview with Harry Veryser, restaurant, Detroit, February 11, 2010.

27. Author interview with Grover Norquist, subject's office, D.C.; May 12, 2010, "And Then There's Buchanan," *Washington Post,* March 9, 1999, A15.

28. "Prosperity Alters Politics in New Hampshire," *Washington Post,* March 21, 1999, A3.

29. Author interview with Tom Piatak, phone, August 19, 2010.

30. Author interview with Pat Buchanan, subject's home, Virginia, May 1, 2010.

31. Author interview with anonymous.

32. "Bauer: The Right Track," *Washington Post,* January 14, 1999, A27.

33. "Independent Conservative Bob Smith Runs Uphill Race on Principle," *New York Times,* September 20, 1999, A12.

34. "Conservatives Shield Bush's Abortion Stand from Right Wing," *Washington Post,* March 20, 1999, A4.

35. "Curiosity in Dole Exceeds Support," *New York Times,* October 7, 1999, A13.

36. "Bradley Pulls Ahead of Gore in Latest Fund Raising Lap," *New York Times,* October 1, 1999, A22.

37. "GOP Hopefuls Differ on Kosovo," *Washington Post,* March 27, 1999, A23.

38. "Numbers Game in Kosovo," *Washington Times,* November 19, 1999, 24.

39. "Bombing Campaign Gives McCain Added Prominence in GOP Field," *Washington Post,* April 7, 1999, A4.

40. "GOP Presidential Hopefuls Work N.H. Crowds," *Washington Post,* July 5, 1999, A4.

41. "N.H. GOP Event Draws 8 Hopefuls," *Washington Post,* May 3, 1999, A12.

42. Author interview with Bay Buchanan, restaurant, Virginia, May 3, 2010.

43. "Politics," *Washington Post,* June 20, 1999, A6.

44. "Buchanan 'Strongly' Leaning to Reform Bid," *Washington Post,* September 13, 1999, A1.

45. Author interview with Scott McConnell, subject's home, D.C., February 15, 2010.

46. Author interview with Pat Choate, phone, August 27, 2010.

47. "Buchanan: No Plans to Leave GOP," *Washington Post,* August 5, 1999, A6.

48. "Buchanan Nears Decision on Reform Party Bid," *New York Times,* September 13, 1999, A8.

49. Author interview with Bay Buchanan, restaurant, Virginia, May 3, 2010; author interview with Pat Choate, phone, August 27, 2010.

50. Author interview with anonymous.

51. "Buchanan's Sister Shepherds Insurgent's Race."

52. "Buchanan: No Plans to Leave GOP."

53. "From Straw to Gold," *Washington Post,* August 14, 1999, C1.

54. "Rivals May Get Thrashed Trying to Trip Bush," *Washington Post,* August 14, 1999, A4.

55. "Bush Wins Iowa Poll," *Washington Post,* August 15, 1999, A1.

56. "Rivals Turn Attack on Victorious Bush," *Washington Post,* August 16, 1999, A1.

TWENTY-FIVE: THE REFORM NIGHTMARE

1. "The Cable Guy," *New York Times,* October 24, 1999, SM74.

2. Buchanan, *A Republic, Not an Empire,* 282.

3. "The Cable Guy."

4. "Buchanan and Anti-Semitism," A14.

5. "Buchanan Takes Offense," *New York Times,* September 24, 1999, A23.

6. "Buchanan: The Most Interesting Candidate," *Washington Post,* August 27, 1999, A29.

7. "The Cable Guy."

8. Christopher P. Gilbert and David A. M. Peterson, "From Ross the Boss to Jesse the Body," in Jelen ed., *Ross for Boss.* 163–182.

9. "The Cable Guy."

10. "Leave Party, Reform Chairman Tells Ventura," *New York Times,* October 2, 1999, A9.

11. "Politics—Buchanan Camp Denies Candidate Is Considering Party Switch," *Washington Post,* June 27, 1999, A6.

12. Author interview with Scott McConnell, subject's home, D.C., February 23, 2010.

13. "Buchanan Nears Decision on Reform Party Bid," *New York Times,* September 13, 1999, A8.

14. Author interview with Bay Buchanan, restaurant, Virginia, May 3, 2010.

15. Author interview with Kara Hopkins, subject's office, D.C., February 23, 2010.

16. "Counting Controversy as Blessing," *New York Times,* October 2, 1999, A9.

17. "The New Patriotism," October 25, 1999, *Boyd Cathey Private Papers.*

18. "Buchanan Kicks Off Insurgent Campaign," *New York Times,* October 26, 1999, A1.

19. "Buchanan Bolts GOP for Reform Party," *Washington Post,* October 26, 1999, A1.

20. "Buchanan's Views on Hitler Create a Reform Party Stir," *New York Times,* September 21, 1999, A22.

21. Author interview with Kara Hopkins, subject's office, D.C., February 23, 2010.

22. Letter, Cathey to Buchanan, October 5, 1999, *Boyd Cathey Private Papers.*

23. Author interview with Frank Powell, subject's home, North Carolina, May 12, 2010.

24. Author interview with Boyd Cathey, subject's home, North Carolina, May 5, 2010.

25. "Reform Party Unsettled by Quest for a Nominee," *New York Times,* September 25, 1999, A10.

26. "Split over Buchanan Splinters Reform Party Convention," *New York Times,* September 26, 1999, 48.

27. Author interview with Tom Smith, home of Boyd Cathey, North Carolina, May 12, 2010.

28. Memo, "Campaigning Outline," Cathey to state activists, undated, *Boyd Cathey Private Papers.*

29. Author interview with Roger Stone, phone, February 12, 2010.

30. "Trump Proposes Clearing Nation's Debt at Expense of the Rich," *New York Times,* November 10, 1999, A19.

31. Author interview with Roger Stone, phone, February 12, 2010.

32. "Trump Set to Join Reform Party," *Washington Post,* October 25, 1999, A4.

33. "Poll Finds Greater Confidence in Democrats," *New York Times,* November 10, 1999, A1.

34. "Buchanan Visits Art Exhibit in Brooklyn and Doesn't Like It," *New York Times,* 6 November 1999, B5.

35. "Campaign Briefing," *New York Times,* February 10, 2000, A28.

36. "Trump and His Portfolio Tour Miami," *New York Times,* November 16, 1999, A22.

37. "Buchanan Finds a Place to Belong," St. Petersburg *Times,* December 8, 1999.

38. "A Question Trails Trump: Is He Really a Candidate?," *New York Times,* December 10, 1999, A33.

39. "Labor's Battle in Seattle," *Washington Post,* December 2, 1999, A03.

40. "The New Radicals," *Newsweek,* December 13, 1999, 36.

41. "Battle in Seattle: No, This Wasn't the '60s All Over Again," *USA Today,* December 7, 1999, 19A.

42. "Senseless in Seattle," *New York Times,* December 1, 1999, 43.

43. "The Battle in Seattle: What Was That All About?," *Washington Post,* December 5, 1999, B1.

44. "The New Radicals," *Newsweek,* December 13, 1999, 36.

45. Author interview with Scott McConnell, subject's home, D.C., February 15, 2010.

46. "A Harlem Stop for (Surprise!) Pat Buchanan," *Daily News,* November 12, 1999, 53.

47. "Counting Controversy as Blessing," *New York Times,* October 2, 1999, A9.

48. "Reform Party's Odd Couple: Fulani and Buchanan," *Washington Post,* November 12, 1999, A9.

49. "The Reliable Source," *Washington Post,* October 27, 1999, C1.

50. "Ventura Quits Reform Party," *New York Times,* February 12, 2000, A1.

51. Author interview with Pat Choate, phone, August 27, 2010.

52. "Reform Bid Said to Be a No-Go for Trump," *New York Times,* February 14, 2000, A18.

53. "What I Saw at the Revolution," *New York Times,* February 19, 2000, A15.

54. "The Third Party," *New York Times,* February 13, 2000, 35.

55. "Wrestling Free in Minnesota."

56. "The $12 Million Man," *New York Times,* February 27, 2000, WK5.

57. "The Reform Party," *New York Times,* February 19, 2000, A11.

58. "Political Briefing," *New York Times,* February 20, 2000, 32.

59. "The Next Stop," *New York Times,* February 2, 2000, A18.

60. "Reform Party Casts an Eye on a McCain-Bradley Ticket," *New York Times,* February 5, 2000, A10.

61. "Journal," *New York Times,* February 12, 2000, A15.

62. "McCain and Perot Stealing Glances," *New York Times,* February 26, 2000, A1.

63. "One Party Quite Divisible," *New York Times,* February 29, 2000, A1.

64. "Political Memo," *New York Times,* March 10, 2000, A18.

65. Author interview with Boyd Cathey, subject's home, North Carolina, May 5, 2010.

66. "Buchanan's Bid Transforms the Reform Party," *Washington Post,* July 23, 2000, A4.

67. Author interview with Boyd Cathey, subject's home, North Carolina, May 5, 2010.

68. Author interview with Tom Smith, home of Boyd Cathey, North Carolina, May 12, 2010.

TWENTY-SIX: PAT BUCHANAN VS. THE FLYING BUDDHISTS

1. "The Reform Party," *New York Times,* June 6, 2000, A20.
2. "Unlikely Ally Ends Her Ties to Buchanan," *New York Times,* June 20, 2000, A21.
3. "Campaign Briefing," *New York Times,* May 16, 2000, A18.
4. "Campaign Briefing," *New York Times,* June 2, 2000, A19.
5. "Campaign Briefing," *New York Times,* May 18, 2000, A26.
6. "California Reform Delegates Reject Anti-Buchanan Move," *New York Times,* June 5, 2000, A16.
7. Author interview with Tom Piatak, phone, August 19, 2010.
8. "Buchanan Hints 'Cop-Bashing' Contributed to Assaults in Park," *New York Times,* June 16, 2000, B4.
9. "The Reform Party," *New York Times,* March 17, 2000, A19.
10. "Campaign Briefing," *New York Times,* April 1, 2000, A8.
11. "Buchanan, in a Change, Calls for End to Sanctions," *New York Times,* December 17, 1999, A26.
12. "Nader Runs Again, This *Time* with Feeling," *New York Times,* April 15, 2000, A1.
13. "Campaign Briefing," *New York Times,* March 21, 2000, A20.
14. "The Vice President," *New York Times,* June 17, 2000, A10.
15. "The Green Party," *New York Times,* June 22, 2000, A28.
16. "Doctors Remove Buchanan's Gall Bladder," *New York Times,* August 19, 2000, A11.
17. "The Reform Party," *New York Times,* July 30, 2000, 24.
18. "Buchanan Campaign Dismisses Effort to Remove His Name from Reform Ballot," *New York Times,* July 31, 2000, A12.
19. "The Reform Party," *New York Times,* August 7, 2000, A16.
20. "The Reform Party," *New York Times,* August 9, 2000, A19.
21. "The Reform Party," *New York Times,* August 7, 2000, A16.
22. "The Reform Party," *New York Times,* August 10, 2000, A18.
23. Author interview with Tom Smith, home of Boyd Cathey, North Carolina, May 12, 2010.
24. "Buchanan's Bid Transforms the Reform Party."
25. "Rift on Buchanan Leads to a Split in Reform Party," *New York Times,* August 11, 2000, A1.
26. "The Reform Parties," *New York Times,* August 12, 2000, A10.
27. Author interview with Bay Buchanan, subject's home, Virginia, February 26, 2010.
28. Author interview with Kara Hopkins, subject's office, D.C., February 23, 2010.
29. Ezola Foster and Sarah Jepson Coleman, *What's Right for All Americans* (Waco, TX: WRS Pub., 1995), 64–65.
30. Author interview with Scott McConnell, subject's home, D.C., February 15, 2010.
31. "The Reform Parties," *New York Times,* August 12, 2000, A10.
32. Author interview with Tom Smith, home of Boyd Cathey, North Carolina, May 12, 2010.

33. "Ezola Foster: Pat Buchanan's Far Right Hand," *Washington Post,* September 13, 2000, 1.

34. David A. Neiwert, *The Eliminationists: How Hate Talk Radicalized the American Right* (New York: PoliPoint Press, 2009), 95.

35. http://www.stormfront.org/forum/t102585/, last accessed October 31, 2010.

36. "Both Halves of Reform Party Prepare for Legal Challenge," *New York Times,* August 14, 2000, A12.

37. Copy of Reform Nomination Speech, August 14, 2000, *Boyd Cathey Private Papers.*

38. "The Reform Parties," *New York Times,* August 13, 2000, 22.

39. "Campaign Briefing," *New York Times,* August 23, 2000, A19.

40. "The Split," *New York Times,* August 25, 2000, A23.

41. "Campaign Briefing," *New York Times,* August 30, 2000, A21.

42. "The Reform Party," *New York Times,* September 12, 2000, A22.

43. "The Reform Party," *New York Times,* September 19, 2000, A21.

44. "Buchanan near the End of a Weak Run," *New York Times,* November 3, 2000, A27.

45. "Campaign Briefing," *New York Times,* November 2, 2000, A28.

46. "Campaign Briefing," *New York Times,* October 27, 2000, A28.

47. "Political Briefing; Buchanan Fights On, for a Future Election," *New York Times,* October 8, 2000, A28.

48. "The Endorsement," *New York Times,* November 3, 2000, A27.

49. "Nearing the End of the Tunnel, Buchanan Glimpses a Sunset," *New York Times,* October 20, 2000, A28.

50. "The 2000 Elections: State by State," *New York Times,* November 9, 2000, A28.

51. Author interview with Tom Piatak, phone, August 19, 2010.

52. http://dir.salon.com/politics/feature/2000/11/10/buchanan/, last accessed October 31, 2010.

TWENTY-SEVEN: PAT TAKES TEA IN THE TWENTY-FIRST CENTURY

1. Author interview with anonymous.

2. Patrick Buchanan, *The Death of the West: How Dying Populations and Immigrant Invasions Imperil Our Country and Civilization* (New York: Thomas Dunne, 2002), 205–26.

3. "Death of the Party," *American Conservative,* May 2010, 26.

4. "Alien Nation," *New York Times,* February 3, 2003, SM13.

5. D. Brooks, "One Nation, Slightly Divisible," *Atlantic Monthly* 288, no. 5 (2001), 53–65; for an alternative view, see James Davison Hunter and Alan Wolfe, *Is There a Culture War?: A Dialogue on Values and American Public Life* (Washington, D.C.: Pew Research Center, 2006).

6. Ann Coulter, *Godless: The Church of American Liberalism* (New York: Crown Forum, 2007), 99–146. For a critique, see Markos Moulitsas, *American Taliban: How War, Sex, Sin, and Power Bind Jihadists and the Radical Right* (New York: PoliPointPress, 2010), 163–98.

7. Bill O'Reilly, *Culture Warrior* (New York: Broadway Books, 2007), 2.

8. "Study Finds Left-wing Brain, Right-wing Brain," *Los Angeles Times*, September 10, 2007, 15.

9. Author's notes.

10. Buchanan, *The Death of the West*, 6.

11. "The Isms That Bedevil Bush," *Middle American News*, March 25, 2008, 9.

12. Buchanan, *Where the Right Went Wrong*, 8.

13. "US Pays the High Price of Empire," *Los Angeles Times*, September 20, 2001, 23.

14. "Whose War?: A Neoconservative Clique Seeks to Ensnare Our Country in a Series of Wars That Are Not in America's Interest," *American Conservative*, March 24, 2003, 11.

15. Author interview with Scott McConnell, subject's home, D.C., February 15, 2010.

16. "Unpatriotic Conservatives," *National Review*, April 7, 2003, 33.

17. "All Those Things to Apologize For," *Washington Times*, June 27, 1995, A23.

18. Gottfried, *Encounters*, 158–59.

19. Shots Fired: Sam Francis on America's Culture War (Vienna, VA: Fitzgerald Griffin Foundation, 2005), xii.

20. "Joseph Sobran, Writer Whom Buckley Mentored, Dies at 64," *New York Times*, October 1, 2010, A17.

21. Author interview with Scott McConnell, subject's home, D.C., February 15, 2010.

22. Patrick Buchanan, *Churchill, Hitler, and "The Unnecessary War": How Britain Lost Its Empire and the West Lost the World* (New York: Crown Publishers, 2008), 116–17, 122–23, 128–30.

23. "Necessary Evil," *American Conservative*, June 2, 2008, 5.

24. Author interview with Kara Hopkins, subject's office, D.C., February 23, 2010.

25. Author interview with Joe Scarborough, phone, August 13, 2010.

26. http://www.huffingtonpost.com/2008/10/06/rachel-maddow-pat-buchana_n_132145 .html, last accessed November 15, 2010.

27. Author interview with Peter Fenn, subject's office, D.C., May 12, 2010.

28. Author interview with Chris Matthews, phone, May 25, 2010.

29. Author interview with Peter Fenn, subject's office, D.C., May 12, 2010.

30. The discovery was made by Christopher Hayes of *The Nation Online*: http://www.the nation.com/blog/sarah-palin-buchananite, last accessed December 19, 2010.

31. "Whose Palin?," *American Conservative*, October 6, 2008, 23.

32. "Sam Francis' Mad Tea Party," *Chronicles*, April 2010, 34.

33. Author interview with Connie Mackey, phone, October 19, 2010.

34. Author interview with Terry Jeffrey, restaurant, D.C., February 21, 2010.

35. Author interview with Greg Mueller, restaurant, D.C., February 21, 2010.

36. Author interview with Jerry Woodruff, restaurant, North Carolina, March 2, 2010.

37. "The Tea Party Tribe," *American Conservative*, April 19, 2010, 23.

38. Patrick Buchanan, *Suicide of a Superpower: Will America Survive to 2025?* (New York: Thomas Dunne, 2011), 397.

39. Thomas Frank, *What's the Matter with Kansas?: How Conservatives Won the Heart of America* (New York: Macmillan, 2004). Frank's thesis is controversial. For an alternative view that says voting is still defined by income, see Andrew Gelman ed., *Red State, Blue State, Rich State, Poor State: Why Americans Vote the Way They Do* (Princeton, NJ: Princeton University Press, 2008).

40. Author interview with Thomas Dunne, restaurant, New York, April 26, 2010.

41. Author interview with Howard Phillips, phone, March 5, 2010.

SOURCES

PUBLIC ARCHIVAL COLLECTIONS

Gerald R. Ford Library, 1000 Beal Avenue, Ann Arbor, MI 48109

Library of Congress (Serial and Government Papers Division), 101 Independence Avenue SE, Madison Building, LM-133, Washington, D.C. 20540-4760

National Archives (Papers of the National Security Council), 700 Pennsylvania Avenue Northwest, Washington, D.C. 20408-0002

New Hampshire Political Library, 30 Park Street, Concord, NH 03301

Richard Nixon Library, 18001 Yorba Linda Boulevard, Yorba Linda, CA 92886-3949

Robert J. Dole Archive and Special Collections, Robert J. Dole Institute of Politics, 2350 Petefish Drive, Lawrence, KS 66045

Ronald Reagan Presidential Library Papers, 40 Presidential Drive, Simi Valley, CA 93065

Roosevelt Study Center (Papers of Richard M. Nixon), Abdij 8, 4331 BK Middelburg, The Netherlands

Southern Historical Collection (Papers of Boyd Cathey), The Wilson Library, University of North Carolina, Chapel Hill, NC 27514-8890

PRIVATE PAPERS

Boyd Cathey

Chuck Douglas

Claes Ryn

Jon Utley

PERIODICALS

The Advocate

The American Conservative

The American Spectator

Anchorage Daily News

The Arizona Republic

Associated Press

The Atlanta Constitution

The Atlanta Journal-Constitution

The Atlantic Monthly

The Boston Globe

BusinessWeek

Chicago Tribune

The Christian Science Monitor

Chronicles

Commentary

Concord Monitor

Confederate Veteran

Congressional Record

Conservative Chronicle

Daily News (New York)

The Dallas Morning News

The Economist

Foster's Daily Democrat (New Hampshire)

The Greenville News (South Carolina)

The Guardian

Harper's

Spartanburg *Herald-Journal* (South
   Carolina)

The Irish Times

Los Angeles Times

Manchester Union-Leader

Middle American News

Mother Jones

The Nation

National Catholic Reporter

The National Interest

National Review

The New Republic

Newsweek

New York

New York Post

The New York Times

News & Record (North Carolina)

Penthouse

The Philadelphia Inquirer

The Portsmouth Herald

The Post and Courier (South Carolina)

The News & Observer (Raleigh)

Reuters

Rolling Stone

The San Jose Mercury News (California)

Southern Partisan

St. Louis Globe-Democrat

St. Louis Post-Dispatch

The State (South Carolina)

Time

The Times and Democrat (South Carolina)

The Times (London)

The Times-Picayune (New Orleans)

Vanity Fair

The Wall Street Journal

The Washington Post

The Washington Times

USA Today

INTERVIEWS

Diana Banister

Charles Black

Brent Bozell Jr.

Bay Buchanan

Pat Buchanan

Shelley Buchanan

Boyd Cathey

Pat Choate

E. J. Dionne

Chuck Douglas

Thomas Dunne

Paul Erickson

Tony Fabrizio

Mike Farris

Peter Fenn

Tom Fleming

Frederica Friedman

Paul Gottfried

Fran Griffin

Richard Hines

Kara Hopkins

Terry Jeffrey

John Judis

David Keene

Annette Kirk

Bill Lacy

Yehuda Levin

Connie Mackey

Chris Matthews

Scott McConnell

Signe McQuaid

Greg Mueller

Grover Norquist

Howard Phillips

Tom Piatak

Frank Powell

Larry Pratt

Scott Reed

Peter Robbio

Claes Ryn

Joe Scarborough

Phyllis Schlafly

Tom Smith

Joe Sobran

Roger Stone

Jon Utley

Harry Veryser

Richard Viguerie

Jerry Woodruff

Carter Wrenn

BIBLIOGRAPHY

Agnew, Spiro T., *Go Quietly . . . Or Else* (New York: William Morrow, 1980).

Aistrup, Joseph A., *The Southern Strategy Revisited: Republican Top-down Advancement in the South* (Lawrence: University Press of Kansas, 1996).

Allitt, Patrick, *The Conservatives: Ideas and Personalities Throughout American History* (New Haven: Yale University Press, 2009).

Ambrose, Stephen, *Nixon: The Triumph of a Politician, 1962–1972* (New York: Simon & Schuster, 1990).

Bandow, Doug, *The Politics of Envy: Statism as Theology* (New Brunswick: Transaction Books, 1994).

Barilleaux, Ryan J. and Mark J. Rozzell, *Power and Prudence: The Presidency of George H. W. Bush* (College Station: Texas A&M University Press, 2004).

Bennett, David Henry, *A Party of Fear: From Nativist Movements to the New Right in American History* (Chapel Hill: University of North Carolina Press, 1988).

Berger, Dan, *Outlaws of America: The Weather Underground and the Politics of Solidarity* (New York: AK Press, 2006).

Berkowitz, Edward D., *Something Happened: A Political and Cultural Overview of the Seventies* (New York: Columbia University Press, 2006).

—— *To Improve Human Health: A History of the Institute of Medicine* (Washington, D.C.: New Academies Press, 1998).

Bochin, Hal, *Richard Nixon: Rhetorical Strategist* (New York: Greenwood Publishing Co., 1990).

Bowman, Karyln and Everett Carll Ladd, *What's Wrong: A Survey of American Satisfaction and Complaint* (Washington, D.C.: AEI Press, 1998).

Braestrup, Peter, *How the American Press and Television Reported and Interpreted the Crisis of Tet 1968 in Vietnam and Washington* (New York: Presidio, 1977).

Bridges, Linda and John R. Coyne Jr., *Strictly Right: William F. Buckley, Jr. and the American Conservative Movement* (Hoboken, NJ: Wiley and Sons, 2007).

Bridges, Tyler, *The Rise of David Duke* (Jackson, MS: University Press of Mississippi, 1994).

Briggs, B. Bruce, *The New Class?* (New Brunswick, NJ: Transaction, 1979).

Buchanan, Patrick J., *A Republic, Not an Empire: Reclaiming America's Destiny* (Washington, D.C.: Regnery, 1999).

—— *Churchill, Hitler, and "The Unnecessary War": How Britain Lost Its Empire and the West Lost the World* (New York: Crown Publishers, 2008).

—— *Conservative Votes, Liberal Victories: Why the Right Has Failed* (New York: Quadrangle, 1975).

—— *The Death of the West: How Dying Populations and Immigrant Invasions Imperil Our Country and Civilization* (New York: Thomas Dunne, 2002).

—— *The Great Betrayal: How American Sovereignty and Social Justice Are Being Sacrificed to the Gods of the Global Economy* (New York: Little Brown, 1998).

—— *The New Majority: President Nixon at Mid-Passage* (The Girard Company, 1973).

—— *Right from the Beginning* (Washington, D.C.: Regnery Gateway, 1990).

—— *Suicide of a Superpower: Will America Survive to 2025?* (New York: Thomas Dunne, 2011).

—— *Where the Right Went Wrong: How Neoconservatives Subverted the Reagan Revolution and Hijacked the Bush Presidency* (New York: Thomas Dunne, 2004).

Busch, Andrew, *Ronald Reagan and the Politics of Freedom* (New York: Rowman & Littlefield, 2001).

Busch, Andrew and James W. Ceaser, *Losing to Win: The 1996 Elections and American Politics* (Lanham, MD: Rowman & Littlefield, 1997).

Bush, Barbara, *Barbara Bush: A Memoir* (New York: Scribner, 2003).

Cannon, Lou, *President Reagan: The Role of a Lifetime* (New York: Simon & Schuster, 1991).

Carter, Dan T., *From George Wallace to Newt Gingrich: Race in the Conservative Counter Revolution, 1963–1994* (Baton Rouge: Louisiana State University Press, 1996).

—— *The Politics of Rage: George Wallace, the Origins of the New Conservatism, and the Transformation of American Politics* (New York: Simon & Schuster, 2000).

Carter, Gregg Lee, *Guns in American Society* (Santa Barbara, CA: ABC-CIO, 2002).

Clarke, Jonathan and Stefan A. Halper, *America Alone: The Neo-Conservatives and the Global Order* (New York: Cambridge University Press, 2004).

Clinton, Bill, *My Life* (New York: Random House, 2004).

Continetti, Matthew, *The K Street Gang: The Rise and Fall of the Republican Machine* (New York: Doubleday, 2006).

Coulter, Ann, *Godless: The Church of American Liberalism* (New York: Crown Forum, 2007).

Critchlow, Donald T., *The Conservative Ascendancy: How the GOP Right Made Political History* (Cambridge, MA: University of Harvard Press, 2007).

Crowley, Monica, *Nixon in Winter: The Final Revelations, Volume 1998, Part 2* (London: I.B. Tauris, 1998).

Cuneo, Michael W., *The Smoke of Satan: Conservative and Traditionalist Dissent in Contemporary Catholicism* (Baltimore, MD: John Hopkins University Press, 1999).

Dallek, Robert, *Lyndon B. Johnson: Portrait of a President* (New York: Oxford, 2004).

—— *Ronald Reagan: The Politics of Symbolism* (Cambridge, MA.: Harvard University Press, 1999).

DeCapua, Sarah and Edmund Lindop, *America in the 1950s* (Minneapolis, MN: Twenty-First Century Books, 2010).

Dionne, E. J., *They Only Look Dead: Why Progressives Will Dominate the Next Political Era* (New York: Simon & Schuster, 1995).

Donaldson, Gary, *Liberalism's Last Hurrah: The Presidential Campaign of 1964* (New York: M.E. Sharpe, 2003).

Drew, Elizabeth, *On the Edge: The Clinton Presidency* (New York: Simon & Schuster, 1995).

Dunn, Charles W., *The Enduring Reagan* (Lawrence: University Press of Kentucky, 2009).

Durham, Martin, *The Christian Right: The Far Right and the Boundaries of American Conservatism* (Manchester, UK: Manchester University Press, 2000).

—— *White Rage: The Extreme Right and American Politics* (New York: Taylor and Routledge, 2007).

Edsall, Mary and Thomas Edsall, *Chain Reaction: The Impact of Race, Rights, and Taxes on American Politics* (New York: Norton, 1991).

Edsall, Thomas, *Building Red America: The New Conservative Coalition and the Drive for Permanent Power* (New York: Basic Books, 2007).

Edwards, Chris R. and John Curtis Samples, *The Republican Revolution 10 Years Later: Smaller Government or Business as Usual?* (Washington, D.C.: Cato Institute, 2004).

Edwards, Lee, *The Conservative Revolution: The Movement That Remade America* (New York: Free Press, 1999).

Einstein, Mara, *Media Diversity: Economics, Ownership, and the FCC* (New York: Routledge, 2004).

Farber, David, *Chicago '68* (Chicago: University of Chicago Press, 1994).

Francis, Sam, *Beautiful Losers: Essays on the Failure of American Conservatism* (Columbia: University of Missouri Press, 1993).

—— *Revolution from the Middle* (Raleigh, NC: Middle American Press, 1997).

Frank, Thomas, *What's the Matter with Kansas?: How Conservatives Won the Heart of America* (New York: Macmillan, 2004).

Franklin, H. Bruce, *Vietnam and Other American Fantasies* (Boston: University of Massachusetts Press, 2000).

Frum, David, *The Right Man* (London: Weidenfeld & Nicolson, 2003).

Gelman, Andrew ed., *Red State, Blue State, Rich State, Poor State: Why Americans Vote the Way They Do* (Princeton, NJ: Princeton University Press, 2008).

Genovese, Michael A., *The Watergate Crisis* (Westport, CT: Greenwood Press, 1999).

Germond, Jack and Jules Witcover, *Mad as Hell: Revolt at the Ballot Box, 1992* (New York: Warner Books, 1993).

Gerson, Mark, *The Neoconservative Vision: From the Cold War to the Culture Wars* (Lanham, MD: Madison Books, 1996).

Gillis, Chester, *Roman Catholicism in America* (New York: Columbia University Press, 1999).

Gooding-Williams, Robert, *Reading Rodney King/Reading Urban Uprising* (New York: Routledge, 1993).

Gottfried, Paul Edward, *Conservatism in America: Making Sense of the American Right* (New York: Palgrave, Macmillan, 2007).

────── *Encounters: My Life with Nixon, Marcuse, and Other Friends and Teachers* (Wilmington, DE: ISI Books, 2009).

Gottfried, Paul and Thomas Fleming, *The Conservative Movement* (Boston: Twayne, 1988).

Graham, Hugh Davis, *Collision Course: The Strange Convergence of Affirmative Action and Immigration Policy in America* (New York: Oxford University Press, 2003).

Grant, George, *Buchanan: Caught in the Crossfire* (Nashville, TN: Thomas Nelson, 1996).

Greenberg, David, *Nixon's Shadow: The History of an Image* (New York: Norton, 2003).

Griffith, Robert, *The Politics of Fear: Joseph R. McCarthy and the Senate* (Amherst: University of Massachusetts Press, 1987).

Haldeman, H. R., *The Haldeman Diaries: Inside the Nixon White House* (New York: Berkley Book Pub. Group, 1996).

Hames, Tim and Nicol C. Rae, *Governing America: History, Culture, Institutions, Organization, Policy* (Manchester, UK: Manchester University Press, 1996).

Hazen, Don ed., *Inside the L.A. Riots: What Really Happened—and Why It Will Happen Again* (Houston, TX: Institute for Alternative Journalism, 1992).

Herrnson, Paul S. and Dily M. Hill eds., *The Clinton Presidency: The First Term, 1992–1996* (London: Macmillan Press, 1999).

Hulsman, John C., *A Paradigm for the New World Order: A Schools-of-Thought Analysis of American Foreign Policy in the Post-Cold War Era* (London: Macmillan, 1997).

Hunter, James Davison and Alan Wolfe, *Is There a Culture War?: A Dialogue on Values and American Public Life* (Washington, D.C.: Pew Research Center, 2006).

Jelen, Ted G. ed., *Ross for Boss: The Perot Phenomenon and Beyond* (New York: SUNY Press, 2001).

Jensen, Richard Jay, *Reagan at Bergen-Belsen and Bitburg* (College Station: Texas A&M University Press, 2007).

Johns, Andrew L., *Vietnam's Second Front: Domestic Politics, The Republican Party, and the War* (Lexington: University Press of Kentucky, 2010).

Johnson, Haynes, *Sleepwalking Through History: America in the Reagan Years* (New York: HarperCollins, 2003).

Kauffman, Bill, *Ain't My America: The Long, Noble History of Antiwar Conservatism and Middle-American Anti-Imperialism* (New York: Metropolitan, 2008).

Kazin, Michael, *Populist Persuasion: An American History* (New York: Cornell University Press, 1998).

Kissinger, Henry, *The White House Years* (London: Weidenfeld & Nicolson, 1979).

Klobuchar, Lisa, *The Iran-Contra Affair: Political Scandal Uncovered* (Minneapolis, MN: Compass Point Books, 2008).

Kopel, David B., *Guns: Who Should Have Them?* (New York: Prometheus, 1995).

Kurial, Richard G. and David B. Woolner, *FDR, the Vatican, and the Roman Catholic Church in America, 1933–1945* (New York: Palgrave MacMillan, 2003).

Ladley, Eric J., *Nixon's China Trip* (Lincoln, NE: Writers Club Press, 2002).

Landers, James, *The Weekly War: Newsmagazines and Vietnam* (Columbia: University of Missouri Press, 2004).

Langguth, A. J., *Our Vietnam: The War, 1954–1975* (New York: Simon & Schuster, 2000).

Lassiter, Matthew, *The Silent Majority: Suburban Politics in the Sunbelt South* (Princeton, NJ: Princeton University Press, 2005).

Lowry, Rich, *Legacy: Paying the Price for the Clinton Years* (Washington, D.C.: Regnery, 2003).

MacArthur, John R., *The Selling of "Free Trade": NAFTA, Washington, and the Subversion of American Democracy* (Los Angeles: University of California Press, 2000).

Macmillan, Margaret, *Nixon and Mao: The Week That Changed the World* (New York: Random House, 2007).

Mailer, Norman, *Miami and the Siege of Chicago: An Informal History of the American Political Conventions of 1968* (London: Weidenfeld & Nicolson, 1968).

Maltese, John Anthony, *Spin Control: The White House Office of Communications and the Management of Presidential News* (Chapel Hill: University of North Carolina Press, 1994).

Mark, David, *Going Dirty: The Art of Negative Campaigning* (Lanham, MD: Rowman & Littlefield, 2009).

Mason, Robert, *Richard Nixon and the Quest for a New Majority* (Chapel Hill: University of North Carolina Press, 2004).

May, Elaine, *The Birdcage: The Shooting Script* (New York: Newmarket Press, 1999).

Mayer, Jane and Doyle McManus, *Landslide: The Unmaking of the President 1984–1988* (New York: Houghton Mifflin, 1988).

McGirr, Lisa, *Suburban Warriors: The Origins of the New American Right* (Princeton, NJ: Princeton University Press, 2001).

Medhurst, Martin J. and Kurt Ritter, *Presidential Speechwriting: From the New Deal to the Reagan Revolution and Beyond* (College Station: Texas A&M University Press, 2003).

Miroff, Bruce, *The Liberals' Moment: The McGovern Insurgency and the Identity Crisis of the Democratic Party* (Lawrence: University of Kansas Press, 2007).

Morgan, Iwan, *Nixon* (New York: Oxford University Press, 2002).

Moulitsas, Markos, *American Taliban: How War, Sex, Sin, and Power Bind Jihadists and the Radical Right* (New York: PoliPointPress, 2010).

Neiwert, David A., *The Eliminationists: How Hate Talk Radicalized the American Right* (New York: PoliPoint Press, 2009).

New, David S., *Holy War: The Rise of Militant Christian, Jewish, and Islamic Fundamentalism* (Jefferson, NC: McFarland, 2001).

Olsen, Keith, *Watergate: The Presidential Scandal That Shook America* (Lawrence: University Press of Kansas, 2003).

O'Huallachain, D. L. and J. Forrest Sharpe eds., *Neo-Conned!: Just War Principles: A Condemnation of War in Iraq* (Norfolk, VA: IHS Press, 2007).

O'Reilly, Bill, *Culture Warrior* (New York: Broadway Books, 2007).

O'Sullivan, John, *The President, the Pope, and the Prime Minister: Three Who Changed the World* (Washington, D.C.: Regnery, 2006).

O'Toole, James M., *The Faithful: A History of Catholics in America* (Cambridge, MA.: Harvard University Press, 2008).

Oxby, Marc, *The 1990s* (New York: Greenwood, 2003).

Parmet, Herbert S., *Richard Nixon and His America* (Boston: Little Brown, 1990).

Perlstein, Rick, *Before the Storm: Barry Goldwater and the American Consensus* (New York: Hill and Wang, 2001).

—— *Nixonland: The Rise of a President and the Fracturing of America* (New York: Scribner, 2008).

Phillips, Kevin P., *Post Conservative America: People, Politics, and Ideology in a Time of Crisis* (New York: Random House, 1983).

Pontell, Henry N., Stephen M. Rosoff, and Robert Tillman, *Profit Without Honor: White-Collar Crime and the Looting of America* (New York: Prentice Hall, 2003).

Raimondo, Justin, *Reclaiming the American Right: The Lost Legacy of the Conservative Movement* (Wilmington, DE: ISI Books, 2008).

Rapoport, Ronald B. and Walter J. Stone, *Three's a Crowd: The Dynamic of Third Parties, Ross Perot, and Republican Resurgence* (Detroit: University of Michigan Press, 2008).

Regan, Donald T., *For the Record: From Wall Street to Washington* (New York: Harcourt Brace Jovanovich, 1988).

Riccards, Michael P., *The Presidency and the Middle Kingdom: China, the United States, and Executive Leadership* (Lanham, MD: Lexington Books, 2000).

Rider, Jonathan, *Canarsie: The Jews and Italian Americans of Brooklyn Against Liberalism* (Cambridge, MA.: Harvard University Press, 1985).

Rozell, Mark J., *The Press and the Bush Presidency* (Westport, CT: Greenwood, 1996).

Russello, Gerald J., *The Postmodern Imagination of Russell Kirk* (Columbia: University of Missouri Press, 2007).

Safire, William, *Before the Fall: An Inside View of the Pre-Watergate White House* (New Brunswick, NJ: Transaction Publishers, 2005).

Scammon, Richard and Ben Wattenberg, *The Real Majority* (New York: Coward-McCann, 1970).

Schier, Steven E., *The Postmodern Presidency: Bill Clinton's Legacy in U.S. Politics* (Pittsburgh: University of Pittsburgh Press, 2000).

Schoenwald, Jonathan M., *A Time for Choosing: The Rise of Modern American Conservatism* (New York: Oxford University Press, 2001).

Schrecker, Ellen, *Many Are the Crimes: McCarthyism in America* (New York: Little Brown, 1998).

Schulman, Bruce J., *The Seventies: The Great Shift in American Culture, Society, and Politics* (Cambridge, MA.: Da Capo Press, 2002).

Schulman, Bruce J. and Julian Zelizer eds., *Rightward Bound: Making America Conservative in the 1970s* (Cambridge, MA: Harvard University Press, 2008).

Scotchie, Joseph, *The Paleoconservatives: New Voices of the Old Right* (New Brunswick, NJ: Transaction Publishers, 1999).

—— *Revolt from the Heartland: The Struggle for an Authentic Conservatism* (New Brunswick, NJ: Transaction Publishers, 2002).

Shirley, Craig, *Reagan's Revolution: The Untold Story of the Campaign That Started It All* (New York: Thomas Nelson Inc., 2005).

Sobran, Joe, *Hustler: The Clinton Legacy* (Vienna, VA: Griffin Communications, 2000).

Strober, Deborah and Gerald Strober, *The Nixon Presidency: An Oral History of the Era* (New York: HarperCollins, 2003).

—— *The Reagan Presidency: An Oral History of the Era* (New York: Houghton and Mifflin, 2003).

Thompson, Hunter S., *The Great Shark Hunt: Strange Tales from a Strange Time* (London: Pan Macmillan, 1979).

Thompson, Hunter S. with Kevin Simonson and Beef Torrey, *Conversations with Hunter S. Thompson* (Jackson: University Press of Mississippi, 2008).

Thompson, Michael J. ed., *Confronting the New Conservatism: The Rise of the Right in America* (New York: New York University Press, 2007).

Troy, Gil, *Morning in America: How Ronald Reagan Invented the 1980s* (Princeton, NJ: Princeton University Press, 2005).

Tufte, Edward R., *Political Control of the Economy: Booms, Busts, Dollars, and Votes* (Lawrence: University Press of Kansas, 1998).

Tyrell, R. Emmett, *Boy Clinton: The Political Biography* (Washington, D.C.: Regnery, 1996).

Viguerie, Richard A., *The Establishment vs. The People: Is a New Populist Revolt on the Way?* (Chicago: Regnery Gateway, 1984).

Weaver, Mary Jo, *What's Left?: Liberal American Catholics* (Bloomington: University of Indiana Press, 1999).

Whitaker, Robert W. ed., *The New Right Papers* (New York: St. Martin's Press, 1982).

Wills, Gary, *Nixon Agonistes: The Crisis of the Self-Made Man* (New York: Mariner, 2002).

Witcover, Jules, *Very Strange Bedfellows: The Short and Unhappy Marriage of Richard Nixon and Spiro Agnew* (New York: Public Affairs, 2007).

Woodward, Bob, *The Choice* (New York: Simon & Schuster, 1996).

Wroe, Ann, *Lives, Lies and the Iran-Contra Affair* (New York: I.B. Taurus, 1991).

Yuill, Kevin L., *Richard Nixon and the Rise of Affirmative Action: The Pursuit of Racial Equity in an Era of Limits* (Lanham, MD: Rowman & Littlefield, 2006).

Zeskind, Leonard, *Blood and Politics: The History of the White Nationalist Movement from the Margins to the Mainstream* (New York: Farrar, Straus and Giroux, 2009).

INDEX